imerick Anthology

D1493886

THE LIMERICK ANTHOLOGY

Edited by Jim Kemmy

Gill & Macmillan

Gill & Macmillan Ltd
Goldenbridge
Dublin 8
with associated companies throughout the world
© Introduction and selection, Jim Kemmy 1996
Copyright in the stories and poems is that of the individual authors and publishers
0 7171 2458 4
Print origination by Graham Thew Design
Printed by ColourBooks Ltd, Dublin

A catalogue record is available for this book from the British Library.

5 4 3 2

The Editor and Publishers wish to acknowledge the
generous financial assistance of Mr Joseph O'Donoghue,
without whom this anthology could not have been
published in its present form.

Contents

Four: People

Five: The County

Six: Sport

Seven: History

Ten: Travellers

Preface

Over the years in reading books and articles about Limerick and its people two pieces of writing have remained firmly in my mind. John Ferrar, Limerick's first major historian, and Kate O'Brien, the city's most famous novelist, lived almost two centuries apart but they had a common bond of enthusiasm and tolerance in their writings.

In the preface to his *History of Limerick*, written in 1787, Ferrar wrote:

> It is near twenty years since the Author published a sketch of the History of Limerick. He was then little acquainted, what a respectable figure this city makes in the History of Ireland.

In her book *My Ireland*, published in 1962, Kate O'Brien, then aged sixty-five years and living in Boughton, near Faversham in Kent, unashamedly told of her emotions as she eagerly counted the number of times the name of her 'dear native place' appeared in the columns of the London *Times* every week:

> As I write these words I am long out of sight of St John's spire, but I imagine and hope that Limerick is fast asleep this minute, and the Shannon running quietly past Barrington's Pier. I read in *The Times* this morning that someone was dead, 'late of Castleconnell, Co. Limerick'. It is surprising how often Limerick is named in this great London newspaper. Over the years I have come to the opinion that the place averages three appearances to six issues! Extraordinary. But this person, 'late of Castleconnell' — I wonder what he last saw, within, as his eyes closed? Had he been a child in Castleconnell and did he play in one of those tangled gardens above the wide, cataracting Shannon? Did he know Doonass across the water, and with his brothers take the ferry-boat above the Falls and walk by those fields under the Hell-Fire Club to picnic on the little lawn of The Angler's Rest? Did he have friends who lived in the Tontines? Did he run in and out of Cusack's Rod and Tackle shop? And did all rush back into his slowing heart the other night?

Most people, particularly those who have lived abroad, will readily understand her feelings and these words will bring memories of childhood, exile and that wasting longing for a glimpse of a person, family, home or place flooding back to mind. In compiling this anthology I have tried to emulate the generous and free-wheeling spirit of John Ferrar and Kate O'Brien.

Many anthologists have described at some length their working methods and the criteria used in their selections. Long and obtrusive introductions are not necessary to explain the contents of such works. Anthologies should speak for themselves and tell their own stories. What the ideal compilation should aim to achieve is best described by the architectural term 'section through'. As a 'section through' of a detailed drawing is designed to cut inside the facade of a structure to reveal an inner and all-encompassing picture, so should a good anthology — whatever its theme — unfold a wide range of contents and its own distinctive qualities.

In the preface to his *History*, John Ferrar gives this attractive description of the vocation of the historian:

> To the love of literary pursuits the world is indebted for the preservation of its antiquities, so pleasing to an enlightened mind. The honest desire of rescuing our History from oblivion, of transmitting remarkable events to posterity, supports the historian in his undertaking, renders him superior to every difficulty, and repays the toil of reading and collating a number of manuscripts and old books.

An anthology is not a history, but as Limerick prepares to celebrate its 800th anniversary as a chartered city in 1997, I am pleased to have had this opportunity of engaging in 'the toil of reading and collating a number of manuscripts and old books' and of 'transmitting' the results to book form.

Here, then, is my 'section through' of Limerick and its people as seen by historians, poets, writers, travellers and observers, local and otherwise, through the centuries.

Jim Kemmy
September 1996

Acknowledgments

I wish to thank the following people who have assisted me in compiling this anthology: Danny Browne, Siobhan Carroll, Michael Collopy, Peadar Cremin, John Curtin, John Cussen, Tom Donovan, Desmond FitzGerald, Knight of Glin, Marian Gaffney, Kevin Hannan, Fred Hourigan, Patsy Kelly, Fr John Leonard, Paddy Lysaght, James McMahon, Ciarán MacMathúna, Tadhg Moloney, Ann Mulqueen, Pat Nash, Ronan O'Brien, Fr Dermot O'Connor, Margaret O'Donoghue, Manus O'Riordan, Michael O'Sullivan, Toddy O'Sullivan and Mainchín Seoighe. I also wish to express my gratitude to Alan McEvoy, Curtain Call Limited, Gerald Lyne and Eugene Hogan, the National Library of Ireland, Dolores Doyle, Brendan Martin, Eileen McMahon, Deirdre O'Dea, Ann Culhane and other members of the staff of the Limerick City Library, Tony Storan, Librarian, Limerick County Library, Larry Walsh, Curator, Limerick City Museum, Chris O'Mahony, Regional Archivist, Shannon Development Company, and Kay McGuinness, Chairperson, Limerick 800 Committee, for their patience in dealing with my persistent requests for help.

I am the Shannon
Eugene McCabe

I am the Shannon, old as Ireland,
Older than history.
I know the secret ages of the moon,
I know the hidden pathways of the sun,
I know rain storms and stars at evening,
I know the changing rumours of the wind,
I know the floating gossip of the tides,
I know snipe and swan and curlew,
Badger, wolf and stag,
The small red fox, the tall red deer,
The blackbird on the hazel bough,
The brown hawk on the dead ash tree,
The black rat on the dripping branch,
The otter swimming free,
I know three great lakes,
One hundred mountains,
One thousand spidered wells,
And five hundred salmon pools,
I know quiet marshlands where long-necked herons call,
Weirs and stony fiords and sounding waterfalls.
I know hills and the plains,
And forests and the sea,
I know the seasons,
I know silence.

Primeval dawn.
No bird of warning,
Till one cry of terror,
And the ancient moon is splattered by a murderous sun.
Night cracks to bloody light,
Rats gibber on my banks,
And timid creatures shrink away.
Wolf howls and eagle shrieks,
Declare the death of innocence.
There is human blood upon my waters.

Ten thousand years before Christ walked in Israel,
The first North men came in wood-rib boats,

With leather sails, camping where I meet the sea,
Nosing up in time to hunt about my lakes and rivers,
Weapons of stone they left, and a high Atlantic fort,
Great earth mounds on a wild hilltop,
Circles and stone-capped dolmens in quiet fields.
On the dark side of the moon their God of death kept court,
Their burial cairns had doorways that faced the rising sun.

From Europe's middle plains came the Celts,
Charioteers, huntsmen, poets and warriors.
Spread through the death-haunted people,
Settled in every corner of the island.
I knew the children of their rape,
And carried them to dark places.
I know . . .
And I know man.

And so it was for a thousand long years.
I knew round towers and castles, cells and cloisters.
I knew wars and hunting, fishing and feasting.
I knew wattles and weirs, stones and bridges.
I knew the first ford of Inish Sibhton.
I knew man spawned on its island.
I know the secret of its name,
Limerick . . . Limerick . . .
Its echoes linger on my tides.
I am the Shannon, old as Ireland,
Older than history.

Extract from *Limerick Pageant*, 1969

ONE

RELIGION

The Fr Scanlan Affair
David Lee and Bob Kelly

In recent years a series of sex scandals have rocked the Irish Catholic Church causing great pain and anguish to clergy and laity alike. But it's not the first time in the history of the Church that wayward priests have violated their vows of chastity and brought grief to their bishops.

In 1756 Fr Patrick Scanlan, parish priest of St Munchin's chapel in Thomondgate, Limerick was excommunicated following revelations that he was having an affair with a woman and had fathered at least one of her two children. Despite attempts by the Bishop of Limerick, Dr Robert Lacy, to remove Fr Scanlan from his post, the turbulent cleric refused to give up his position as parish priest of St Munchin's. Defying the bishop's authority with the assistance of a violent mob, Fr Scanlan rebelled against the Church, establishing his own 'independent state' in Thomondgate.

The scandal first came to light a year previously in 1755 when rumours began to circulate that Fr Scanlan was on very familiar terms with a certain Elizabeth Fitzgerald and was the father of her baby child. When word of these rumours reached the ears of Bishop Lacy, who had recently moved into Limerick from Athea, Co. Limerick, he confronted Scanlan and urged him to break off the relationship with Elizabeth and arrange for her to leave town.

But Scanlan proved stubborn and made a point of maintaining the relationship with his mistress. Acting on the adage that attack is the best form of defence, he even put it about town that the real father of Elizabeth's child was the Bishop himself! The source of this accusation was, according to Scanlan, the very priest who had heard Elizabeth's confession.

Following this turn of events Bishop Lacy attempted to run Elizabeth out of town by telling people to have absolutely nothing to do with her; however, Fr Scanlan still kept his mistress installed in Limerick.

Amidst these developments, charges and counter-charges, Bishop Lacy and his senior clergy, in an effort to establish the facts of the case, spent the third week of February 1755 taking sworn statements from witnesses, both for and against Fr Scanlan. One of these witnesses, Brigid Horan, alleged that Fr Scanlan had had an improper relationship with her five years previously and had impregnated her with child. Her testimony was corroborated by other witnesses.

Despite the allegations made against Fr Scanlan, many of his parishioners still remained loyal to him.

Relations between Fr Scanlan's supporters and the Bishop deteriorated to such an extent during this period that a crowd composed of the people and the gentry of St Munchin's parish expressed their solidarity with the priest by stoning the Bishop. During this incident Fr Scanlan just stood silently by and made no attempt to intervene and disperse the unruly gathering. The Bishop retaliated by placing the parish chapel 'under interdict' (a Roman Catholic disciplinary measure withdrawing most sacraments and Christian burial from a person, parish or district) for two months.

In early March Bishop Lacy, after studying all the sworn statements by witnesses for and against Scanlan, decided to suspend him from his office as parish priest for a year — the Bishop reserving the right to shorten or lengthen the sentence as he saw fit.

But Fr Patrick Scanlan wasn't going to take this lying down — he cared not a feather or a fig for his Bishop and was willing to defy his authority to the utmost. He appealed first of all to the Archbishop of Cashel, but as His Grace did not deal with the matter as speedily as Scanlan would have liked, he then appealed to the Archbishop of Armagh, as Primate. This action was taken against the advice of his superiors, who claimed that Armagh's jurisdiction did not extend to Munster.

This process of appeals complicated the case still further and ensured that it lasted throughout the rest of 1755 and on into 1756.

The scandal erupted again on March 4th, 1756 when the Bishop of Limerick charged Fr Scanlan with a series of clerical crimes, including making defamatory remarks about the Bishop and maintaining a 'criminal conversation' (an illicit sexual relationship) with Elizabeth Fitzgerald, despite previous warnings to desist.

Refusing to answer the charges put to him, Fr Scanlan stated that he would be appealing to the Papal Nuncio in Brussels (at that time, the Papal Nuncio resided in Brussels) against whatever action the Bishop decided to take against him, then, or in the future. Angered by these remarks, Dr Lacy suspended the wilful priest from his clerical duties 'ab officio et beneficio' (without office or benefits) thus depriving him of his position and livelihood as a parish priest.

Showing the utmost contempt for the Bishop's authority, Fr Scanlan said Mass at St Munchin's on the following Sunday, and continued to carry out his pastoral duties as normal. More than a little bit peeved by all this, Bishop Lacy then sent two of his priests to the Thomondgate chapel on Sunday, March 17th with his written orders to interdict the chapel and inform the congregation that any person who assisted Fr Scanlan at any religious service, or other function, would be excommunicated.

Incensed by this intervention, Fr Scanlan openly declared from the pulpit that he would pay no more obedience to the Bishop than he would to the 'meanest of the flock'. Raising up a storm, he publicly incited the congregation against the two clergymen who were:

'Insulted by the rabble of a flock said Scanlan had about him, their lives were treaten'd, the Bishop's written orders were forceably taken from them . . . and they were driven out of the chapel.'

Scanlan had placed himself at the head of a determined revolt against his Bishop's authority.

A Woman Scorned

It appears that the relationship between Patrick Scanlan and his lady friend had turned sour in the meantime, for what reason we don't know. Several weeks after the two priests had been ejected from the chapel Elizabeth came to town demanding financial support for her two children. But when her temperamental and volatile lover refused to give her any more maintenance money she immediately went to the Bishop's house and made a full and frank confession of her sins in the presence of Bishop Lacy, the Rev. Michael Hoare and the Rev. James White, the author of the *White Manuscript*.

Placing herself on oath, Ms Fitzgerald gave a detailed account of the affair she had enjoyed with the sexually active priest from the time they first met. The woman scorned also presented the Bishop with clear evidence that Fr Scanlan had promised to pay her six guineas a year maintenance during her lifetime, or during the life of their daughter, Margaret.

Scanlan, hearing that his estranged mistress was revealing all to the Bishop, 'raised a mob against her', according to the Rev. James White, an eyewitness to all these scenes of passion and violence.

Pursued by the mob, Elizabeth fled to the safety of the Mayor's house where her life was protected with the utmost difficulty. That night she was obliged to flee the city for fear of losing her life.

As unprecedented and bizarre as these incidents were, they were exceeded by events that took place later that year.

Sunday May 9th, 1756 saw Bishop Lacy go in person to St Munchin's chapel during Mass to forbid the assembled flock, under pain of incurring excommunication, to assist Scanlan at Mass or to receive any sacraments from him. Despite these threats the congregation, emboldened by their previous defiance of Dr Lacy's authority, insulted the Bishop to his face and unceremoniously bundled him out of the chapel, much to the delight of their rebel leader.

Shortly after this disgraceful incident, Dr Lacy, exasperated beyond all measure, went to the altar of St Mary's chapel, dressed in full Episcopal regalia, and there, 'in writing, excommunicated said Patrick Scanlan . . . and at the same time he quenched the candles and rung the bell.' He also, with bell, book and candle, and with all solemnity, excommunicated all those who would in the future support Scanlan.

Casting Scanlan out of Mother Church proved a far easier proposition than trying to evict the mutinous cleric from his Thomondgate stronghold. On July 4th Bishop Lacy attempted to take possession of St Munchin's chapel and install a new priest, the Rev. Rowland Kirby. But once again Dr Lacy was thwarted in his aims by the insolent cleric, for, according to an account in the *White Manuscript*:

'Patrick Scanlan being surrounded by a great mob was ready to commit all kind of outrages in order to support his illegal possession, and even many shots were fired by Protestants he had with him, to deter the Bishop from the attempt of possession.'

Forced to retreat, Bishop Lacy formally installed Fr Kirby in a derelict house in St Munchin's parish, where he said Mass.

The Papal Nuncio, hearing of the turn of events in Limerick, instructed the Archbishop of Cashel to establish a Church tribunal to investigate and adjudicate on the dispute, provided that Scanlan first submit to Bishop Lacy's authority. But when the Archbishop met the rebel priest at Hospital in County Limerick in August 1756, he found him still obstinate in his refusal to comply with his Bishop's instructions, a stance which undermined Scanlan's credibility and further injured his case in the eyes of the Church. The tribunal subsequently had to be postponed.

The stand-off continued until December 1756 with Scanlan still retaining possession of St Munchin's. Matters came to a head on Saturday December 4th, when Fr Scanlan was summoned to St Mary's chapel by the Archbishop of Cashel who, on the Papal Nuncio's orders, pronounced sentence of 'Apostolical Excommunication' (final excommunication, with no going back) on the headstrong priest.

No sooner had sentence been pronounced than Scanlan's stubborn defiance crumbled to dust and he abjectly submitted himself to the Nuncio's orders and promised perfect obedience to Bishop Lacy. Confessing the error of his ways, regretting his past disobedience, Scanlan, brought to heel at last, surrendered the keys of his chapel that very same evening to the Bishop.

The next day, being a Sunday, Scanlan attended Mass at St Munchin's and exhorted all who had supported him in his late rebellion to humbly submit themselves to the Church and do whatever penance was required of them so that they may be cleared of excommunication. With Scanlan now out of the way the Rev. Rowland Kirby took over as parish priest of St Munchin's.

Scanlan gave no reason for his *volte face* and for his total and sudden submission. His former parishioners, as a penance, heard Mass on the following two Sundays outside the chapel and on the third Sunday they were absolved from the censure of excommunication at the church door.

At an ecclesiastical court held in Limerick in May and June 1757, to formally investigate the whole Scanlan affair, Bishop Lacy's actions during the dispute were vindicated, his sanctions against the Thomondgate priest were found to be legal and the court declared that Scanlan's appeals against his Bishop's actions were frivolous.

So ended what surely must be one of the most unusual and controversial events in Limerick diocesan history. According to Archdeacon John Begley in his *History of the Diocese of Limerick*, Patrick Scanlan lived in Limerick for many years after his trial and his death occurred on 29th March, 1774.

From *Georgian Limerick*, edited by David Lee and Bob Kelly, Limerick Civic Trust, 1996

Bishop Charles Graves
Alfred Perceval Graves

I remember my father as a spare, well-proportioned man, a little below the average height but with a dignity of carriage that made him appear taller. He had that shade of blue eyes which usually goes with auburn hair. His forehead was high and dome-shaped, the nose aquiline, the mouth straight and stern, though it relaxed at times into an engaging smile. His hands were small yet capable, with long, slender fingers. He was most particular about his dress, and orderly in all his habits. Had he not been, he could not have got through anything like the amount of work which he accomplished in so many directions. He was so fine and well-grounded a scholar, that he was able to converse freely in Latin with one of the brothers Grimm whom he met while travelling on the Continent, and as an old man he would quote Homer or Plautus with equal felicity.

He was better known as a mathematician, attaining European reputation as an original discoverer. Chasles, the French geometer, acknowledged his indebtedness to him for having added greatly to the results of his own researches. It may be that his classical tastes were responsible for the elegant form in which he presented his new algebraic and geometrical formulae and theorems, which have been described as instances of the 'Poetry of Mathematics'.

He could read six or seven modern languages, and was an interested student of English Literature. He also learned to speak Modern Irish. He was the secretary to the Brehon Laws Commission, took a leading part in the translation into English of the Old Irish Brehon Laws, made important discoveries about the authorship of the Book of Armagh, and was for long the leading authority on Oghams, the early Irish cryptic inscriptions which Brash and other Irish antiquaries had entirely misinterpreted.

He was a founder of the Trinity College Choral Society; played cricket for the Phoenix Club and for his own University; was an expert trout and salmon fisher, taking great pleasure in tying his own flies . . .

When my father was appointed Bishop of Limerick I was in my one-and-twentieth year. The Episcopal Palace, last occupied by Bishop Griffin, was very much out of repair, but Westfield, the residence of Archdeacon Hare, was kindly put at my father's disposal. This was situated on the far side of the Shannon opposite to the cathedral, and we had to cross a toll-bridge to get home from the station. Our neighbours were Major and Mrs Vandeleur and their children, and the Hon. Robert and Mrs O'Brien of the Inchiquin family, to which Smith O'Brien belonged.

After my father's installation he set to work to acquaint himself thoroughly with his diocese, which was a very large one, consisting of three divisions, Limerick, Ardfert, and Aghadoe. Fortunately Parknasilla lay within the diocese, and from there he worked the Ardfert and Aghadoe districts. The town of

Limerick was the natural centre of the remainder of his diocese, and from it he radiated in every direction, chiefly on horseback. He was a good rider, and had as a boy been intended for the army. Not that the family regiment was a cavalry one; but in those days, and I believe the tradition holds, every young Irishman of position learnt to ride . . .

While . . . my father neglected no part of his diocese, his main activities were concentrated on Limerick. I lived to see many proofs of his uplifting influence. For on my return to it, years later, I found more carefully conducted and more thoughtful services in the parish churches and well-attended morning prayer in the cathedral instead of what used to be a sparse congregation. For by this time my father had drawn many young and earnest Irish clergy into his diocese and he and my sisters had rallied round our organist, Dr Rogers, a fine body of professional and amateur singers, which made Limerick Cathedral a centre of the best church music. Socially our Limerick days in the sixties were delightful ones. What with fishing and boating and archery and picnic parties and cricket matches by day and dances and concerts by night we young people had rare times. Nor can I honestly say that the expression 'Limerick lasses', implying the beau-ideal of Irish beauty, was not justified in those days. For I remember counting at one Limerick ball a full score, any one of whom would have been the belle of a London ballroom. When my uncle Robert paid his first visit to Cooper Hill he told me he felt he ought to have been a Rembrandt to have done justice to the ten beautiful sisters to whom he was there introduced . . .

In the summer of 1899, a few months before the birth of my son Charles, my father died at the age of eighty-seven. The Palace passed into other hands and, as Parknasilla had already been sold, we no longer had a home in Ireland. But we were anxious to leave behind us in Limerick a worthy memorial of my father. This took the form of a beautiful Irish-Celtic Cross with inscriptions in Irish, Latin and English verse by Dr Hyde, Professor Tyrrell, and myself.

From *To Return to All That: An Autobiography*, Jonathan Cape Limited, 1930

'I promised or prophesied that before long they would all sing. To get them to do this was not easy. Many could not read. So I read out a verse of a hymn, made them all repeat it, and then I sang the verse alone in the pulpit to their breathless admiration. I told them I knew nothing about music, but had just ear enough to get a tune correctly and voice enough to sing it somehow, and that I thus made a fool of myself publicly to encourage them. They took courage; some sang modestly and correctly, others were very loud and out of tune. Yet by perseverance we succeeded in learning the Tantum Ergo and several hymn tunes pretty well; so that before the end of the first year they had become the wonder of the city. The harmonium was brought near the pulpit and the choir gathered round to lead. We had singing classes on Wednesday evenings.'

From this lively description we can easily understand what a vast amount of labour fell to the lot of the pioneers. But we may also gather from it that there was great good will. By degrees order was established, and sooner than we should expect, the working of the Confraternity went on without a hitch, although not with the precision and regularity with which we are now familiar. Fr Bridgett took to himself the lion's share of the work, and did it in so masterly a manner as to place all members, past, present and future, under an obligation of gratitude to him. However, he did not lack willing helpers. In addition to the officials of the Confraternity, who, then as always, gave their indispensable services gratuitously and cheerfully, he had at his command the Fathers of the community, who one and all esteemed it a privilege to be allowed to assist in the great work. The most efficient helper was without doubt Fr Harbison, whose power to stir the hearts of the men was truly remarkable. When, at length, after nine months, the Confraternity was established on a firm basis, Fr Bridgett retired from the Directorship to give way to a not less zealous and even more enthusiastic Director in Father Hall, who took up office 5th November, 1868. This date may be regarded as the end of the foundation period. It will be of interest to set down here the muster roll of the Confraternity as it then stood.

St John's Division — 34 Sections and 940 members.

St Michael's Division — 36 Sections and 967 members.

From *Golden Jubilee of the Arch-Confraternity of the Holy Family, Mount St Alphonsus, Limerick, 1868–1918*

The Redemptorist Arch-Confraternity

It was under the patronage of Our Lady of Perpetual Succour that a mission for men was opened in the Church of St Alphonsus on New Year's Day, 1868. This mission, which was preached by Fathers Bridgett, Harbison, Cameron, Connolly, Geoghegan, Gibson, Johnson, and Livius, was the immediate preparation for the establishment of the Confraternity. It is not easy, after a lapse of 50 years, to form an idea of the enthusiasm with which the men of Limerick attended this mission. We can only guess what it must have been from the figures and bare facts left us by the chronicler of the time. He tells us that the confessionals were surrounded by waiting crowds, that 8,000 men received Holy Communion in the Church of St Alphonsus, and that on the day of the close 1,400 men and boys received the Sacrament of Confirmation. In the following words he describes the vast crowd at the close of the mission:— 'An enormous throng of men occupied all the available space in the Church, from which many of the benches had to be removed to afford more accommodation. And more than this: so great was the crowd, that it was literally one thickly packed mass from the Altar steps to the railings in Henry Street and even as far as the Military Road.' As to the success of the mission we have a competent witness in the person of the Most Rev. Dr Butler who thus expressed himself:— 'This is the miracle wrought by Our Lady of Perpetual Succour — surely a far greater miracle than the cure of a blind boy or the healing of a cripple.' This was indeed a great miracle; but, as we shall see, it was soon to be followed by something still greater.

The way was now prepared for the actual founding of the Confraternity. On Monday, 20th January, 1868, and the two following days Fathers Harbison and Bridgett explained its object and rules to crowded congregations. Their invitation to men willing to join met with a splendid response; for no fewer than 1,400 men had themselves enrolled, and many more followed their example within a few weeks. The Bishop, who came to address the men on the 3rd February, had reason to congratulate them on the good beginning they had made. New recruits still continued to present themselves in such numbers, that it was soon found that the Church, large as it was, could not accommodate all the members at the same meeting. Consequently, in addition to the meeting on Tuesday evening, an overflow meeting was held on Sunday afternoon. As, however, this arrangement proved unsatisfactory, Monday evening was substituted for Sunday afternoon. It was thought that when the first fervour had time to cool down, there would be no longer any need for a second meeting in the week. Contrary to expectations, the fervour increased, and it was soon realised that the Monday meeting had come to stay. On Tuesday evening the members from St Michael's Parish (in which the Church of St Alphonsus is situated) had their meeting and came to be known as St Michael's Division. The members from the parishes of St John, St Mary, St

Munchin and St Patrick met on Monday evening, and were called St John's Division. From the very beginning down to the present day both divisions have rested on a footing of perfect equality.

When strangers, unacquainted with the Confraternity, are present for the first time at any of its functions, they seldom fail to express their astonishment at the perfect discipline of the men and unvarying regularity with which everything proceeds in that vast congregation. The men themselves take it as a matter of course that the working of the Confraternity should run as smoothly as clockwork. But, as we often forget, when admiring an accurate clock, the labour and pains expended on it, to bring it to perfection, so, too, when we see the order and discipline of the Confraternity, we seldom think at how great an expense of skill, patience and hard work the early Directors and their zealous band of self-sacrificing helpers made it a wonder of perfect organisation. It will, we trust, be of interest to present-day members, if we recall some of the details of their first efforts to establish the admirable order, which is now characteristic of the Confraternity. These details will be all the more acceptable from the fact that they are furnished by one whose name will ever be revered by the men of the Confraternity, namely, Father Bridgett, the founder and first Director. He introduces his narrative by speaking of a method that may be followed when small confraternities have to be marshalled. Then he continues:—

'But this simple method was impossible in our case; the numbers were far too large. The church was packed; the men could not move about without great difficulty; we did not know the city with its back streets, and thus a more laborious and studious method had to be followed. Books had been filled with the names taken down. We cut them up into slips, each slip containing one name, and made a great heap of them. I invited several postmen to my help and they made about a dozen districts out of the city and suburbs on which they agreed, and then distributed the big heap into twelve smaller heaps, so far as they could. I say *so far as they could*, for they soon found that they could not recognise half the localities. There were "Flag Lanes" and "Pump Courts" into which no postman had ever penetrated. I had to call in several well-known rent collectors to assist me in finding these hidden recesses. Then, again, many addresses were so imperfect or so badly written that we could not arrange them. The next distribution was of the twelve minor heaps into sub-divisions of thirty each; for we had agreed to give three large benches of the nave, or four small benches of the aisles, to each section and to limit the numbers to thirty.

'When this division was made, I got about fifty copy books. On the first leaf was written the name of the patron saint, and the streets and lanes assigned to that section. Then the names were all copied from the slips in fair round hand into the books. Several clerks helped me in this work, one reading and the other writing, and then after a time, changing places. But as these men could only come in the evenings, I employed an old lawyer's clerk. He not only filled up the copy books,

but performed the more laborious task of drawing up an Index book giving the name alphabetically with occupation and address, and adding the name of the section. Such a book was soon found indispensable.

'It is easier to marshal men on paper than to drill them in flesh and blood. When Tuesday came, I explained the principle of division and its purpose: the purpose being that the attendance might be registered, and that the member living in the same locality might come to know each other, and assist each oth[er] when sick, dying or dead, the principle of division being in general that locality. Then I cleared some benches on the Gospel side and declared that th[ey] were for the Section of St Alphonsus, in which I had placed young men from [one] of the drapers' houses. These soon came forward. But all did not run so smoo[th.] One difficulty arose from the number of similar names. I have this mor[ning] glanced at the original alphabetical Register. I find ten Kings — a large nu[mber] for a republic like our Confraternity. I find ten Sextons — enough to bury [us.] But these are rare names. Take the letter K. There are 39 Kellys, 35 Ken[nedys] besides 12 Kennys and 8 Kennellys. What a confusion when these nam[es are] called out in a vast church in the midst of movement! Then the Macs a[nd] Macnamaras! It seems that some Celts nowadays drop their Macs or [O's] altogether and are contented to be called simple Sheahan instead [of] Sheahan and Doherty rather than O'Doherty. But, on the other hand, [there are] some who drop the clan or family name and cling to the Mac; so tha[t "Patsy] Mac" or "Biddy Mac" is in Limerick a common abbreviation fo[r] MacNamara or Bridget MacMahon. However, I find in our first Inde[x the] Macnamaras written full. Now imagine the scene on these first nights [in] trying to get men into their places. I want to put a certain Macnama[ra in the] Section of St Brendan. I begin to read in a loud voice: "Macnar[a." A] hundred voices cry out: "Here, Father," and two hundred legs stand e[rect.] "Macnamara, Patrick." Fifty men sit down disappointed and fifty [cry: "Here,] Father." Once more: "Patrick Macnamara, Tailor." Twenty-five s[it down;] twenty-five still cry: "Here, Father." At last: "Patrick Macnamara[, Mungret] Lane, Boherbuoy" — and so I get my man, and he fights his wa[y through the] crowd, amidst considerable laughter, to the vacant place. Or just [as likely I did] not get him. He was not there that night and I had all my troub[le for nothing.] But suppose I did get him into his place — was all over? Not at al[l. Perhaps he] had forgotten the name of his section or the exact part of the ch[urch where I] placed him, and how could I find out? I could not search thro[ugh 40] and 50 books till I found one that would suit him. So I found it [necessary to keep] an alphabetical Register, and when a man forgot his section o[r his place] when his name was called, we looked him up in the Register[, wrote] on a paper the name of his section and of his Prefect, and se[nt him to make] his acquaintance. This first classification was so difficult tha[t I was in the] pulpit till nearly 11 o'clock at night on the first three or fou[r

The Redemptorist Arch-Confraternity

It was under the patronage of Our Lady of Perpetual Succour that a mission for men was opened in the Church of St Alphonsus on New Year's Day, 1868. This mission, which was preached by Fathers Bridgett, Harbison, Cameron, Connolly, Geoghegan, Gibson, Johnson, and Livius, was the immediate preparation for the establishment of the Confraternity. It is not easy, after a lapse of 50 years, to form an idea of the enthusiasm with which the men of Limerick attended this mission. We can only guess what it must have been from the figures and bare facts left us by the chronicler of the time. He tells us that the confessionals were surrounded by waiting crowds, that 8,000 men received Holy Communion in the Church of St Alphonsus, and that on the day of the close 1,400 men and boys received the Sacrament of Confirmation. In the following words he describes the vast crowd at the close of the mission:— 'An enormous throng of men occupied all the available space in the Church, from which many of the benches had to be removed to afford more accommodation. And more than this: so great was the crowd, that it was literally one thickly packed mass from the Altar steps to the railings in Henry Street and even as far as the Military Road.' As to the success of the mission we have a competent witness in the person of the Most Rev. Dr Butler who thus expressed himself:— 'This is the miracle wrought by Our Lady of Perpetual Succour — surely a far greater miracle than the cure of a blind boy or the healing of a cripple.' This was indeed a great miracle; but, as we shall see, it was soon to be followed by something still greater.

The way was now prepared for the actual founding of the Confraternity. On Monday, 20th January, 1868, and the two following days Fathers Harbison and Bridgett explained its object and rules to crowded congregations. Their invitation to men willing to join met with a splendid response; for no fewer than 1,400 men had themselves enrolled, and many more followed their example within a few weeks. The Bishop, who came to address the men on the 3rd February, had reason to congratulate them on the good beginning they had made. New recruits still continued to present themselves in such numbers, that it was soon found that the Church, large as it was, could not accommodate all the members at the same meeting. Consequently, in addition to the meeting on Tuesday evening, an overflow meeting was held on Sunday afternoon. As, however, this arrangement proved unsatisfactory, Monday evening was substituted for Sunday afternoon. It was thought that when the first fervour had time to cool down, there would be no longer any need for a second meeting in the week. Contrary to expectations, the fervour increased, and it was soon realised that the Monday meeting had come to stay. On Tuesday evening the members from St Michael's Parish (in which the Church of St Alphonsus is situated) had their meeting and came to be known as St Michael's Division. The members from the parishes of St John, St Mary, St

Munchin and St Patrick met on Monday evening, and were called St John's Division. From the very beginning down to the present day both divisions have rested on a footing of perfect equality.

When strangers, unacquainted with the Confraternity, are present for the first time at any of its functions, they seldom fail to express their astonishment at the perfect discipline of the men and unvarying regularity with which everything proceeds in that vast congregation. The men themselves take it as a matter of course that the working of the Confraternity should run as smoothly as clockwork. But, as we often forget, when admiring an accurate clock, the labour and pains expended on it, to bring it to perfection, so, too, when we see the order and discipline of the Confraternity, we seldom think at how great an expense of skill, patience and hard work the early Directors and their zealous band of self-sacrificing helpers made it a wonder of perfect organisation. It will, we trust, be of interest to present-day members, if we recall some of the details of their first efforts to establish the admirable order, which is now characteristic of the Confraternity. These details will be all the more acceptable from the fact that they are furnished by one whose name will ever be revered by the men of the Confraternity, namely, Father Bridgett, the founder and first Director. He introduces his narrative by speaking of a method that may be followed when small confraternities have to be marshalled. Then he continues:—

'But this simple method was impossible in our case; the numbers were far too large. The church was packed; the men could not move about without great difficulty; we did not know the city with its back streets, and thus a more laborious and studious method had to be followed. Books had been filled with the names taken down. We cut them up into slips, each slip containing one name, and made a great heap of them. I invited several postmen to my help and they made about a dozen districts out of the city and suburbs on which they agreed, and then distributed the big heap into twelve smaller heaps, so far as they could. I say *so far as they could*, for they soon found that they could not recognise half the localities. There were "Flag Lanes" and "Pump Courts" into which no postman had ever penetrated. I had to call in several well-known rent collectors to assist me in finding these hidden recesses. Then, again, many addresses were so imperfect or so badly written that we could not arrange them. The next distribution was of the twelve minor heaps into sub-divisions of thirty each; for we had agreed to give three large benches of the nave, or four small benches of the aisles, to each section and to limit the numbers to thirty.

'When this division was made, I got about fifty copy books. On the first leaf was written the name of the patron saint, and the streets and lanes assigned to that section. Then the names were all copied from the slips in fair round hand into the books. Several clerks helped me in this work, one reading and the other writing, and then after a time, changing places. But as these men could only come in the evenings, I employed an old lawyer's clerk. He not only filled up the copy books, but performed the more laborious task of drawing up an Index book giving the name alphabetically with occupation and address, and adding the name of the section. Such a book was soon found indispensable.

'It is easier to marshal men on paper than to drill them in flesh and blood. When Tuesday came, I explained the principle of division and its purpose: the purpose being that the attendance might be registered, and that the members living in the same locality might come to know each other, and assist each other when sick, dying or dead, the principle of division being in general that of locality. Then I cleared some benches on the Gospel side and declared that these were for the Section of St Alphonsus, in which I had placed young men from one of the drapers' houses. These soon came forward. But all did not run so smoothly. One difficulty arose from the number of similar names. I have this morning glanced at the original alphabetical Register. I find ten Kings — a large number for a republic like our Confraternity. I find ten Sextons — enough to bury us all. But these are rare names. Take the letter K. There are 39 Kellys, 35 Kennedys, besides 12 Kennys and 8 Kennellys. What a confusion when these names are called out in a vast church in the midst of movement! Then the Macs and the Macnamaras! It seems that some Celts nowadays drop their Macs or their O altogether and are contented to be called simple Sheahan instead of Mac Sheahan and Doherty rather than O'Doherty. But, on the other hand, there are some who drop the clan or family name and cling to the Mac; so that "Paddy Mac" or "Biddy Mac" is in Limerick a common abbreviation for Patrick MacNamara or Bridget MacMahon. However, I find in our first Index Book 99 Macnamaras written full. Now imagine the scene on these first nights when I was trying to get men into their places. I want to put a certain Macnamara into the Section of St Brendan. I begin to read in a loud voice: "Macnamara"! One hundred voices cry out: "Here, Father," and two hundred legs stand erect. I go on: "Macnamara, Patrick." Fifty men sit down disappointed and fifty say: "Here, Father." Once more: "Patrick Macnamara, Tailor." Twenty-five sit down and twenty-five still cry: "Here, Father." At last: "Patrick Macnamara, No. 5 Pump Lane, Boherbuoy" — and so I get my man, and he fights his way through the crowd, amidst considerable laughter, to the vacant place. Or just as likely I did not get him. He was not there that night and I had all my trouble for nothing. But suppose I did get him into his place — was all over? Not at all. Next week he had forgotten the name of his section or the exact part of the church where I had placed him, and how could I find out? I could not search through 1,500 names and 50 books till I found one that would suit him. So I found it necessary to have an alphabetical Register, and when a man forgot his section or had been absent when his name was called, we looked him up in the Register and wrote for him on a paper the name of his section and of his Prefect, and sent him off to make his acquaintance. This first classification was so difficult that I remained in the pulpit till nearly 11 o'clock at night on the first three or four meetings . . .

'I promised or prophesied that before long they would all sing. To get them to do this was not easy. Many could not read. So I read out a verse of a hymn, made them all repeat it, and then I sang the verse alone in the pulpit to their breathless admiration. I told them I knew nothing about music, but had just ear enough to get a tune correctly and voice enough to sing it somehow, and that I thus made a fool of myself publicly to encourage them. They took courage; some sang modestly and correctly, others were very loud and out of tune. Yet by perseverance we succeeded in learning the Tantum Ergo and several hymn tunes pretty well; so that before the end of the first year they had become the wonder of the city. The harmonium was brought near the pulpit and the choir gathered round to lead. We had singing classes on Wednesday evenings.'

From this lively description we can easily understand what a vast amount of labour fell to the lot of the pioneers. But we may also gather from it that there was great good will. By degrees order was established, and sooner than we should expect, the working of the Confraternity went on without a hitch, although not with the precision and regularity with which we are now familiar. Fr Bridgett took to himself the lion's share of the work, and did it in so masterly a manner as to place all members, past, present and future, under an obligation of gratitude to him. However, he did not lack willing helpers. In addition to the officials of the Confraternity, who, then as always, gave their indispensable services gratuitously and cheerfully, he had at his command the Fathers of the community, who one and all esteemed it a privilege to be allowed to assist in the great work. The most efficient helper was without doubt Fr Harbison, whose power to stir the hearts of the men was truly remarkable. When, at length, after nine months, the Confraternity was established on a firm basis, Fr Bridgett retired from the Directorship to give way to a not less zealous and even more enthusiastic Director in Father Hall, who took up office 5th November, 1868. This date may be regarded as the end of the foundation period. It will be of interest to set down here the muster roll of the Confraternity as it then stood.

St John's Division — 34 Sections and 940 members.

St Michael's Division — 36 Sections and 967 members.

From *Golden Jubilee of the Arch-Confraternity of the Holy Family, Mount St Alphonsus, Limerick,* 1868–1918

One More for the Road!
Patrick Conlan, OFM

A Third Train for the Third Order

The friar appointed to visit the Irish province in 1879 by the minister general was a German, Gregor Janknecht. He was appalled by what he considered the low level of religious observance among the Irish Franciscans . . . Fr Janknecht got his chance . . . in 1883 . . . a plan was formulated which would eventually result in a total reform of the Irish Franciscans . . . For the next ten years the Ennis community would live a sort of twilight existence, hoping against hope that the Black Friars would be allowed to recruit and continue . . . During these ten years the community usually consisted of three priests and two or three tertiaries. They had their occasional high-lights, such as a Third Order Pilgrimage from Limerick on 12 August 1894. Fourteen hundred came on two special trains, accompanied by the band of the Limerick Industrial Schools. They marched from the station to the Friary for prayers and thence to the Abbey, where Fr Lee, Adm. of St John's, Limerick, gave a talk on the history of the friars in Ennis. The events there concluded with the hymn 'God Save Ireland' and the pilgrims were free until it was time for Vespers and Benediction in the Friary. For some strange reason it took three trains to bring them back to Limerick!

From *The Franciscans in Ennis*, The Lilliput Press, 1984

A Letter from Rabbi Levin
July 1904

The Hebrew Congregation of Limerick,
Synagogue Chambers,
63 Colooney Street

The Memorial of the Reverend Elias Bere Levin, 18 Colooney St, Limerick on behalf of The Hebrew Community in Limerick.

Memorialist is the Jewish Minister at Limerick and as such entrusted with the spiritual, and to some extent temporal welfare of his people.

To the General of The Redemption Order now visiting.

Up to a very recent time the Jews of Limerick have had no cause to complain of any unjust or oppressive treatment from their Christian fellow Citizens, and enjoyed the same facilities as every other citizen, and for which the soul of Ireland has always been remarkable, namely that trade was not to be obtained by Religion or politics, but by fair and honourable dealings, and that every honest trader could count on the support of those who differed from him in religion, or politics, just as much as those who agreed with him.

Unfortunately this has of late changed, and now, though we still trade with our Christian fellow Citizens, they no longer trade with us, and treat us with ill will, and occasionally the rougher element has used actual violence towards us, and our debts due to us for goods sold, are practically now irrecoverable.

I do not think it deemable in the interest of the good feeling which I respectfully urge your Excellency to restore, that I should enter on any explanation of the causes which produced for us — terrible result.

There are a small number of our people, who, seeking refuge in Ireland (which is famous all over the world for its hospitality to strangers, and its uplifting the cause of the oppressed) are now deprived by circumstances over which they have no control, from earning the bare necessities of life.

I respectfully ask your Excellency, that during your visit to Limerick, you will be pleased to point out to the Catholic Citizens of Limerick that a Jew is one of God's creatures entitled to their brotherly love and consideration which is at the root of all true religious feeling, and practise those things it may be just that the Christian shall give such preference to those of his own religion, though the fact that we are Jews should not prevent them also dealing with us.

I regret I have to say to your Excellency that at present it is useless for a Jew to keep open his shop for any trade, for though the Catholic people who were their customers will no longer deal with them, under the mistaken idea that in so depriving us of our means of living, they are complying with some religious requirement of which they would be breaking the requirements if they were to trade with us.

I therefore ask your Excellency, during your stay in Limerick, to address such remarks on this subject to your people, as will remove from them the idea, that we are under the ban of your Church and will give them to understand, that there is no objection from any religious grounds to them dealing with any honest trader, whether Christian or Jew.

If your Excellency would accord me the honour and pleasure of an interview, I shall avail myself of the honour with very great pleasure, and shall call on you whenever and wherever you name, either alone or accompanied by one or more of our Elders.

It is necessary to the very existence of my little flock, only Twenty-four families, that their trade shall be restored and relieved from the terrible blight which has now fallen on it, owing to the mistaken view of our Christian fellow Citizens that they are forbidden by their religion to deal with us.

Respectfully Yours
Elias Bere Levin
18 Coloney Street
Limerick

Jews Minister
at Limerick

From a copy of Rabbi Levin's letter in the possession of the Editor

'Make No Mistake About It, My Lord Bishop of Limerick'
Paul Blanshard

Ireland has not produced either in the South or in the North the kind of society described in the first chapter of this book as the American ideal — a society of tolerance and good will where men of different faiths can live together as equals, educate their children together, marry across religious boundaries without discrimination, and refuse to use sectarian advantage for political power. On the contrary, the Irish Catholic policy on church and state has produced a society of deep religious divisions characterised by conflict and suspicion. Far worse, it has produced in Southern Ireland a society where cultural freedom and, to a certain extent, genuine political freedom have been sacrificed to clerical dictatorship. Without labouring our points at great length, it seems fair to make certain inductions from the evidence.

In a nation in which the Catholic hierarchy controls the organs of public opinion, formal political democracy is not an adequate defence against clerical dictatorship. The Irish Republic has complete political democracy, but democracy cannot rise higher than its source, and its source is public opinion. When the priests control all elementary education and indirectly almost all of the press, they exercise a veto power over the whole national life. Because of this condition, the Irish Republic is an exhibit of mutilated democracy . . .

Michael Davitt, founder of the Irish Land League, son of an American mother, and one of the greatest of the Irish Catholic revolutionists, saw the issue clearly when he challenged the dictatorship of the Irish priests as well as British rule. In a famous controversy in 1906 with the Catholic bishops of his country, Davitt wrote: 'The growing experience of progressive civilisation is coming to see that the American system of universal and free secular education is the best all-round plan yet devised.' When Bishop O'Dwyer of Limerick blasted him with five columns of pastoral rebuke in the *Freeman's Journal*, Davitt was not dismayed. He was conscious that the future belonged to those who believed in complete democracy and complete tolerance. In a letter to the press, he wrote a sentence which I have used as the epigraph of this book — a sentence which may well be applied to two present-day countries in which Irish Catholic power is struggling with modern conceptions of freedom and tolerance, Ireland and the United States: 'Make no mistake about it, my Lord Bishop of Limerick, Democracy is going to rule in these countries.'

From *The Irish and Catholic Power*, Derek Verschoyle Limited, 1954

Two Fanaticisms
Frank O'Connor

I don't know why I should always have had a soft spot in my heart for Limerick. Of course, my family came originally from that county, but that was in the eleventh century, and I am no believer in racial memories. Probably it began in an internment camp during the Civil War, for here I hit it off admirably with a whole hutful of Limerickmen. They were a tough, argumentative, clannish lot with very good voices, who amused themselves in the evenings with part-singing, a recreation they were alone in enjoying.

It was as well I had friends among them, because our mess-leader was a Limerickman, and I might otherwise have starved, but no Limerickman dared exploit even a Limerickman's pal. When a hunger-strike was declared and I opposed it and became violently unpopular in the camp, they made me sleep in their hut for safety. It must have been something of a strain on them to see me return three times a day from the dining hall, and they always asked fondly after the menu, but they would not let a pal be knocked about by any Dublin jackeen.

Since then I have always felt at home in the city. I have no doubt whatever that if you had been brought up in it, it would seem a hell-hole worse even than Cork. At any rate, my Limerick cousins assure me that the great pleasure of living there is that you know *everybody's* business, which is my definition of hell; but knowing nobody's business except your friends', and not caring a rap whether or not anyone knows yours, you can be as happy here as in any Irish town.

Limerick is much more like Belfast than Cork. All the religious orders in Ireland have established themselves there, even the Jesuits, who are popular nowhere else, and my poor unfortunate Galway friend cannot find a soul who will admit to any doubt of orthodox religion. The religious orders run confraternities which march to church behind their bands, and exclusion from one of these confraternities is almost equivalent to social extinction . . . Jews, evangelists and strolling players have all at various times suffered from these outbursts of demented religion . . .

In most Irish cities nationalism has always come first, religion second; but in Limerick, where the two fanaticisms are almost equally balanced, they produce conflict on a very considerable scale . . . Another famous local nationalist was a baker. The Bishop at that time was a toady called O'Dwyer, who had been appointed by Rome and was determined on crushing nationalist opposition (later he changed his tune and became something of a national hero). When the baker stood for election to the Corporation, O'Dwyer turned the whole power of the Church against him. In spite of this, he was elected. It became even worse when he was nominated for the mayoralty. Then everything O'Dwyer could do in the way of intrigue and threats was done, but the unfortunate councillors had a second loyalty beside their loyalty to the Church, and to O'Dwyer's chagrin the baker was elected. His first business as Mayor was to attend High Mass at the cathedral with the Corporation. A special chair was reserved for him, and he appeared there in his mayoral robes. O'Dwyer was sitting in the Bishop's throne. When the Mayor appeared he sent a message ordering him out of the cathedral. The Mayor rose and left, but the Corporation had gone as far as it could go and it skulked behind . . .

There are a good many fine houses in the county, apart from those grouped about Castleconnell. The loveliest of them, Shannongrove, is only a short distance from Limerick on the Askeaton road. It is a house of Queen Anne date, with a high roof and wide, ornamented chimneys which look like the trousers of a blue-jacket standing on his head, and stable buildings with Dutch gables . . .

There is another Queen Anne house at Ballyneety on the Bruff road, though this has little to recommend it but a good doorway and a flight of what I understand are called 'water-lily' steps. These are steps in a curve, each stone of which is also curved — obviously the invention of a temperance advocate who determined to break the leg of anybody leaving his house under the influence of drink. At the other side of the road is the ruined home of Boss Croker, with statues 'all standing naked in the open air'. There was a proposal to bring Hercules to Limerick, but a committee of inspection, having studied him carefully fore and aft, decided that he would never do for the confraternities. Where Jews, salvationists and actors had not escaped, what chance had poor old Hercules?

From *Leinster, Munster and Connaught*, Robert Hale Limited, 1949

Christmas in the Presentation Parlour
Kate O'Brien

I had five aunts. So had my brothers and sisters, the same five in name and place . . .

Aunt Mary had a soldierly quality, and was naturally a controller of events and persons. As quite a young nun she was elected to the various officeships of the religious life, from sacristan to Bursar, to Mistress of Novices.

When she was still quite young there took place, as every five years by the Presentation Rule, an election for the office of Reverend Mother . . .

Let me recall Aunt Mary in the Parlour. Christmas Day would be a good occasion. It was our first ceremony on that day, our first worldly ceremony, that is. We had all been to eight o'clock Mass at our parish church, St John's Cathedral. Father would have no going to midnight Mass. The riff-raff of the town was loose at that hour, he said, and he would not have his children meet it. And in the churches crowded by the poor and the dirty we might get fleas, or worse afflictions. Let him not be judged un-Christian for this — for he was not. He was only a clean-habited and affectionate man who wanted to keep us in good health and as long as possible unaware of violence and uproar in life. So instead of the fun and novelty of the midnight ceremonies we had the bleak morning rigours of ordinary Mass and Communion, fasting and frozen. The novelties were only the exquisite alto boy's voice in *Adeste Fideles* after the Consecration — and before the *Credo* there were the ten minutes of the Administrator's Christmas sermon. I have heard bad sermons all over the world, and I believe a good sermon to be the whitest of white blackbirds; I have listened only to two that I remember for merit. But for sheer agonising badness, flatness, inexcusable platitudinous fatuity those Christmas sermons from the various head priests of St John's Cathedral over my years of childhood and girlhood — and I was an attentive listener — take all the cakes and every imaginable biscuit. They were agonising, that is all I can say. And some of those flinty, dead, unholy voices I can hear now this minute, as I write.

Well, God has forgiven the well-meaning men, if I have not. And afterwards there was breakfast — wonderful and picturesque and decorated breakfast, with candles lighted and frilled cold dishes on the sideboard, and wrapped-up presents heaped at every place — and a deep sense of relief and benevolence.

Afterwards there came the campaign of the Parlour. On Christmas Day Aunts May and Fan held high reception for us from noon to three o'clock . . . So, breakfast over, we younger ones were not given half enough time to brood over our presents; we had to be upstairs, changing into our newest and best, and setting off hours too early, 'to bag the Parlour'. This was Father's idea — and over such a matter this kindest of men was a tyrannical fusspot. So off we had to go, feeling fools, in dressed-up instalments, to take up our positions, much too soon for the aunts, in the Parlour.

Father himself, who took everything to do with Christmas with the most generous seriousness, would not leave the house until the post came. The sending of Christmas cards — and presents, may I add, for he was princely — but the sending of cards was only equalled in pleasurable seriousness for him by his reception of the cards and greetings of his friends — and of ours! (Useless to hope for a private message from anyone at Christmas. Father, in sheer pleasure, had to see and consider all that came to his house.) So he waited, alone, for the postman — who arrived intoxicated before one o'clock, and very certainly did not leave our house without some further cheer. Then, and only then, Father would have himself driven to the convent, and come smiling and waving up the long garden — I can see him now — with a Gladstone bag. Our Christmas post, which would be publicly and ruthlessly opened, by him and Fan and Auntie Mick and Sister Bernardine, in the Parlour — and thoroughly discussed and disputed and assessed, every silliest card of it . . .

However . . . back to the Parlour. A large, square Georgian room, with two fine broad windows giving on to the visitors' garden, two doors facing each other, one from the hall, the other through which the nuns came to us but beyond which we might not travel. A handsome Georgian fireplace. A tinny little piano. A number of comfortable but severe Victorian chairs. Plants in brass pots. Two portraits of two bishops of Limerick on the walls. (The Bishop of Limerick was always, *ex officio*, the governor of any Presentation house.) Some prints and engravings of religious subjects from old masters. A highly polished floor. A rep-covered Victorian sofa. A central table to which, on Christmas Day and other days, many kinds of refreshment were borne by Sister Lucy and Sister Philomena.

A very pleasant parlour. But on Christmas Day one could not see it very well, because by one o'clock it was thronged. Nine of us, Katty's children, for a start, ranging — let us take a date at random — from twenty years to five. That means that Mother — Katty — is more than five years dead, and that her name can at least be spoken without instant tears, between the elders. Nine of us fidgeting around; Father on the sofa with his Gladstone bag; Fan safely planted near him, between him and the window, cushioned, shawled and happy, as eager as dear Tom about the Christmas post in the opened bag. Auntie Mick, who will not stay long, across the window from Fan, upright and elegant, talking to Mother Ligouri, and dealing very firmly with Gerard, the youngest of us whom she detests and who seems to love annoying her. He pulls and teases now at her exquisitely rolled and delicate silk umbrella; his fingers are chocolate-stained. But with Father so near she will not give him the brutal slap and insult that he would get on her own ground.

Music Ho! The little piano is overworked on Christmas Day. Our sister Clare, a teenager, is unable to bear the out-of-tuneness of it. She is a natural musician, and has absolute pitch. However, on Christmas Day she tries to control her impatience. Most of the family can sing, and if they can, today they must do so for the nuns.

Now, the funny thing is that, like our father who had a sweet, light tenor voice, most of our family could sing in tune, and with sufficient volume and taste to be bearable performers. But two, Clare and Gerard, had in fact musical and singing talents of distinction. In the general Christmas parade for the aunts, however, there was no differentiation, and we all performed in some way, God help us, and as we were Katty's children we were all marvellous.

So the Christmas Day concert, while Father smiled and nodded and went on through the post — everyone's post; while this priest and that young nun peeped in and asked Reverend Mother (Aunt Mary) if they might listen awhile to all the wonderful talent of her nieces and nephews — until at last the Bishop of Limerick, in a lesser parlour waiting for Aunt Mary, was shown brilliantly in — and brilliant he was and looked, Edward Thomas O'Dwyer — so the concert went on. Broken only by applause, and by the episcopal entrance. Father, who loved Bishops and Princes of the Church — only imaginatively and with no experience of them — was delighted to have Aunt Mary place the deaf prelate beside him. He knew him well, and mounted him. Bishop O'Dwyer, who would allow none of his priests to hunt, was a great horseman.

So there they sat, shouting at each other. Bishop O'Dwyer shouted high and shrill anyway, and Father's only attack on the deaf — in this case useless — was to bellow.

And as they bellowed my sister Clare, persuaded by some gentle nuns near the piano, began to sing.

She sang 'At the mid hour of night . . . ' Father heard her when she began, and stopped shouting. The Bishop, glad enough no doubt to end an interchange he had not head nor tail to, subsided into some note-taking, with a gold pencil on the back of an envelope. So I can hear the young, sad voice now, overcoming us all. She was already full contralto. She had had lessons from a local musician, but I think they meant nothing to Clare. I always thought, as I listened to her singing, that she was self-taught. She sang out of some knowledge that no Limerick teacher gave her. She sang, as few singers do, like a musician. She sang out of the centre of music. Often when we were young she sang ridiculous songs, but she never sang ridiculously. She gave musicianship to everything she sang. And that musicianship was her own — she did not learn it from any of her Limerick teachers.

'At the mid hour of night . . . ' The young, rich voice, its purity seeming to contradict the great sorrow of the theme, still insisted that it knew what it sang. I think that Father, some Christmas card in his fidgety hand, could hardly bear the desolate and ghostly song — and yet he loved it.

Aunt Mary would break it up gently, patting Clare's shoulder, and asking her to play 'The West's Awake' for Jack to sing, or 'The Battle-Eve of the Irish Brigade'.

'We must have something lively on Christmas Day,' she would say. But Fan's tears fell faster for these songs than for ' . . . when stars are weeping . . . ' the long line of which bored her a little — whereas she was a patriot always before the first shout; and 'Hurray! Let England quake!' was very much her idea, even on Christmas Day and from her enclosed convent.

The Bishop rose and we with him, dropping all on one knee for his blessing — and a minute later one could watch him pacing down the garden, silky, silver hair blowing, pink hand cupping his good ear as he conversed with Aunt Mary, this Reverend Mother whom he admired extremely. His carriage horses champing, and even if the wind was cold he would linger with this nun — and *hear* what she said. An autocrat mostly disliked by his priests, a man of iron principle and courage as he was to prove in political troubles yet ahead, and one who expected to be listened to and obeyed, he often listened and often, I think, without knowing it obeyed when this young nun, his mere subaltern, spoke. It was known, and he always made clear, that he thought highly of her powers in office. But he was a man with an unexpected regard for the brains of women. He proved that in his long liking for the society of two unusually brainy nuns of Laurel Hill Convent, in Limerick. I was educated there, and I know how rarely intelligent were those two Latinists, Mother Lelia and Mother Thecla — and I know too how he liked to visit them, to tackle them about Latin, about the revival of Irish, about Irish history and Ireland's future. His twanging, unpleasantly pitched voice was nevertheless clear and cultivated, and we could hear him from far off if it pleased him to walk into our garden classroom of an afternoon. Then he would take Horace out of Mother Thecla's hand, and singing out the Ode would turn mockingly on me or on Nellie Dundon or whomsoever, for a lightning scan. No use being scared; the thing was to make a stab at the lines — and he never mocked, always bent his good ear down attentively. Then after a few minutes he would slam the book shut, wave dismissal at us, and take Mother Thecla off into the garden in loud, learned argument, often talking Latin to her, to our deep edification.

Aunt Mary had no Latin, but she had wits and qualities he sought and too often missed among his fellow creatures. When he died his chaplain gave her, as a souvenir, a slim, shallow lacquered box — a useful and pleasant desk box, for pencils, sealing wax, etc. And when she in her turn died, Fan gave it to me, because she knew that I agreed with Aunt Mary in admiring our difficult bishop, Edward Thomas of Limerick . . .

Auntie Mick made a stately exit, and was escorted from the parlour and down the garden by some anxiously polite young nun.

With her gone and the Bishop, the pace of feast-day quickened in the parlour. Blushing novices slipped in to wish happy Christmas to Reverend Mother's 'lovely family', and with any luck to hear May, the eldest of us, sing 'The Snowy-Breasted Pearl', looking the while so like the heroine of her song; or Nance recite

'O'Rourke's Request' brilliantly; or Father Thornhill, our handsome, heavy cousin, oblige with a great long roar of 'Dark Rosaleen' (I also had to make a fair fool of myself, for I was an accomplished reciter, and I think, looking back, that unless someone had upset me beforehand, I enjoyed my own ghastly performances — of 'Only Daisies', or something). Anyway I do believe those nuns enjoyed us all; the five boys were good at entertainment; they could sing — except Michael; they could do little bits from school plays; Tom could recite 'Eugene Aram'; they could conjure; Father could juggle oranges or apples — and he could sing.

But so could some of the vain, shy, visiting curates — and so could Sister Bernardine. Thus, the programme was crowded. However, enraptured or not, people talked and moved about through performances — and ate Turkish delight too if it suited them, and drank port. So the strain was light.

And Aunt Mary, Reverend Mother, governed all.

From *Presentation Parlour*, William Heinemann Ltd, 1963

Confraternity Bell
John Liddy

What was once
The rallying bell,
Final whistle
Of unfinished matches,
Signal to withdraw
From a kiss,
Holy gong that drew me
Like a magnet uphill
Past dog-eat-dog
Housing estate,
Cat-wired
Barrack railing,
Cherry blossomed
Footpaths
Soft as carpets
Leading
To the power and glory
Of a thousand candles
In a packed church . . .

Is now the bell
I no longer heed,
Less than holy gong
That made me ponder
The wickedness
Of a kiss,
Declared
My every innocent act
A sin,
Haunted
My every search
For different shades
Of black and white,
Prevented
What could have been
The music of angels
In my heart.

From the *Limerick Socialist*, Vol. 6, No. 10, October 1977

The Most Maligned Place
David Hanly

Before talking about where I was going to, it would be as well to sketch in where I was coming from. Limerick. The most maligned place in Ireland. 'A medieval dungheap' its most renowned painter, Sean Keating, called it back in the sixties. It is remembered for its 'pogrom' which is supposed to have occurred at the beginning of the century . . .

At any rate, as Dallas is stigmatised the world over for what happened to JFK so is Limerick's history stained forever by what happened back then.

But my memories as I left the city for Dublin in 1962 were not so spectacular. (It was Donal Foley who regaled me with Limerick's 'shameful past', and I had a long and bitter row with him because of his ignorance in the matter.) No, my memories were visceral, ineradicable, and mostly pleasant. They had nothing to do with 'social' Limerick, which is supposed to be the most snobbish in the country: I started telling snobs very early on in life what I thought of them, and it's just possible that this is the reason why I've never experienced Limerick snobbery with the intensity that others have.

Mind you, it is impossible not to notice some appalling contradictions: the worthy burghers who were at the altar rails every morning, but worked their staff to the bone and paid them a miserable and unChristian pittance at the end of the week. The Redemptorists never railed against *that*, and why would they, since every one of these well-heeled merchants was a 'pillar of the Confraternity'.

It would be very disingenuous to talk of Limerick back then without mentioning the Arch-Confraternity of the Holy Family, 'the largest sodality in the world'. At one stage, every male in the city seemed to be a member. The effect on their minds was utterly paralysing: each week they were ranted at by trained professionals; the tirades — which purported to be spiritually uplifting — were bigoted, insular and profoundly anti-intellectual, and there was no counterpoint, because, of course, Limerick was not given a university college.

What effect all this had on me I leave to others to judge (I do know that it left me with a deep and abiding loathing of dogma of any kind). So, I was leaving all of that. I was also leaving the Shannon River at Plassey, on whose tributary, the Groody, I caught my first trout.

I took away memories of days spent in solitude at the Black Bridge or the Garrison Wall (it was at the Black Bridge that I read in one day Russell Braddon's *Naked Island*), and before that of family outings with jars of Matterson's meat paste for the sandwiches, on afternoons that were so hot the cattle went into the Shannon up to their eyeballs, and the day often ended to the sound of a Down's Syndrome teenager singing 'The Ring your Mother Wore' across the river, surrounded by a caring family.

Plassey was, and still is, a magical place to me: it is from the Black Bridge that I want my ashes scattered when all is over; I know it won't matter a tinker's curse to me then whether they're thrown into the Shannon or the Elbe, but it matters to me now to know that I will end up back there.

That is a most cursory sketch of what I was leaving that day in 1962 when I sat into the car driven by a small but perfectly formed Protestant named Derek, with whom I used to work during the summer in Matterson's bacon factory, now — like the other two bacon factories — gone. I left without the faintest trace of regret.

Going to Dublin was a perfectly natural reward for all those years of study: I would be a junior ex in the Department of Industry and Commerce in a city where I could come and go as I liked. What could be more wonderful?

From *The Sunday Tribune*, 3 January 1988

Eamonn Casey: Years of Innocence
Joe Broderick

The Casey family's move to Adare was a leap into the twentieth century. Adare was no hidden village, but a thriving town in the Golden Vale, situated on a main thoroughfare leading to the city of Limerick. The creamery handled great quantities of milk, produced by pedigree Holsteins . . . John Casey was accepted as a personality in the town and rubbed shoulders with the cream, so to speak, of the local gentry.

Being a careful and exacting manager, both he and the business prospered. Within the space of three years he had built a substantial two-storey house on the outskirts of the town. The wide front door with its leadlights, the generous hallway and elegant stairs were evidence of good taste and good fortune. Most houses in Adare at that time were low thatched cottages. It was no doubt an exciting day for the Casey children when they moved into their new home, just two doors from the Christian Brothers School. Eamonn was six or seven years old, and all his childhood memories were to be associated with the place . . .

He also recalls how their father would get them up out of bed each morning for Mass and down on their knees every night for the Rosary. They were always relieved when their dad got home late from the creamery and mother led the Rosary, since she added fewer trimmings. John Casey had a string of litanies and invocations which they could hear him recite walking up and down the yard behind the house on a dry night. He could see the sanctuary lamp in the Brothers' oratory and said he felt he was praying in the presence of the Blessed Sacrament.

On Sundays they were herded into Mass and took an entire pew for themselves.

Often enough they would go to a second Mass on Sunday, as far as Rathkeale several miles away, because John Casey insisted on hearing the sermon of a 'famous canon' who preached there. After dinner on Sundays he would read the *Irish Catholic* aloud to the family for an hour. Years later, when Eamonn Casey was working as a priest in London, his father would send him this Catholic periodical every week — 'to make sure I didn't lose the faith,' quipped Eamonn . . .

Sunday was set aside also for a drive in the country. The Caseys were among the few who owned a car in those days. A little Anglia it was, and not all of the ten children fitted into it at one time. You were selected for the ride on your ability to add a new song to your repertoire. John Casey loved to hear the children sing and knew a lot of songs himself, mostly of the Mother Machree variety much in vogue at the time. Motivated by the promise of Sunday outings, Eamonn built up a store of these ditties which he would publicly warble with relish, given half a chance, for the rest of his life . . .

Micheál and Eamonn were Mass servers. Observing them, the curate, Fr Culhane, was convinced that Eamonn was the one that had 'a feel for being a priest', and Eamonn was sure he was right. He never really wanted to be anything else. Not surprising then that, one fine day, the curate called at the creamery and said: 'Mr Casey, I've booked Eamonn into St Munchin's.'

'My father came home and told me that Fr Jim Culhane had booked me into the Diocesan Seminary and asked me if I'd go. Of course, if Fr Culhane had asked me to climb to the pinnacle of the cathedral, I would have done so.'

John Casey's original idea for his two eldest sons was to send them to Blackrock College in Dublin; in fact he had already spoken to the priests there. In the upshot, Micheál went to Dublin and, after high school, worked for a couple of years before discovering that he too had a 'feel' for the priesthood. He was to volunteer for the 'mission fields' and study at All Hallows while his brother was at Maynooth . . .

It was an era of faith. Most of the 'plain people of Ireland' had learnt to submit to the Will of God as revealed through both papal encyclicals and the decrees of Éamon de Valera. The year of Eamonn Casey's birth was the year de Valera led the Fianna Fáil party into the Dáil (Irish parliament) and began his march back to power. It is most likely that John Casey supported him, as most people did in Limerick. Indeed it is not unthinkable that the future bishop's name might have been inspired, in part at least, by admiration for him.

Be that as it may, Irish children grew up as if under the protection of de Valera's cloak. His mind, his austere personality, his carefully worded constitution affected all aspects of life during the thirties and forties. The universe he had built seemed stable and unalterable; it did not tremble even on the outbreak of world war. Ireland remained neutral and at peace . . .

Eamonn Casey has described the untroubled atmosphere of his youth.

'We had a sheltered life. It was idyllic in one sense . . . Growing up I never had to question the future.'

He did not even seriously question his own personal future. He slipped into the priesthood as the most natural thing in the world . . .

'I saw the priesthood as something that brought a lot of relief and support and happiness to people.'

A pause, and then he added: 'My vocation was never challenged until I went to Maynooth.'

From *Fall from Grace*, Brandon Book Publishers, 1992

The Curse of St Munchin
A. S. O'B.

There were saints who achieved immortal deeds
In times that are long gone by.
Ah! Why are our times so far removed
From saints and from sanctity!

St Munchin vowed to build a church —
He was strong of heart and limb;
And the faith that surmounts all obstacles,
Was largely given to him.

Now, mark the difference between
Us and such saintly elves —
They made cathedrals unto God,
We, railways for ourselves.

St Munchin found a ponderous stone —
He toiled below and above it;
But vain the crow-bar, and vain the spade,
Not an inch could St Munchin move it.

'Now help me, thou who passest this way —
What one cannot do, two can;
I labour to build in thine own city
For I know thee a Limerick man.'

'Oh! doting fool,' the Limerick man,
Thus the saint his scoffings began on:
'I would that the stone were tied round thy neck,
And thou cast into the Shannon.'

Thus the scorner spoke — but a stranger came,
And to him the saint did cry,
'Stranger, thou art sent hither to do
An act of piety.

Bend thy back, put forth thy strength,
And raise this rock with me,
So may all good angels bring thee aid
In thine own extremity.'

The stranger strove and the stone was raised,
And he passed on his journey home;
Not the first or the last who had blest his kind,
And gone to a nameless tomb.

Now St Munchin aloud cursed Limerick
With a curse of prophetic bear;
They tell how the tide of the Shannon ebbed
That cleaving curse to hear.

'Because ye have scorned my holy work,
And laughed at my toil and my danger;
And that which should have been done by you,
Ye have left to be done by a stranger.

Strangers shall gather your city's wealth —
Strangers shall flourish there —
While idle visions distract your thoughts
And then work at your despair.'

Since those words were spoken that church was built —
Ages have passed and gone —
But a cloud hangs over the city yet,
And all men sorrowing own —

How her towns-folk have often no dinner to eat,
While strangers two courses for luncheon;
And how we witness in every street,
Sad signs of the curse of St Munchin.

From *The Limerick Chronicle*, 27 August 1845

TWO

THE GARRISON

Nocturnal Disorders
Thomas Crofton Croker

Limerick is as notorious for its nocturnal irregularities as for its memorable sieges, many instances of which may be produced. Before the freaks of Johnny Connell, Mr Hayes, whose memory is recorded in the cathedral of that city as
'DAN HAYES, AN HONEST MAN AND LOVER OF HIS COUNTRY',
has thus described his departure from the scene of his juvenile excesses, under the title of 'The Farewell'.

> 'Ye gentle virgins, set your hearts at ease,
> No more the town's disturbed with riotous Hayes;
> No more in Barrack Street his sword he draws,
> Nor murders horses, nor bravades the laws;
> No more inspired with 'rack he scours the streets
> To swear and play the devil with all he meets;
> No more the windows clink with clattering stones,
> Nor dying pigs emit untimely groans;
> The peaceful street, no more with clamour rings,
> Nor nightly fiddlers ply their sounding strings.'

Previous to the midnight vagaries of 'Buck Hayes', or 'Count Hayes', as he was sometimes called, we find Dr Smyth, the Bishop of Limerick, complaining by his letter of the 27th of October, 1710, of similar wanton proceedings.

'On the 12th of September, about one or two in the morning, several persons with musical instruments, . . . sang a song, which (I am informed by those who heard it most distinctly) was a very scandalous one. Afterwards, I heard them repeat the words, 'confusion and damnation', which, I suppose, was when they drank confusion and damnation to Dr Sacheverel and all his adherents, and all of his principles, as I was informed they did by a gentleman, who says he opened his casement and heard them. They staid before my house a considerable time, and (the same gentleman informed me, whose depositions are taken before the mayor and other justices) drank other healths, among which was the health most profanely called 'The Litany Health', wherein they prayed that plague, pestilence, and famine, &c., might fall on all (and among them particularly on all archbishops and bishops, &c., to the best of his remembrance, and as he verily believes) who should refuse to drink the glorious memory of King William. The former of these healths was likewise drank at one Alderman Higgins's, and neither of them drank at any other houses appears by depositions taken as before. The persons concerned in this (as appears upon oath) were Major Cheater, at that time commanding officer in chief of the garrison, Captain Plasto, Lieutenant

Mason, Lieutenant Barkly, and Lieutenant Walsh, all belonging to Sir John Whittingar's regiment, and Captain Blunt of Colonel Rooke's regiment. After this, on the 21st of this month, about four, as I conceive, in the morning, I and my family were again disturbed by several persons who passed by my house, and made a strange unusual noise, by singing with feigned voices, and by beating with keys and tongs (as it appears on oath) on frying-pans, brass candlesticks, and such like instruments. Afterwards, on the 24th instant, about the same hour, I was startled out of my sleep (as I was each time before) by a hideous noise made at the corner of my house by the winding of horns, and the following of men, and the cry of a pack of dogs. I lay some considerable time in bed, in hopes they would soon have gone away, but finding they did not, I got out of my bed and opened my window, and stood there for some time in hopes of discovering who they were (for it was a moonshiny night), but could not. At length the dogs, in full cry (to the number, I believe, of twenty-three or twenty-four couple, or thereabouts) ran by my house, and in some time after returned again, and soon after in the same manner ran back again, making the same noise. After they had passed by my house the first time, I called to the centinel at my door, and asked him who those men were, and what they were doing; who answered me that they were officers, who had got a fox and dragged him along, and sent the dogs after him. Who these persons were, who were guilty of the second and third riots, appears by the depositions taken before our justices of the peace. I cannot but observe that Major Cheater, with others of that regiment (as I think appears by my depositions), was always one; and in the second riot, was accompanied by Lieutenant Barkly.

'The gentlemen who put the first great affront upon me having owned their fault and asked my pardon I should never have mentioned it to their prejudice, had it not been for the repeated indignity they have put upon me since; which, if continued, will oblige me to remove with my family out of town, till the gentlemen come to a better temper.

'Besides these abuses which I have mentioned, I and my family have been frequently alarmed and awakened in the dead of night by soldiers (as they afterwards appeared to be), who feigned themselves to be spirits, some by stripping themselves naked, and others by putting on white garments, and throwing stones at the centinel at my door, and at other times by throwing stones on the slates of my house, which made an unusual noise when they were tumbling down; and one night particularly the centinel was so much affrighted, and made such a noise, that I was obliged to rise out of my bed to encourage him, and to assure him they were no spirits.

'All this having been done since the first abuse that was put on me, and never before having received any such abuses by any officers or soldiers since my first coming to this town, there having been always a good understanding betwixt us, and the officers of all former regiments having been at all times very obliging and courteous to me, which I think myself bound in justice to acknowledge; for these reasons I cannot but believe that these later outrages were the result of some resentments occasioned by the first abuse, and that the first abuse was occasioned by an opinion they conceived that my principles did not in all things agree with their own.'

(Signed) 'Tho: Limerick.'

Speaking of the enjoyments of the people of Limerick at fair time or on festival days, Fitzgerald and McGregor notice in their history, a fondness for music of the fiddle or bagpipe. 'Amongst the airs selected upon these occasions, "Patrick's Day", and "Garryowen", always hold a distinguished place' . . .

In Fitzgerald and McGregor's *History of Limerick*, when noticing the customs and amusements of the lower orders, it is stated that the tradesmen formerly marched in grotesque procession on Midsummer-day, and that 'the day generally ended in a terrible fight between the Garryowen and Thomond Gate boys — the tradesmen of the north and south suburbs'.

From *Popular Songs of Ireland*, collected by Thomas Crofton Croker, George Routledge and Sons, 1886

The Night Watch
J. F. S.

If England boasts her noble guards,
And Germany her Uhlans:
If Scotland views with fond regard
Her highlanders in tartans:
Old Limerick too may view with pride —
May ask what guards may match
That gallant group, by danger tried,
Her famous old Night Watch.

Through many a land their praise has passed,
Through many a clime their fame
A brilliant halo round them cast,
Undying is their fame.
All visitors from foreign lands
Unsatisfied depart,
Unless a sight of this brave band
Has gratified their heart.

And artists, too, quite anxious seem
Their features to portray,
And of their photographs they deem
The sale would right well pay,
For all throughout the world wide
Such men 'twere vain to seek —
In aspect, dress, and martial stride
They're perfectly unique.

In brawl or scuffle, row or fight,
In this our ancient town,
On many a dark and dismal night
They've won a high renown:
Upon their beat they never sleep,
Nor do they e'er repair
To sheltered nooks and doorways deep
To smoke and ponder there.

But all night long, through fair and foul,
They wander to and fro,
And here they peep and here they prowl
In search of hidden foe;
With lusty lungs and piercing tone
The fleeting hours they roar;
''Phast three' they cry when 'tis but one;
''Phast one' when it is four.

The temperance too I must extol,
Of these old Limerick rangers —
To liquoring up and alcohol
They are teetotal strangers.
And hence it is they're never found
Incapable or tipsy,
Or stretched unconscious on the ground,
Ah! no, they hate the whiskey.

But why do I their praises chant!
On every side they're rung;
Nor shall they to their graves depart
Unhonoured and unsung.
Long, long they'll shine in history's page
Amid time's greatest heroes;

Their fame shall live in every age
And lasting be as Nero's!

From *The Limerick Chronicle*, 30 November 1875

Starting School
Christopher Isherwood

(Kathleen and Frank were Christopher Isherwood's mother and father. The book *Kathleen and Frank* tells their story through their letters and Kathleen's diary, with a commentary in the third person by Christopher Isherwood.)

[On January 7th, (1912) Kathleen saw Roden House, her seventeenth, and this, as she wrote later, proved to be the very one she wanted:]

There wasn't *a doubt of it* from the first moment, when the woman who had the keys came across with a shawl over her head and let us in mysteriously through a gate in the wall, followed by other shawled people waiting to see what we should do! High grey walls bounded the house on two sides, covered with creepers — really the backs of the cottages in the lane, but only one had a window on the garden, discreetly wired over, where the nice peasant (who had the keys) lived.

In front of the house were prim little beds with box borders and a fountain and an apple tree, and a long glass veranda ran the whole length of the house and above were seven windows in a long row. Inside, it was the quaintest place. Downstairs only a kitchen, servants' hall, pantry, dining-room. But upstairs it was all surprises — little passages and endless doors running in and out, giving one the impression of a network of rooms, some quite a good size, you hardly knew where you were — so unexpectedly did rooms thrust out in all directions, going right through to another lane at the back, looking to the Barracks, in the midst of the most slummy cottages where everyone threw everything out of the window!

I suppose it must have been much larger at some time, as evidently blocked-up doorways must have led into the adjoining cottages and been part of the original house. And it belonged to two old Miss Warmleightons who had lived here from their childhood when the Military Road was nothing but fields, and instead of the big Technical School nothing but a big orchard led away from the upper garden, but still the steps are left leading down into the onetime orchard, and the old iron gate and the square pillars and urns guarding it. I have always wanted *urns* on pillars and an old iron gate! And the Technical School is quite a long way off. There was something very romantic too and un-obvious about it all, and so unlike the regular soldiering house. Indeed, no soldier has ever discovered it.

January 27. Bright and sunny but very cold. News that the furniture had reached Cork but I suppose it won't come on till Monday. We went for a lovely walk to Lax Weir over the fields, where a raised path above river and bogs winds away to the weir, lovely views of Limerick looking back, the cathedral tower etc. and flat green meadows in every direction away into blue and misty distances . . .

February 11. Did not go out all day and spent a day of rest and leisure in our new drawing room watching the birds from the sofa and reading. Such a cheerful lookout — the iron gate with the urns on the top of the crumbling pillars, and the spreading apple tree close to the window and the quaint box-bordered beds below, and trees in the distance and the Technical School and a church spire, and seagulls and blackbirds and sparrows and chaffinches all flying, hopping and making nice noises.

February 19. Dreadful day with smoke, the chimneys were bad yesterday but simply outrageous today. The Nursery and Drawing room were unbearable and the whole place was covered with blacks. I took C to school and fetched him and we went into the town after. He is going to the Girls High School where there are also a few little boys. I like Miss Mercer the head, also Miss Croston in whose class C is.

February 21. Christopher very pleased with his school which I hope will make him much more independent and tomorrow he is going to walk there alone. When C came out of school we went down to the town and back along by the river to watch the loading and unloading of the ships.

February 22. Smoke, though less violent, continues to cover everything with smuts and the rooms are cloudy with smoke, it is so tiresome. C to school alone from the Technical School and walked back all the way by himself.

February 24. Bright day. Christopher has whole holiday on Saturdays. He and I went to do Sunday marketing and looked into the old Market which has sort of cloisters running all round supported by Doric pillars and behind which a great trade in old clothes is done, a great deal of colour and clusters of women in funny little donkey carts. The women manage to arrange their black shawls to give an almost eastern effect, often folding them across the lower part of their faces so that little more than their eyes are visible . . .

March 25. C top of his class . . . The hedges are all getting quite green and the pink of the apple blossom is beginning to show in the big old tree outside the window. I love the house . . .

July 4. The usual grind of shopping. Never in any place has the housekeeping been so tiresome as here. In afternoon we drove up to the Market Fields for the Church Lads Brigade sports. A most fortunate afternoon for it. Frank inspected. I gave away the prizes!

July 17. Interviewed policeman about the children in the lane, lawless little hooligans who bang at the door (which we have to keep locked, now that Frank is away) and dash in the moment it is open to try and steal the apples and pick the flowers for sheer mischief's sake, not for the love of either! The Irish seem most *hopelessly* lawless and murders are overlooked in a way to make an Englishwoman's blood boil.

July 26. An interesting talk with Miss F, who told me quite mediaeval stories about the state of things in Ireland. They think if Home Rule really comes they will be too much at the mercy of all sorts of incapable and dishonest people to make it possible to go on living here . . .

September 28. Nurse and C to the moving pictures at The Gaiety, the new place of entertainment at St George's Street about which C has been excited for weeks.

[Thus Christopher's lifelong devotion to the movies began, as an indiscriminate appetite for *any* two-dimensional happening on a lighted screen in a dark theatre. He finds it hard to remember individual film actors or films from the Limerick days, but he is certain he saw John Bunny, Francis X. Bushman, Lillian and Dorothy Gish, Annette Kellermann, the Keystone Cops, Mae Marsh, Mabel Normand, *The Spoilers, Judith of Bethulia,* the Italian version of *Quo Vadis* and episodes from many serials including Pearl White's *The Perils of Pauline.*] . . .

October 17. To the town before lunch. Every other shop, nearly, has suffered from the riots of last week and has smashed glass. From starting politically on the grounds of the big Unionist meeting, it ended by being a religious riot. The Roman Catholics especially attacking all the Protestant shops and the Archdeacon's house and the church next door, into which they threw nearly a thousand stones. The Archdeacon was chased and cut about the face. The priests finally came out on Saturday and addressed the people, imploring them to cease, and they did . . .

1913.
February 19. Took C to his first dancing class at the George. Thirteen children and a very alert little teacher from Cork.

March 17. To see Miss Mercer in morning. She is giving up the High School on account of her health. Talked of Christopher and I told her of our intention of sending him to Miss Burns on account of the society of a few other little boys. She said as far as education was concerned she feared it was time wasted and that to send him to England would really be better. We parted very solemnly. His education is a great problem and difficulty here . . .

April 7. Took Christopher to Miss Burns's school, Mount Saint Vincent Cottage, up the Military Road next to the Convent, only six or seven children but the majority are boys. Do hope it will be a success.

[This change of schools was, of course, made in the hope that Christopher would become more masculine in male society. Kathleen took it for granted that his growing interest in girls was due to a girlishness in himself and nothing more. But perhaps she was wrong. Perhaps Christopher was actually exhibiting slight heterosexual tendencies which could have been strengthened and confirmed, if he had been sent to a co-educational school in his teens. Perhaps he could have worked his way up to a George Sand-Alfred de Musset type of affair with a girl like Mirabel! Well, thank goodness for St Edmund's School and Repton, if they did indeed have anything to do with tipping the balance in the opposite direction. Despite the humiliations of living under a heterosexual dictatorship and the fury he has often felt against it, Christopher has never regretted being as he is. He is now quite certain that heterosexuality wouldn't have suited him; it would have fatally cramped his style . . .

   That autumn, after their return to Limerick, Kathleen comments on the growing tension in Ireland. The Home Rule Bill was now almost certain to become law and Ulster was determined to resist it, fearing the rule of a government of Irish Catholics.]

They have appointed all the members for their own government should Home Rule come in force and intend governing themselves should Ireland separate from the Imperial Parliament. They are backed by funds and a trained army of volunteers who mean fight without any doubt.

[Meanwhile, in Limerick (October 12th):]

The statue in the Crescent is decorated with mottoes of FAITH AND FATHERLAND and a dozen or so young men dressed in saffron coloured kilts and stockings appeared in a long procession which with many bands marched through the chief streets, representing the Home Rule demonstration. They were afterwards addressed by Redmond. The general opinion seems to have been that they were rather a disappointed looking band, but the day was depressing . . .

October 29. One of the popular ideas is that, if Home Rule comes and the English leave, the Irish American millionaires will then come back and flood the country with money, build mills and have fine ships up and down the Shannon.

[On November 1st, Frank and Kathleen were invited to stay at Curragh Chase, once the home of Aubrey de Vere, the schoolmate of Byron, whose sonnets (e.g., *The Rock of Cashel*) were called by Wordsworth, 'the most perfect of our age' and of his son Aubrey Thomas de Vere, also a poet (*Florence MacCarthy's Farewell to her English Lover*) who had entertained Tennyson, Coventry Patmore and Watts; Watts had done an outline on the stairs for a fresco of Dante meeting Beatrice. Kathleen admired the house, which was built in the grand manner:]

The long room which opens out of the hall is called The Saloon, there are busts all down the room and tall french windows open on to the broad stone terrace, just now the woods beyond the lakes are perfectly gorgeous with the colouring of autumn and the mountains to the south the most wonderful blue.

[The present owners of the house had what seemed to Kathleen and Frank an amusing eccentricity; they ran it on Daylight Saving Time:]

All through our visit they kept explaining what the time was, according to *them*, which made the hours of meals very confusing! They get up at 8 and call it 8, go to bed at 9 and call it 10, or at 10 and call it 11. Of course the scheme is that it should be universal, even so it seems unnecessary to put the clock on! . . .

(On December 3rd they all left for England again.)

From *Kathleen and Frank*, Methuen & Co. Ltd, 1971

Drunken Thady
(A Legend of Limerick)
Michael Hogan

Before the famed year ninety-eight,
In blood stamped Ireland's wayward fate;
When laws of death and transportation
Were served, like banquets, thro' the nation —
But let it pass — the tale I dwell on
Has nought to do with red rebellion;
Altho' it was a glorious ruction,
And nearly wrought our foes' destruction.
There lived and died in Limerick City,
A dame of fame — Oh! What a pity
That dames of fame should live and die,
And never learn for what, or why!

Some say her maiden name was Brady,
And others say she was a Grady;
The devil choke their contradictions!
For truth is murdered by their fictions.
'Tis true she lived — 'tis true she died,
'Tis true she was a bishop's bride,
But for herself, 'tis little matter
To whom she had been wife or daughter.
Whether of Bradys or O'Gradys!
She lived, like most ungodly ladies;
Spending his reverend lordship's treasure
Chasing the world's evil pleasure;
In love with suppers, cards, and balls,
And luxurious sin of festive halls,
Where flaming hearts, and flaming wine,
Invite the passions all to dine.
She died — her actions were recorded —
Whether in heaven or hell rewarded
We know not, but her time was given
Without a thought of hell or heaven.
Her days and nights were spent in mirth —
She made her genial heaven of earth;
And never dreamt, at balls and dinners,
There is a hell to punish sinners.
How quick time throws his rapid measure
Along the date of worldly pleasure?
A beam of light, 'mid cloudy shadows,
Flitting along the autumn meadows;
A wave that glistens on the shore,
Retires, and is beheld no more;
A blast that stirs the yellow leaves
Of fading woods, in autumn eves;
A star's reflection on the tide,
Which gathering shadows soon shall hide —
Such and so transient, the condition
Of earthly joys and man's ambition.
Death steals behind the smile of joy,
With weapon ready to destroy;
And, tho' a hundred years were past,
He's sure to have his prey at last.
And, when the fated hour is ready,
He cares not for a lord or lady;

But lifts his gun, and snaps the trigger
And shoots alike the king and beggar.
And thus the heroine of our tale,
He shot, as fowlers shoot a quail;
And, 'mid the flash of pomp and splendour,
He made her soul the world surrender.
She joined her father's awful forms
'Mid rolling clouds and swelling storms;
And, lest the muse would be a liar,
I'm led to think she went no higher.
But now I have some secret notion,
She did not like her new promotion;
For if she did she would remain,
And scorn to come to earth again.
But earth, the home of her affection,
Could not depart her recollection!
So she returned to flash and shine,
But never more to dance or dine!
The story of her resurrection
Flew out in many a queer direction!
Each night, she roamed, with airy feet,
From Thomond Bridge to Castle-street;
And those that stayed out past eleven,
Would want a special guard from heaven
To shield them, with a holy wand,
From the mad terrors of her hand!
She knocked two drunken soldiers dead,
Two more, with battered foreheads, fled;
She broke the sentry-box in staves,
And dashed the fragments in the waves!
She slashed the gunners, left and right,
And put the garrison to flight!
The devil, with all his faults and failings,
Was far more quiet in his dealings,
(Notwithstanding all that he lost),
Than this unruly, rampant she-ghost!
No pugilist in Limerick town,
Could knock a man so quickly down,
Or deal an active blow so ready
To floor one, as the Bishop's Lady!
And thus the ghost appeared and vanished,
Until her ladyship was banished

By Father Power whom things of evil
Dread as mortals dread the devil!
Off to the Red Sea shore he drove her,
From which no tide nor time can move her,
From numbering sands upon the coast
That skirts the grave of Pharaoh's host!
A lady of her high-born station
Must have acquired great education
For such a clerkship — numbering sands,
With no account-book, save her hands!

But, ere the priest removed the Lady,
There lived a 'boy', called 'Drunken Thady'!
In Thomond-gate, of social joys,
The birth-place of the 'devil's boys'!
Thade knew his country's history well,
And for her sake would go to hell!
For hours he'd sit and madly reason
Upon the honours of high treason!
What Bills the House had lately got in,
What Croppies nimbly danced on nothing!
And how the wily game of State
Was dealt and played in ninety-eight!
How Wexford fought — how Ross was lost!
And all to Erin's bloody cost!
But had the powers of Munster 'risen,
Erin had England by the weasan'!
He told long tales about those play-boys,
Called Terry Alts and Peep-o'-day Boys
Who roused, at night, the sleeping country,
And terrified the trembling gentry!

Now who dare say that Irish history
To Thady's breeding was a mystery?
Altho' the parish priest proclaimed him
And first of living devils named him!
In heart he was an Irish lumper,
But all his glory was a bumper!
He believed in God, right firm and well,
But served no heaven and feared no hell!
A sermon on hell's pains may start him,
It may convince but not convert him!

He knew his failing and his fault
Lay in the tempting drop of malt;
And every day his vice went further,
And, as he drank, his heart grew harder.
Ah, Thady! Oft the parish priest
Called you a wicked, drunken beast!
And said you were the devil's handle
Of brazen, bare-faced, public scandal!
An imp — without the least contrition —
At whiskey, discord and sedition!
That drinking was your sole enjoyment,
And breaking doors your whole employment!
That you — at every drunken caper —
Made windows change their glass for paper!
That, sure as closed each Sunday night in,
You set near half the parish fighting!
That, with your constant, droughty quaffing,
You broke Moll Dea and Biddy Lavin!
And drove the two poor widows begging,
For not a drop you left their keg in!
If Satan stood, with his artillery,
Full at the gates of Stein's Distillery;
With Satan's self you'd stand a tussle
To enter there and wet your whistle!

In vain the priest reproved his doings —
Even as the ivy holds the ruins —
He cautioned, counselled, watched, and tracked him,
But all in vain — at last he whacked him;
And with a blackthorn, highly seasoned,
He urged the argument he'd reasoned.
But Thady loved intoxication,
And foiled all hopes of reformation;
He still raised rows and drank the whiskey,
And roared, just like the Bay of Biscay.
In every grog-shop he was found,
In every row he fought a round;
The treadmill knew his step as well
As e'er a bellman knew his bell;
The jail received him forty times
For midnight rows and drunken crimes;
He flailed his wife and thumped her brother,
And burned the bed about his mother,

Because they hid his fine steel pike
Deep down in Paudh Molony's dike!
The guard was called out to arrest him,
Across the quarry loch they chased him;
The night was dark, the path was narrow,
Scarce giving room to one wheelbarrow;
Thade knew the scanty passage well,
But headlong his pursuers fell
Into the stagnant, miry brook,
Like birds in birdlime sudden stuck.
The neighbours said the devil steeled him,
For if the garrison assailed him
Inside King John's strong castle-wall,
He would escape unhurt from all!
All day he drank 'potheen' at Hayes's,
And pitched the King and law to blazes!
He knocked his master on the floor,
And kissed Miss Lizzy at the door!
But ere his drunken pranks went further,
The host and he had milla murdher!
The window panes he broke entire,
The bottles flew about the fire;
The liquor, on the hearth increasing,
Caught fire and set the chimney blazing!
The reverend sage this deed admonished,
The congregation stood astonished —
He said that Thady was an agent
Employed on earth by hell's black Regent!
And if he wouldn't soon reform,
His place and pay would be more warm!
His vital thread would soon be nicked,
And into Hades he'd be kicked!
Even there he would not be admitted,
Except the porter he outwitted!
For, if he got inside the wall,
Most likely, he'd out-devil 'em all!
The people heard the sad assertion,
And prayed aloud for his conversion!
While Thady in the public-house
Was emptying kegs and 'brewing' rows!
For him the priest prognosticated
A woeful doom and end ill-fated!

And truth hath rarely disappointed
The sayings of the Lord's anointed!
But many a one in heaven takes dinner,
Who died a saint and lived a sinner!
'Twere better far, and safer surely,
To live a saint and die one purely!
All ye who're ready to condemn
A fellow-child of clay, like him!
Try if yourselves need no repentance,
Before you pass the bitter sentence!
And ere you judge your brother, first
Remember that yourselves are dust!
But if your conscience tells you then
That your own heart is free from sin —
Cry, with the Pharisee, 'Thank God!
I am not like that wicked clod!'

But to our story of this queer boy
Thady the drunken, devil-may-care-boy!
'Twas Christmas Eve — the gale was high —
The snow-clouds swept along the sky;
The flaky drift was whirling down,
Like flying feathers thro' the town.
The tradesman chatted o'er his 'drop',
The merchant closed his vacant shop
Where, all day long, the busy crowd
Bought Christmas fare, with tumult loud.
The grocer scored the day's amounts,
The butcher conned his fat accounts;
The farmer left the noisy mart,
With heavy purse and lightened heart.
In every pane the Christmas light
Gave welcome to the holy night;
In every house the holly green
Around the wreathed walls was seen;
The Christmas blocks of oak entire
Blazed, hissed and crackled on the fire;
And sounds of joy from every dwelling,
Upon the snowy blast came swelling.

The flying week, now past and gone,
Saw Thady earn two pounds one!

His good employer paid it down,
And warned him to refrain from town;
And banned the devilment of drinking,
But Thady scorned his sober thinking;
He fobbed the coin, with spirit light,
To home and master bade good-night,
And, like a pirate-frigate cruising,
Steered to the crowded city, boozing!

The sweet-toned bells of Mary's tower,
Proclaimed the Saviour's natal hour!
And many an eye with pleasure glistened!
And many an ear with rapture listened!
The gathered crowd of charmed people
Dispersed from gazing at the steeple,
The homeward tread of parting feet,
Died on the echoes of the street;
For Johnny Connell, that dreaded man,
With his wild-raking Garryowen clan,
Cleared the streets and smashed each lamp,
And made the watchmen all decamp!

At half-past one the town was silent,
Except a row raised in the Island,
Where Thady — foe to sober thinking —
With comrade boys sat gaily drinking!
A table with a pack of cards
Stood in the midst of four blackguards,
Who, with the bumper-draught elated,
Dashed down their trumps, and swore, and cheated!
Four pints, the fruits of their last game,
White-foaming, to the table came;
They drank, and dealt the cards about,
And Thady brought 'fifteen wheel out!'
Again the deal was Jack Fitzsimons',
He turned them up, and trumps were diamonds;
The ace was laid by Billy Mara,
And beat with five by Tom O'Hara;
The queen was quickly laid by Thady,
Jack threw the king and douced the lady!
Bill jinked the game and cried out, 'Waiter!
Bring in the round, before 'tis later!'

The draughts came foaming from the barrel;
The sport soon ended in a quarrel;
Jack flung a pint at Tom O'Hara,
And Thady levelled Billy Mara;
The cards flew round in every quarter,
The earthen floor grew drunk with porter;
The landlord ran to call the Watch,
With oaths half Irish and half Scotch.
The Watch came to the scene of the battle,
Proclaiming peace, with sounding wattle;
The combatants were soon arrested,
But Thady got off unmolested.

The night was stormy, cold and late,
No human form was in the street;
The virgin snow lay on the highways,
And choked up alleys, lanes, and byeways.
The North still poured its frigid store,
The clouds looked black and threaten'd more;
The sky was starless, moonless, all
Above the silent world's white pall.
The driving sleet-shower hissed aloud —
The distant forest roared and bowed;
But Thady felt no hail nor sleet,
As home he reeled thro' Castle-street.
The whistling squall was beating on
The battered towers of old King John,
Which guarded once, in warlike state,
The hostile pass of Thomond-gate.
The blinding showers, like silvery balls,
Rustled against the ancient walls,
As if determined to subdue
What William's guns had failed to do!
Old Munchin's trees, from roots to heads,
Were rocking in their churchyard beds;
The hoary tombs were wrapt in snow,
The angry Shannon roared below.
Thade reeled along, in slow rotation,
The greatest man in Erin's nation;
Now darting forward, like a pike,
With upraised fist in act to strike;
Now wheeling backward, with the wind,
And half to stand or fall inclined;

Now sidelong, 'mid the pelting showers,
He stumbled near the tall round towers:
With nodding head and zig-zag feet,
He gained the centre of the street;
And, giddy as a summer-midge,
Went staggering towards old Thomond Bridge,
Whose fourteen arches braved so clever,
Six hundred years, the rapid river;
And seemed, in sooth, a noble picture
Of ancient Irish architecture.

But here the startled muse must linger,
With tearful eye and pointed finger
To that dark river once the bed
Of Limerick's brave defenders dead —
There half the glorious hope she cherished,
In one sad hour, deluded, perished;
The fatal draw-bridge opened wide,
And gave the warriors to the tide;
The flood received each foremost man,
The rear still madly pressing on;
'Till all the glory of the brave
Was buried in the whirling wave;
And heroes' frames — a bloodless slaughter —
Choked up the deep and struggling water.

Now Thady ne'er indulged a thought
How Limerick's heroes fell or fought;
This night he was in no position
For scripture, history, or tradition.
His thoughts were on the Bishop's Lady —
The first tall arch he'd crossed already;
He paused upon the haunted ground,
The barrier of her midnight round.
Along the bridge-way, dark and narrow,
He peered — while terror drove its arrow,
Cold as the keen blast of October,
Thro' all his frame and made him sober.
Awhile he stood in doubt suspended,
Still to push forward he intended;
When, lo! Just as his fears released him,
Up came the angry ghost and seized him!

Ah, Thady! You are done! — Alas!
The priest's prediction comes to pass —
If you escape this demon's clutch,
The devil himself is not your match!

He saw her face grim, large and pale,
Her red eyes sparkled through her veil;
Her scarlet cloak — half immaterial —
Flew wildly round her person aerial.
With oaths, he tried to grasp her form,
'Twere easier far to catch a storm;
Before his eyes she held him there,
His hands felt nothing more than air;
Her grasp pressed on him cold as steel;
He saw her form but could not feel;
He tried not, tho' his brain was dizzy,
To kiss her, as he kissed Miss Lizzy,
But prayed to Heaven for help sincere —
The first time e'er he said a prayer.

'Twas vain — the Spirit, in her fury,
To do her work was in a hurry;
And, rising with a whirlwind strength,
Hurled him o'er the battlement.
Splash went poor Thady in the torrent,
And rolled along the rapid current,
Towards Curragour's mad-roaring fall
The billows tost him, like a ball;
And who dare say, that saw him sinking,
But 'twas his last full round of drinking?
Yet, no — against the river's might
He made a long and gallant fight;
That stream in which he learned to swim,
Shall be no watery grave to him!
Near, and more near he heard the roar
Of rock-impeded Curragour,
Whose torrents, in their headlong sway,
Raged mad as lions for their prey!
Above the Fall he spied afloat
Some object, like an anchored boat,
To this, with furious grasp, he clung,
And from the tide his limbs upswung.

Half-frozen in the stern he lay,
Until the holy light of day
Brought forth some kind assisting hand
To row poor Thady to the strand.
'Mid gazing crowds, he left the shore
Well sobered, and got drunk no more!
And in the whole wide parish round,
A better Christian was not found;
He loved his God and served his neighbour,
And earned his bread by honest labour.

From *Lays and Legends of Thomond*, M. H. Gill & Son, 1880

The Mister
Siegfried Sassoon

By the time I had been at Limerick a week I knew that I had found something closely resembling peace of mind . . .

Toward the end of my second week the frost and snow changed to soft and rainy weather. One afternoon I walked out to Adare and saw for the first time the Ireland which I had imagined before I went there. Quite unexpectedly I came in sight of a wide shallow river, washing and hastening past the ivied stones of a ruined castle among some ancient trees. The evening light touched it all into romance, and I indulged in ruminations appropriate to the scene. But this was not enough, and I soon began to make enquiries about the meets of the Limerick Hounds.

No distance, I felt, would be too great to go if only I could get hold of a decent hireling. Nobody in the barracks could tell me where to look for one. The genial majors permanent at the Depot were fond of a bit of shooting and fishing, but they had no ambition to be surmounting stone walls and big green banks with double ditches. Before long however, I had discovered a talkative dealer out at Croom, and I returned from my first day's hunting feeling that I'd had more than my money's worth. The whole thing had been most exhilarating. Everyone rode as if there wasn't a worry in the world except hounds worrying foxes. Never had I galloped over such richly verdant fields or seen such depth of blue in distant hills. It was difficult to believe that such a thing as 'trouble' existed in Ireland, or that our majors were talking in apprehensive undertones about being sent out with mobile columns — the mere idea of our mellow majors going out with mobile columns seemed slightly ludicrous.

But there it was. The Irish were being troublesome — extremely troublesome — and no one knew much more than that, except that our mobile columns would probably make them worse.

Meanwhile there was abundance of real dairy butter and I sent some across to Aunt Evelyn every week . . .

It was a fine morning and there was quite a large crowd at the cross roads, where the hounds were clustering round the hunt servants on a strip of grass in front of an inn . . .

Powerless to intervene I followed them to the inn. The Mister's popularity became immediately apparent. Everyone greeted him like a long-lost brother, and I also became aware that he was universally known as 'The Mister'.

They all seemed overjoyed to see The Mister, though most of them had seen him out hunting three days the week before; and The Mister responded to their greetings with his usual smiling detachment. He took it for granted that everybody liked him, and seemed to attribute it to their good nature rather than to his own praiseworthiness . . . For the moment, however, his only wish seemed to be that the whole world should drink his health. And they did. And would have done so once again had time permitted. But the hounds were about to move off, and The Mister produced his purse with a lordly air, and the landlord kept the change, and we went out to find our horses.

Had I been by myself I should have been sitting on my hireling in a state of subdued excitement and eagerness, scrutinising the hounds with a pseudo-knowing eye, and observing everyone around me with the detached interest of a visiting stranger. But I was with The Mister, and he made it all feel not quite serious and almost dreamlike. It couldn't have been the modicum of cherry brandy I'd sipped for politeness' sake which made the proceedings seem a sort of extravaganza of good-humoured absurdity.

There was The Mister, solemnly handing his immense flask to the groom, who inserted it in a leather receptacle attached to the saddle . . .

Even The Mister's horses seemed in a trance-like condition, although the bustle and fluster of departure was in full swing around them . . .

'You'll be following to bring him home,' said The Mister to our motor-driver, who replied that sure to God it was the grandest hunt we'd be having from the Gorse. We then jogged sedately away . . .

A quarter of a mile away the tail end of the field could be seen cantering up a green slope to the Gorse. It was a beautiful still morning and the air smelt of the earth.

"Ark!' exclaimed The Mister, pulling up suddenly. (Dropped aitches were with him a sure sign of cerebral excitement.) From the far side of the covert came a long-drawn view-halloa, which effectively set The Mister in motion. 'Go on, boy, go on! Don't be waiting about for me. Holy Mother, you'll be getting no hunting with them Egyptians!' So I went off like a shot out of a gun, leaving him to ride the hunt in his own time. My horse was a grand mover; luckily the hounds turned towards me, and soon I was in the same field with them. Over the next forty minutes I can only say that it was all on grass and the banks weren't too formidable, and the pace just good enough to make it exciting. There was only one short check, and when they had marked their fox to ground I became aware that he had run a big ring and we were quite near the Gorse where we found him . . .

The Mister was now in a glow of enthusiasm and quite garrulous. 'Sure that mare you're riding is worth five hundred guineas if she's worth a penny bun,' he ejaculated, and proceeded to drink the mare's health from that very large flask of his.

As I have already suggested, there was something mysterious about The Mister — a kind of innocence which made people love him and treat him as a perennial joke. But, so far, I knew next to nothing about him, since he took it for granted that one knew everything that he knew; and the numerous hunting people to whom he'd introduced me during a rather dull and uneventful afternoon's sport took everything about The Mister for granted; so on the whole very little definite information about anything had emerged . . .

Mrs O'Donnell . . . had given us a 'high-tea' after hunting which had made dining in the mess seem almost unthinkable. It had been a banquet. Cold salmon and snipe and unsurpassable home-made bread and honey had indeed caused us to forget that there was a war on; while as for Mrs O'D. herself, in five minutes she made me feel that I'd known her all my life and could rely on her assistance in any emergency. It may have been only her Irish exuberance, but it all seemed so natural and homely in that solid plainly-furnished dining-room where everything was for use and comfort more than for ornament.

The house was a large villa, about a mile from the barracks — just outside the town. There I sat, laughing and joking, and puffing my pipe, and feeling fond of the old Mister . . .

Mentally, I became not unlike The Mister, whose motto — if he ever formulated anything so definite as a motto — was 'we may all of us be dead next week so let's make the best of this one'. He took all earthly experience as it came and allowed life to convey him over its obstacles in much the same way as his horses carried him over the Irish banks. His vague geniality seemed to embrace the whole human species. One felt that if Hindenburg arrived in Limerick The Mister would receive him without one tedious query as to his credentials. He would merely offer to mount him, and proudly produce him at the meet next morning. 'Let me introduce me friend Marshal Hindenbird,' he would say, riding serenely up to the Master. And if the Master demurred, The Mister would remark, 'Be reasonable, Master. Isn't the world round, and we all on it?'

He was a man who had few forethoughts and no afterthoughts, and I am afraid that this condition was too often artificially induced . . . In The Mister's case it didn't matter much; he was saddled with no responsibilities, and what he felt like next morning was neither here nor there. He looked surprisingly well on this regime, and continued to take the world into his confidence. (He was either solemnly sober or solemnly tipsy; his intermediate state was chatty, though his intermediate utterances weren't memorable.) . . .

I was getting formal permission from the Assistant-Adjutant to go out hunting the next day . . . The meet was twenty-three miles away, which made it all the better for the purpose. So it was arranged. The Mister was mounting me, and we were to call for him with the erratic Ford car at Mrs O'Donnell's house (which was where he lived).

It was a pouring wet morning and blowing half a gale . . . Mrs O'Donnell came out on to her doorstep, and while we were waiting under the porch for The Mister, she asked me to try and bring him straight home after hunting. 'The O'Hallorans are coming to dinner — and of course we are expecting you to join us. But Mrs O'Halloran's a bit stiff and starched; and The Mister's such a terrible one for calling on his friends on the way back; and it isn't barley water they offer him.' At this moment The Mister came out, looking very festive in his scarlet coat and canary waistcoat. He was optimistic about the weather and I tried to feel hopeful that I should bring him home 'the worse' for nothing stronger than water.

The maid now appeared carrying The Mister's hat box and flask; he was helped into an enormous overcoat with an astrakhan collar which Mrs O'Donnell turned up for him so that his countenance was almost completely concealed. He then put on an immense pair of fur gloves, pulled his voluminous tweed cap down over his nose, and gave Mrs O'Donnell a blandly humorous look which somehow suggested that he knew that whatever he did she couldn't be angry with him. And he was right, for he really was a most likeable man. 'Now Mister,' she said, 'bear it well in your mind that Mrs O'Halloran and her daughter are dining with us this evening.' . . .

On my last day in Ireland I went out in soft sunshiny weather for a final half-day with the hounds. The meet was twelve miles off and I'd got to catch the 4.30 train to Dublin, so I had to keep a sharp eye on my watch. The Mister was mournful about my departure . . . I felt a bit mournful myself as my eyes took in the country with its distant villages and gleams of water, its green fields and white cottages, and the hazy transparent hills on the horizon — sometimes silver-grey and sometimes that deep azure which I'd seen nowhere but in Ireland.

We had a scrambling hunt over a rough country, and I had all the fun I could find, but every stone wall I jumped felt like good-bye for ever to 'this happy breed of men, this little world', in other words the Limerick Hunt, which had restored my faith in my capacity to be heedlessly happy. How kind they were, those friendly fox-hunters and how I hated leaving them.

At half-past two The Mister and I began to look for Clancy's car, which contained his groom and was to take us home. But the car was on the wrong side of a big covert, and while we were following it, it was following us. Much flustered, we at last succeeded in encountering it, and Clancy drove us back to Mrs O'Donnell's in a wild enthusiastic spurt.

Mrs O'Donnell had a woodcock ready for my tea, and I consumed it in record time. Then there was a mad rush to the station, where my baggage was awaiting me, plus a group of Fusilier friends. The Assistant-Adjutant was at his post, assuring the engine driver that he must on no account start without me, mail-train or no mail-train. With thirty seconds to spare I achieved my undesirable object, and the next thing I knew was that I was leaning out of the carriage window and waving good-bye to them all — waving good-bye to warm-hearted Mrs O'Donnell — waving good-bye to the dear old Mister.

From *The Complete Memoirs of George Sherston*, Faber and Faber, 1937

Bishop O'Dwyer's Letter to General Maxwell

November 10th, 1915

Sir: The treatment which the poor Irish emigrant lads have received at Liverpool is enough to make any Irishman's blood boil with anger and indignation. What wrong have they done to deserve insults and outrage at the hands of a brutal English mob? They do not want to be forced into the English army and sent to fight English battles in some part of the world. Is not that within their right? They are supposed to be free men, but they are made to feel that they are prisoners who may be compelled to lay down their lives for a cause that is not worth 'three rows of pins' to them.

It is very probable that these poor Connaught peasants know little or nothing of the meaning of the war. Their blood is not stirred by the memories of Kossovo and they have no burning desire to die for Serbia. They would much prefer to be allowed to till their own potato gardens in peace in Connemara. Small nation-alities and the wrongs of Belgium and Rheims Cathedral and all the other cosmopolitan considerations that rouse the enthusiasm of the Irish Party, but do not get enough recruits in England, are far too high-minded for uneducated peasants, and it seems a cruel wrong to attack them because they cannot rise to the level of the disinterested Imperialism of Mr T. P. O'Connor and the rest of the New Brigade.

But in all the shame and humiliation of this disgraceful episode, what angers one most is that there is no one, not even one of their own countrymen, to stand up and defend them. Their crime is that they are not ready to die for England. Why should they? What have they or their forbears ever got from England that they should die for her? Mr Redmond will say a Home Rule Act on a Statute Book. But any intelligent Irishman will say, a simulacrum of Home Rule, with an express notice that it is never to come into operation.

This war may be just or unjust but any fair-minded man will admit that it is England's war, not Ireland's. When it is over, if England wins, she will hold a dominant power in this world and her manufacturers and her commerce will increase by leaps and bounds. Win or lose, Ireland will go on in her old round of misgovernment, intensified by a grinding poverty which will make life intolerable. Yet the poor fellows who do not see the advantage of dying for such a cause are to be insulted as shirkers and cowards and the men whom they have raised to power and influence have not one word to say on their behalf.

If there is to be conscription, let it be enforced all round, but it seems to be the very intensity of injustice to leave English shirkers by the million go free and coerce the small remnant of the Irish race into a war which they do not understand, and which, whether it is right or wrong, has but a secondary and indirect interest for them.

I am, dear Sir, your obedient servant,
Edward Thomas
Bishop of Limerick

From *Our Catholic Life*, Christmas 1966

The Soldier Hunter

To our Readers

This Publication, which we intend to have on Sale weekly, has been called into existence for the purpose of giving publicity to some of the many scandals that occur nightly in our city; and as its name implies, those girls who parade the streets and avenues with soldiers will have the privilege of a free advertisement as to their conduct and identity.

We are out to clean up the town. Social Hygiene, if you will, is our objective.

The outskirts of the city are barred at night to all decent citizens. The Dock Road, the Back Road, the Avenues, Rosbrien, Prospect, the Circular Roads, the Canal Banks, the Roxboro' Road, etc., are dens of infamy where immorality stalks naked and unabashed. Riotous and indecent behaviour is the nightly order of some of the city streets. We are sick and tired of hearing appeals from the Pulpit, and lamentations from private individuals on these points. We are well aware that the clergy have been active within and without the Church, in the crowded street and the lonely suburb; that they have undergone the danger which they could not be expected to undergo, that they have been doing police work as well as priests' work. We admire their zeal and their interest in the morality of our girls. No doubt they have done much good. We trust they will not misunderstand our action in coming in with a new idea and a method in which we have every confidence.

What is this New-Found-Out?

Simply the Bull's-Eye Lantern and the Lime-Light. We are out to discover who *are* the soldier hunters. We will give them timely notice and warning. If they persist we will turn on the light and keep it playing round them, until for very shame they must hide their heads and make a virtue of necessity. We shall confirm the strong in virtue, support and shelter the weak, but we shall scourge the shame-faced and the vicious. Parents who discharge their duties towards their children need have no fear of us, but woe betide the man or the woman that does not show the care that a reasonable person should exercise, and that religion demands. Mistresses must look after maids and, if they fail, mistress and maid will be flailed together. It is the one thing left to bring responsible people to a sense of duty. This may be a sorry state of affairs, but it is a fact. Let the Mary Annes, and the Mary Kates, and the Mary Joes look out, for our method is of the 'rough on rats' order.

Cowardly Assault

In reference to the cowardly assault made upon one of our city clergy by a Welsh Fusilier, the following letter appeared in the local Press during the past week:—

St Michael's, Limerick, 16th Feb., 1918.
Dear Sir — Would you be good enough to give publicity to the fact that one of the parochial clergy was violently assaulted on Friday evening by a brutal Welsh soldier. The clergyman in question happens to be the military chaplain, and was only discharging his duty when he sought to protect a girl of 16 years of age against the lustful passion of this low clod-hopper.

Respectable citizens and ratepayers have complained to me of the unseemly conduct of soldiers and young girls on our city footpaths at night.

I warn the authorities, both military and civil, that they have a duty to perform, and that if they neglect to perform it there is every danger of serious breaches of the public peace.

I remain, dear sir, yours faithfully,
W. Dwane, Adm.

P. S. — I think I can safely count on the support of the young men of Limerick for the parish clergy in their efforts to uphold public morality.
— W. D.

To All Whom It May Concern

Our staff will parade the streets and patrol the bye-ways, and if the cat jumps out of the bag it will be hard on the rats anyway. We shall pay special attention to the gates of the various military barracks that are bye-words for lowness and looseness at present.

The Drugged Sweet

Incredible though it may seem, here in Catholic Limerick, many a young innocent girl has been made the victim of the lowest class of outrage by some of those demons in human form who, khaki-clad, seem to think women and young girls have no other business in this world other than to accompany them in their lonely walks. Quite recently in a back road, known as the Long Avenue, a young girl, in the company of a British soldier, was offered chocolates by him, and finding a peculiar taste from the sweets declined to eat them. Luck was on her side, and probably had she used those chocolates she would now have sunk to the same depths of depravity as many others who were foolish enough to trust to the honour of the 'defenders of small nationalities and despoilers of womanly virtue'.

To Dolly

Who strolls along O'Connell Street
With measured step and dainty feet
And strives each soldier-man to greet?
Our Dolly.

Her blouse is low, her skirt is quaint
Her blush is hidden under paint
She's half a d — l and half a saint,
Our Dolly.

Now list' to me, my gentle Sir,
Before the trees begin to burr,
We'll knock the devil out of her,
Our Dolly.

From *The Soldier Hunter*, Vol. I, No. 1, Saturday, 23 February 1918

A War-Ravaged Town
Robert Graves

In the middle of December the cadet battalions were wound up, and the officers, after a few days' leave, sent back to their units. I had orders to rejoin the Royal Welch Third Battalion, now at the Castle Barracks, Limerick, but decided to overstay my leave until the baby was born. Nancy expected it early in January 1919, and her father took a house at Hove for the occasion. Jenny, born on Twelfth Night, was neither coal-black nor affected by the shocks of the previous months. Nancy had no foreknowledge of the experience — I assumed that she must have been given some sort of warning — and it took her years to recover from it. I went over to Limerick, and there lied my way out of the overstaying of leave.

Limerick being a Sinn Fein stronghold, constant clashes occurred between the troops and the young men of the town, yet little ill-feeling; Welsh and Irish always got on well together, just as Welsh and Scottish were sure to disagree. The Royal Welch had the situation comfortably in hand; they made a joke of politics and turned their entrenching-tool handles into shillelaghs. Limerick looked like a war-ravaged town. The main streets were pitted with holes like shell-craters and many of the bigger houses seemed on the point of collapse. Old Reilly at the antique shop, who remembered my grandfather well, told me nobody built new houses at Limerick now; the birth-rate was declining and when one fell down the survivors moved into another. He also said that everyone died of drink in Limerick except the Plymouth Brethren, who died of religious melancholia.

Life did not start in the town before nine in the morning. Once, at about that time, I walked down O'Connell Street, formerly King George Street, and found it deserted. When the hour chimed, the door of a magnificent Georgian house flew open and out came, first a shower of slops, which just missed me, then a dog, which lifted up its leg against a lamp-post, then a nearly naked girl-child, who sat down in the gutter and rummaged in a heap of refuse for filthy pieces of bread; finally a donkey, which began to bray. I had pictured Ireland exactly so, and felt its charm as dangerous. When detailed to search for concealed rifles at the head of a task force, in a neighbouring village, I asked Attwater, then still adjutant, to find a substitute; explaining that as an Irishman I did not care to be mixed up in Irish politics. That January I played my last game of rugger: as full-back for the battalion against Limerick City. We were all crocks and our opponents seemed bent on showing what fine fighting material England had lost by withholding Home Rule. How jovially they jumped on me, and rubbed my face in the mud! . . .

I rode a few miles from Limerick to visit my uncle, Robert Cooper, at Cooper Hill. He was a farmer, a retired naval commander, and the Sinn Feiners had begun burning his ricks and driving his cattle. Through the window he showed me distant herds grazing beside the Shannon. 'They have been there all winter,' he said despondently, 'but I haven't had the heart to take a look at them these three months.' I spent the night at Cooper Hill, and woke up with a sudden chill, which I recognised as the first symptoms of Spanish influenza.

Back at the barracks, I found that a War Office telegram had come through for my demobilisation, but that all demobilisation among troops in Ireland was to be stopped on the following day for an indefinite period because of the Troubles . . . I decided to make a run for it.

From *Goodbye to All That*, Jonathan Cape Limited, 1957

The Limerick Night Watch
Michael Hogan

Now solemnly in yonder tower
The clock proclaims the midnight hour
With strokes sonorous and sublime;
The muffled watchman tells the time,
As down the street with drawlings droll
He saunters with his pounding pole.
The inky heaven still grows more dark;
Lone banshees wail and bitches bark,
And tree-tops beneath the storm's mad mirth
Bend down and kiss the shuddering earth
And then spring back with howl and hiss
As if disgusted with the kiss.
From earth still Luna keeps aloof;
Slates fly along the rattling roof
And crashing loudly on the flags
Awake affrighted hakes and hags,
Who see destruction in night's mirror
And cross themselves in abject terror,
And shout, as deep in prayer they bend,
The world is coming to an end.
But hark! what midnight sound is that?
Which makes my heart go pit-a-pat,
Makes me awhile my breath suspend
And every hair stand on its end?
Hark! hark I hear, but not quite loud,
The rustling of a shimmering shroud;

From whence comes yon advancing light
So vivid, fitful, broad and bright
Eclipsing the sweet queen of night?
Now more intense still grows the glare.
Hallo! hush! who the devil is there?
What fiend creates this huge uproar?
Who knocks so loudly at the door?
Is it a lawless prowling thief?
If so, by heavens he'll come to grief;
His napper with a knife I'll notch,
And hand him over to the 'Watch',
The grand protectors of our town
Maligned by every cur and clown
Because at times they take a glass,
And shelter many a bonnie lass
At night beneath their cosy coat,
That covers them from toe to throat.
Snails have their shells, and crabs their rocks,
The soldier has his sentry-box,
The wily weasel has his hole,
So has the rat, the mouse, the mole,
But watchmen in this moral town
Have nothing but a flimsy gown
Around their shivering shoulders cast
To shield them from the wintry blast.
Is it, Sirs, any wonder then
That these maligned, meek, moral men
To shield themselves from shower and storm
Should long for girls to keep them warm?
Some girls indeed cannot control
Their passion for the pounding pole
And answer with smiles fair and fond
The beckonings of a watchman's wand.

From A *Political Satire on the Corporation and Other Sordid Citizens* by Oliver Twist, Bard of the Brand (Michael Hogan), *circa* 1875

Entertaining General Lucas
Michael Brennan

Liam Lynch had captured a British Brigadier General named Lucas near Fermoy. Early in July Seán Finn and some of his men crossed the Shannon near Bunratty and handed over Lucas to me for 'safe keeping'. This was a frightful imposition, but they promised it was only for a few days, so I couldn't refuse. We kept Lucas for some weeks in Cratloe (at Ernest Corbett's), in Clonmoney (at Brennan's), at Tullyvarriga (now the Shannon Airport), at Hastings' and in Doonass at Hartigan's. His presence completely immobilised us as we daren't do anything which would involve raiding by the British. In addition, he was an expensive luxury as he drank a bottle of whiskey every day which I hated like hell to pay for. I was very sorry for him and more so for his young wife in England, who was very ill partly after a baby, but mostly, I imagine, from shock. Through Jack Coughlan, who worked in Limerick Post Office, I arranged a system whereby Lucas wrote to his wife and got a letter from her every day. I put him on his honour that he would make no use of this facility to harm us or to escape and I gave him his letters unopened. He could understand being able to send letters, but receiving them impressed him very much with the machine we appeared to control. He was keen on exercise and he spent most of his day saving hay, while he played bridge every night until about 2 a.m.

Getting some signs of activity, we moved suddenly to Doonass and we only escaped being caught in a general 'round up' by a few hours. They had no knowledge of Lucas being in the district, but that wouldn't have made any difference if we hadn't moved.

I kept appealing to GHQ to get rid of our prisoner but all I got was news that East Limerick would take him over soon. In Doonass the same routine held and the hold-up of the Brigade continued. Hartigan's House was on the bank of the Shannon and the local men offered to take Lucas 'stroke-hauling' for salmon some night if he wished. This was apparently poaching and his strait-laced English mentality was at first horrified at the suggestion. He raised it with me again, however, and he seemed keenly interested but uneasy at the possibility of being caught poaching. I gave him positive assurances against this and eventually he decided to risk it. Late at night we got into a boat and Seán Carroll of Castleconnell and some of his men pulled us out into the middle of the rapids. Both banks of the river were of course strongly guarded. The boat was held in the strong current for about two hours while Lucas cast for salmon but without result. Every now and then he expressed anxiety as to the possibility of the river bailiffs discovering us, but Carroll reassured him. When we got back Lucas said he could understand our feeling of security from police interference as he presumed we had taken the necessary precautions, but he would like to know why 'Seán' (the only name he had for Carroll) was so certain that we were safe from interference from the Bailiffs. I didn't know, but I promised to find out the next day. I got the information and passed it on to Lucas. 'Seán' was the Head Bailiff. This seemed to be the most astonishing bit of information Lucas had ever got.

We had brought Lucas to Doonass on a promise to have him taken over by the East Limerick. After another week's appeal they asked us to bring him to Caherconlish which would be more convenient for them. We took the road again one night in a horse and trap escorted by cyclists, but when we reached Caherconlish no arrangement had been made. The local Commandant, Dick O'Connell, put us into the doctor's house near the village (the family were away in Kilkee) and asked us to stay for a few days. We had realised by now, of course, that nobody wanted Lucas, as his presence held up all activities. We also knew that GHQ and the Dáil Government were very embarrassed by him. Threats had been made publicly that he would be held against other prisoners and obviously we couldn't play this game indefinitely against the British. When a Dublin visitor commented: 'Why the hell doesn't he escape', I saw the solution of the difficulty.

We spent three days in Caherconlish and then moved to a vacant house near Herbertstown, Bruff. We took Lucas for long walks across country and I noted with satisfaction that he studied the topography carefully from every hilltop. Up to this we had always left a man outside his bedroom window at night and now when the room was on the ground floor we withdrew this man. At first nothing happened (he may have suspected a trap), but when we got up on the second morning our prisoner was gone. Later, we learned he had gone straight across country until he met the main Limerick–Tipperary road where he waited until lorries came along. He hailed them and was picked up and a few minutes later they ran into an ambush laid by Dan Breen. Lucas was wounded there, but only slightly.

From *The War in Clare 1911–1921: Personal Memoirs of the Irish War of Independence*, Four Courts Press/Irish Academic Press, 1980

The Killing of Winifred Barrington

Fuller particulars obtained of the fatal ambush show that the motor car contained a party of five — two ladies, Miss Winifred Barrington, Miss Coverdale, Major Biggs, District Inspector RIC, Captain Tamgouse, Oxfordshire and Buckinghamshire Light Infantry, and Mr William Gabbett, Mount Rivers, Newport. It would appear that Miss Barrington and Miss Coverdale, who was a guest at Glenstal Castle, Murroe, the seat of Sir Charles and Lady Barrington, proceeded to Newport in the afternoon, where they met Mr Gabbett, who is a friend of the Barrington family. Miss Barrington rode on a pony and Miss Coverdale cycled. On the way they were met not far from Glenstal by Sir Charles, who had only just returned from London. Sir Charles addressed his daughter, and asked her to be home for dinner. When Miss Barrington and her lady friend reached Newport they were joined by Mr Gabbett, Major Biggs, and Captain Tamgouse. It was suggested by one of the party that they should go fishing for the evening, and the suggestion was complied with. The pony and bicycle were left in Newport, and the party of five set out in a private motor, and the evening was spent fishing in the Newport river beyond Killoscully.

On the return journey, and when between Killoscully and Newport, at about half past seven o'clock, the car was suddenly ambushed. Major Biggs was driving, and Miss Barrington was sitting next him, the other three being seated behind . . .

A lady witness stated that she was at Newport on the date in question with the deceased, Miss Barrington, a civilian and an officer, and the late Captain Biggs. They motored to a house where they had tea. On the return journey, and when they got to Coolboreen bridge, fire was opened from both sides of the bridge and behind. Captain Biggs, who was driving, was hit in the throat, and the car stopped after going a few yards. The three men jumped from the car and ran up the road. Miss Barrington was thrown on to the road and remained there. The firing went on, and seven or eight shots struck the back of the car where witness was, and she was wounded. She saw Captain Biggs running about ten yards from the side of the car and then drop, with the civilian and officer standing alongside him on his right. The officer then got through a hedge and fired his revolver at the attackers whom she saw running away. The firing continued, and she heard the civilian say, 'Stop, stop: there is a lady in the back of the car.' The civilian then went to help Miss Barrington, who was lying on the side of the road, and witness stood up in the car with her hands up. She then saw about five or six men come up. The leader asked how many were in Biggs' car and who was lying on the road. Witness told him it was District Inspector Biggs. He then asked where the other was, and she replied that she did not know. She told him there was a girl lying on the other side of the road, and he said it served them right for driving with the military. At that time Miss Barrington was unconscious but alive. She asked for help, and the reply she got was that it served them right. She saw in all about a dozen men there, and some of them before they left went up to where Captain Biggs was lying and fired at him. Witness remained with Miss Barrington until the military arrived, and before the attackers left they fired over their heads.

From *The Limerick Chronicle*, 17 and 19 May 1921

THREE

LAND AND LABOUR

The Bottom Dog

'We must look at life in all its aspects from the point of view of the "Bottom Dog" — the oppressed — be it nation, class, or sex.'

Vol. 1   No. 1   20th October, 1917

Introductory

In making his bow (wow) to the public The Bottom Dog wishes to offer a word by way of explanation. For a long time he has been the butt of ridicule and odium as well as the target for the cheap sneers of those whose hands are raised against him. He has grown tired of continually grumbling, and bemoaning his unenviable lot. He has seen for himself in the struggle that the 'Every-man-for-himself-and-the-weakest-to-the-wall' dictum still holds sway. Coming forth from his obscurity to study at closer range the ways of mortals and give vent to his feelings, he trusts that the bones of contention, which he encounters will be readily overcome. Grown weary of his mess of pottage he is out for better fare. If The Bottom Dog bites occasionally and makes himself felt, it will not be his fault; rather will it be the fault of the opponent, who seeks to wipe his feet on him, or kick him about like a football. He believes in the truth of the old saying that 'Every Dog has his day' but at the same time he must assert that The Bottom Dog's day appears to be a long way off, shrouded in the misty future. To work at hand then — hastening the day of the Bottom Dog.

A Manly Demand

A six hour day, five working days per week and £1 a day, is Tom Mann's programme. Some of our local 'sweaters' will collapse when they hear this.

The Gibson Girls

Grave murmurs of discontent are heard from the girls employed at Gibson's, Mulgrave Street. They get something like 7/- or 8/- a week and have to work from 8 'till 8; some nights even as late as 11 or 12. Quite recently we heard that a gentleman bearing the unmistakeable signs of a Factory Inspector called one night but did not succeed in gaining admission, the lights in the establishment being extinguished and the girls there told to hide themselves. When leaving for home that night late they were cautioned if they were asked why were they working so late to state they were coming from a wake of a relative of one of their fellow-workers! If these long hours and miserable wages continue there will soon be a few 'wakes' and some vacant places in Gibson's. The Agent had better wake up and treat the girls as well as he treats his dogs. The girls too must get into a Trade Union.

The Bottom Dog's Share

He makes everything,
He makes overcoats and freezes,
He builds palaces and lives in shacks,
He builds automobiles and walks home,
He makes fine tobacco and chews scraps,
He makes carriages and pushes a wheel barrow,
He makes meerschaum pipes and smokes clay,
He digs the gold and has his teeth filled with cement,
He makes patent leather shoes and wears brogans.

Vol. 1   No. 2   27th October, 1917

Plots

We believe that the right note was struck at the Plotholders' meeting on Sunday night by the Chairman, Mr Stevenson, when he stated that to settle the housing problem satisfactorily the money expended on a patchwork scheme would be useless. 'Leave the slums alone to the owners to rot, and go into the country where habitable dwellings could be erected with a garden, large or small, attached.' The prolongation of the unfortunate war has taught the workers that if money can be found to slaughter human beings it can and should be found to decently house the wage-earner, the best asset to the nation.

The B.D. bared his teeth at the Corporation meeting when he saw a big number of the self-styled labour representatives leave before the resolution forwarded by the Plotholders' Executive, demanding more land for plots, was come to, thus knocking the resolution on the head. The B.D. knows full well that some of our City Fathers are above handling a spade — they leave it to the common workman or the serf as they would have him. The B.D. doesn't believe in this and says it is far nobler and manly to handle a spade and extract from mother earth some of the treasures in the shape of food than living on one's wits and 'backsheese'. And these call themselves Labour Men. Ye Gods! Heel up Dog!!

Vol. 1   No. 3   3rd November, 1917

Local Trade Union Activities

Last week we referred to the pressing need of organisation. Skilled workers who belong to their respective Trade Unions know full well what a tower of strength their Unions are to them — how their lot has been bettered and the status made secure against all attack. Unfortunately one class of worker, the unskilled and the semi-skilled man or woman, is practically only now waking up and commencing to realise that his or her only hope of advancement lies in Trade Unionism. The ordinary labourer has been down in the dust simply for want of unity and organisation. Within the past month a much-needed move has been made to effectively organise the latter class of worker in Limerick and . . . as a result, big strides have been made by the Irish Transport and General Workers' Union . . . The Union has also taken in hand the organising of the women, who, to say the least of it, are as a whole paid an un-Christian low wage for a working week of over-long hours. The girls at the Shannon Laundry have had their weekly wages increased by 1/6 and 1/-. A big meeting of women and girls working at Messrs Cleeves, Lansdowne, was held under the auspices of the Transport Union on Thursday night week and the following evening these workers, numbering between 300 and 500, got 2/6 each increase. So, the good work goes merrily on. When every worker — male and female — is thoroughly organised, then the Bottom Dog hopes to come into his own.

Concerning Cannocks

While on the prowl last week the B.D. went up O'Connell Street to see what time it was by Cannock's Clock. He learned the time as well as some interesting information concerning the owners of the clock. He is not surprised now on hearing that Cannock's are able to pay a nine per cent dividend. Where does it come from? Listen to this and then put on your thinking cap: Cannock's employ thirty girls in their dressmaking Department and the weekly wages of these thirty girls comes to the magnificent total of eight pounds per week! £8 between 30; rather should it be £30 between 8. One of these thirty girl workers is fourteen years with the firm and all she has is seven shillings a week!

The Boys at Boyd's

The B.D. asked for a bone from one of the above, but the reply was in the negative, as he was told bones — even backbones — were out of the question on 18/- a week. These workers have only 18/- and 20/- a week. They get a bonus, intended to be taken off after the war. It is paid them in a separate envelope marked 'war bonds' in red ink, the colour symbolic of the blood of workers shed in a world conflict to amass wealth and territory for the idle rich.

Vol. 1   No. 4   10th November, 1917

The Housing Problem

As the Bottom Dog knows full well the worker's lot is not a happy one. He has to work long hours for low wages and has to house himself and his family in 'houses' and surroundings a disgrace to civilisation. And we need not go outside our own city to prove this. We will content ourselves at the moment with the figures given in the 1915 Report of the Medical Officer of Health (Dr McGrath). From it we find there are *1,669 houses unfit for human habitation in the city*, 692 owing to

dilapidated condition and 977 owing to want of ordinary sanitary accommodation. According to the same authority 681 should be closed up absolutely. From
statistics available it is proved that with the exception of the poor of Dublin, the
Limerick poor are the worst housed people of the large cities of Ireland . . . Time
has shown us that the wealthy, to which the slum owner and the sweater belong,
will not do anything to remedy this shameful state of affairs under which the
working class is forced to exist, (not live, as they can't be said to 'live'). It is only
for the workers themselves to do what they can in the matter. It is therefore with
much pleasure we learn that at a Conference in the Mechanics' Institute on
Sunday last, composed of representatives of the Limerick Trades Council, the
Federated Labour Council, the Town Tenants' Association and the Plot-Holders'
Association, the subject was fairly fully dealt with and steps taken to form a
Committee from the bodies to formulate a scheme for better housing for Limerick
workers.

Limerick Labour Rally

We wish every success to the public meeting to be held in the City on tomorrow
(Sunday). Though primarily intended for unskilled and semi-skilled workers it
will have a special interest too for skilled workers, because it is only by organising
every available worker — man, woman, boy and girl — that it can ever be hoped
to better their lot and give them an opportunity of obtaining a decent living. In
most instances the wages paid in the City are a veritable disgrace alike to the
employers directly responsible and those other professing energetic citizens who
prate so much about having the welfare of the City at heart. It is about time surely
that we got rid of cant and humbug and got down to business. We, workers, must
realise that our one sure means of salvation from our present unenviable
condition lies in our own solidarity; we can only expect help from our own class.
We will get nothing by fawning and acting the slave — the cap-in-hand, 'Please
your Honour' attitude. We have had an overdose of this in Ireland.

The Galbally Farmer
Darby Ryan

> One evening of late as I chanced for to stray,
> The town of Tipperary I struck on my way,
> For the praties to dig and to work by the day,
> I hired with a Galbally farmer.

The hire that was going, a shilling a day,
I took it, I own, tho' shameful to say,
No mention of grub — nor even of tay —
Or a drink for the road from my hirer.

His name was O'Leary, a man hard and mean,
With the face of a miser, mangy and lean;
I was soon made aware of the fool I had been
To hire with that Galbally farmer.

Now Darby was scraggy and wore a hard hat,
I gazed at his get-up, but he gave me no chat;
His eyes, altho' bleary, could see like a cat,
When watching for a poor *spailpín fánach*.

Said the crabby ould caffler as he mounted his steed:
'To the Galbally mountains we're posting with speed.'
My feelings, don't doubt it, were gloomy indeed,
As I struck at a trot out behind him.

Before leaving the town 'twas painful to see
How he acted the clown on his shaggy stageen,
He tore up the street on its head at full speed,
To show off his antics on horseback.

What a sight was O'Leary and the *garran* he rode,
Going through Tipperary in his claw-hammer coat;
Tho' my feelings were dreary and heavy my load,
I couldn't but laugh at the ould codger.

I followed the lead of the daft *angishoir*,
As he capered and wheeled up wild Galteemore —
No need to reveal the kind feelings I bore
Towards generous Darby O'Leary.

The way that he took wound south on the dale,
Below *Sliabh na Mac* thro' a green flowery vale;
How glorious it looked, were one in the vein
To enjoy all its beauty so charming!

The road it got steep, and was full of rough stones
That scalded my feet and rattled my bones;

The pain grew severe — how I suffered, *mo bhron*!
Trudging that night towards Barna.

I asked at the Gap how far we'd to go —
The night it got dark, and my steps became slow —
I was hungry and tired and my spirits were low,
How I needed a drop to revive me!

He told me the distance from there to his place —
As he sat on his nag, a scowl on his face —
Would be less than it was, had I kept the pace
That he set for me leaving Tipperary.

He loosened the reins and gave head to his steed,
And I, altho' lame, had to follow his lead;
'Twas vain to complain, he paid me no heed,
Or cared how I dragged on behind him.

When we came to his house, I looked at it first,
It seemed like the ruins of an ould preaching church.
Oh, cruel was my fate, I was left in the lurch,
In the clutches of Darby O'Leary.

'Tis well I remember, 'twas Michaelmas night,
To a hearty good supper he did me invite —
Bad spuds and sour milk that would physic a snipe,
Or give you the woeful disorder.

The niggardly rascal looked on with a frown,
While I was admiring my shabby shake-down,
A tick of wet chaff, all dirty and brown,
And a quilt since the time of the Damer.

I was tired and distressed from my long and hard tramp,
And found when undressed a bed worse than damp;
I'd no hope of a sleep for it seemed the ould scamp
Kept the fleas in his doss in starvation.

The following morning before the daylight,
I was roused up by Darby, all flurry and fright,
Had to weed his big garden, till late into night,
When even the ghosts had been quartered!

From work without cease and food that was bad,
When the darkness came on, I was weary and sad,
Parched for a *deoch*, I touched the old lad,
But as well look for down on a badger.

'Twas early next morning I opened my cell,
And left without warning this happy hotel;
His praties and *blathach* I pitched them to hell —
And likewise kind Darby O'Leary.

I worked in Kilcommon, I worked in Kenmore,
I worked in Knockcarron and Soloheadmore,
Nicker, Rathcannon and Boheranore
With dacent respectable people.

I worked in Tipperary, the Rag and Rosgreen,
The moat of Kilfeacle, and the bridge of Aleen,
But such cruel tribulations I never have seen
As I got from that Galbally farmer.

And now it is time for to finish my song;
I hope that the reign of his breed be soon gone,
So, here's to that day — for it won't be too long —
And bad cess to you Darby O'Leary!

From the *Labour Party Conference Magazine*, 1995

The Story of Sarah McGowan

The ways of the average employer are many. He is an astute gentleman at all times, but especially so when there is a danger of his pocket suffering. Of course he doesn't like that his employees should look for an increase in their wages, and neither does he like to see them organise for their own protection and defence, although he joins up with his fellow employers in wealthy Federations in order to safeguard himself and his pocket, and try and break up Trades Unionism on the part of his workers. We have heard that since the Irish Transport and General Workers Union started organising in Limerick, certain employers are thinking out ways and means, to smash the Union. We will give one instance which has come to the B.D.'s ears. Twelve girls employed by George McKern and Sons, Ltd, Printers, &c., joined the Union, and at their request a demand was put in for a 5/- increase in their wages, which ranged from 5/- to 11/- for an employee thirteen years with the firm. The Manager, an individual with the very Irish name of Eakins, told the girls that he would give them 2/6 increase each, on condition that they left the Union, and he would also pay them a sum equal to the amount they paid into the Union; that if they did not leave the Union they would not get an increase, and furthermore he would dismiss them. Under pressure eleven of the girls agreed and got the 2/6 increase. One young girl, named Sarah McGowan, to her everlasting credit be it said — refused to leave the Transport Union and was therefore dismissed by Eakins. The girls who accepted the bribe to leave the Union are, perhaps, more to be pitied, than blamed. They may think that they did the wise thing, but the paltry thirty pieces of copper which they sold themselves for and turned their back on their victimised self-respecting comrade, can be taken off in the morning by Eakins, as the girls have no Union now behind them to fight their cause.

From *The Bottom Dog*, Vol. 1, No. 5, 24 November 1917

From: **Limerick Town**
John Francis O'Donnell

Here I've got you, Philip Desmond, standing in the market-place,
'Mid the farmers and the corn sacks, and the hay in either space,
Near the fruit stalls, and the women knitting socks and selling lace.

There is High Street up the hillside, twenty shops on either side,
Queer, old-fashioned, dusky High Street, here so narrow, there so wide,
Whips and harness, saddles, signboards, hanging out in quiet pride.

Up and down the noisy highway, how the market people go!
Country girls in Turkey kerchiefs — poppies moving to and fro —
Frieze-clad fathers, great in buttons, brass and watch seals all a-show.

Merry, merry are their voices, Philip Desmond, unto me,
Dear the mellow Munster accent, with its intermittent glee;
Dear the blue cloaks and the grey coats, things I long have longed to see.

Even the curses, adjurations, in my senses sound like rhyme,
And the great, rough-throated laughter of that peasant in his prime,
Winking from the grassbound cart-shaft, brings me back the other time.

Not a soul, observe you, knows me, not a friend a hand will yield,
Would they know, if to the landmarks all around them I appealed?
Know me? If I died this minute, dig for me the Potter's Field!

* * * * *

'Pshaw! You're prosy.' Am I prosy? Mark you then this sunward flight:
I have seen this street and roof tops ambered in the morning's light,
Golden in the deep of noonday, crimson on the marge of night.

Continents of gorgeous cloudland, argosies of blue and flame,
With the sea-wind's even pressure, o'er this roaring faubourg came.
This is fine supernal nonsense. Look, it puts my cheek to shame!

Come, I want a storm of gossip, pleasant jests and ancient chat;
At that dusky doorway yonder my grandfather smoked and sat,
Tendrils of the wind-blown clover sticking in his broad-leafed hat.

There he sat and read his paper, Fancy I recall him now!
All the shadow of the house front slanting up from knee to brow;
Critic he of far convulsions, keen-eyed judge of sheep and cow.

* * * * *

Many a night from race and market down this street six brothers strode,
Finer, blighter, truer fellows never barred a country road.
Shouting, wheeling, fighting, scorning watchman's law and borough code.

* * * * *

Rolled the waggons, swore the carters, outside in the crowded street,
Horses reared and cattle stumbled, dogs barked high from loads of wheat;
But inside the room was pleasant, and the air with thyme was sweet.

Others now are in their places, honest folks who know us not;
Do I chafe at the transition? Philip 'tis the common lot —
Do your duty, live your lifetime, say your prayers and be forgot.

From *Poems*, Ward and Downey, 1891

The Limerick Soviet
Jim Kemmy

The period from 1917 to 1919 was a time of world revolutionary turmoil and stirring working class struggles never since repeated. The traumatic effect of the Bolshevik Revolution of October 1917 and the disturbed aftermath of the First World War transformed Europe into a boiling cauldron of political and industrial unrest. In 1919 a wave of revolt and protest swept across the continent bringing a soviet in Munich, an insurrection in Berlin, a commune in Budapest, a general strike in Vienna, risings in Vratca and Plovdiv, the occupations of factories by Turin workers, the struggles for a forty-hour week in Glasgow and Belfast and big strikes in Liverpool, Southampton, Tyneside and London.

Ireland experienced some of the tremors of this upheaval. A combination of external and internal influences found expression in working class activity in different parts of the country. In Limerick, many workers, led by the officers and executive committee of the United Limerick Trades and Labour Council, had grown in political and nationalistic consciousness. This development had been sharpened by a number of events, notably, the effects of the 1913 Dublin Lockout, the influence of the writings of James Connolly and the participation of the Citizen Army in the 1916 Rising. James Larkin, speaking at the 1914 annual conference of the Irish Trade Union Congress, in thanking those who had helped the locked out Dublin workers, made a special reference to the Limerick Pork Butchers who had 'sent more every week in proportion to their strength than any other union'.

This new awareness found an outlet in the appearance on 20 October 1917 of Limerick's first working class paper, *The Bottom Dog*. This weekly publication was written and circulated by some of the leaders of the Trades Council and continued for 48 editions to November 1, 1918. Labour Day was celebrated by Limerick workers for the first time on 1 May, 1918, when over 10,000 workers marched through the streets. A press report described the event: 'it was a striking display of the strength and solidarity of organised labour in the city, and the appeal of the Trades and Labour Council to celebrate the day was most successful'.

The demonstration ended with speeches from three platforms at the Markets Field, where the assembled workers passed a resolution, to the sound of a trumpet. The first part of this resolution read: 'That we the workers of Limerick and district, in mass meeting assembled, extend fraternal greetings to the workers of all countries, paying particular tribute to our Russian comrades who have waged such a magnificent struggle for their social and political emancipation'. Thus it can be seen from the language used in the text of the resolution that the Russian Revolution had repercussions in Limerick and the expression of solidarity by the city's workers shows the extent of their developing class consciousness.

During this period, the Irish Transport and General Workers Union campaigned vigorously to organise general workers into its young Limerick branch. But other forces were also at work. The rise of Sinn Féin to political power brought another potent influence into working class consciousness. So the two emergent political expressions of nationalism and socialism struggled to assert themselves and these forces were soon to merge in a general strike of the city's workers, in April 1919, that became widely known as the Limerick Soviet.

The first moves that led to the strike began on 21 January, 1919, when a member of Sinn Féin and an Irish Volunteer, Robert J. (Bobby) Byrne, was sentenced to twelve months' imprisonment with hard labour after a revolver and ammunition had been found at his house. Byrne had been branch president of the Post Office Clerks' Association until he was dismissed from his job for his political activities. He had also been a delegate to the Trades Council. In prison Byrne led his republican colleagues in a campaign of disobedience to secure political status and better treatment. This campaign culminated in a riot at the prison. Police reinforcements were sent for and the prisoners were beaten. On 14 February, following a meeting of the Trades Council, a resolution was passed, and later distributed throughout the city in leaflet form, protesting against the treatment being meted out to the prisoners.

This protest was ignored and the prisoners went on hunger strike to try to secure their objective. After three weeks, Byrne was in a weak condition and was removed to the hospital at the Limerick Union. He was placed in a general ward under a heavy armed guard. Plans were made for his rescue by the Volunteer leadership and, at 3 p.m. on Sunday, 6 April the attempt was made. An attack was made on the ward and, in the ensuing melee, Byrne was shot through the chest and died at 8.30 p.m. the same evening. One of the policemen guarding Byrne was killed, another seriously wounded and others received injuries.

The death of the policeman was not an isolated incident but part of a general strategy of guerrilla harassment and attacks on the British military forces and the police. The British administration in the country was in the process of breaking down before the rising tide of Irish nationalism. In March 1919, a month before the Limerick strike, in a report marked URGENT and stamped SECRET, the Inspector General of Royal Irish Constabulary informed the Chief Secretary's Office for Ireland that 'In the prevailing discontent with the existing form of Government, should the extremists decide to take independent action, they could rely to a considerable extent on the co-operation of Labour organisation, and that they would certainly find a large number of fanatical Irish Volunteers through the country, ready to do their bidding. Ireland is unquestionably in a highly inflammable condition and in my opinion at no time was there more urgent necessity for the presence of an overpowering military force.'

It was against this highly charged background that the funeral of Robert Byrne took place. The funeral itself was a tense and crowded occasion with an estimated

15,000 people, including the Mayor and Corporation and Sinn Féin sympathisers from Limerick and the surrounding counties, coming together for the event.

On 9 April, three days after Byrne's death, the British military authorities took a further step to deal with the explosive situation: the city of Limerick was proclaimed a special military area under the Defence of the Realm Act, with the terms of the proclamation to take effect from Tuesday, 15 April.

Strong resentment, spurred by the active nationalist forces, manifested itself among the workers against these restrictions. A special meeting of the Trades Council was called on 13 April and was attended by representatives of thirty-five trade unions. The decision of the meeting was that the workers should not be forced to work under the conditions of the proclamation. A general strike of all the city's workers was declared and the Limerick Soviet was under way.

A strike committee was elected to control the city and sub-committees were appointed to take charge of propaganda, finance, food and vigilance. The strike was called at 11.30 p.m. on Sunday, 13 April, and, with the help of a sympathetic printing works in Cornmarket Row, which worked night and day during the strike, within two hours the city was covered with the following proclamation:

> Limerick United Trades and Labour Council Proclamation. The workers of Limerick assembled in Council, hereby declare cessation of all work from 5 a.m. on Monday, April 14, 1919, as a protest against the decision of the British Government in compelling them to procure permits in order to earn their daily bread.
>
> By order of the Strike Committee Mechanics' Institute. Any information to the above can be had from the Strike Committee.

So the strike began and an estimated 15,000 workers obeyed the call. Through a unique coincidence, journalists from all over the world were then in Limerick to report on the proposed transatlantic flight by Major Wood, who had planned to land in the city for re-fuelling. Consequently, within twenty-four hours, the striking Limerick workers had captured headlines in newspapers throughout the world. For the duration of the strike these journalists gave their readers a blow-by-blow account of the operation of the soviet.

Four depots were established to supply food at fixed prices and the work of collecting and distributing the food was carried out by four City Councillors. Certain shops were allowed to open and labour was provided for bakeries, gas and electricity works and other essential industries. Only vehicles displaying the notice, 'Working under authority of the Strike Committee', were allowed to travel on the streets. Approval was given to some firms to save perishable goods and to transport such goods as coal, butter and flour from the docks and the railway station. Any company not carrying out instructions or engaging in profiteering or the unequal distribution of food was immediately closed down. James Casey, a printer, one of the strike leaders and treasurer of the Trades Council, has written:

'It was generally admitted that the city was never guarded or policed so well previously. The people, for once, were doing their own work, and doing it properly . . . There was no looting and not a single case came up for hearing at the Petty Sessions.'

At the end of the first week, the strike committee had not received the anticipated amount of outside financial support. The committee, faced with dwindling food supplies and a serious shortage of money, attempted to head off a crisis by deciding to design and print its own money. Thousands of pounds, in denominations of 10/-, 5/- and 1/- notes, were issued.

The strike committee continued its work against a variety of difficulties and pressures. Daily discussions failed to bring enough support from the Irish TUC or from workers in other parts of the country.

On Thursday, 24 April, following discussions with the Roman Catholic Bishop of Limerick, Dr Hallinan, and the Mayor of Limerick, Alphonsus O'Mara, the workers' solidarity began to crumble. The strike committee, under strong pressure, shifted ground. After a long meeting, John Cronin addressed a big meeting outside the Mechanics' Institute, the headquarters of the strike committee in Lower Glentworth Street, and announced the terms of the decision taken. He called on all workers who could resume work without military permits to do so, and those who could not to continue 'in their refusal to accept this sign of subjection and slavery'.

The abrupt end to the strike caused much discussion and controversy in Limerick. In an editorial headed, 'The Strike — and After', the local paper, *Munster News*, commented: 'The struggle would have dragged on for some time longer had not his Lordship, Most Rev. Dr Hallinan and the Mayor, as representing the spiritual and temporal interests of the citizens, sent a joint letter to the Trades Council on Thursday, requesting the immediate end of the strike; and that the ready compliance with that request was wise will be readily acknowledged by everyone who has at heart the interests of Limerick as a whole — interests that suffered severely during the continuance of the strike.'

While the contents of the joint letter sent by the Bishop and the Mayor were not publicly disclosed, it is clear that the Bishop's intervention was the decisive factor in finishing the strike. A report in the *Irish Times* stated:

'The opinion is undoubtedly entertained that the early attitude of the Roman Catholic clergy in supporting the strikers was not consistently pursued. It is thought that their views on the situation completely changed when they learned the drastic plans submitted by the Labour Executive to force the issue. They naturally discountenanced extreme measures and the Executive knowing that the people would be guided by their clergy, wisely abandoned their plans . . . '

From the *Labour Party Conference Magazine*, 1995

From: **Maiden Street Ballad**
Michael Hartnett

Now before you get settled, take a warning from me
for I'll tell you some things that you won't like to hear —
we were hungry and poor down in Lower Maiden Street,
a fact I will swear on the Bible.
There were shopkeepers then, quite safe and secure —
seven masses a week and then shit on the poor:
ye know who I mean, of that I am sure,
and if they like, they can sue me for libel.

They say you should never speak ill of the dead,
but a poet must say what is inside his head;
let drapers and bottlers now tremble in dread:
they no longer can pay men slave wages.
Let hucksters and grocers and traders join in
for they all bear the guilt of a terrible sin:
they thought themselves better than their fellow-men —
now the nettles grow thick on their gravestones.

So come all you employers, beware how you act
for a poet is never afraid of a fact:
your grasping and greed I will always attack,
like Aherne and Barry before me.
My targets are only the mean and the proud
and the vandals who try to make dirt of this town,
if their fathers were policemen they'd still feel the clout
of a public exposure in poetry.

But now to get back to the story at hand
about the street of my youth where my bum was once tanned:
when you hear what I'll tell you, then you'll understand
why I smile now whenever I go there.
'Tis said that in Church Street no church ever stood,
and to walk up through Bishop Street no bishop would,
and 'tis said about Maiden Street that maidenhood
was as rare as an ass's pullover.

And then I left home, and I started to roam
making my living by the writing of poems:

until I got wed ('twas the wife who proposed)
and I had to stop gallivantin'.
We've a son and a daughter, a cat and a hen,
a dog and an acre of weeds to fence in
and we dwell in the shade of Tom White's green hill
in exile out foreign in 'Glantine.

I have told ye no big lies, and most of the truth —
nor hidden the hardships of the days of our youth
when we wore lumber jackets and had voucher boots
and were raggy and snot-nosed and needy:
so now — there you have it, the long and the short —
and there may be some people that I have forgot:
if you're not in this ballad, be thankful you're not,
but anyway, buy it and read it.

So now to conclude and to finish my song:
it wasn't composed to do decent men wrong
if I had known it would go on so long
I'd have finished before I got started.
And in times to come if you want to dip
back into the past, through these pages flip,
and if you enjoy it, raise a glass to your lips
and drink to the soul of Mike Hartnett!

From *Maiden Street Ballad*, Observer Press, 1980

'The Whole City's on Strike'
Ruth Russell

At Limerick Junction we were locked in our compartments. There were few on the train. Two or three school boys with their initialled school caps. Two or three women drinking tea from the wicker train baskets supplied at the junction. In the yards of the Limerick station, the train came to a dead stop. Then the conductor unlocked compartments, while a kilted Scotch officer, with three bayonet-carrying soldiers behind him, asked for permits. At last we were pulled into the station filled with empty freight trucks and its guard of soldiers. Through the dusk beyond the rain was slithering.

'Sorry. No cab, miss,' said a constable. 'The whole city's on strike.'

That explained my inability to get Limerick on the wire. From Kildare I had been trying all morning to reach Limerick on the telephone. All the Limerick shops I passed were blinded or shuttered. In the grey light, black lines of people moved desolately up and down, not allowed to congregate and apparently not wanting to remain in homes they were weary of. A few candles flickered in windows. After leaving my suitcase at a hotel, I left for the strike headquarters. Between it and me, there loomed a great black mass. Close to it, I found it was a tank, stencilled with the name of Scotch-and-Soda, and surrounded by massed barbed wire inside a wooden fence. On the bridge, the guards paraded up and down and called to the people:

'Step to the road!'

At the door of a river street house, I mounted gritty stone steps. A red-badged man opened the door part way. As soon as I told him I was an American journalist, the suspicious look on his face vanished. With much cordiality he invited me to come upstairs. While he knocked on a consultation door, he bade me wait. In the wavering hall light, the knots in the worn wooden floor threw blots of shadow. On an invitation to come in I entered a badly lit room where workingmen sat at a long scratched table. In the empty chair at the end of the table opposite the chairman, I was invited to sit down. As I asked my questions, every head was turned down towards me as if the strike committee was having its picture taken and everybody wanted to get in it.

'Yes, this is a soviet,' said John Cronin, the carpenter who was father of the baby soviet. 'Why did we form it? Why do we pit people's rule against military rule? Of course, as workers, we are against all military. But our particular grievance against the British military is this: when the town was unjustly proclaimed, the cordon was drawn to leave out a factory part of town that lies beyond the bridge. We had to ask the soldiers for permits to earn our daily bread.

'You have seen how we have thrown the crank into production. But some activities are permitted to continue. Bakers are working under our orders. The kept press is killed, but we have substituted our own paper.' He held up a small sheet which said in large letters: The Workers' Bulletin Issued by the Limerick Proletariat.

'We've distributed food and slashed prices. The farmers send us their produce. The food committee has been able to cut down prices: eggs, for instance, are down from a dollar to sixty-six cents a dozen and milk from fourteen to six cents a quart.

'In a few days we will engrave our own money. Besides there will be an influx of money from England. About half the workers are affiliated to English unions and entitled to strike pay. We have, by the way, felt the sympathy of the union men in the army sent to guard us. A whole Scotch regiment had to be sent home because it was letting workers go back and forth without passes.

'And — we have told no one else — the national executive council of the Irish Labour party and Trade Union congress will change its headquarters from Dublin to Limerick. Then if military rule isn't abrogated, a general strike of the entire country will be called.'

Just here a boy with imaginative brown eyes, who was, I discovered later, the editor of the *Workers' Bulletin*, said suddenly:

'There! Isn't that enough to tell the young lady? How do we know that she is not from Scotland Yard?'

In order to send my wire on the all-Ireland strike, I stumbled along dark streets till I came to the post office. Lantern light was streaming from a hatchway open in the big iron door in the rear. 'Who comes?' challenged the guards. While I was giving a most conversational reply, a dashing officer ran up and told me the password to the night telegraph room. Streets were deserted when I attempted to find my way back to the hotel. At last I saw a cloaked figure separate itself from the column post box against which it was standing. I asked my way and discovered I was talking to a member of the . . . Watch. Limerick is the only town in the British Isles that retains the ancient custom of a civilian night guard. While the strike was on, there were, during the day, 600 special Royal Irish constables on duty in Limerick. But, at night, in spite of unlit streets, the 600 constables gave place to the sixty men of the Watch . . .

In order to pictorialise the predicament of the Limerick workers to the world through the journalists who were gathered in Limerick waiting the hoped-for arrival of the first transatlantic plane, the national executive council devised this plan. One bright spring afternoon, the amusement committee placed poster announcements of a hurling match that was to be held just outside of Limerick at Caherdavin. About one thousand people, mostly Irish boys and girls, left town. At sunset, two by two, girls with yellow primroses at their waists, and boys with their hurling sticks in their hands, marched down the white-walled Caherdavin road towards the bridge. The bridge guard hooped his arm towards the boat house occupied by the military. Soldiers, strapping on cartridge belts, double-quicked to his aid. A machine gun sniffed the air from the upper storey of the boat house. Scotch-and-Soda veered heavily bridgewards. A squad of fifty helmeted constables marched to the bridge, and marked time. But the boys and girls merely asked if they might go home, and when they were refused, turned about again and kept up a circling tramp, requesting admission. Down near the Broken Treaty Stone, in St Munchin's Temperance hall, in a room half-filled with potatoes and eggs and milk, women who were to care for the exiles during their temporary banishment, were working. A few of the workers' red-badged guards came to herald the approach of the workers, and then sat down on a settle outside the hall.

St Munchin's chapel struck the Angelus.

The red-badged guards rose and blessed themselves.

From *What's the Matter with Ireland?*, New York, 1920

The Sandmen
Kevin Hannan

Sand was dredged from the river by the sandmen, a hardy breed who came from a number of old Limerick families in the heart of the 'Parish' and were engaged in the work for centuries. The sandmen never changed their methods of work but sallied forth, to the very last, with the gear bequeathed to them by their great grandfathers.

For all their hard work and meagre earnings they appeared content with their labouring lot. While their hardiness could be attributed to the physical fitness demanded and maintained by their active lives, their contentment was bolstered by their dietary, which was spiced with regular quotas of that favourite of the pint-drinking epicure, packet and tripe, and by their generous partiality for the pint itself, which has long been the elixir and sustenance of many of those in energetic occupations.

The sand barge, or cot, as it was more commonly known, was the ugly duckling of all small river craft. Simple in structure, it was about thirty feet long and five feet in the beam. Squared and sloped fore and aft, it had a small jib and hand-winch astern for raising the loaded dredge after it had been pushed into the river bed by the single operator standing on the gun'le. There were several anchors and grapnels, plenty of rope, and, of course, the essential wooden bailer, or 'skeef'.

Power and steering were provided by a heavy sweep set in a socket over the stern. When circumstances permitted the craft was bow-hauled by one of the two-men crew. It was altogether a lubberly and ungainly vessel, yielding to control with only the greatest apparent reluctance, and exerting the crew's energies to the full. The labour of loading and hauling the sand was increased considerably by the need for almost constant bailing out of water draining from the load. Circumstances often so combined as to make it imperative for the winch-man to bail with one hand and raise the dredge with the other at the same time.

Up to about seventy years ago, all sand was taken from the stretch between the Lax Weir and the Island Point. Unloading took place at the appropriately named Sand Mall. Breaches or gaps along the river wall facilitated the work; these had gates which were closed at night for the protection of children and others . . . The Mall was characterised almost from its foundation by the heaps of wet sand along the roadway, and the general activity of the sandmen and carters.

After the abandonment of the dredging in the Island Point area, all work was carried out at the deep below Plassey Bridge, and cargo was unloaded at the old canal harbour, close to the Lock Mills. This venue was less hazardous than the former one, and permitted use of much larger cots. Only small loads of four or five tons at a time were taken in the Island Point area.

Different types and grades of sand and gravel lodged in certain areas along the watercourse and were known intimately to the sandmen, who anchored their cots directly over the sand deposits as if by intuitive perception. Gravel was raised principally in the winter time when the seasonal dearth in building activity cut back the demand for sand. Most of this gravel was used in the surfacing of driveways and garden paths of the 'big houses' in and around the city, where it was considered a rare delight to walk on the crunchy multicoloured carpets from the shores of Clouncaree, or the mouth of the Clare Blackwater.

The construction of the Shannon Scheme marked the turning point in the fortunes of the sandmen. Sand was required in such unprecedented quantities for this great engineering feat, that only the opening up of pits in Limerick and Clare could supply the needs. River sand was still in demand, however, and the ancient trade was carried on until the mid-'fifties, when the last load was brought to the old sand quay by Mike Shanahan . . .

Simple economics, modern machinery and transport called the tune, and the curious, legendary occupation had to come to an end, just like the nailers of 'Change Lane, and the chairmakers of the Irishtown. The sandmen had made a contribution to the local scene just like the others. The end was silent, if not altogether painless, and another era was closed.

Some of the sandmen emigrated and others found employment in the building industry. It is certain that the work in their new jobs was not as tough or as dangerous as their old occupation — and they were certainly better paid.

Despite the rigours of the trade, most of the sandmen were healthy and long lived. They were highly respected in the community in which they lived, and many excelled in different branches of sports and athletics. The record of the great athlete, Rory Frawley, in winning five Munster Senior Cup medals while playing with Garryowen calls for special mention.

The Crowes, the Frawleys, and the Shanahans are no longer summoned to their daily labour by the hoarse cry of the early morning heron and the riverside bird chorus is lost in the clear air. There is a strange loneliness since the sandmen left — strange to those who remember the shadowy figures, and their long hours of back-breaking work delving the golden store.

From *The Old Limerick Journal*, No. 8, 1981

The Limerick Rake
Anonymous

I am a young fellow that's aisy and bold,
In Castletown Conners I'm very well known,
In Newcastle West I spent many a night
With Kitty and Judy and Mary.
My father rebuked me for being such a rake,
And spending my time in such frolicsome ways,
But I ne'er shall forget the good nature of Jane,
Agus fágaimid siúd mar atá sé.

My parents had reared me to shake and to mow,
To plough and to harrow, to reap and to sow,
But my heart being too airy to drop it so low
I set out on a high speculation.
On paper and parchment they taught me to write,
In Euclid and grammar they opened my eyes,
And in multiplication in truth I was bright,
Agus fágaimid siúd mar atá sé.

If I chance for to go to the town of Rathkeale,
The girls all around me do flock on the square,
Some buy me a bottle and others sweet cakes
To treat me unknownst to their parents.
There is one from Askeaton and one from the Pike,
Another from Ardagh my heart has beguiled,
Though being from the mountains her stockings are white,
Agus fágaimid siúd mar atá sé.

To quarrel for riches I ne'er was inclined
For the greatest of misers must leave them behind.
I'll purchase a cow that will never run dry
And I'll milk her by twisting her horn.
John Damer of Shronel had plenty of gold,
And Devonshire's treasure is twenty times more,
But they're stretched on their backs among nettles and stones,
Agus fágaimid siúd mar atá sé.

This cow can be milked without clover or grass
For she's pampered with corn, good barley and hops,

She's warm and stout, and she's free in her paps,
And she'll milk without spancel or halter,
The man that will drink it will cock his caubeen,
And if anyone cough there'll be wigs on the green,
And the feeble old hag will get supple and free,
Agus fágaimid siúd mar atá sé.

If I chance for to go to the market of Croom
With a cock in my hat and my pipes in full tune,
I'm made welcome at once and brought up to a room
Where Bacchus is sporting with Venus.
There's Peggy and Jane from the town of Bruree
And Biddy from Bruff and we all on a spree,
Such a combing of locks as there was about me,
Agus fágaimid siúd mar atá sé.

There's some say I'm foolish and more say I'm wise,
But being fond of the women I deem it no crime,
For the son of King David had ten thousand wives
And his wisdom was highly regarded.
I'll till a good garden and live at my ease,
And each woman and child can partake of the same,
If there's war in the cabin themselves they may blame,
Agus fágaimid siúd mar atá sé.

And now for the future I mean to be wise,
And I'll send for the women that acted so kind,
And I'll marry them all on the morrow by and by
If the clergy agree to the bargain.
And when I'm on my back and my soul is at peace
All the women will crowd for to cry at my wake,
And their sons and their daughters will offer their prayers
To the Lord for the soul of their father.

From *Irish Street Ballads*, collected and annotated by Colm O Lochlainn, The Three Candles Ltd, 1939

The Best Stonecutter in the Country
Seamus Murphy

'I don't care what you think, but the best man this country ever produced in our line was a stonecutter by the name of O'Dowd, and a Limerick man to boot.' So began Nedgill one day at dinner-hour.

'To see that man working was a treat. He made stone-cutting look simple and you would wonder why the blazes you had to serve seven years to it. I don't know how he did it, but he had a system of working which left everyone else standing. I saw him get up a big apex stone about a ton weight and tear into it like 'twas beerstone. You know the work there is on an apex-stone — all angles. Well he had it blocked out while another man would be marking it on. He was the best man I ever saw to use a hammer-point, every blow down to the maker's name! And a skim over with a skew-chisel and he was out. 'Twas enough to make any man give up the trade and go peddling bootlaces, because you'd be ashamed of yourself working near him.

'What used to beat me was that you got the impression he was taking it easy and sure he'd be walking away from you. I remember we were doing a moulded cornice for a bank, and big stones they were. It was overhanging the building so the beds had to be big enough to hold it and we were all banked together on it. That was the way they used to test the men in them days — all of us trying to best one another. It should never have been allowed because it always caused trouble among the men. For the first day we'd all be watching to see who was going to make the pace, and then one of us would start going it and 'twas every man for himself, each fella going about the job in his own way and taking all the short cuts he knew.

'You know the way it goes — you get the rake of the moulding with the template, block off the waste and put in a chase a bit stiff of the line and claw-tool it down. Then you get in the lines of the moulding and put in the ends. I was always a bit nervous of getting down a face too quickly; I like a bit on for the skew-chisel. Now and then I leave a bit too much on and it means making a face twice over. It is hardshipping to try and skew-chisel a quarter of an inch off a bed. You want a mallet point.

'But, to get back to the cornice—'

'Take off another length of it now,' said the Gargoyle, 'you wiped out that course in no time and, as far as I can see, O'Dowd couldn't hold a candle to you.'

'Let me finish what I was saying,' said Nedgill, 'you never lost it — always butting in on a man! Well, we were all on the cornice. I think there were six of us. We had a man from Waterford, a man from Dublin, from Ballinasloe and Tralee, along with myself and O'Dowd — 'twas like an inter-county competition! And they were all good men.'

'Including yourself,' said the Gargoyle.

'Yes,' said Nedgill, 'I'm one of the best men in Ireland yet.'

'How do you know that?' asked the Gargoyle. 'Sure you never worked outside of Cork, and that's only a small part of Ireland.'

'No more old buck out of you, now,' said Nedgill, 'if you're not interested, the other men are.'

We appealed to the Gargoyle to shut up, now that the story had taken on a competitive aspect we were all attention.

'Well, the Ballinasloe man was the first to get ahead, he was used to the Ballinasloe stone and could cut it like cheese. At the end of the second day he was walking into them. Then the Dublin man showed up. He was a man with a good head on him and he never made the mistake of wasting time marking on the guide lines; he always saw his job finished the first minute he took it up. I learned a lot from him. Anyway there wasn't much to choose between us after three days' work, and there was over a week's work in each stone.

'None of us took much notice of O'Dowd. He'd only been jobbed a few days before and we didn't know exactly what he was made of. But by the time we were finished with that cornice we'd good reason to know. He finished his job a day and a half ahead of me, and I was a good few hours ahead of the rest — and into the bargain his job was better masoned than mine. I needn't tell you we were lepping mad at the beating we got and to give the foreman his due he said it was astonishing how any man could have got away with it. "Nedgill," he said, "you are well over a day ahead of what I allowed for the working of these stones, and, at that rate, the Limerick man is two and a half days ahead. I wonder did he get a kind bit of stone, or did he come in over the wall and do a bit at night? It's a mystery to me anyway."

'I agreed because I had never in all my natural days worked so close and along with that I had no trouble, everything went smooth from the start but in the end I was left standing. The foreman had a smack for me. "'Twill look bad," he said, "on the time-sheets. What will the boss say? An unknown man from Limerick wiping the floor with the rest of ye."

'Then I had a brainwave. I thought of Padna. At that time he was in his prime, the best man in this town, or any town outside, for that matter. "You're right," said the foreman, "I'll banker him with Padna. We'll have to uphold the honour of Cork."

'"But not on the cornice," said I, "the Limerick man will make the next bit of that with his eyes shut and Padna hasn't worked any of it." "I'm fly for that," said the foreman. "I'll give them one of the bases for the columns, and there's at least ten days' work on one of them with the beds made."

'He bankered them and tipped Padna off: "For the sake of the old town, don't leave us down or 'twill be all over the country and we'll never live it down."

'Anyway they got started. We were all excitement wondering how our man would fare. "Don't stir from the banker," says I, "if you have any tools to sharpen let them on the rub stone and I'll do them for you. And I won't talk to you on the job. Come up to the house in the evening and we'll work out all the short cuts possible."

'After about five days I noticed Padna looking a bit down in himself so I arranged with the other men that we give him a few pints in the evenings to keep his heart up. So we used all waltz into Miss O's and try to cheer him up by telling him how well he was going about the job and that we were all depending on him. But 'twas no use, he seemed to have got it into his head that the Limerick man was just a little bit too good for him, though, to give Padna his due, he worked like a nigger and never let up for an instant.

'Then I got an idea. I suggested to the other men that the best thing at all to keep him in form would be a visit to the Turkish Baths. 'Twas agreed, and I took him along the next evening to the old baths in Maylor Street. The baths were old-fashioned, compared with what they are now. You undressed in an outer room and then proceeded to the wash-house, where you filled a basin with warm water. A dipper with a handle was provided and you poured the warm water over you and then went into the sweating room.

'I gave Padna two pints before we went in as he was a bit nervous. Anyway, stark naked we went into the wash-house. I filled the dipper with water from the stone basin and poured it over Padna — merciful Heaven, he let a roar out of him that nearly brought the house down. Instead of being warm, the water was icy cold! I'll never forget Padna's language. The attendant rushed in and ordered us out for misconduct.

'On the eighth day Padna was looking very shook in spite of everything. The sweat was streaming down his face, making channels in the dust on it. Just before lunch he collapsed at the banker. He had worked himself to a standstill and made no impression at all on the Limerick man.'

'I'd believe it,' said the Gargoyle. ''Twas given up to O'Dowd as being the best stonie that ever worked in this part of the country. 'Tis all in the method.'

From *Stone Mad*, Routledge & Kegan Paul, 1966

The House of Darby O'Leary
Pat Feeley

The county of Limerick can be divided in two parts: the great sweep of almost unbroken flat country that forms the greater part of the county and the small western corner of hills and rough country that encompasses the Mullaghareirk mountains. The two parts are different not only physically but also economically and culturally. The fertile plain was, and is, the stomping ground of the strong farmer. The hill country is a land of small farmers and labouring men. Here the best land is on the hillsides and along the rivers. Elsewhere there are bogs, rushes in the low-lying fields and furze bushes in many places. This upland place was densely populated for all of the nineteenth century and for most of this century. The County Limerick farmers looked to the landless men of this place and other similar places to till their fields and reap their corn.

Up until the late eighteen twenties, the hill country of west Limerick had no proper road system. It was sealed off from the outside world. The forces of law and order could penetrate it but with difficulty. It was a Gaelic world and it still is. The last native speaker of Irish died in Mountcollins in the 1960s. In sharp contrast the lowlands of the county were anglicised fairly early on. The great pool of men and women, all in search of work, gave the farmers great power. You worked with them or you went hungry. But they wrought no improvement to the state of the poor, Arthur Young, the agriculturalist, thought. He visited Adare in 1766 and described the people 'as not better off than 20 years ago . . . Have a potato garden, of which one half to three fourths of an acre carries a family through the year.'

One would think that the decimation brought by the Famine and the mass flight out of the country that followed would have so reduced the number of the farm labourers that those remaining behind would have been in a better position to bargain. But Karl Marx, in *Capital*, wrote: 'That the relative surplus population is today as great as before 1846, that wages are just as low and that the oppression of the labourers has increased.'

Farm servants were hired in different ways. In the hill country young people from the same family might hire out to the same farmer, one after another as they came of working age. Successive hiring out to the same farmer was, of course, an indication that he was a good employer. In such instances it was common for the farmer to come to the cottage of the servant to do the hiring.

But there were two big hiring fairs in the county, one in Newcastle West and the other in Kilmallock. Both towns were on a railway line. The Newcastle fair was held from early January to late February. It took place in the Square. Farmers coming there to hire servants came from north Cork, north and east Kerry and from all over the County Limerick. They took up positions in key spots to observe those presenting themselves for hire. The servant girls wore long black shawls that enveloped them from head to toe. The servant boys also wore dark clothes, with caps and hobnail boots. Colour and song were provided by ballad singers, three-card-tricksters and vendors of sweets, drinks and cakes. The farmers were looking for physique, stamina and health. The work, the wages, the food and the sleeping accommodation were what concerned the servants. A hiring was usually sealed with coin and with a drink. The fair ended about 6 p.m. The hiring fair of Newcastle was at its peak in the 1920s, when as many as three hundred people could be seen on a day offering themselves for hire. But after the last world war, the fair began to decline and died out altogether at the end of the 1940s.

Paddy Roche of Mountcollins was probably as representative of the Limerick servant boy of the early century as one could find. Ten years, he said, he spent working for the farmers. For his first year's work, he was paid £16 and £32 for his last year. He worked with farmers within a fifteen mile radius of his home. This was in keeping with thinking in the hills, where they preferred their children to hire with farmers of their own culture than with the hard, rich farmers of east Limerick. Paddy hired on the eleven month system from 1 February to Christmas Eve. In some houses the food was good up to Saint Patrick's Day and after that it deteriorated. This was because the hiring fairs in Newcastle ended in mid-March and there was little further hiring of servants. One farmer gave him a bed in a loft over a stable. He slept little, with the pounding and neighing of the horses. This farmer was in line with the mediaeval practice of humans sleeping close to the animals for body warmth. In another house he was given a settle-bed in the kitchen. This had a number of inconveniences for him: he could not go to bed until the family had gone to bed and if there were visitors in the house, he was obliged to remain in an outhouse until they had left. In the mornings he had to be dressed and out of the house before the farmer's wife came down to light the fire, and on Sundays he had to dress for Mass in one of the outhouses. The farmer could dismiss him for standing under a tree from a shower. There were many wettings but the farm servant was not allowed to sit at his master's fire. One of the first things that Paddy did, therefore, when he went to a new district was to try and strike up a relationship with one of the cottiers so that he would have a fire to dry his wet clothes. If he was unsuccessful in this, he might not sit at a fire from February until he returned home to Mountcollins at Christmas.

Girls were hired out young and were more vulnerable than boys. The servant girl's work was generally lighter. In the mornings she put out the ashes and lit the fire, milked the cows, separated the milk, fed the calves and then had breakfast. In a good house this would consist of tea and bread and a boiled egg. She had to do all the usual household chores.

At sowing time in spring and at harvest time in the autumn, women and girls were expected to work in the fields with the men. As one woman put it: 'You did what you were asked or turned your face homewards.' Girls of thirteen or fourteen were expected to do the work of men. The servant girl working around the house often experienced the full brunt of the snobbery and class distinction from the farmer's wife or daughters. During the year the female servant was given money for clothes, shoes and stockings and this was deducted at Christmas when the balance was paid to the girl or her father.

There was a saying in the Athea area in west Limerick: 'She came home at

Christmas with £11 and a bun in the oven.' Young women and girls were sometimes made pregnant by the farmer, by one of his sons or by a labourer. Though to be fair, in many households, the farmer's wife took great care to see that no sexual relationship developed between members of the family and the female servants. 'It was a class crime', as one farmer told me, 'for a farmer to marry his servant girl.' The puritanical sexual code that dominated the lives of people helped to protect the farm girls from the sexual abuse that their sisters experienced in other countries.

Ownership of land was central to the life and thinking of the east Limerick farmer. This is illustrated in a story told. Two Limerick farmers were in a pub discussing a local tradesman. The first farmer said the tradesman was a decent fellow, a good type. The second farmer said nothing. The first man made some further complimentary remarks. The second farmer then responded saying: 'Ah, sure he's only a man of straw.' He had no land.

Those that emigrated to the New World in the second half of the nineteenth century had to work hard but they earned more than they could have ever earned at home. And they were free, independent and proud in a democratic society. Some of this is to be found in a letter written by John Costello of Caherconlish, County Limerick to his father near the close of the last century. He said: 'Men here are not starved with the hunger like half the gentlemen's men are at home. There are no gentlemen here. If a farmer in Ireland made 3 or 4 thousand dollars in a year like I made here, you couldn't walk the roads with them. You would have to go inside the fence or they would ride over you. I would like to know what the boys want to be wasting their time around Croagh. There is nothing to do there but to go work for somebody, and sooner than I would work for a farmer in Ireland I would cut off my good right hand.'

The farm servants were turning their backs to their masters. In the years following the anti-fascist war, Britain was booming with work for everyone. Irishmen crossed the sea in droves to work in the construction industry. For the women there was work in shops, hospitals and factories.

The epitaph for the servant boy system in County Limerick was written by Patrick McNabb in *The Limerick Rural Survey 1958–1964*. The Limerick farmer was said to be without hired labour and to be dependent on his own family. The farm workers, McNabb said, had demanded the wages and working conditions of their urban counterparts. The farmer 'more or less successfully resisted the attacks of the workers but only at the price of losing them altogether'. The survey showed that migration from the county for the period 1941 to 1951 was highest for farm workers at 33%, as compared to 17% for farmers' sons and 2% for farmers.

'The Galbally Farmer' is the best known Limerick song on the relationship between farm labourer and farmer.

From the *Labour Party Conference Magazine*, 1995

The Men of Park
Richard Ross-Lewin

Shadows of evening softly fall
On tower and spire, cathedral wall.
Sons of the earth, of toil and moil,
Delving and digging the deep rich soil,
Patiently working from dawn till dark,
Such are the lives of the men of Park.

I've passed them by in the early day,
When the city folk in their slumbers lay,
When the dew shone white on the grassy lawn,
And the cocks 'gan crow at the rising dawn,
And the blithe notes rang from the soaring lark,
And there at their work were the men of Park.

And when at even the vesper bell
Is tolling, tolling o'er brake and dell,
And the birds are speeding their homeward flight
Seeking for cover ere gath'ring night
Out in the gardens you still may mark
The toiling, moiling men of Park.

Oh! say not our sons are an idle race —
Thriftless, shiftless, lazy and base,
Industries start to keep them at home,
Never again from their isle to roam,
And stay their flight in the emigrant bark,
To work for their homes like the men of Park.

Alas! too many afar have flown
From the older city and Treaty Stone,
Away far over the ocean tide
In foreign land where waves divide,
Where the strange streams flow yet they fain would hark,
To old Shannon's voice, like the men of Park.

No time for politics labouring there
Neath these lovely, lonely hills of Clare,

Ever and always they seem content,
For hearth, and home, and a well-earned rent,
And rest but comes when they're stiff and stark,
To the sturdy, homely men of Park.

From *Poems by a County of Clare West Briton*, George McKern & Sons, 1907

The Battle of the Tail-Race
Michael McCarthy

At 11.30 on Monday, July 11, 1932, the full fleet of the Abbey fishermen numbering 24 boats, each containing two men, gathered at St Thomas' Island. On the stroke of midnight the fleet approached the tail-race. An official of the Fishery Board shouted to the fishermen from the bank that fishing inside a particular mark was prohibited. The warning went unheeded and the fishermen continued on their course. Bailiffs in three motor boats patrolled the mouth of the tail-race. Gardaí were also on duty in launches. Hundreds of onlookers lined the banks. Slowly the angling cots arrived and some of them nosed over towards the bailiffs' hut to extend their line in order to make it more difficult for bailiffs and police to prevent their entry to the canal. The turbines at Ardnacrusha had been turned on at full strength creating a tremendous current which made the handling of the light fishing boats more difficult. The next few moments are described by William Lysaght in his book *The Abbey Fishermen*, 'there was a moment of hesitation, but with a cry of "Up Garryowen" and a few deft strokes of their paddles, Randy and Lully Hayes sent their boat surging in between the chains behind one of the launches. This was the signal for concerted action. In a matter of minutes all the boats were inside — the battle was on.' Some boats made to go upstream towards the Power Station. The bailiffs followed. The crowd cheered the fishermen on. From Parteen Bridge stones were thrown at the boat injuring one bailiff, Thomas O'Connor, though not seriously. Nine nets were seized. The names of 42 men were taken by the gardaí. Three boats, reportedly heavily laden with fish, escaped. Four or five shots were fired in the air to disperse the crowd. The last net was seized close to 3 a.m. and then the boats returned to their base at the Sandmall.

On the following day, Tuesday, the fishermen planned their strategy for that night, and at 8 p.m. the full group assembled at the Sandmall. Almost immediately they dipped their paddles and set out for the tail-race forty-five minutes away. Peadar O'Donnell, the former Sinn Féin TD for Donegal, was present that night as a reporter for *An Phoblacht* and gives an eye-witness account of the events:

'I arrived at the tail-race one of the war evenings; a wet evening but crowds of Limerick folk were there waiting for the fishermen to come. Police in great numbers; a dark bundle of a dozen men over near a shed were pointed out as the bailiffs. And a-lack-a-day, the man in charge of the bailiffs was one who had a great reputation among the Volunteers. I felt terribly ashamed for him as I drew near to the crowd of the bailiffs. I talked to him: what I said doesn't matter, I suppose. Then I did a meeting of the bailiffs. I asked them to go on strike for the night and I put my heart into the talk, while bewildered policemen with horned, stumpy necks pushed into the crowd. And I would recognise again one face full of enthusiasm when I seemed to be winning the bailiffs. But I lost.' At this point the fishermen appeared in view and approached the tail-race. The crowd cheered. Peadar O'Donnell continues his account: 'The bailiffs went to their motor boats: the war was on. Just picture it: two powerful motor boats full of well-coated bailiffs wait while frail two-men shells of boats go quickly into the tail-race. Out go the nets. And the crowd cheers. When a salmon strikes the cheers become a roar. Suddenly the motors are set going and in come the bailiffs' boats. The scene suddenly becomes sickening; the motor boats crash in among the coracles and grappling hooks reach out. There is a crash and a man of the McNamaras is overboard; clothes, boots and all, he is down the mill-race of the flood. But the bailiffs hang on to their prey, the boat and the nets. McNamara swims ashore. The crowd rush to the water's edge and there is excitement. Policemen with drawn batons move about, some imploring, some threatening. One policeman reminds me of Mickey James in *Rat-Pit*: I expected him to invite us to sniff the scent of the dead men on his baton. Suddenly there is a stampede: military with fixed bayonets are clearing the embankment: police are using batons. I picked up a docker out of the dirt of the road into which he had been hammered by police. I witnessed this incident from the start: the docker, another of the McNamaras, just would not run: he was sulky, grudging, but that was all. He was struck with a baton: I saw a policeman box him, another kicked him, kicked him heavily. A man in a rain-coat — I was told he was a police officer — was in the group that hammered the man. I got the man from the police and I drove him into Limerick: his face was bleeding, his clothes were a mess. But the man was quite gentle: he just wouldn't run from the police. I saw a few other incidents that were shameful to the police, and in any case the man in the rain-coat was there: policemen seem to think that the presence of an officer demands roughness from them: they reminded me of a buck-navvy gaffer when the travelling ganger appears. I saw incidents where guards were considerate.'

The curtain of darkness brought an end to the baton charging and stone throwing for one night. In all 17 boats and 10 nets were seized; 10 boats escaped. Forty-eight names were taken. The confiscated nets and boats were put in a military lorry and brought to Sarsfield Barracks. During the night a party of military patrolled the banks of the tail-race.

From *The Old Limerick Journal*, No. 7, 1981

The Farm Labourers
Patrick McNabb

The class structure is complicated by the change in the social conditions of the working class. The traditional class system remains intact, but the workers no longer accept it. There is, as yet, no new stratification of the society, because the worker cannot breach the stronghold of the farming class. It may be that the only way in which he can realise his new aspirations is to emigrate. On the other hand, the farming class are on the defensive and many of their social attitudes may be related to the emancipation of the workers. It is necessary, therefore, in order to understand the contemporary social situation, to examine in greater detail the development of the farm working class.

The farm workers as a group are the most migratory. The net migration rate for farm workers during the period 1941–1951 was 33%, as compared with 17% for farmers' sons and 2% for farmers. In view of the heavy decline among farm workers, it seemed worthwhile to investigate how the farm worker plans his own future and that of his children and whether his plans imply dissatisfaction with his position in the community and with the existing social institutions.

The majority of workers interviewed, although they termed themselves farm workers and were called such by farmers, worked part of the year on the roads or at other unskilled jobs. Full-time farm workers were exceptional and were drawn mainly from the over-40 age group. Usually these were single men who had worked and lived on the same farm for many years. Married workers favoured casual employment and moved from farm to farm. The same pattern could be observed for younger workers living at home . . .

Until 1930, when wages and conditions of work were fixed by law, the common method of recruiting farm labour was by hiring. On the 17th of March, boys and girls from the upland regions of Kerry or West Limerick gathered in the market-places of East Limerick towns and offered themselves for hire. If they were minors, the parents bargained with the farmer. The period of hire was from St Patrick's Day to the end of November. Conditions of employment included board and lodging and a lump sum ranging from £15 to £30 per year, depending on the quality and experience of the worker. The money was paid either to the parents or the worker at the end of the year. The farmer could deduct a certain amount for clothes and pocket-money given to the worker during the year. There were no fixed hours of work and days off depended on the good will of the farmer.

The hiring system continued in a limited way for many years after the introduction of fixed wages, and it is claimed that the last hiring fair took place in Kilmallock in 1939. Many of the workers interviewed had been hired in their youth. Their chief complaint was that they were excluded from any participation in the life of the farm family and had harsh conditions of work.

'We suffered nothing but hardship, working long hours with poor diet.' A woman said: 'I remember working on a farm where the mistress was so mean she would save the left-overs for us. I was so hungry that I ran away.'

According to farm workers, relationships between the two classes on the whole were not good. They admitted that some farmers were 'thorough gentlemen' but these were a minority. In fact a typical comment was that 'the dogs were treated better than us'. Some statements showed a certain acceptance of their depressed condition.

'One thing I must say about my mother; she was hard, but she never let me go cheap.'

'We were slaves, but in our own way we were happy.'

The last statement is identical with the sentiments expressed by the old generation of American Negroes.

However, conditions of work seemed less important to the worker than his position on the social ladder. As one man said: 'It is not the work that would pinch you, but class distinction.'

As evidence of class distinction, the workers described the domestic arrangements in the farm house. In very large farm houses the family dined in a separate room. This seemed to cause less friction than the custom in smaller houses where the workers dined with the family in the kitchen. The workers sat at a separate table, were given inferior food, used different crockery and, in some cases, were not given cutlery. After the evening meal, they were not encouraged to stay in the kitchen. During winter-time this caused much hardship, as there was no warm place to rest in the evenings. Even their bedroom was not a refuge, as this was usually an unheated outhouse. One got the impression of a life of hopeless drudgery. Workers described how, at the end of the day, they were too tired to take off their clothes or say their prayers before going to bed. One recalls the phrase 'we were slaves, but we were happy'. It may seem strange that the worker tended to minimise the importance of the harsh conditions of life and at the same time stressed class distinction. A possible explanation is that the harshness of life was eased by the frequency and closeness of human contact in a period when the number of farm workers was high and the very primitiveness of their lives created a sense of solidarity and trust. Living in close proximity to the farmer underlined the difference in status and made important such things as dining at separate tables.

From *The Limerick Rural Survey 1958–1964*, edited by Rev. Jeremiah Newman, Muintir na Tíre Rural Publications, 1964

FOUR

PEOPLE

Sylvester O'Halloran (1728–1807)
J. B. Lyons

The eldest son of Michael O'Halloran of Cahirdavin, County Clare, Sylvester O'Halloran was born on 31 December 1728. Very little is known about his childhood and youth except that his mother's kinsman, Sean Claragh McDonnell, a man accomplished in Greek, Latin and Irish, was one of his earliest instructors and that with his brother, Joseph, who later joined the Society of Jesus, he attended a school in Limerick run by the Reverend Robert Cashin, a Protestant clergyman. Facilities for further education were inadequate in eighteenth-century Ireland and the doors of Dublin University were closed to young O'Halloran who was a Catholic, so he sought his professional education in Leyden, Paris and London . . .

He returned to Limerick in 1749. A contemporary has left us a graphic portrait of O'Halloran: 'The tall, thin doctor in his quaint French dress, with his gold-headed cane, beautiful Parisian wig and cocked hat . . . ' He must have presented a strikingly elegant figure in that provincial city, and sartorial perfection is rarely known to hinder success. He had only to wait; sooner or later it would come . . .

In 1752 Sylvester O'Halloran married Mary O'Casey of Ballycasey, County Limerick, and they had four children. His wife pre-deceased him by many years. Her death in 1782 grieved and dispirited him . . .

Sylvester O'Halloran's publications included A New Treatise on the Glaucoma or Cataract (1750); A New Method of Amputation (1765) and A New Treatise on the Different Disorders Arising from External Injuries of the Head (1793). His Proposals for the Advancement of Surgery in Ireland which was published as an appendix to the treatise on gangrene is generally regarded as having been extremely influential in bringing about the foundation of the Royal College of Surgeons in Ireland.

Far from allowing professional commitments to set him apart from the life of the city, O'Halloran seems to have engaged to a not inconsiderable degree in public affairs as well as energetically pursuing a special preoccupation with Irish history. He was President of the Free Debating Society in 1772 . . .

At a meeting held in Limerick in 1783 to enquire into the state of the Shannon navigation Sylvester O'Halloran was among those appointed to the Citizens of Limerick Committee. In the following year a long letter from his pen was printed in the Dublin Evening Post championing the cause of Catholic Emancipation. He was a prolific letter writer . . .

His historical books, Ierne Defended (1774), An Introduction to the Study of the Antiquities of Ireland (1770), and A General History of Ireland (1774) made him widely known. Gilbert included him in The Medical Review and a Gaelic poet, Thomas O'Meehan of Clare, also wrote a poem in his praise.

His histories did not receive universal acclaim. One gentleman, indeed, advised him to 'drop any more scribbling, and mind the Systole and Diastole of the human body, which I suppose you are better acquainted with than history'. Nevertheless, they were standard reference works during the latter part of the century, and distinguished visitors to Limerick made a point of calling on the author.

He helped to found the County Limerick Infirmary and was one of the surgeons to the hospital. He seems to have been in considerable demand as a consultant in Munster. In 1802 he was among those who formed the Limerick Medical Society. At a meeting of this body in 1806 the proceedings of the College of Physicians and Faculty of London with respect to medical reform, transmitted at the desire of the Government through Surgeon O'Halloran, were duly considered.

Old age advanced relentlessly. The Reverend J. Hall, who visited Limerick in 1807, wrote in his *Tour of Ireland*: 'I found Dr O'Halloran the celebrated antiquarian to whom I had been introduced, old, infirm and confined to his chair.'

Such is our last sad glimpse of Sylvester O'Halloran, defeated physically by time but still mentally active. He died in Limerick on the night of Tuesday 11 August 1807, at his residence on Merchant's Quay. His remains were laid in a vault in Killeely Cemetery.

From *Brief Lives of Irish Doctors*, Blackwater, Dublin

The Benns of Broad Street
Alfred Browne

If the Labour Party has its roots in the Methodist social conscience of the nineteenth century, then Tony Benn can claim an impeccable ancestry.

Religious dissent comes with the first Benn of whom there is any trace, the Reverend William Benn, of Dorchester in Dorset, who was one of 2,000 Anglican clergymen to fall victim of the Five Mile Act of 1665. This followed on the Act of Uniformity of 1662, which had rejected the Puritanism of the Commonwealth in favour of High Church views, by forbidding any non-conforming clergyman to come within five miles of any town of which he had been a minister, or to act as tutor or schoolmaster. Virtually exiled for his Puritanism, William Benn went to Limerick, in Ireland, to begin what turned out to be a long Congregational tradition — a seventeenth-century engraving of the dissident clergyman was a treasured possession of the nineteenth-century Benns.

Certainly, the Benns have Irish connections, though the current head of the family might wish they had begun in some other way than they did, with the granting of a licence of land in Ireland by Oliver Cromwell to William Benn just ten years before his expulsion.

In Limerick William was among other Protestant refugees, from France, Alsace and Germany and evidence of intermarriage is suggested by the names of some of his descendants. Julius, with its German overtones, was a popular name among the Benns — a Julius Caesar Benn was baptised in Limerick in 1718 — and the Benn fondness for preserving connections in second names, as witnessed by the appearance of 'Wedgwood' later, is presumably the reason why Julius Delmege Benn, baptised there in 1838, was given his French middle name.

The first direct ancestor of Tony Benn to have his life recorded in detail was his great-grandfather, Julius, a Congregational minister. He was born at Cheadle, near Manchester, in 1826, the son of a quilt maker who had returned to England from Limerick. His mother died when he was quite small, and when his father married again, stepmother and stepson failed to get on together. Julius, still not in his teens, decided to run away to sea.

He got as far as Liverpool, thirty miles away, where, family tradition has it, a Quaker, moved by a sudden urge to walk along a quayside, found the small boy, hungry, penniless, cold and miserable, on the point of suicide. In the fashion of nineteenth-century tracts the Quaker said to himself on seeing the boy, 'Surely this is one of the least of these, my brethren,' touched Julius on the shoulder and spoke aloud, 'Friend, follow me.' Julius did, to a new home and education.

Whatever the truth of this account, based on a tale Julius later in life told his children, it seems the situation was resolved on a family basis. Young Julius went to live with an uncle, Francis Benn, who had a haberdasher's shop in Broad Street, Limerick.

While there he fell under the sway of one of the brilliant non-conformist ministers of the nineteenth century, John de Kewer Williams, who was to become a lifelong friend and influence. He outlived Julius and conducted the funeral service after Julius's tragic death.

The Hungry Forties were upon Ireland and Williams founded a society for helping the least fortunate people of that most unfortunate country. Under the unprepossessing title of 'The Eclectic Society' he pressed for educational and social reform. Whatever the society's effects in relieving distress it had a profound effect on its members, all of whom, except one, became Congregational ministers themselves. Its influence on Julius seems not to have fitted him for trade in the eyes of his employer . . .

Whatever the truth of that, he seems to have had in good measure the Benn trait of being able to make his way in the world, whether in terms of reputation or material prosperity or both. All the Benns seem to have had the ability to lift themselves by their own bootlaces and generally chose wives from similarly able families.

From *Tony Benn: The Making of a Politician*, W. H. Allen, 1983

Merryman Comes to Town
Frank O'Connor

Architecturally, the little city of Limerick is one of the pleasantest spots in Ireland. The Georgian town stands at the other side of the river from the mediaeval town which has a castle with drum towers and a cathedral with a Transitional Cistercian core and a fifteenth century shell, all in curling papers of battlements. Across the bridge are the charming Custom House with its arcade cemented up by some genius from the Board of Works; Arthur's Quay falling into a ruin of tenements, and a fine long street of the purest Georgian which ends in a double crescent. There is no tablet in Clare Street to mark where Bryan Merryman, the author of *The Midnight Court* died, nor is there ever likely to be, for Limerick has a reputation for piety . . .

What Merryman aimed at was something that had never even been guessed at in Gaelic Ireland; a perfectly proportioned work of art on a contemporary subject, with every detail subordinated to the central theme. The poem is as classical as the Limerick Custom House; and fortunately, the Board of Works has not been able to get at it . . . Merryman never wrote again. He went to live in Limerick with his daughter and her husband, a tailor, and died suddenly there in 1805. Why did he go there? Most probably because what Professor Corkery sneers at as 'his much-enlightened soul' longed for some sort of intellectual society, which in twentieth century Clare it might still long for. To say the man was 150 years before his time would be mere optimism — think of Professor Corkery! Did he expect to find among Limerick Protestants a cultured group who would understand him? If they ever heard of him they forgot to mention the fact. Perhaps it was their neglect which compelled him to realise the futility of trying to make Irish the language of contemporary thought. He had that sort of clear, objective intelligence which rarely attaches itself to lost causes, and he may well have turned with a wry smile from the dream of a modernised Gaelic Ireland to the teaching of trigonometry . . .

Merryman was ignored by Georgian society in Limerick, but in death he has taken a terrible revenge. The great, wine-coloured Georgian cliffs are being steadily eaten away by Rathmines Romanesque and Ruabon Renaissance. Nowhere else in Ireland has Irish Puritanism such power. Leaning over the bridge in the twilight, looking up the river at the wild hills of Clare from which old Merryman came down so long ago, you can hear a Gregorian choir chanting *Et expecto resurrectionem mortuorum*, and go back through the street where he walked, reflecting that in Limerick there isn't much else to expect.

From *The Midnight Court: A Rhythmical Bacchanalia from the Irish of Bryan Merryman*, translated by Frank O'Connor, Maurice Fridberg, 1946

A Poet's Grave*
T. J. Dunbar

How still this solemn place of gloom!
The gaunt, bare trees, their leaves have shed;
Where winter shrouds grey spire and tomb,
And tablet sacred to the dead.

Beneath yon solitary mound,
Where one white daisy rears its breast;
With yew and cypress clustered round,
The world-tired Poet lies at rest!

No more shall toil, or daily strife,
Wake his calm dreaming, slumber-won;
Cold, lone, neglected as in life,
Sleeps Erin's chiefest minstrel son!

No titled pomp, nor wealth had he —
Yet all his toiling life, he sung
Of Youth, and Love, and Chivalry,
And Beauty, when the world was young.

Though poor and hard his lot below,
To all mankind he could afford,
Kind friendship's gift; in weal or woe,
The rapture of a kindly word.

Dear Bard, whose worth lived all unknown,
While sweet the strains thy wild harp made;
No humble tribute stands, nor stone,
To mark the spot where thou art laid.

Yet, from the distant city gay,
Here, where December's chill winds rave;
One kindred spirit comes to lay,
This laurel chaplet on thy grave.

Great singer of the South! whose name,
By future tongues shall reverenced be —

Graved in the golden scroll of Fame,
Though once the cold world frowned on thee!

* The grave of Michael Hogan, the Bard of Thomond

From A *Garland of Verse*, Sealy, Bryers and Walker, *circa* 1910

The Palatines
D. L. Kelleher

Ardnacrusha, colonised temporarily by German technicians in the Shannon electricity works in 1928, was not the first settlement of Germans near Limerick. In 1709 the English Queen Anne invited the Protestant Lutherans who had been driven from the German palatinate to settle in Ireland. They would impart, she hoped, a stiffening of *morale* to the native Irish, would check the 'rudeness and explosive manners' of the aborigines with an infusion of German thoroughness and that tincture of dourness that is always an aid to empire. They were conveyed in transports provided by England, and three thousand of them planted round Rathkeale and Adare. Each soul was granted eight acres of land, with a rental of five shillings an acre after the first twenty years of rent-free tenure. Every man, too, was provided with a good straight-barrelled musket and certain hints as to whom he might shoot, such as always went with gift-muskets in Ireland. These musketeers were known as the 'true blues', an ambiguous title as their blue sequel proves.

Something went wrong with the settlement very soon, and, in a couple of generations, the Germans had sadly degenerated from their national good brown beer standard to the level of common Irish *usquebagh*. John Wesley, the little preacher with a wig, a black stuff gown and a charming voice, came round on his horse on one of his Irish missionising tours. He rode out to Court Matrix, where he found 'the Germans, having no minister, had become eminent for drunkenness, cursing, swearing and utter disrespect for religion', as he mildly put the case in his *Journal*. That kind of 'eminence' was induced by despair at their economic situation, for even their German thoroughness could not pull them alive through the general ruin of Ireland all around them. Literally they had been sold a swindle when they were inveigled into this colonising attempt, aimed rather against the local population than at any amelioration of the destiny of the foreigners. 'At Ballygarane,' continued the truthful Wesley, 'as they could not get food and raiment, with all their diligence and frugality, part are scattered up and down the kingdom, and part are gone to America.'

From *Ireland of the Welcomes*, The Irish Tourist Association, Inc., 1943

Gerald Griffin and Lydia Fisher
John Cronin

The year 1829, which saw the publication of his most enduring fiction, was to prove memorable for Griffin for other reasons also. It was in this year that he formed the warmest personal association which was ever to come his way outside his immediate family circle. It was a characteristically cruel irony that the woman who aroused his ardour was of a different religious persuasion and, in any case, already happily married. She was Lydia Fisher, wife of James Fisher and daughter of a well-known writer, Mary Leadbeater (1758–1826), author of *Cottage Dialogues Among the Irish Peasantry* (1814) and *The Annals of Ballitore from 1768–1824*. The Fishers were Quakers and lived near Limerick. At the time of their first meeting Lydia Fisher was about thirty, some three years older than Griffin himself. She too had done some writing, though she did not achieve her mother's fame.

It was Griffin's journalistic pieces which first brought him to the notice of the Fishers. They read and admired some of the Irish sketches which he had written for the London journals but, as has already been noticed, these were all published either anonymously or under pseudonyms so that it was some time before the Fishers knew the name of the writer whose work they had been admiring. They then came to know him through his more serious publications, first of all *Holland-Tide*, then *Tales of the Munster Festivals*, and particularly through *The Collegians*. After publication of his best-known novel Gerald was invited to visit the Fisher home and 'having spent an evening there, he returned to Pallaskenry, delighted beyond expression with his new acquaintances'. It is clear from such letters as survive that at this point Gerald fell in love not just with Lydia but with the entire Fisher family and he did so because he found them 'a literary oasis in what I thought a desert of utter and irreclaimable dullness'. Recently returned as he was from London and Dublin, elated with the success of his most ambitious work so far, he was delighted beyond measure to find close to his Irish home a highly congenial family who shared his intellectual and literary interests, who admired his writing and welcomed him warmly into their happy family circle.

The letters which survive from this period bubble over with boyish pleasure in his new-found friends . . .

Apart from the letters the only further clues are supplied by the verses which Gerald addressed to Lydia from time to time . . . and we can form a fairly accurate judgment on the nature of Gerald's feelings for Lydia Fisher and of the progress of his attachment by reading the letters and verses together. When we do this what emerges is an emotional graph strangely analogous to the curve of Griffin's literary career. That is to say that the affair begins ardently, then sours for a while before finally mellowing into a more pedestrian form, until it is finally stamped out by the scrupulously perfectionist Griffin who climaxes the affair by refusing to see Lydia when she calls on him at his Dublin monastery. In a similar mood, he climaxed his literary career by burning his manuscripts. This wilful self-abnegation is his only final solution to all his dilemmas . . .

Daniel Griffin, usually so cautious about what he includes in the *Life*, gives us some remarkably revealing verses which indicate clearly that Gerald had certainly confronted the full implications of his feelings for Lydia Fisher:

> Yet, all pleasing rise the measure
> Memory soon shall hymn to thee,
> Dull for me no coming pleasure,
> Lose no joy for thought of me.
> Oh, I would not leave thee weeping,
> But, when falls our parting day,
> See thee hush'd, on roses sleeping,
> Sigh unheard, and steal away.

He must have realised very clearly that only 'forms of deadly promise' could emerge from any attempt on his part to indulge his feelings for her. It was a particularly cruel stroke of fate that caused him to fall in love with a married Quaker, a dutiful wife and mother. Daniel concludes the *Life* with some verses which provide Gerald's own very precise definition of the relationship along with an acute perception of his own character:

> Remember me, Lydia, when I am departed,
> Live over those moments when they, too, are gone;
> Be still to your minstrel the soft and kind-hearted,
> And droop o'er the marble where he lies alone . . .

> And say, while ye pause on each sweet recollection,
> 'Let love like mine own on his spirit attend:
> For to me his heart turned with a poet's affection,
> Just less than a lover, and more than a friend . . .

> Yet peace to his clay in its dreary dominion,
> I know that to me he was good and sincere;
> And that Virtue ne'er shadowed, with tempering pinion,
> An honester friendship than Death covers here!'

He loved her deeply, knew his case was hopeless, sublimated his feelings for her in a display of warm affection for her children, her husband and herself. When his prudishness came to the fore he felt guilty about it all and cold-shouldered his friends and subsequently repented of his churlishness. All the time, he valued Lydia and James Fisher as intelligent friends who loved his writings and provided for him a welcome oasis of culture in an intellectual desert. The two families visited each other, corresponded regularly, valued each other's friendship greatly.

Had Lydia been free to marry, how differently the whole story might have ended! The night before he left his brother's home for the last time, to join the Christian Brothers, he wrote:

> I believe we both give each other credit for that strong and lively interest in all that concerns the happiness of either, without which friendship is but a name. In parting with my old desk, which has accompanied me through almost all my labours in the literature of the world, for which, perhaps, I have worked at least quite as hard as it deserved, it occurred to me that you would attach some value to what would be worthless in the eyes of most others — so I leave it for you, dear Lydia, and in it your letters, and my own hateful share of the correspondence. Of the latter, I opened one or two, and found them so odious that I was not much tempted to proceed . . . If we do meet again in this life, dear Lydia, as I hope we often may, I trust it will be with unaltered feelings of confidence and friendship. Our dear Lucy said she never knew any one so like a *real* sister as you were, and such, dear Lydia, I beg of you to continue always to me and mine. I fear you will think this letter cold, as my manner has often been, even when my feelings were farthest from indifference.

It says so much, this last, sad, dismissive letter which is so clearly intended as a final severing of his ties with her. His desk is to be hers — a touching gesture certainly, but inside it are all her letters to make the gift a painful one. His letters to her are now 'hateful' and 'odious' to him. His self-disgust is so absolute that he must emphasise it by repetition. And Lucy enters the letter, in a significantly magisterial role, to define their relationship for them yet again as brother and sister, lest any dangerous misunderstandings should arise. Passion and duty have clashed and duty has emerged victorious but the price in frustration, pain and self-disgust has been high. It is small wonder that he could not endure to have the relationship reopened in even the most formal manner and could not bear to see her when she called later at his monastery in Dublin.

From *Gerald Griffin (1803–1840): A Critical Biography*, Cambridge University Press, 1978

Seán South of Garryowen
Sean Costelloe

'Twas on a dreary New Year's day as the shades of night came down,
A lorry load of volunteers approached a Border town;
They were men from Dublin and from Cork, Fermanagh and Tyrone,
But the leader was a Limerick man, Seán South of Garryowen.

And as they moved along the street up to the barrack door,
They scorned the danger they would meet, the fate that lay in store.
They were fighting for old Ireland's cause, to claim our very own,
And the foremost of that gallant band was South of Garryowen.

But the sergeant foiled their daring plan, he spied them thro' the door;
Then the Sten guns and the rifles, a hail of death did pour;
And when that awful night was past, two men were cold as stone;
There was one from near the Border and one from Garryowen.

No more he'll hear the seagull cry o'er the murmuring Shannon tide,
For he fell beneath the Northern sky, brave Hanlon at his side,
He has gone to join that gallant band of Plunkett, Pearse and Tone.
A martyr for old Ireland, Seán South of Garryowen.

From *The Irish Catholic*, 10 January 1957

Lola Montez
Horace Wyndham

> 'When you met Lola Montez, her reputation made you automatically think of bedrooms.'
> Aldous Huxley

In a tearful column, headed 'Necrology of the Year' a mid-Victorian obituarist wrote thus of a woman figuring therein:

'This was one who, notwithstanding her evil ways, had a share in some public transactions too remarkable to allow her name to be omitted from the list of celebrated persons deceased in the year 1861.

'Born of an English or Irish family of respectable rank, at a very early age the unhappy girl was found to be possessed of the fatal gift of beauty. She appeared for a short time on the stage as a dancer (for which degradation her sorrowing relatives put on mourning, and issued undertakers' cards to signify that she was now dead to them) and then blazed forth as the most notorious Paphian in Europe.

'Were this all, these columns would not have included her name. But she exhibited some very remarkable qualities. The natural powers of her mind were considerable. She had a strong will, and a certain grasp of circumstances. Her disposition was generous, and her sympathies very large. These qualities raised the courtesan to a singular position. She became a political influence; and exercised a fascination over sovereigns and ministers more widely extended than has perhaps been possessed by any other member of the *demi-monde*. She ruled a kingdom; and ruled it, moreover, with dignity and wisdom and ability. The political Hypatia, however, was sacrificed to the rabble. Her power was gone, and she could hope no more from the flattery of statesmen. She became an adventuress of an inferior class. Her intrigues, her duels, and her horse-whippings made her for a time a notoriety in London, Paris and America.

'Like other celebrated favourites who, with all her personal charms, but without her glimpses of a better human nature, have sacrificed the dignity of womanhood to a profligate ambition, this one upbraided herself in her last moments on her wasted life; and then, when all her ambition and vanity had turned to ashes, she understood what it was to have been the toy of men and the scorn of women.'

Altogether a somewhat guarded suggestion of disapproval about the subject of this particular memoir.

Three years after the thunderous echoes of Waterloo had died away, and 'Boney', behind a fringe of British bayonets, was safely interned on the island of St Helena, there was born in barracks at Limerick a little girl. On the same day, in distant Bavaria, a sovereign was celebrating his thirty-fifth birthday. Twenty-seven years later the two were to meet; and from that meeting much history was to be written.

The little girl who first came on the scene at Limerick was the daughter of one Ensign Edward Gilbert, a young officer of good Irish family who had married a Señorita Oliverres de Montalva, 'of Castle Oliver, Madrid'. At any rate, she claimed to be such, and also that she was directly descended from Francisco Montez, a famous toreador of Seville. There is a strong presumption, however, that here she was drawing on her imagination; and, as for the 'Castle Oliver' in sunny Spain, well, that country has never lacked 'castles'.

The Oliver family, as pointed out by E. B. d'Auvergne in his carefully documented *Adventuresses and Adventurous Ladies*, was really of Irish extraction, and had been settled in Limerick since the year 1645. 'The family pedigree', he says, 'reveals no trace of Spanish or Moorish blood.' Further, by the beginning of the last century, the main line had, so far as the union of its members were blessed by the church, expired, and no legitimate offspring were left. Gilbert's spouse, accordingly, must, if a genuine Oliverres, have come into the world with a considerable blot on her 'scutcheon.

Still, if there were no hidalgos perched on her family tree, Mrs Gilbert probably had some good blood in her veins. As a matter of fact, there is some evidence adduced by a distant relative, Miss D. M. Hodgson, that she was really an illegitimate daughter of an Irishman, Charles Oliver, of Castle Oliver (now Cloghnafoy), Co. Limerick, and a peasant girl on his estate. This is possible enough, for the period was one when squires exercised 'seigneurial rights', and when colleens were complacent. If they were not, they had very short shrift.

Mrs Gilbert's wedding had been a hasty one. Still, not a bit too hasty, since the doctor and monthly nurse had to be summoned almost before the ink was dry on the register. As a matter of fact, Mrs Gilbert must have gone to church in the condition of ladies who love their lords, for this 'pledge of mutual affection' was born in Limerick barracks while the honeymoon was still in full swing, and within a couple of months of the nuptial knot being tied. She was christened Marie Dolores Eliza Rosanna, but was at first called by the second of these names. This, however, being a bit of a mouthful for a small child, she herself soon clipped it to the diminutive Lola. The name suited her, and it stuck.

From *The Magnificent Montez: From Courtesan to Convert*, Hutchinson & Co., 1935

Sir Peter Tait
Kevin Hannan

Sir Peter Tait, whose life story reads like a fairy tale, was Limerick's famous 'rags-to-riches' hero.

He was born in Shetland in 1828, his father was Thomas Tait from Tingwall. While in his early teens Peter left his island home to seek his fortune. He arrived in a sloop at Limerick harbour in 1846 and secured a position as a draper's apprentice at the firm of Cumine and Mitchell (afterwards Cannock's) . . .

Apprentices 'lived-in' at the large stores at the time, but most were left off during the slack period from October to April. Thus young Peter Tait found himself on the streets of a strange city with only a few shillings in his pocket. His offer to the management of the firm to work, without pay, for his bed and board having been turned down the enterprising young man bought himself a hawker's basket and went from door to door of the lanes and streets of the city selling small articles of haberdashery. His enterprise prospered, and in a short time he was selling articles of drapery, mainly to sailors disembarking at the harbour after long voyages.

In a remarkably short time Tait had made enough money to open his own business in a premises in Bedford Row, where he employed a number of women making shirts and caps. (In those years everyone wore a cap.) Soon he was back in his old firm, not as an apprentice, but as full partner. The firm was now 'Cannock and Tait'.

At this time the Singer sewing machine had just been perfected, and the ambitious young Shetlander saw the potentialities of its use. Limerick being a garrison town, Tait was well aware of the great difficulties and expense in providing uniforms for a whole regiment at a time when every stitch had to be made by hand. Full of confidence and expectation he consulted the Lord Lieutenant in Dublin, and explained his plan to manufacture army uniforms quickly and cheaply by a revolutionary system of employing a number of workers each performing a different operation in the manufacture of the garment. This man was so impressed with Tait's idea of mass producing uniforms that he prevailed upon the war office to support the project. Tait was given a contract to equip a regiment with uniforms, to be supplied to the Central Military Stores in London. He succeeded so well in fulfilling his undertaking that the authorities gave him an unlimited contract to supply the army in general.

Tait was now well and truly on the road to prosperity. He purchased an old auxiliary workhouse in Lord Edward Street, and worked there for some time before erecting one of the most modern factories in Europe on the site.

In due course Tait supplied uniforms to the forces engaged in the Civil War in America, breaking the Yankee blockade of the American ports on one memorable occasion with his steamship 'Evelyn', one of his three ships which transported his finished uniforms from the port of Foynes to America and England. His other vessels were 'Elvey' and 'Kelpie'.

By this time Tait was a rich young man with many of his early ambitions already realised, so he decided to settle down in earnest. He married Rose Abraham, the beautiful daughter of Thomas Abraham, of Fort Prospect, the splendid mansion not far from the South Hill House, where he settled down with his bride.

That the young tycoon never allowed success to go to his head was evidenced in the hawkers basket which he kept hanging in the hall at South Hill as a reminder to himself and all visitors to the house of his early days as a struggling waif.

Tait was also an outstanding success with the people of Limerick. He subscribed to every charity, and made his name synonymous with acts of benevolence in all directions. He was a good employer, and treated his workers generously. He was elected Mayor in 1865, and held the office for three years. In 1867 the citizens decided to erect a fitting memorial to him in recognition of his services to the city; this is the handsome clock tower in Baker Place, known as 'Tait's Clock'.

Like many a good man that went before him, Peter came a 'cropper' when he entered politics. He stood as a Tory candidate in the '67 general election, and was defeated. After this event his popularity began to wane, but many who disagreed with his politics were really sorry for him. The big man might have recovered if he had learned the lesson of his election defeat, but he succumbed to the temptation to enter as a candidate in a by-election in his native Shetland in 1873. He was defeated, and also lost in a general election. The shattering effect of these disasters resulted in a loss of interest in his business concerns.

After a few years Tait retired to England (he had a house in London), and left the control of his factory to his brother, Robert, who, lacking his knowledge and ability, caused the business to decline. It was afterwards rescued from closure by a group of local businessmen who stepped in and set up a new company.

Tait, for ever the adventurer, found his restless spirit too difficult to control: we find him in the late 1880s failing in a cigarette manufactury, which he established in India.

Sadly the greatest benefactor that Limerick ever knew died at Batoum, South Russia, on December 15, 1890, leaving only £50 to the world.

From the *Limerick Leader*, 30 September 1989

The Death of a Cabin-Boy
Jim Kemmy

Few people today will have heard of Patrick O'Brien. His name has not entered any of our major works of local history. There is not even a plaque or stone to his memory.

Patrick O'Brien had a short life. He was born in Killaloe and died, aged 15 years, on 18 December, 1835. His life ended in the most appalling and terrifying circumstances.

As a boy labourer Patrick O'Brien had worked at the local docks stacking timber. When the Limerick ship, 'The Francis Spaight', sailed for St John's, New Brunswick, on 25 November, 1835, he signed on as a cabin-boy. The ship, which a few years earlier had taken 300 poor emigrants from Limerick to Quebec, was set to return with a cargo of timber.

The ship came to grief on the night of the 3 December when, during a snowstorm, it was upended by strong gales, and three of the crew of eighteen were lost overboard. When dawn broke it was found that all provisions had been washed away, the fresh water fouled, and that only the cargo of timber was keeping the ship afloat.

Apart from the bottles of wine and what rain-water the crew could gather in their handkerchiefs, no food or drink remained. On 18 December, after sixteen days of excruciating cold, hunger and thirst, the captain of the ship, Thomas Gorman, called the remaining members of the crew together.

With no sign of rescue in sight, it was decided that one of the crew should be killed to keep the rest alive. Lots were drawn, and it was found that Patrick O'Brien, a widow's son, had drawn the shortest lot. It was later suggested that the lottery had been rigged against him.

However, young O'Brien bravely bared his wrists but when the veins were cut the blood refused to flow. Eventually the cook was compelled to cut the boy's throat.

The rest of the story is equally gory. Three other crew members were similarly put to death, after two of them had become deranged, and they, too, were devoured by their shipmates.

On 23 December, the eleven surviving crew members were rescued by the brig 'Agenora'. The captain of 'The Francis Spaight' was engaged in eating the liver and brains of his cabin-boy when rescued.

After their return to Limerick, the captain and crew were tried for murder and acquitted.

The ship owner, Francis Spaight, in a public appeal for the survivors and the relatives of those that had perished wrote:

'It is only necessary to state here that the surviving sufferers have arrived in Limerick in a state of abject wretchedness, and some of them are mutilated by the frost and otherwise rendered helpless, as to be unable not only to obtain bread, but to labour for it during the rest of their lives. Without food, without clothing, and without hope, unless from the present appeal, they and the families of their deceased shipmates, implore the bounty of the citizens.'

Thomas Gray, in his 'Elegy', wrote of 'the short and simple annals of the poor'. Patrick O'Brien's life was short and simple, and he was killed on Christmas week, in 1835.

From the *Labour Party Conference Magazine*, 1995

Robert Dwyer Joyce
John Boyle O'Reilly

There is one remarkable feature absent from modern Irish poetry, from the work of poets born in Ireland and other countries: the song-maker is rare, and becoming rarer. Allingham has written only a few songs; McCarthy not many; Alfred Perceval Graves a good many, and very good ones. In America the poets of the Irish have had only one eminent song-maker, Dr Robert Dwyer Joyce. His volume 'Songs and Poems', is a most notable book of songs, written mainly to old Irish airs, which adds to their value and charm. Joyce had in a high degree the melody-sense and the brief one-idead and richly-chased song method. His ballads are stirring songs, as anyone knows who has ever heard the chorus of 'The Iron Cannon' or 'The Blacksmith of Limerick'. In 'Deirdre' and 'Blanid', both noble epics, the songs interspersed are the high-water mark of Joyce's genius. We range the fields of literature to find more exquisite songs than 'Forget me not', and 'O, Wind of the West that Bringest'. Not only sweet to the ear but to the soul, the cry of the little blue-eyed blossom in the deadly embrace of the 'bitter-fanged strong East wind':—

'O woods of waving trees! O living streams.
In all your noontide joys and starry dreams,
Let me, for love, let me be unforgot!
O birds that sing your carols while I die,
O list to me! O hear my piteous cry —
Forget me not! Alas! Forget me not!'

Joyce's life was a poem in its unrealities, achievements, agony and gloom. He died in the strength of manhood, beloved by the friends whom he had made, proudly secretive, but beyond hope, and heartbroken. He was so strong, so wise, and so harmless to man or woman, that his life, under fair conditions, would have been as fair and natural as the flow of a river. He wrote his songs in his happier years. He composed as he walked in the crowded city streets. On his daily rounds as an over-burdened physician, the strongly-marked face was usually pre-occupied, the sight introverted. He was always 'making a song', or working some of his characters in or out of difficult positions. A friend met him once in Boston and was passed unnoticed. He stopped the Doctor by touching his arm, and the spell was broken. 'Oh man!' cried the poet, with his rich Limerick utterance, 'I was getting Deirdre down from the tower! She's been up there for three months, with the ladder stolen; and I couldn't think how I was ever to get her down, without a balloon.'

But in the streets, too, the chill of the secret grief would strike his heart like a breath from the grave, and the powerful form would shudder with the spirit's suffering. It was then he wrote the woeful nameless little song in 'Blanid', which I have called in this collection 'The Cry of the Sufferer'. There was no dainty seeking after artificial misery when Joyce wrote these lines:—

> 'The measured rounds of dancing feet,
> The songs of wood-birds wild and sweet,
> The music of the horn and flute,
> Of the gold strings of harp and lute
> Unheeded all shall come and go —
> *For I am suffering, and I know!*
>
> No kindly counsel of a friend
> With soothing balm the hurt can mend;
> I walk alone in grief, and make
> My bitter moan for her dear sake,
> For loss of love is man's worst woe,
> *And I am suffering, and I know!*'

Dr Joyce won a distinct and deserved renown in America's literary capital. Respect and affection met him in the street, the garret, and the drawing-room. Old Harvard honoured him with a degree. The poor, among whom he laboured unceasingly, and to whom he gave unstintedly of money and gratuitous attendance, repaid him with love. A physician, who took his vacant place and much of his practice, and who did not know Joyce, has since said:— 'He was an extraordinary man, and a very good man. His charity was never-ending. I find traces of it in every poor street and tenement house I visit.'

From *The Poetry and Song of Ireland*, edited by John Boyle O'Reilly, Gay Brothers & Co., 1887

John Francis O'Donnell
Richard Dowling

Now the young poet [J. F. O'Donnell] made up his mind to adopt writing in some form as a career. He accordingly acquired a knowledge of shorthand, and for about two years acted as reporter on the *Munster News*, published in his native city. In after life he never forgot the phonographic art. He was the first man I ever knew well who could write verse on the spur of the moment. I shall never forget the astonishment with which I saw him exercise the two arts conjointly. He and I were chatting, between night and morning, about a poem which he had conceived the idea of while we talked. He said, 'Wait a minute,' pulled a letter out of his pocket, and began writing with great rapidity on the back of it. 'How is this?' he asked, after a few minutes, during which his hand had not ceased to move over the paper. He read the poem out. I said what I thought, and asked to see the MS. 'It won't be of much use to you,' said he, with a laugh, as he threw the paper across the table. The sheet was covered with characters that looked to me like Arabic dancing mad, which he assured me was fairly good phonography, for a man out of practice. 'And can you always write verse as quickly as that?' I asked. 'Well,' he said, 'I can make the verses as quickly as that, but they have to be copied or written out in longhand. When I am very particular, I jot down the poem nearly as fast as you saw me just now, throw the paper into a drawer, never think of it for a couple of weeks, then take it out and finish.' 'Why,' said I, 'you write verse as fast as prose!' 'Faster,' said he; 'as a matter of speed, I could turn out a column of verse sooner than a column of prose.'

But the experience of O'Donnell's method of work which amazed me most of all I had in the *Nation* office. I went out into the composing room and found him seated on the only chair, smoking and writing, with his paper on the 'stone', a large high table of slate or metal where the pages of newspapers and books are imposed or arranged in the proper order for printing. A very large and extremely noisy machine was in full work below, in sight of the composing room, there being a wide, long opening in the floor to let light down to the nethermost regions. 'What on earth are you doing here?' I shouted above the din. 'I — I — I — ,' he answered, he had a slight impediment in his speech, 'I am doing my poem for this week.' 'What! in this awful racket?' I shouted incredulously. 'Yes,' he said; 'I like the noise. It soothes me,' and he went on with the poem.

From Introduction to *Poems* by John Francis O'Donnell, Ward and Downey, 1891

The Bard Bows Out
Michael Hogan

My mother thought of a new plot of torment and humiliation to my goaded and perplexed heart. She brought a basket of periwinkles along with some shell-dilisk to the other side of the street, nearly opposite my door, and there she sat to vend her beggarly merchandise. The shabbiest pauper that ever strayed from a poorhouse looked a Queen in comparison to her. She had attired herself in a Babel of old rags that were actually confusing each other as they fluttered around her wretched form. They appeared like a mass of ivy leaves on an old wall quivering and shaking in the wind. I knew she had no other object in rigging herself thus, and coming there, than to shame and scandalise me. What could I do? I couldn't use force to remove her, neither could I employ the law to do it. Killely Glebe House was at that time untenanted, and there at the lawn wicket she located herself on neutral premises, and no one had the authority to turn her away.

I was almost sure the cold weather would finally expel her, but in this speculation I was deceived. For two years she occupied that bleak position, and never quitted it for even an hour up to the very moment I left my cottage, to return to it no more. Then she gave up her miserable occupation, well satisfied and in high glee. During those two provoking years she left no device untried to outrage my patience. She tried to prevent many persons from dealing in my shop, under the threatened penalty of her avenging curse. She slandered, belied and denounced me to every one that passed by. The bad Neighbours exulted at her unnatural villainy and used to bring her scraps of food, by way of alms, just to taunt and humiliate me. To avoid looking at these disgusting scenes I often ran into the city and remained away all day.

Every morning before she attended her periwinkle mart, she gave a round of begging about the neighbourhood — With a little tin plate in her hand she begged for tealeaves to restew for breakfast. This mean piece of hypocrisy would make me laugh but I was too much hurt. All those shabby tricks were performed to cloak the robbery she perpetrated in my house. I saw she was deceiving the public as she had deceived myself, and I did not envy them for it. Yet I was mad to think that her lying stories were able to rouse up such wild sea of prejudice against me, but I bore it with a silent immovable resolution. I waited for the advocacy of Time, the alleviator of all injuries and evils.

And now in the midst of all my perplexing difficulties the crushing news of the venerable Archdeacon Goold's sudden death reached me. My best prop — my noblest, truest, steadiest friend whose munificent heart and hand were always open to me. His unexpected demise was the most desperate affliction of all I had encountered yet. Now I had real reason to give up the world's conflict and fold my arms in dumb despair. For two gloomy months I could not be held responsible for word or action of mine, for my existence was like that of a moody maniac or a night-walking somnambulist. But no one knew the deep heart-ache that made me strange and silent. I was heedless, reckless and stolidly indifferent to everything . . .

Something whispered in the ear of my mind that I could not stay long in my native land except at the risk of becoming degraded by the shelter of the abominable poorhouse. As soon as my volumes would all be sold off I saw nothing before me but the Atlantic ocean with America at the other side.

I always entertained a settled horror against going to America with all its boasted freedom and enormous wealth. I knew there never could be a flower garden for my soul in that tremendous land of strange, heterogeneous nationalities. But like my ancestors in the days of Cromwell, I had my choice, either to go to Hell or Connaught, and as neither of those two places held out anything but the very quintessence of atrocity to my thoughts, I resolved on going to the Land of Dollars as the least of the evils.

As if to stimulate my resolve in quitting my native land for ever the Nationalists of Limerick began to show me the cold shoulder. Their patriotic principles were so lofty I was far too humble for their dignified notice; and so they shunned me to show the seasoning nobility of their patriotism. In the meantime I received intelligence of the sudden demise of another unflinching friend of mine, the Rev. Edward O'Shaughnessy, PP of Milltown Malbay, Co. Clare. He was at Lahinch when he died. He was a genuine Saggort Aroon of the grand old type, who was always prepared to share his last pound with me, like the faithful and elegant Father Jerry Vaughan of Barefield, Ennis, whom death had also snatched away a few years before.

A friend in New York had offered to send me a sailing ticket, I wrote my acceptance, the ticket came and I at once prepared to face the wild Atlantic. All interest and love of home had turned into bitter hatred in my heart. My whole nature was poisoned and disgusted against my own worthless people. I longed for thousands of miles to intervene between myself and them. I spent the Sunday before I left, taking a last farewell of the Shannon and its shamrock banks; the scenes of all the loving daydreams of my life. I visited the weird and solitary Avon Down and lay until sunset on its mossy banks, feasting my soul with sorrowful reflections. I was homeless, friendless and alone in the land I loved as heaven; and was soon to become a forlorn exile for ever. It was the evil work of those who took treacherous advantage of my simple confidence. I felt all the dark enormity of their baseness and their hideous ingratitude; and the detestable weight bowed down my embittered spirit to the dust. As I returned to the city along by the side of the river, St Mary's glorious 'Bells of the Legend' pealed out an enchanting diapason over the blue bosom of the Shannon.

I stood enraptured drinking into my heart every tone of their delightful melody. I had heard their majestic chimes since my childhood, but until then, I never heard them ringing with such deep mournful sweetness. I imagined they were playing me a farewell anthem, and I blessed them with all my soul. When the chimes ceased I turned to take a last look at Thomond Cottage across the river. I felt uncontrollably a burning malediction shooting from my eyes on the fraudulent party who had usurped my room and my right there. But I quickly walked away in tears leaving the matter in the just hands of Heaven that only saw the cruel wrong that was inflicted on me in that quarter.

On the following Wednesday I left Limerick for Queenstown. I bade adieu to no one for no one came to bade adieu to me. Altho' the city was thronged with patriots and nationalists yet I did not see the face of one of them coming near. I took their absence as another proof of their magnanimous devotion to Ireland and her cause. A few years ago I would have a host of them around me on such an occasion as this.

But now I did not miss them when I remembered the changeful and brittle tempers of that sensitive article called Irish patriotism. The parting with my poor erring wife was painful and distressful. In an agony of sorrow she owned it was all her fault — she did not guard herself against the wicked machinations of old Betty Cromwell, and now a just punishment, in losing me, had fallen on her for acting on the corrupt and evil counsel of that fearful old witch.

I released myself from her as gently as I could and bade her a friendly goodbye. I made my way towards the train as fast as I could hurry on. My memory shrinks to ponder on that dreary and desolate day. I had no luggage but a travelling bag in which I packed a few shirts, four pairs of stockings, some handkerchiefs, forty-four copies of the *Lays and Legends*, the MS of *The Snow Queen* and a copy of poems recently composed. Oh how my spirit fainted at the bare idea of going to America. I felt like one under sentence of death on his way to the place of execution. But that iron edict of destiny was on me and I could not turn back.

My heart may bleed and burst but my spirit would still be unconquered and unquenched, altho' I had no love of life to sustain me in the ordeal. Luckily for me there were two other passengers with whom I was well acquainted bound for America along with me. Under the failing state of my eyesight I never would have ventured along on shipboard amongst strangers. But the company of those two persons encouraged me for they promised to stay near me to the end of the voyage. On Friday, September 19th 1886, I departed from Queenstown on board the steamship *Britannia*. It was 3 o'clock a.m. when the gigantic vessel impelled by her tremendous machinery glided steadily out into the mighty Atlantic. It was dinner time and all the passengers had disappeared from deck to enjoy their meal. I remained alone, leaning against the bulwark, intently watching the retiring shores of my native land. Oh, the blood-sweating agony of that terrible hour!

From *Memoirs* by Michael Hogan, *Limerick Weekly Echo*, 30 April and 6 May 1972

Eamon de Valera
Tim Pat Coogan

Aboard the SS *City of Chicago*, 'Dev was brought to Ireland, in 1885, by an uncle who at that time was about eighteen years of age.' Kate Coll's living conditions must indeed have been 'hardly ideal' if they caused her to send her only child on such an arduous journey — back to a one-roomed thatched cottage — in the care of her teenage brother. Even the journey's last lap in Ireland, from Killmallock to Bruree, had its hardships. On 20 April 1885, the child was 'carried over the hills by his uncle in his arms as that was the shortest walking way to Bruree at the time' . . .

Symbolically enough the Colls were moving up in the world as de Valera arrived in Bruree, with the result that he had the unpleasant experience, for a child, of waking up in an empty house the morning after he arrived. The others — his grandmother, Uncle Patrick and Aunt Hannie — had forgotten about him in the excitement of inspecting the new three-room slate-roofed cottage, with a half acre of ground attached, which had just been awarded them by the state. Despite his initial scare de Valera subsequently took a pride in being 'the last occupant of his family home', even if it was a one-roomed, mud-walled cabin with an open fire around which cooking and sleeping took place.

The move to the new house almost had fatal consequences for the young de Valera. There was a loft over the kitchen, and one morning the child was preparing to descend from it by ladder when his attention was distracted by the blood on a newly plucked goose-wing feather and he fell to the floor beneath. He became aware of his grandmother standing over him, calling out: 'Is he dead?' . . .

Another influential figure shortly to be removed, albeit less drastically, from de Valera's life was that of his fifteen-year-old Aunt Hannie. For about a year after he arrived in Bruree she played a mothering role, lacing his boots and dressing him up in his American velvet suit. He became 'particularly fond' of his aunt. But the same economic situation that had driven her sister Kate to America drove Hannie there in 1886. Her mother's tears mingled with those of young Edward as they waved her goodbye at Bruree railway station. At the age of four he was being left behind in a strange country, bereft of the presence that had helped to make up for the loss of his father and mother.

One of the first manifestations of that strangeness that he became aware of was to have a profound effect on his entire life and career: it was the Irish language. His grandmother's friends used to speak in Irish around their firesides. He did not learn Irish as a boy and when, later in life, he took it up he learned the Connemara dialect. As a child he had not realised that the old people were speaking the Decies dialect, and he came to regret not learning this living link with his early life . . .

His first teacher, Thomas MacGinn, had to rely on a boy who lived near the Colls, Tom Mortell, for the spelling of his name. Consequently, he was entered on the rolls as 'Eddie Develera'. He was generally known as 'Eddie Coll'. His strange-sounding Spanish name puzzled the villagers; by a process of elimination they decided that, since it was neither Irish nor English, it had to be French — France being the foreign country uppermost in folk memory because of French involvement in the 1798 rebellion. It is recorded that, when he had grown a little older, he foiled an attempt by two other boys to hi-jack his uncle's jennet and car. Admiring the way in which one lad defeated two, a bystander called out: 'Ha! Ha! The Frenchman will do for ye!' . . .

The Coll household did not provide a great deal in the way of childish entertainment. His official biography had to concentrate on one annual event to provide a paragraph on 'Eddie's pleasures': 'The race-meeting at Athlacca with its "thimble riggers", "three-card tricksters", the man in the barrel who kept bobbing his head up and down while people tried to hit him with a thrown wattle, "pigs crubeens", more sweets and cakes and, of course, the races themselves — all this was top entertainment.' And, if this 'top entertainment' was not enough to sustain a lad for a year, when the heady delights of Athlacca began to fade Bruree also provided a 'forge and the cooper's yard, producing an endless supply of firkins and barrels . . . And on top of all this 'Bruree village church was a centre of much excitement'. This last was probably true enough because the parish priest, Father Sheehy, who would have been the leading figure in the village anyhow, was doubly famous for his nationalist sermons and for having served a prison sentence on account of his Land League activities. De Valera, who served Mass for him, has described sitting with his fellow altar boys 'drinking in every historic detail. Father Sheehy, eyes closed and long nose reaching his lips, retailed the golden exploits of bygone days, as if in ecstasy.' . . .

De Valera developed one unusual pastime which does not appear on the official list of 'Eddie's pleasures': digging for springs. 'In the long summer evenings he and a companion often spent hours at this work. It would seem a peculiar method of enjoyment, and indeed an unprofitable one,' comments his sympathetic but puzzled biographer. But de Valera was so keen on this activity that he rigged up 'something in the shape of a bell which he affixed to the top of a hawthorn tree . . . The first to arrive would pull the string and the loud metallic sound of the time-saving apparatus resounded through the ether, a reminder to the absent youth that operations had commenced.' From his late teens another loud sound came to be associated with him: the crack of a shotgun cartridge. He became so fond of fowling that neighbours remarked he seemed to have a different gun every time he came home. Prophetically he said: 'I'm afraid I shall be a soldier. I have such a love for guns.'

Perhaps one reason why there is so little flesh on the bones of de Valera's memory is because it was consciously, or unconsciously, selective. In later life, for political reasons, he idealised the ethos of the peasant patriarchy; he never ever referred to the reality of the brute sexuality and near slavery that lay behind that patriarchy, and which bore particularly heavily on women . . . De Valera, although he invariably showed a studied courtesy to women, never showed any disposition to improve their lot in society . . .

His 'hard though good uncle' Patrick was obviously a man of some political talent. He served on the Killmallock Board of Guardians for three three-year terms, and was active throughout Munster in the labour movement. He thrashed the lad when he 'mitched' from school. Physical punishment was commonly meted out for misbehaviour, or what was deemed to be misbehaviour: for example, using the good reins (normally kept for driving the donkey to Mass on Sunday) to make a swing. Patrick Coll's reaction to his nephew's mitching seems to have been prompted by anger at wasting time which might have been spent on the farm, rather than at lost educational opportunity — for he ensured the boy took the fullest possible part in the labouring work of the Coll holding. In class II de Valera is recorded as being present on thirty-six days fewer than the most regular boys.

One of de Valera's most famous speeches to the Dail during a perfervid moment in his career gave details of his chores:

> There was not an operation on the farm, with perhaps *one* exception, that I as a youngster had not performed. I lived in a labourer's cottage, but the tenant in his way could be regarded as a small farmer. From my earliest days I participated in every operation that takes place on a farm. One thing I did not learn, how to plough, but until I was sixteen years of age there was no farm work from the spancelling of a goat and milking of a cow, that I had not to deal with. I cleaned out the cowhouses. I followed the tumbler rake. I took my place on the cart and filled the load of hay. I took milk to the creamery. I harnessed the donkey, the jennet and the horse . . .

But despite all this toil, from his earliest days he seems to have been sufficiently other-directed and self-motivated to put in the study required to get him promoted from one class to another. Gallagher recorded an anecdote which shows how, even at the age of twelve, de Valera had his eyes set on wider horizons than Bruree. He and a boy some four years older were digging potatoes one day when the other boy announced that he was going to Limerick to a job. To de Valera, going to Limerick 'seemed like a great adventure and he said bitterly to himself, "and I am to remain digging potatoes all my life."' . . .

De Valera's grandmother died in 1895, her loss being somewhat mitigated for him by the fact that Hannie had come back to Ireland once more to nurse her. It was at this stage that the boy gave a major display of that determination and self-belief that was to be the hallmark of his adult career. With the illness and death of his grandmother, his labouring chores were increased considerably: cooking was added to his list of duties. He even prepared the wedding breakfast when his Uncle Patrick went through with the marriage that he had seemingly been hesitating over while his mother was alive . . .

The biography tells us he had a hidden agenda. He wanted to persuade his uncle to send him to Charleville Christian Brothers' School which, unlike Bruree, offered the possibility of studying for an exhibition that could carry him on up the educational ladder. 'At last uncle Pat agreed to the scheme since de Valera was willing to walk the seven miles there when necessary' . . . his two years at Charleville were a test of character that he passed with honour.

He had got the idea of going to the school in the first place through the example of an older boy at Bruree who had gone on to win an exhibition there.

But this lad's home was three miles nearer to Charleville than Knockmore, and whatever inducements Kate brought to bear on Patrick Coll these did not include the provision of a bicycle. Eamon de Valera was only fourteen years old on 2 November 1896 when he started at Charleville. He may have got to school by train, but there was none back to Bruree until three hours after school ended. His biography tells how 'often on the long walk home from Knockmore he would rest exhausted against a fence, longing to throw away the heavy pile of school books. But he persisted as so often later in life.' And persist he did, to such effect that in the summer after he enrolled at Charleville he was allowed a trial run at the exhibition examination, which he passed with honours. Owing to his youth he then had a year in hand, which he put to such good use that the second time around he got honours in all his subjects and was awarded an exhibition of £20 a year for three years.

His subjects were English, French, Greek, Latin, arithmetic, geometry and algebra. In retrospect it seems curious that one who throughout much of his life was preoccupied with history did not include that subject in his studies . . . The simple truth was that in his school days de Valera saw politics as an interesting phenomenon outside the reality of his daily existence. This reality was that he would break stones or dig potatoes, whether Home Rule came or not, if he did not apply himself to getting a higher education. But in the end the fact that he got one came about not so much through his own diligence as because of a chance conversation in a railway carriage between two priests.

He failed to get a place at two Co. Limerick schools, the Jesuit-run St Munchin's and Mungret College. But one day the local curate, Father James Liston, rode up to the door of Knockmore on his horse, and called out: 'Eddie, I have news for you.' The news was that while on a holiday train journey that year he had met Father Larry Healy, the President of Blackrock College. During the meeting he had told Father Healy about his bright young parishioner, and when de Valera was refused by the Jesuits he decided to write to the President. Father Healy turned up trumps . . . and so Edward de Valera arrived safely in Blackrock to a sympathetic welcome from a member of the 'French' congregation who spoke with a reassuringly broad Tipperary accent — Brother Mary Paul McGrath.

Brother McGrath's reception of the determined but confused and very gauche sixteen-year-old set the tone for what was to become for de Valera a lifelong relationship with the College. On his first night in the dormitory the boy in the bed beside him wept with homesickness. De Valera was amazed. For his part, 'he felt joy rather than sorrow'. Here he was in an environment of study, free of the drudgery of Knockmore and the long walks from Charleville. An eloquent assessment of his home life came at Christmas, when he opted to stay on at the college with the clerical students, who only returned home at the summer break.

From De Valera: Long Fellow, Long Shadow, Hutchinson, 1993

The Limerick Field Club
Patsy Harrold

The summer snowflake is only one example of the many species of flora which continue to enrich the city and its environs. The combination of the damp climatic conditions, the limestone bedrock, the alluvial soil of the tidal river and the likelihood that foreign ships may have brought some 'outside' seeds to the city through its port has given Limerick a rich crop of wild flowers. And we owe a debt of gratitude to the Field Club for documenting the full range of this selection. Reading the old *Journals*, one discovers that not only did the club publish a regular series of botanical articles but that it also had its own herbarium.

It was the end of the era of great Victorian collectors and enthusiasts, and a time when R. D. O'Brien, George Fogerty, R. A. Phillips, Miss S. C. Bennis, Helen Laird, Eleonora Armitage and many more members of the Limerick Field Club went on regular rambles about the city and county in search of unusual flora. Fortunately for us, the results of their explorations are fully recorded in the pages of their *Journal*.

What sort of people were these amateur botanists and what stirred them to spend their spare time rooting about in disused quarries, rubbish dumps, muddy ditches and quiet backwaters? They were gentle, romantic adventurers, who were driven on in their searches by the magical excitement of discovering a new species of wildflower. The descriptions of their explorations, for all their Victorian idiosyncrasies and quaint turns of phrase, have an essential quality which is seldom found in modern scientific writing — a burning love of the natural order of things, and an awareness of beauty, without which the simple appreciation of life can often be lost in a welter of cold and clinical language. In short, they never lost their sense of wonder and were not inhibited in expressing this wonderment in their writings.

Though we have become more conscious of the need to preserve our environment, we all too often take our wild flowers for granted. But it is not too late to renew our interest in this neglected area of botanical studies.

In many respects, little has changed in this timeless, hidden world and Limerick has much to offer to the botanist in the attractions of its wild flowers: wallflowers still decorate our medieval ruins; valerian grows in profusion on Georgian walls, and, no sooner is a building demolished, than the whole derelict area is clothed in the sweet-smelling flowers of the butterfly bush, *Buddleia davidii*.

The Limerick Field Club, through the explorations and writings of its members, has left us a rich heritage. It is a heritage to explore and enjoy.

From *The Old Limerick Journal*, No. 20, 1986

Donogh O'Malley
Proinsias Mac Aonghusa

Donogh O'Malley was born into a well-off Limerick middle-class family in January 1921. He received a typical conservative middle-class education at two Jesuit schools, at Limerick and at Clongowes Wood in Co. Kildare, and later at University College, Galway. His family keenly supported Cumann na nGaedheal but turned against that party in the early thirties. When he died in March 1968 he was the most popular Fianna Fáil Minister . . . Contrary to many appearances he had used his time and energy to advantage and his 47 years were far from wasted.

Donogh O'Malley came to Dáil Éireann for the first time in May 1954 with the reputation of being 'a holy terror'. His capacity for alcohol was staggering and his desire for it more than equalled the capacity. Stories of some of his more colourful exploits preceded him to Leinster House so that the staff, if not the members, had some idea of what was in store for them. The stories were far from being exaggerated; the reality was quite as terrifying as any Limerick-based tale of his past activities. Some of his activities within weeks of the election would put Brendan Behan in the boys' place: O'Malley when involved in serious drinking never looked as if he were a boy on a man's errand. As with so many of his other activities, when he was truly drinking he gave his mind and heart to it and was highly impatient of any interruption . . .

But whatever was being said and seen in Dublin, Limerick loved him and he developed a real hold on people's affections as well as on the city's Fianna Fáil machine. In June 1961 he became Mayor of Limerick — amazingly the third O'Malley brother to hold the office. The late Desmond O'Malley was Mayor from 1941 to 1943 and Michael O'Malley held the office in 1948–49.

Seán Lemass succeeded Éamon de Valera as head of the 26-Counties Government in June 1959 and two years later Fianna Fáil, under his very forceful leadership, won a General Election: no viable alternative was on offer. To the expressed surprise of a great many people he placed Donogh O'Malley in charge of the Office of Public Works as Parliamentary Secretary to the Minister for Finance. It was a gamble, perhaps a typical Lemass gamble. It ultimately paid off but there were great growing pains, coupled with a many-sided incident, which brought discredit upon the administration of justice in the state. One evening O'Malley had a good many refreshments. He then got into a car and drove it up O'Connell Street. Unfortunately he drove on the wrong side of the street. When ultimately the car came to a stop a Garda approached and asked him if he had not seen the arrows. The Parliamentary Secretary's contemptuous reply is said to have been: 'If I had seen the arrows sure I'd have seen the ____ Indians!' The law was not amused. A prosecution was initiated and, in spite of fantastic and desperate pressures being brought to bear upon him, the Garda refused to withdraw the summons. His point was that every man was equal before the law. Late one afternoon when the ordinary courts at Chancery Place had closed for the day and the public and, more important, the reporters, had gone home, a court-house was quietly opened and Donogh O'Malley, member of the administration which controlled the courts, was surreptitiously tried. He was convicted and fined. A week later the Garda in the case was dismissed from the force. Certain Ministers, though not O'Malley, went to considerable trouble to blacken his character and to ensure that the matter received as little public notice as possible. So many members of the Opposition had had cases 'fixed' for themselves and their friends that they were not in a position to raise too loud an outcry about the matter. It was as shocking an example of the realities of Mafia-type politics in the 26-Counties as had been seen for many years. There were no further prosecutions of Ministers or Parliamentary Secretaries. The message had been clearly put across to the police that certain men regarded themselves as being above the law and were in a position to enforce that belief.

That terrible happening led to a change in Donogh O'Malley's life that ultimately had the most fortunate consequences for thousands of young people and will have great good consequences for hundreds of thousands of young people yet to be born. O'Malley achieved the near-impossible and in so doing showed what tremendous willpower he possessed and what amazing strength of character he had. He gave up the drink. It is practically impossible to overestimate the change this wrought upon his life. Much of his time for many years had been spent with a bottle, now the bottle was finally set aside and a new life started to be built . . .

He knew there was no point in opening up long-drawn-out discussions about the feasibility of free secondary education for all capable of availing of it. He used the *fait accompli* method of getting his way and he succeeded. His threat to leave the Government if his scheme was not in operation for the following school year startled people. But he meant it. It is a credit to O'Malley and to Fianna Fáil and to hard-working civil servants and to thousands of teachers, that there was no necessity for him to carry out his threat. If many thousands of Irish children are now getting more extensive education than they would otherwise have received they can thank Donogh O'Malley for it, and also spare a kind thought for the far-seeing Seán Lemass who saw O'Malley had vision and ability and took a chance on him. His schools transport system is another monument to him which has changed the whole Irish countryside and, by and large, changed it for the better.

From *Scene*, 1968

Untamed Spirit: Séamus Ó Cinnéide
Micheál Ó Siochrú

According to Irish folklore, the gates of Heaven remain opened during the Christmas season, so that whoever should die at this time could enter unimpeded. Even a poet could slip past an off-duty St Peter.

Winged breakers and ethereal strings
And wild intangible things
Clamoured in the bedlam of your mind
As you hiked the shining roads of Clare,
Hobo and wandering bard and raconteur.
With azure opened tent and basketful of lore —
Picnic for the soul —
You thirsted for adventure
And, with senses too sensitive
And arms too long,
You strove to embrace it all at once,
Glutton at life's banquet table,
You drank down pints of mellifluous conversations,
Ingredients for distillation of your poem,
But bubbles gurgled frantically,
Your pen too slow
To drain the overflow.
You sought solace among the ruins
Of ancient Iniscealtra
But centuries of Shannon legends
Were trapped in your whirlpool,
Story upon story pleading to be told,
Knowing well your affinity with the waters.
You were pagan in your worship
At Nature's altar
And in the end
It all came right,
You took your final hike
At Christmastide.

From *Séamus*, edited by Seán Ó Morónaigh, An Chistin, 1994

William Moloney
D. A. Binchy

By the time I first knew him Osborn Bergin had long severed his connection with the Gaelic League . . . he was by then thoroughly disillusioned by the compulsion and commercialism that had — in his view at least — destroyed the disinterested idealism of the original Gaelic Revival. Yet, though he had broken with the Gaelic League and was profoundly sceptical about the value of the policies adopted by a native government to revive Irish, Bergin never lost his love of the language . . .

His earlier poems in Irish, a selection from which was published in 1918, are best known; but he also wrote verse in several other languages — English, Latin, Greek, Sanskrit, and even one poem in Arabic, addressed to his friend and fellow-polyglot W. J. Moloney . . .

William Moloney was the Limerick schoolboy to whom Bergin addressed a congratulatory poem after he had won both the Irish and Greek medals at the Intermediate examination of 1901. He subsequently left Ireland and became Reuters correspondent in several countries, acquiring *en route* French, German, Italian, Norwegian, Arabic, Hindi and Urdu. Over the years Bergin and he corresponded in various languages, but chiefly in Irish, which Moloney continued to speak and write with remarkable fluency. Ultimately he became Chairman of Reuters, and after his retirement in 1942 lived in Hampshire. He was one of the most charming and witty conversationalists I have ever met, and his life-long friendship with Bergin was a strong bond between us. By a sad coincidence the news of his death reached me while I was preparing this lecture.

From the *Osborn Bergin Memorial Lecture*, March 1968

Frank Ryan
Michael O'Riordan

By December 1936 the first group was on its way to Spain. It was led by Frank Ryan, who prior to the departure made a public press statement:

'The Irish contingent is a demonstration of revolutionary Ireland's solidarity with the gallant Spanish workers and peasants in their fight for freedom against Fascism. It aims to redeem Irish honour besmirched by the intervention of Irish Fascism on the side of the Spanish Fascist rebels. It is to aid the revolutionary movements in Ireland to defeat the Fascist menace at home, and finally, and not the least, to establish the closest fraternal bonds of kinship between the Republican democracies of Ireland and Spain.'

Thus was declared the credo of all the Irishmen who went to fight in the International Brigades in the years 1936–37–38.

Frank Ryan, the spokesman and commander of the Irish in the Brigades, personified as no one else did the best militant and revolutionary characteristics of the Irish people. He was born at Elton, Knocklong in County Limerick on September 11th, 1902. Both his parents were national teachers; his father exercising a very formative patriotic influence on him as a youth. Educated at the local national school he made contact with the Irish Volunteers, being accepted at the age of 16 years into the East Limerick Brigade by Seamus Malone. In 1920 he secured a scholarship to St Colman's College, Fermoy, County Cork. There his national feelings were further cultivated by frequent historical and political talks that one of the lecturers used to give to the students. His military training was also further developed when he and some other students used to climb the college walls at night in order to take part in the secret 'drilling' parades of the local IRA unit.

From there he went to University College Dublin to study for a degree in Celtic Studies and Master of Arts. It was not until 1925 that he was able to secure his degree because of his participation in the Irish War for independence. When the Civil War broke out he was on a visit to his family home. He straightaway left to participate in the fighting with the Anti-Treaty forces in Kilmallock. He was later arrested by the Treatyite Government and lodged in the Internment Camp at Harepark, County Kildare in the period of 1922–23, being one of the last of the prisoners to be released.

On his release he returned to his studies at UCD and there continued his Republican activities. He had a burning enthusiasm for every organisation that strove for the political, cultural and social liberation of Ireland. He was one of the founders of the UCD Republican Club and became Auditor of the Cumann Literardha Na Gaeilge (Gaelic Language Literary Society) in the College. In later years he became an active figure in the Gaelic League being a member of Craob Moibhi and Craob na Cuig Cuighi, writing many articles under the pseudonym of 'Seachranaidhe'. He was also the Chairman of the 'Sean Cole' Gaelic Football Club.

In the Irish Republican Army he blossomed out to become one of its leading personalities. He was the Editor of An Phoblacht (The Republic) which he made into an eagerly read weekly radical national journal. He was also one of the founders of the Dublin Branch of the National Union of Journalists. For his activities he was arrested many times. In 1928–29 he was arraigned on the charge of possessing seditious documents. There were three trials — on each occasion the jury disagreed and he was therefore freed of the charge. It was this failure of the Government to secure conviction by juries that led them to abolish trial by jury and to set up a Military Tribunal.

On December 8th, 1931 he was imprisoned with other Republicans in Arbour Hill Military Prison. The fact and the conditions of their imprisonment became one of the issues in the 1932 March General Election. On the day of the defeat of the Cosgrave Government the new Ministers-elect of the de Valera Government went immediately to the prison to see the prisoners. There they saw Ryan and the others lying naked in their cells. The next day they were released and were greeted by a mass meeting of welcome at College Green. After his release Frank Ryan returned to his work at the editorial desk of An *Phoblacht* and to his position as a leader of the Irish Republican Army. In 1933 he was Director of Organisation of Fianna Eireann, the Republican Boy Scout Movement.

To his forthright opposition to British Imperialism, and to native capitalism in Ireland, he had coupled a deep detestation of Fascism. When the Republican Congress was formed he was its Joint Secretary along with George Gilmore. He was a respected figure even outside the Republican and Anti-Fascist movements because of his integrity and fighting personality, and for his active interests in all matters relating to Ireland.

He was also a versatile organiser. Armistice Day in Ireland of the thirties was always an occasion, with the inevitable reaction by Republicans of the seizing of Union Jacks and the poppy wreaths. In November 1934 Frank Ryan organised a counter demonstration of another kind. To the annual anti-poppy day meeting, there marched to an audience of 10,000 in Abbey Street in Dublin a procession of Irish veterans of World War I wearing their medals and carrying slogans of opposition to War and Fascism — and British Imperialism. Speakers like Bob Smith (Royal Tank Corps), and Tom Ellis (Royal Garrison Artillery), shared the same platform as Roddy Connolly (son of James Connolly), Peadar O'Donnell and Frank Ryan himself. The ex-service men for that unique occasion were mobilised by two first world war veterans — who were close friends of Frank Ryan — Sam Nolan and Danny McGregor.

To Spain in that month of December along with Frank Ryan went other outstanding figures in the Irish Republican and Communist movements.

From *Connolly Column*, New Books, 1979

Two Letters
Seán South

Cinema 'Stars' and their Attitude to Communism
A 'Red' List

(To the Editor, *Limerick Leader*)

3rd January, 1949

A Dhuine Uasail — Allow me, through your columns, to enlighten some film fan(atic)s with regard to the true character of those individuals whom they have placed on pedestals of hero worship. I am sure that if they fully realised the dangers resulting from the stream of insidious propaganda which proceeds from Judaeo-Masonic controlled sources, and which warps and corrupts the minds of our youth by implanting therein a false philosophy and concept of life, they would not hesitate to rise and strike.

American Catholics have risen to the occasion by banding unitedly together in organisations whose policy it is to boycott both the films in which any of the undermentioned take part, and also the theatres which present them.

The recent successful campaigns against the showing in Ireland of 'Duel in the Sun' and 'Forever Amber' bear eloquent testimony that we have a public opinion capable of exerting itself when called upon. Yes, 'when called', but what would happen should the call come too late?

Now is the time for action!

Useless and unavailing it will be for us to cry as we lie in chains!

Attack is the best means of defence.

On the other hand, however, maybe, we, descendants of those forefathers who fought and died so unselfishly, so heroically, so courageously, for **Faith and Fatherland**, are going to betray and forsake that gloriously noble heritage by succumbing, like slaves, to the modern attacks against God and country — attacks aided financially and morally by those whom our youth, through ignorance, strive to imitate.

In the issue at present at stake in the world today nobody can sit on the hedge — he that is not with Christ is against Christ.

I sincerely hope that the publication of the list hereunder of Communist Film Stars, and those who, we say, euphemistically, have 'Communist Tendencies', will have the desired effect:—

James Cagney, Joan Bennett, Betsy Blair, Humphrey Bogart, J. Edw. Bromberg, Eddie Cantor, Charlie Chaplain, John Cromwell, Edward Dmytrik, George Colouris, Phillip Dunne, Melvyn Douglas, Douglas Fairbanks Jnr, Sylvia Fine, Henry Fonda, John Garfield, Betty Garrett, Paulette Goddard, Ira Gershwin, Ben

Hecht, Paul Henreid, Katharine Hepburn, John Houseman, Marsha Hunt, Moss Hart, Walter Huston, William Holden, Olivia de Haviland, Rita Hayworth, Danny Kaye, Gene Kelly, Alexander Knox, Arthur Lubin, Fritz Lang, John H. Lawson, Burt Lancaster, Anatole Litvak, Myrna Loy, Peter Lorre, Frederick Marsh, Burgess Meredith, Groucho Marx, Harpo Marx, Larry Parks, Gregory Peck, Vincent Price, Edward G. Robinson, Paul Robeson, Adrian Scotta, Joseph Sistrom, Robert Siodmack, Irwin Shaw, Frank Sinatra, Sylvia Sydney, Gail Wagner, Cornel Wilde, Orson Welles, Billy Wilder, Jane Wyatt.

(The above list, as is obvious, is composed of only the principal Red stars in the Hollywood firmament. Almost one-third of all the actors and actresses in Hollywood hold membership in the Communist Party.)

In view of the above and of the fact that some of the aforementioned people have publicly associated themselves with Communism by attending party public meetings, by nominating election candidates, by perversely lending their God-given talents to the Anti-God activities of the Communist Youth Organisations — in view of this it is incompatible that Irish Catholics can conscientiously choose for 'amusement' pictures by their attendance at which they indirectly finance Communism and keep in their positions, to use their evil influence against God and man, those traitors who have sold themselves to the diabolical and inhuman task-master — Atheistic Communism.

I thank you, Mr Editor, for the valuable space you have given me in your paper.
Seán Sabhat
32, Sráid Annraoi, Luimneach.

The 'Red' Virus being Spread by Cinema
Communism and Film Industry

(To the Editor, *Limerick Leader*)

24th January, 1949

A Dhuine Uasail — With reference to my letter — published in your issue of the 10th instant — dealing with communist film 'stars' etc., I wish to trespass once again in your columns to present some further comments on the Communist influence in Hollywood . . .

To illustrate these Communist strides in this direction, suffice it to quote that 'the Communists have made every effort, with a considerable degree of success in some instances, to dominate and direct such basic unions as the Screen Writers' Guild, the Screen Readers' Guild and the Screen Analysts' Guild'.

Again, the Committee [on Un-American Activities] reports that through infiltration into key positions where Communists and fellow-travellers can be advanced, aided and promoted in their careers, Communist propaganda experts are able to engage in smearing, sabotaging and hampering anti-Communist writers, actors, composers, and other creative composers, and are able to conduct an intellectual and psychological reign of terror among liberal minded workers in the arts.

Readers have now some idea of the powers possessed by Communists in Hollywood. They probably know now into whose hands they place the moulding of their children's minds when they allow them to go indiscriminately to pictures . . .

For those who have read my first letter, who have then shrugged their shoulders and commented — 'Sure, what business is this of ours?' . . . Let no one misconstrue or misinterpret the implications contained in this letter. This is not just merely a question of whether or not pictures should be shown on Sundays. It is — whether or not pictures should be shown at all. If Hollywood, etc., persist in feeding us with pictures which 'are occasions of sin: reduce young people along the ways of evil by glorifying the passions; show life under a false light; cloud ideals; destroy pure love; respect for marriage, affection for the family' (Pius XI — Vigilianti Cura) — If they do persist in giving us bad pictures, then, in my opinion, we can profitably do without the motion industry.

For readers desirous of procuring further details of Communism and the films, I recommend *The Catholic Voice* (published by the Mercier Press) and *Confessions of Stalin's Agent* by Kenneth Goff.

Before concluding, I wish to make it clear to all that the list published on January 10th is not a complete one.

Once again I thank you, Mr Editor, for the valuable space you have allowed me.

Is mise, le mór-mheas,
Seán Sabhat,
47, Sráid Annraoi, Luimneach.

From the *Limerick Leader*, 10 and 24 January 1949

The Death of Feathery Bourke
Seán Bourke

So, 'Feathery' Bourke is dead. He died peacefully in his bed just over a week ago and was buried in his mother's plot at Mount St Lawrence's Cemetery on a dull and dreary Monday afternoon after three o'clock Mass at St Michael's Church.

Michael Bourke was born nearly eighty years ago, one of a family of four brothers and one sister. In due course the others all fled the nest in the natural way of things, but Feathery stayed behind with his mother and became the natural choice to inherit her extensive property, her money, and the scrap business which was to become the centre of his life for more than sixty years, and which gave him the nickname that he was to take to the grave with him.

He was a wealthy man, having made his pile, like so many other scrap dealers, in time of war. At one time he would have bought anything that was re-saleable at even a penny profit, from a rabbit skin to an old steam engine; from a jam jar to a bundle of rags — having first thoroughly searched the rags to ensure that they were not weighted-down with rocks. Many a wartime schoolboy trotted to the Tivoli Cinema to pay homage to Hopalong Cassidy and Buck Jones on the proceeds of these transactions. And as for the source of the various items of 'scrap': most of the boys (including this writer) were not unduly concerned with the ethics of acquisition.

But for the last ten years of his life Feathery Bourke became less and less preoccupied with the business of scrap and concentrated more and more on the proceeds of his various properties in Limerick and Dublin. He still walked six days a week from his lodge near the Bishop's estate in the North Circular Road (he actually sold the estate to the Bishop) to his dilapidated little shop opposite the city market-place. Here he would sit for eight hours a day forlornly watching a rapidly-changing world go by, an affluent world of plastic and pre-cast concrete in which there was little demand for scrap of any kind, and in moments of boredom he would pore over a small mountain of tenancy agreements and deeds of title with a magnifying glass clutched in the three remaining fingers of his right hand.

In these last years Feathery's shop had become little more than a place of pilgrimage for his numerous nephews and their wives and children, as they paused briefly in Limerick on their way to and from distant lands, to gaze in wonder at this last tenuous link with their forefathers and the past.

This writer, who was also a nephew, was passing Feathery's shop shortly before he died. 'Excuse me, young man,' said Feathery, 'but do you know anything about electricity?' 'I do indeed,' I assured him. He then told me that he was having trouble with his lights. After a brief examination it was clear to me that the whole place was in imminent danger of going up in flames. There were bare wires all over the place and the domestic fuse had a piece of 'fuse' wire in it that was as thick as a broom handle, with the result that the main fuse had long since burned out. I went shopping and came back with some new flex and fuses and switches. After a couple of hours I had rendered the place safe.

'You should have no more trouble now,' I said finally, and started to leave. 'Wait, I must pay you,' Feathery said. 'You will not,' I told him. (In fact, the materials had cost me only about two pounds.) But Feathery insisted. He put his three-fingered hand into the pocket of his ancient greasy raincoat, bent over double, and searched around in the lining, down in the region of the hem near his ankles. Slowly he straightened up and withdrew a dirty canvas bag with a pull-through cord at the neck. He opened the bag, inserted his three-fingered hand, felt around inside, withdrew his hand, and then, with the air of a man embarrassed by his own generosity, he pressed his hand into mine and disappeared quickly into his inner office. I looked down at my palm. It contained ONE SHILLING!

From *The Old Limerick Journal*, No. 2, 1980

Seán South
John Jordan

I intend no disrespect to the memory of South, when I say that it* is . . . designed to appeal to certain quarters with fixed ideas as to what constitutes the best kind of Irish Catholic Republican . . . This book is important because the blue-print for a certain kind of image is almost too perfect . . . the 21-year-old Republican was, perhaps unwittingly, lending himself to witch-hunting, a fact no less shocking than that the disciple of Tone and Pearse should have been associated with attacks on Article 44.

But I think I have said enough to indicate the way Seán was going, the way he had to go, given his premises of an Ireland united, Gaelic and Catholic, and the interpretations he put on these terms. The fact that he could have acted on his convictions as recently as 1957 is what makes his case so curious as in the image projected by Mr Seoighe: devout Catholic, fanatic Gael, anti-foreigner (foreigners are English, Masonic, Jewish, Communist) and yet professed heir to Tone, an eighteenth century deist with more than a touch of anti-clericalism in him, of Pearse, a man of liberal culture . . . and of James Connolly, whose 'Labour in Irish History' is unquestionably a Socialist document.

This handsomely-produced book is not only a tribute to South but a document on the nature of Irish schizophrenia. And that lonely death on January 1st, 1957, is an indictment of our national vice of double think. The sacrifice should not have been in vain.

* *Maraíodh Seán Sabhat Aréir* le Mainchín Seoighe, Sáirséal agus Dill, 1964

From *Hibernia*, July–August 1964

Nurse Lily Flanagan
David Hanly

Often, when recalling aspects of my boyhood, I have described myself as accident-prone. But I have always used the phrase reluctantly, because it fails to evoke that perfect picture of a childhood that was a continuum of profound shocks to the body: I did not, it seems to me, live in harmony with my childhood environment, but engaged in constant, unexpected skirmishes with it until, rather late in life, I came to terms with it, made peace with it.

I'm sure this is so much nonsense, and that my childhood was no more hapless than the next: my summers were sunny and prolonged, there were adventures of epic proportions in the 'quarry' in the Fairgreen. I was happy. Nevertheless, memory is an arbitrary editor, and I can summon a litany of such shocks. I fell out of trees in pursuit of birds' eggs; I stepped on invisible shards of glass — always when wearing wellingtons; I ran into layered concrete blocks, opening my knee so that my patella came through, gleaming and pearl-white. I had so many needles inserted in so many places that I felt that any day the stitching would come apart and those nearest me would be showered with frogs and snails and puppy-dogs' tails.

Inevitably, my stricken face became a familiar one to the casualty nightingales of Barrington's. But these were all one-night-stands, so to speak, although I was rarely able to stand on the night in question, more often being lifted into and out of a neighbour's car.

But I did, once, spend a protected time as an in-patient in Barrington's. I was eight. I was playing soccer one summer evening in 'The Park' at the top of the Fairgreen, when the ball went between the legs of a cart-horse who was grazed there when his day's work was done. I went to retrieve it, and have no memory of the pain as his hoof crashed through my face, cutting a trench through flesh and gums and sending my just-grown second teeth flying in bits over the park.

Joe Slattery hoisted my unconscious form on to his back and carried me down to my house, which was No. 13, an appropriate number, as far as I was concerned. I recovered consciousness in Bill O'Shea's Ford Prefect, suffocating in my own blood. Then I became oblivious once more. When I awoke again, I was lying in bed looking like someone auditioning for *The Curse of the Mummy's Tomb*. My mouth was filled with cat-gut, parts of which in the following weeks I wore away with my tongue.

I was not allowed any visitors, because the prevailing wisdom at the time — for reasons which have never made any sense to me — was that parental or any other kind of visit would be a bad thing. So I was held up to the window of the ward for my parents to gaze up at my bandaged head. They stood by the wall of the Abbey River, the avaricious gulls a screeching and wheeling garland about their heads.

The idea, I suppose, was to reassure them: the picture of the midget mummy at the window probably had quite a different effect.

It was my first time away from home, and my introduction to hospital life. My memories of sights and smells and tastes are as vivid as if I had experienced them 24 hours ago. The food was like nothing I've tasted before or since, but I cannot tell whether it was the quality of the bread or the presence of all that stuff in my mouth: eating anything at all was a feat, and drinking was an experiment each time (it still is, I'm glad to say).

I was far too young to understand what had happened to me, and how deeply it would affect my behaviour in the company of others — especially girls — for a long time afterwards. It was strange, uncomfortable, and lonely. But what made it all bearable was how I was treated by the staff, and one in particular. The little figure in the corner bed, covered in bandages and full of nervous curiosity, became something of a pet, and it was probably my treatment in Barrington's all those years ago that began my lifelong habit of falling in love with nurses. They are, I believe, the most undervalued, underpaid and ill-treated of all of society's workers, and, working long hours with people at their least attractive, they maintain a humorous amiability that is a wonder to behold.

The object of my adoration in Barrington's was a tall, dark-eyed, willowy beauty named Lily Flanagan. She must, I know, have taken some time off to sleep and tend to other matters in her own life and, since I was in a large ward, there were plenty of others constantly demanding attention. But for me she seemed perpetually on call. I was aware too — with that perfect sensitivity that children have for these things — that my calls were answered not with a tired impatience but with smiling and gentle affection, the kind that a child most naturally expects and receives from his own mother.

I find it hard to credit that in the straitened times in which hospitals now find themselves, nurses have time to show concern and affection for individual patients of the order of which Nurse Flanagan showed to me: efficiency is the order of this day. Nevertheless, scarcely creditable or not, those attributes still manifest themselves, as I found during recent brief encounters with the angels of the wards. And I was glad to note, on a final visit to Barrington's before it closed its doors for ever to the plain people of Limerick, that I was not alone in my appreciation of Lily Flanagan's wonderful and selfless work: on a wall plaque listing the prize-winning nurses year by year, her name is to be found taking the honours back then in the early 1950s.

Those are my memories of Barrington's: brisk, affectionate care by an undiffer-entiating staff; masterly surgery by Dr Michael Roberts; bread that tasted like boiled insoles; needles coming at me day and night and from everywhere. And then of course there were the hourly bulletins on my condition, my face shredded and headbones smashed by the horse's hoof. I did not find out about these bulletins until much later. The first said there was little hope that I would survive.

They were wrong there. The second said I would pull through, but would lose my right eye. That was wrong, too. The last prognosis was that my eye would be saved but my mind would be permanently damaged. There is a body of opinion that would have that last bulletin to be correct. Be that as it may, my memory, at any rate, remains undamaged and undimmed, especially my memory of Nurse Lily Flanagan.

I honour her.

From *The Old Limerick Journal*, Barrington's Edition, No. 24, Winter 1988

Dirty Linen
Maureen McAteer

Nightly he loosed the cord
Around the ragged coat,
Closed imaginary curtains,
Parked rickety crutches
Beside porter-sodden bones,
Where a thin stream of hissing steam
Escaped from the Good Shepherd Laundry.

This hot corner 'Dan the Divil'
Called home.
At a nearby hatch
Sometimes when handing in soiled linen
To a serene, cream-clad Sister
I glimpsed lumpy, aproned women
Toiling sweat-soaked in a bleach-laden fug.

Once I asked what ordained who drudged
And who donned a pristine habit
But could never prise an answer
From portcullis'd, adult lips,
So I assumed it was a sort of steamy tabernacle
Where the hunted or the haunted hid,
After mothers threatened errant daughters

With incarceration in the Magdalen,
Until I learned it was a place

Where those who fell from grace,
Or were just too sassy for the fifties,
Were spirited behind high walls,
To conceal the waxing of clandestine couplings
So de Valera's Ireland

Could scale the airy slopes
Of the high moral ground.
Small matter that women withered,
Shirts were starched, sheets shriven,
And outside the convent's high walls,
The lonely cries in the night
Went unheeded and unheard.

From *Women's Work* VII, The Works, 1996

Steve Coughlan

Steve Coughlan has ensured a constant supply of favourable publicity for himself by his championing of local causes. He has, however, in periods of temporary personal eclipse resorted to bizarre methods in order to keep himself in the public eye. In 1952, for instance, just after his mayoralty and his first failure to enter the Dail, he embarked on a strange venture.

On September 22, 1952, Coughlan arrived home from Nice in the South of France. A short while before that he had embarked on a sales trip to Vienna to enquire about a processed dry food chemical industry. Of this he merely said 'there will be more about that later'. Stevie had a more exciting revelation in hand; he announced that he had formed a new limited company. His partners in the company were a French inventor called Monsieur Bloque and Mr Alfred James Deane, better known as Man Mountain Deane, the ex-British wrestling champion. This strange trio had purchased a 'non-skid device' which Coughlan announced would shortly be tested in Limerick. On October 8 Stevie announced that the test would be carried out on the Dock Road by Spike Rhiendo, the famous motor racing champion. On October 11 Stevie once again reached the front page of the *Limerick Leader* when he revealed that the stretch would be treated with oil, grease and similar lubricants and that several prominent local citizens and churchmen had been invited to watch the demonstration. On the following day Spike Rhiendo did his duty and the car did not skid. However, on October 18 Stevie played his card. He announced that the non-skid device was to be made in Limerick. Limerick at the time was suffering from severe unemployment and Stevie's new factory was gratefully hailed in the local press which carried main headlines on the news. Shortly afterwards during another test again in front of a 'distinguished' gathering — the car turned over a number of times and the whole non-skid device idea was quickly forgotten.

In later years Stevie has lost none of his flair for publicity. In 1967, for instance, when a meat factory was closed in Limerick Stevie did not attack the closure in the Dail. Instead he turned up during another debate in a dishevelled state, was greeted with cries of 'you're drunk' from government benches and shouted incoherently about the factory's closure. He was removed forthwith from the house by ushers. This garbled intervention did not save the jobs of the workers in Limerick but it earned him the praise of the local press and the gratitude of the newly unemployed.

He is also a highly emotional person. This has its political benefits and drawbacks. When combined with a high degree of emotional stress and slight over-indulgence in alcohol it can lead him to make statements which have been well nigh politically suicidal for him in the Labour Party. But it also allows him leeway to make speeches and pleas which no other politician could possibly get away with. Few other politicians can become enthused by the various Irish dairy products and retain his credibility, but Stevie recently benefited from a front page straight report in the *Limerick Leader* of an address he made to the National Dairy Council. An extract from the *Limerick Leader* read: 'Some of us are inclined to take this liquid product for granted, but if we are to lay the foundation for a future generation, and avoid being decadent, we must look to the fundamentals, and give milk our first consideration . . . In my home which comprises my wife, two boys and a girl and myself we drink 10 pints of milk a day, and we eat 3 lbs of cheese a week. The cow is truly our second mother.' Only Stevie could get away with that.

At all times and occasions Stevie has been capable of high flown, flowery emotion . . . He has frequently used his emotion to further his political ambitions. During the last election his primary tactic was a plea to give him his pension. From house to house he pleaded, with some justification, that he had two more years to go in the Dail before he qualified for his pension and surely the poor people of Limerick would not turn him out of office on to the streets.

Like most gombeen politicians Stevie has not infrequently utilised the more reactionary and less rational of his constituents' prejudices to gain electoral favours . . .

Coughlan's source methodically harps on the backward political attitudes of some of his constituents but this has no fixed ideological right wing base. When the occasion demands it Stevie can swing on the political pendulum to any position left, right or centre.

Coughlan's weakness as a politician has only become evident in the last four years. He has shown himself to be excessively attached to power in Limerick. His reaction to any real or imagined challenge to his status has been unbalanced and often hysterical. Similarly his reaction to challenges in the local Labour Party have been unwarranted and have exposed his susceptibilities rather than confirmed his unchallenged position . . .

His fanatical parochialism is capable of evoking hysteria in his 'I am Limerick' complex. Illusions, tears and denunciations flow freely. Once embroiled in a controversy he is too stubborn to retract even in the face of overwhelming reason and fact.

But despite it all — his prejudice, parochialism, irrationality, ruthlessness and emotionalism — Stevie is basically loveable. He has replaced his soul-brother Donogh O'Malley in the hearts of many Limerick people and even if on a national level his politics are often despicable and his antics laughable, his innate generosity and big-heartedness to his own, his very own people absolves him of much.

From *Nusight*, May 1970

Unbound Poet
Michael Hartnett

In 1955 I wrote a very bad piece of verse which was published in the *Limerick Weekly Echo*. I was thirteen: I wrote the piece for no good reason, unless it were to make up for my poverty. One of my teachers descended on me wrathfully; it was a copy of the work of that great poet, T. D. Shanahan, he said. The headmaster, Frank Finucane, defended me. The other teacher challenged me to write a set poem in two weeks. Frank Finucane called his class to a halt, and with his encouragement I finished the poem in ten minutes. The other teacher retreated, and never spoke to me again. So, at thirteen, I found that being a poet in Ireland is, contrary to what the Americans think, an incongruity.

That was in Newcastle West, Co. Limerick . . . I left the national school in 1956 and lost an ally. Secondary school came then, and I wrote many poems (all, fortunately, lost) and made a new enemy, my English teacher. For five years I was beaten more often for 'meditating the Muse', as he called it, than for lack of learning. But my poetry changed for the better, not because of the school, but because I partook of an old Irish custom: the girl I loved at the time entered a convent. This, and the claustrophobia of Newcastle West, its rich and its poor, its bullying priest, turned me to write about myself. Any oppression I encountered was not direct. I was oppressed by what was inherent in the town's way of life, the patronising society that doled out bread and boots to the poor; the reading of subscriptions from the pulpit, the quashed scandals, dark secrets about the 'Troubles', and I was a poor man's son in a secondary school, a place I had no right to be, as I was often reminded.

So the poetry went on. I had published another bad piece of verse in the *Irish Weekly Independent* and got a guinea for it. This brought me some small recognition in the town, as a few people there read that paper. As the Dublin literati never really appreciate a poet unless the *Observer* or *Sunday Times* mention him, so the people of Newcastle West would not believe I was a poet unless they saw it 'down in black and white' in a Dublin newspaper.

I left home in 1961 and went to London, out of pure instinct. I worked as a tea-boy in a factory there, every scrap of poetry melting away. Then the coincidences began. I met a friend from home. He introduced me to his uncle, who was working on the *Sunday Review*; he read some of the poetry I had brought with me and liked it. Shortly afterwards my photograph appeared in the *Sunday Review*, captioned with an awful pun, 'Teaboy of the Western World'. A short article said I was a poet. The *Sunday Review* had a good circulation in Newcastle West; I had achieved my myth, because in small towns in Ireland, unless a man has a nickname (a reputation, good or bad), he hardly exists at all.

I returned home and was accepted. Coincidence rested awhile. I got a job as a postman; the poetry, which rose to meet the occasion of acceptance, now dwindled again.

I was badly read at this time, and had no knowledge of modern poetry, although I had read Yeats. I thought that at his death in 1939 Ireland had faded out of the literary picture, and from reading the English Sunday 'heavies' I thought England, especially London, was vibrant with poetic life. Of course, I was totally wrong. But I did not feel up to London again, and I had a fine job cycling around the countryside, finishing just after midday, and was beginning to be lulled into the soft security of my own myth.

Then the second coincidence came. I got a wild letter and numerous poems from Dublin from a young man called Paul Durcan early in 1962. He had read the article in the *Sunday Review*. He wanted my opinion of his work, and also to see some of mine. His poems were mad, rich and full of classical allusions. I was delighted! There was another poet in Ireland! I sent him some of my poems, which I had written in 1958/59, and heard no more for a long time.

One day I went to Galway to see a girl. Paul Durcan arrived in Newcastle West, I had missed meeting my first poet and was furious, but calmed down when my mother told me he had come in a car. So he was rich — and ordinary; from his poems I had expected him to come on a yak, at least. Then one morning in September I was sorting the letters in the post office and there was one for me with a Dublin postmark and in a strange hand. It praised my poetry, said six of my poems were accepted for *Poetry Ireland*, and it also invited me to a reception to mark the launching of the magazine. So on September 12th, 1962, I borrowed a suit, hitch-hiked to Dublin, and set off to discover the literary world.

From *The Old Limerick Journal*, Vol. 16, Autumn 1983

A Newcastle Reading
Vincent Buckley

One day in 1981, Michael Hartnett rang me from Newcastle West in County Limerick, and asked would I read there. Certainly. What pay would I ask? I didn't know, and said so, and was surprised when Michael mentioned eighty pounds. How would he get that? Well, there was a thriving arts committee in the town, and they would expect to get a good crowd. He would read with me, unpaid, and local musicians would play.

Newcastle West is Hartnett's hometown, a substantial smallish town on the main road south from Limerick to Tralee. As many such towns were, it was once a British garrison town, and at the time of the famine, three quarters of its population of several thousand were paupers; it was the poor law centre for the area. Such things give a town a permanent underlying sickness of will, and Newcastle West seemed to have some traces of such a sickness, although it has a good library and a certain prosperity coming from the industrial development on the river Shannon, some miles to the north . . .

I was to read in the building which gives the town its name, the banqueting hall of the now destroyed castle of the Fitzgeralds, Earls of Desmond and Norman magnates of this whole area. The hall is very handsome, but very dilapidated. If some mad, lovable, posterity-infatuated millionaire would do it up, it would be the greatest place in the world for a poetry reading, especially with musicians. As it is, you read seated in a stone window embrasure; the acoustics are excellent; the possibilities are great, and the local people who serve on the committee see them clearly even if, like most Irish people, they are unwilling to promise themselves too much.

On the appointed night, nobody had arrived fifteen minutes after starting-time; there were doors to be opened, lights to be turned up, a hundred chairs to be brought and set up; so Gabriel FitzMaurice's wife Brenda kept me company in Lynch's bar next to the hall while these things were done. It was a small dark friendly bar, and we sat and chatted as the time wore on. Every so often Gabriel would enter, looking fierce, and start on a pint of stout; then he would dash off, and Michael would enter looking quite distracted, and toss down a whiskey. An hour and a half after starting-time, I said to him, 'What does it matter, Michael? Let's call it off. I don't mind.' But that was psychologically impossible; and there was a further complexity, which I never fully understood, and which Michael felt he had to deal with: musicians had been engaged to play, but only one had turned up, characteristically, in the pub, had said to us, 'Are there no musicians here? I was told there would be musicians here,' and ignored all Gabriel's bluff suggestions that, if only he gave a lead, the others would gather. Giving a lead is not a Limerick sport. I could see the man's attitude quite clearly, and I said to

Gabriel and Michael, 'O leave him alone. He doesn't want to play. Forget it.' He kept smiling slyly, and watching everyone.

Michael became sick of this, and rushed off, returning with two teenagers, a banjoist and an accordion player. They were Munster junior champions in their instruments; they would play. They did; they were marvellous, and played with enormous vitality to the audience of about a dozen, whom I read at as vigorously as I could. Even the second point of honour that was bothering Hartnett was cleared up; for I said to him, 'Forget money; I'll read for the train fare,' and, later, 'Look, I'll read for nothing.' It wouldn't have been the first time. But he would not have it. He rushed off fiercely once more, and returned to shove into my hand a roll of pound notes, every one of which I swear had passed across a bar counter that night. He must have gone to every place in town. I knew without counting how many would be in that bundle. It was a quintessentially Irish gesture, solution, and sense of honour. But it was also an Irish problem, that of the promises not kept, the suspicious doubts allowed to run ahead of performance, the earlier engagement quietly discovered.

At reading's end, it was back to Lynch's bar, now crowded with jovial people who had failed to attend the reading, were full of curiosity about it, and of congratulations to those of us who had survived it. The young musicians took one orange juice each, and played tune after tune until after midnight. The banjoist sat on one side of the narrow door to the outside lavatory, and I sat on the other; everyone who wanted to use it had to push between us, and as each passed, the banjoist, without casting a single glance anywhere but at his own brimming soul, would flick the banjo upright, so that part of the time he played vertical, and part diagonal. Once going, and once coming. Gabriel FitzMaurice played along with them. One after another, charming people approached me and enquired of genealogy, poetry, music, and of course Australia. Each had 'heard I was in town'. They could not be described as poetry groupies, for they were far more interested in the idea of poetry than in the reality. But they were interested in the idea. This could be seen in the way they treated Michael Hartnett as a local laureate, and solicited comments from visiting strangers on his wider fame.

In this, they were representative of the whole culture, in all its ambivalence. Poetry was treated with reverence and neglect. And that expressed itself in many ways.

From *Memory Ireland: Insights into the Contemporary Irish Condition*, Penguin Books, 1985

Remembering Séamus Ó Cinnéide
Desmond O'Grady

I was deeply saddened to hear of the death of Séamus Ó Cinnéide. We were old friends going back forty years when we would meet with Kitty Bredin, Gerard 'The Poet' Ryan and other friends in Arthur O'Leary's house for the poetry circle evenings. Since then I have been living abroad. Whenever I returned on a visit to Limerick Séamus was one of the first people I would look up. He wasn't difficult to find, because he was a prominent cultural figure in Limerick for as long as I can remember.

On these occasions, the Poet Ryan and I would spend our talking times on historical walks of the city. Séamus would expound his endless knowledge of Limerick's history, ancient and modern, with enthusiastic gesticulations as we progressed, with healthy pub stops for refreshments, the while pausing to parley briefly with the countless citizens he knew about something or other. He knew and loved his city more than any Limerick person I've ever met.

Séamus didn't walk, he strode purposefully. I had to push myself to keep up with his stride and his story. The Poet Ryan lagged an ever lazier third, whose principal participation was the persuasion of Séamus to stop for refreshments, when we would get a gossipy history of the pub itself and its relation to other pubs as if they were all Limerick people, past and present.

In between he would take giddy gallivants about his reading of international modern poetry, painting and theatre with concerned advice on what I should do about my writing, Jack Donovan his painting, Richard Harris his acting career. And all this in sophisticated Gaeilge-Béarla as if reminding me of my responsibility to my own language. He talked, too, of his own writing in both languages and of the artistic activities and aspirations of the city.

He was blessed with prestigious creative energy. He read everything, knew everybody. The last time I talked with him he was tracking down the Limerick O'Connell side of the wife of the American poet, Ezra Pound.

Over the years when I would meet him on a brief return visit he would immediately continue our last conversation as if I had never been away, as if after a mere pause to say something to a passerby, and end by suggesting a walk-talk or gossip-gallivant in the country.

He always asked after Harris, Kate O'Brien and Michael Hartnett and gave me his own Limerick gossip. As we grew older he began to look to me more and more like an aspect of Samuel Beckett. I even told Beckett, the year of his Nobel Prize, that he had a living stand-in in Limerick who could go to Stockholm in his stead, that way avoiding the publicity Sam shied away from.

All my Séamus meetings were like that: off the clock, off the wall, off the top of the head, with gusto in geometric directions that only the pair of us appreciated with zany but serious glee. Happy! He, being ten years my senior, big-brothering me.

The last time I was in Limerick I had only a couple of hours. I asked for Séamus. My brother told me he'd heard he wasn't well. I thought, 'I'll see him next time.' Now there won't be a next time. But that doesn't sadden me. He is still with me live in our mutually odd way of it. His company was always uplifting.

I hope that what he left of his own writing will be conscientiously edited and published as part of the record of Limerick's cultural history. I send these heart-felt and happy memories of Séamus to his family and friends, when Séamus and I next meet we will send a heavenly multilingual postcard to you all.

From the *Limerick Leader*, Saturday, 3 April 1993

Gurky McMahon was Buried Today
Seán Bourke

Thomas (Gurky) McMahon was born in 1890, before the 'gasoline buggy' or the cinematograph were invented, when a glass of stout cost a penny, a whiskey twopence, and the fare to America was ten pounds sterling. He died yesterday, aged eighty years, and was buried today at Mount St Laurence Cemetery.

Gurky McMahon was a legend in his own lifetime. He was making Limerick laugh before Hope and Groucho Marx and Durante were ever heard of and long before the toothy Rowans and Martins were born.

We stood at the gate of the cemetery as the cortege came up Mulgrave Street, not daring to quote any of his famous jokes, but remaining silent out of long respect. As the hearse drew nearer a whispered and urgent enquiry — a suppli-cation almost — to the sexton to re-assure ourselves that this was really *his* funeral. And a stab of bitter sorrow to be told that it was.

No more than twenty mourners shuffled silently behind the hearse, self-conscious it seemed at their own lack of numbers, and three modest wreaths rested on the coffin. Up at the front the undertaker's man, black-clad and straight as a rod, walked past with measured solemnity.

The doctors, solicitors, and shop-keepers might not have known Gurky McMahon, but there is hardly a working man in Limerick who did not claim the privilege of his acquaintance. For Gurky was essentially a working class hero, a docker who toiled relentlessly for a spartan existence against the gruelling odds and grinding poverty of his day, and all the time he preserved his compassion and legendary humour — a working class humour, simple, unsophisticated.

Gurky, leaving his brand-new house in the then brand-new Island Field to go to a nearby shop for a pint of milk in a jug and on his way back forgetting which was his own house, because they all looked the same, and saying to a group of children playing on the street: 'Come here, young fellas. Did ye see e'er a man coming out of one of those houses along there with a milk-jug in his hand, and could you show me the house he came out of?'

Gurky in England, returning in the evening from work for his dinner in a Birmingham lodging house. There is a small steak-and-kidney pie and one solitary potato on his plate. Gurky sits down, picks up a fork and prods the potato. Looking up at the landlady he says: 'That's grand, ma'am. You can throw the rest of them up now!'

There were hundreds of such stories bandied about the pubs and clubs of Limerick (and of Manchester, Birmingham and London) during the 'thirties, 'forties and 'fifties. And, of course, as with all legendary figures, there was much more attributed to Gurky McMahon than he could reasonably be expected to have achieved.

But Gurky's brand of humour was, like all humour, the product of his age and passed with the passing of that age. Born before the motor car was invented, he died when men's footprints were on the moon.

On the outer edge of the small group of mourners at the graveside, two old men, contemporaries of Gurky, and deaf with the years, reminisced loudly into each other's ears with cupped hands, whilst the elderly white-haired Canon slowly intoned the De Profundis in the new vernacular.

And in the clear March sky above the cemetery the vapour trail of a modern jetplane on its way to America seemed symbolically to underline the ending of an era.

As we drifted silently out of the cemetery, a neighbour's child smilingly asked: 'Whose funeral were you at?'

'Gurky McMahon's.'

'Who is he?'

Thomas (Gurky) McMahon had outlived his own legend. But did you ever hear about the time Gurky went up the town to buy a new shovel . . . ?

From the *Limerick Leader*, 6 March 1971

Heaney in Newcastle West
Vincent Buckley

Michael Hartnett comes from there [Newcastle West], and he had gone back there to write poetry in the onset of early middle age. Having written a *Farewell to English*, he now writes in Irish, a language which he also speaks with congenial companions like Gabriel FitzMaurice. He reserves English for the odd ballad on local events, and these he publishes and circulates locally. He is an amusingly intense man. As we walked to the hotel where we were to attend some meeting, he said, 'Don't say anything against Heaney in this town.' 'I wouldn't dream of it,' I said. 'Why do you mention it?' It appeared that, some months earlier, Heaney had given a reading there, and had then stayed at the bar until very late drinking with his local admirers and other clean-minded types. Among these was the town bore, who as the night wore on annexed Heaney more and more. Heaney coped courteously with all this, but the speaker was so boring that the other drinkers moved slowly away from him. At last, in the middle of a sentence, the poor bore collapsed, and slid slowly down the bar to lie at Heaney's feet. He looked around, called to the nearest deserter, 'Would you mind giving me a hand?' and, with the volunteer thus chosen by the Chinese system, carried the man over and laid him carefully on a couch. 'They've never stopped talking about it,' said Hartnett. 'Heaney's king around here.'

It must have been on this occasion that, when he was signing copies of his works, Heaney was presented with a photocopy of a whole volume. Pirated. 'What did you do?' I asked him when I heard of it. 'O I signed it,' he said. 'Why not?' Then he brooded awhile, and added, 'It often happens in the States.'

From *Memory Ireland: Insights into the Contemporary Irish Condition*, Penguin Books, 1985

FIVE

THE COUNTY

The Tithe War
W. R. Le Fanu

In 1831 came the tithe war, and with it our friendly relations with the priests and people ceased. The former, not unnaturally, threw themselves heart and soul into the agitation. The Protestant clergy were denounced by agitators and priests from platform and from altar, and branded as the worst enemies of the people, who were told to hunt them like mad dogs from the country; they were insulted wherever they went, many were attacked, some were murdered. It is hard now to realise the suddenness with which kindness and good-will were changed to insult and hate; for a short time we were not so badly treated as some of the neighbouring clergy, but the people would not speak to us, and scowled at us as we passed.

Of Doon, a parish which adjoined Abington, our cousin, the Rev. Charles Coote, was rector. At the very commencement of the agitation he had given much offence by taking active measures to enforce the payment of his tithes. It was thus his fight began. He had for years been on the most intimate and friendly terms with Father H—, the parish priest, who held a considerable farm, for which Mr Coote would never allow him to pay tithe. When the agitation against tithes began, Father H— preached a fierce sermon against them, denouncing Mr Coote from the altar, telling the people that any man who paid one farthing of that 'blood-stained impost' was a traitor to his country and his God. 'Take example by me, boys,' he said; 'I'd let my last cow be seized and sold before I'd pay a farthing to that scoundrel Coote.' On hearing of this, Mr Coote wrote to ask him whether the report he had heard was true; he replied that he was proud to say that it was true, adding, 'You may seize and sell my cattle if you can, but I'd like to see the man that would buy them.' Coote, who was a brave and determined man, was so indignant that he resolved to fight it out with the priest. He gave orders to his bailiff, and next morning at break of day, before any one dreamt that he would make the attempt, one of the priest's cows was taken and impounded. Public notice was given that, on a day and hour named, the cow would be sold in Doon; counter notices were posted through the country telling the people to assemble in their thousands to see Father H—'s cow sold. Mr Coote went to Dublin to consult the authorities at the Castle, and returned next day, with a promise from the Government that they would support him.

Early on the morning fixed for the sale, I was sitting at an open window in our breakfast-room, when my attention was roused by the sound of bagpipes playing 'The Campbells are Coming'. On looking in the direction whence the sound came, I saw four companies of Highlanders, headed by their pipers, marching down the road, followed by a troop of lancers and artillery with two guns.

On this little army went to Doon, where many thousands of the country people were assembled. At the appointed hour the cow was put up for sale. There was a belief then prevalent among the people that at a sale unless there were at least three bidders, nothing could be sold; under this mistaken idea, a friend of the priest bid a sum, much beyond her value, for the cow; she was knocked down to him, he was obliged to hand the money to the auctioneer, and the tithe was paid. During all this time, except shouting, hooting at the soldiers, and 'groans for Coote', nothing was done; but when the main body of the troops had left the village shots were fired, and volleys of stones were thrown at four of the lancers who had remained after the others as a rear guard. They fired their pistols at their assailants, one of whom was wounded. The rest of the lancers, hearing the shots, galloped back and quickly dispersed the crowd. It was weary work for the troops, as the day was very hot and bright, and their march to and from Doon was a long one, that village being certainly not less than fifteen miles from Limerick. On their return they bivouacked and dined in a field close to us, surrounded by crowds of the peasantry, many of whom had never seen a soldier before; after a brief rest the pipes struck up, 'The Campbells are Coming', and they were on their march again. So ended this, to us, memorable day.

The next morning, as we were at breakfast, the room door opened; an old man came in; he fell on his knees and cried, 'Oh, wirasthru, my little boy is killed, my boy is shot! Sure the craythur was doin' nothing out of the way when the sogers shot him. Oh, Vo! Vo! What will I ever do widout my little boy!' 'What can I do for you, my poor man?' said my father. 'Ah! then it's what I want your honour to give me a bit of note that'll get him into the hospital in Limerick.'

My father at once gave him the order for his son's admission. He departed invoking blessings on us, and shedding tears of gratitude.

As we afterwards found, the 'little boy' was a youth of six and twenty, who had got a slight flesh wound in the leg. They never brought him to the hospital, but they paraded him, all day, through the streets of Limerick, lying in a cart, covered with a blood-stained sheet; to the back of the cart a board was fixed, on which, in large letters, was this inscription, 'These are the Blessings of Tithes.' From that day Mr Coote was a marked man.

Whenever he or any of his family were seen they were received with shouts and yells, and cries of 'Mad dog! Mad dog! To hell with the tithes! Down with the tithes!' One afternoon, when we returned from a visit to the rectory at Doon, we received a message from our parish priest to say that if we went there any more we should be treated as the Cootes were. Accordingly on our return from our next visit to them, shouts and curses followed us all the way home; from that day forward, when any of us (or even our carriage or car) was seen, the same shouts and cursing were heard in all directions . . .

At this time none of us went out alone, and we were always well armed. This the people knew, and did not actually attack any of us except on two occasions. On one of these my sister, who till a few months before had been idolised by the people for her goodness to them and untiring work amongst them, thought that if she and two girls, cousins, who were with us at the time, drove out by themselves, they would not be molested, especially as she had recently been in very delicate health. So taking advantage of an hour when the rest of the family were out, they went for a drive, when not only were they received with the usual hooting, but were pelted with mud and stone. One of the girls had a front tooth broken and they were glad to get home without further injury, and never again ventured to go out without protection.

The other attack happened thus. My father had been persuaded by some friends to try whether offering a large abatement, and giving time, might induce some of the farmers to pay at least some part of the tithes then due. A number of circulars offering such terms were prepared. These my cousin, Robert Flemyng, and I (little more than boys at the time) undertook to distribute, and to explain the terms to the farmers whose houses we proposed to visit. On our first day's ride nothing worth mentioning beyond the usual hooting occurred. Some of the houses were shut against us as the inmates saw us approach; at some few we were not uncivilly received, but were distinctly told that under no circumstances would one farthing of tithes ever be paid again.

On the following day we rode to a different part of the parish, to visit some farmers in the direction of Limerick. As we turned off the main road down a by-road leading to the village of Kishiquirk, we saw a man standing on a hillock holding in his hands a spade, high in air, then lowering the spade and giving a shrill whistle, then holding up the spade again. We knew this must be a signal, but for what we couldn't think. When we reached the village, a considerable and very threatening crowd was collected there, who saluted us with 'Down with the Orangemen! Down with the tithes!' As this looked like mischief, we drew our pistols from our pockets, and each holding one in his right hand, we rode slowly through the throng. As we got near the end of the village a woman called to us, 'What are ye riding so slow for? Push on, I tell you; they are going to kill ye!' We did push on, and with some difficulty, by riding one after the other, got past a cart which was hastily drawn across the road to stop us. On we galloped, showers of stones after us as we went. About a quarter of a mile further on another but smaller crowd awaited us; they were not on the road, but just inside the mound fence which bordered it. On this mound they had made ready a good supply of stones for our reception, but, seeing us hold our pistols towards them, they did not venture to throw the stones till just as we had passed them, when they came after us volley after volley. Many a blow we and our horses got, but none that stunned. One man only was on the road, and, as we got near him, I saw him settling his spade in his hand as if to be ready to strike a blow. I presented my pistol at him. 'Don't shoot me,' he called out; 'I'm only working here.' But just as I passed him he made a tremendous blow at me; it missed me but struck the horse just behind the saddle. The spade was broken by the violence of the blow. Down went the horse on his haunches, but was quickly up again, and on we went. Had he fallen,

I should not have been alive many minutes; he brought me bravely home, but never recovered, and died soon afterwards.

From *Seventy Years of Irish Life, being Anecdotes and Reminiscences*, Edward Arnold, 1893

Know ye not that Lovely River
Gerald Griffin

Know ye not that lovely river?
Know ye not that smiling river?
Whose gentle flood,
By cliff and wood,
With wildering sound goes winding ever.
Oh! often yet with feeling strong,
On that dear stream my memory ponders,
And still I prize its murmuring song,
For by my childhood's home it wanders.
Know ye not, &c.

There's music in each wind that flows
Within our native woodland breathing;
There's beauty in each flower that blows
Around our native woodland wreathing,
The memory of the brightest joys
In childhood's happy morn that found us,
Is dearer than the richest toys,
The present vainly sheds around us.
Know ye not, &c.

Oh, sister! when 'mid doubts and fears,
That haunt life's onward journey ever,
I turn to those departed years,
And that beloved and lonely river;
With sinking mind and bosom riven,
And heart with lonely anguish aching;
It needs my long-taught hope in heaven
To keep this weary heart from breaking!
Know ye not, &c.

From *The Poetical and Dramatic Works of Gerald Griffin*, James Duffy, 1891

Rockites and Whiteboys
Mainchín Seoighe

In all parts of Limerick men flocked to the banner of a mysterious chief called Captain — or, sometimes, General — Rock. Raids for arms, skirmishes, and attacks on the houses of the gentry, were the order of the day. The Athlacca district was caught up in the turmoil, as contemporary newspaper reports show. For example, the Limerick News of Thursday, February 21st, 1822, reported that on:

Sunday night, fifty men dashed in the hall door of Mr Bolster's house at Tullerboy, near Athlacca, in this county, and entering his bedroom, caused him to surrender his only musket; resistance was in vain, as the fellows intended to burn the house. They destroyed the windows, and did other injury to the dwelling, tho' they left untouched some bank notes.

The house that Bolster lived in is now the property of John Brennan — it was previously owned by Michael Mullins.

The same issue of the Limerick News that reported the raid on Bolster's house also reported that: 'Yesterday morning detachments of the Rifle Brigade marched to do duty at Athea, Athlacca, Abbeyfeale and Glin.' Elsewhere in that particular issue, the Limerick News, referring to the Rifle Brigade, had this to say: 'This corps is particularly adapted for the country, and the peasantry seem to view them already with emotions of terror, from the idea of their being under the appellation of sharp-shooters.'

One wonders where the members of the Rifle Brigade, sent to do duty in Athlacca, were on the night of Monday, February 25th, 1822. The Limerick News of Thursday, February 28th, 1822, reporting on certain events of that night, had this story to tell:

On Monday night, Carew O'Grady, Esq., with Sergeant Fraser, a detachment of the 93rd Highlanders, some members of his family, and a few trusty assistants, proceeded through Manister to Boherard, and being attracted by a vast conflagration and the firing of shots, advanced in double quick to Athlacca church, which was, on their arrival, entirely in flames, and shortly after totally consumed.

Mr O'Grady's party was delayed near Manister in a search for arms and ammunition, which unhappily prevented an engagement, as Mr Croker's steward, who sat up for the protection of the Glebe House, Mr Bolster, and all others concur in stating that he would certainly have fallen in with the party had he been ten or fifteen minutes earlier. These miscreants, about fifty or sixty in number, well armed, placed Mr Bolster (brother of the gentleman the attack on whose house we mentioned in our last) upon his knees, and he owes his life to the approach of the military. Mr O'Grady's party succeeded in taking two prisoners, one within the churchyard, and would certainly have achieved more, but were precipitately hurried from the scene and the village adjoining it, by another fire, to which they quickly advanced, and which proved to be the burning of the barracks at Ballyagran.

Despite what the *Limerick News* had to say, it is unlikely that the attacking party intended to kill Bolster. If, as reported, they had left the scene ten or fifteen minutes before Carew O'Grady's force arrived, they would have had ample time to kill Bolster if they had so wished. It is also unlikely that O'Grady's men captured two of the attackers, since there is no further reference in succeeding issues of the paper that would bear that out.

The church that was burned in Athlacca in 1822 was the Protestant church. It was burned by the followers of Captain Rock, and not for any strictly religious reasons, but because it was the church that was frequented by the landlords, and the ascendancy, and their retainers. That there was a certain social content in the thinking of the Rockite leadership seems clear from an item in the *Limerick News* of Thursday, March 28th, 1822, which told that:

A written notice was posted between Athlacca and Croom, and was taken down by the Rifle Brigade on Saturday — it was signed by Captain Rock, and orders that no person should hold two farms, and threatening destruction to several who are named, for not conforming to former orders.

Another item in the same issue of the *Limerick News* told that 'A cow was shot on the lands of Rathcannon in this county by the insurgents on Saturday.' And on April 4th, 1822 the same paper reported that:

One of the deluded peasantry, who acknowledged that he was prominent in the present disturbances in the neighbourhood of Athlacca, voluntarily came forward on Sunday last to the Rev. Mr Croker, and delivered him a gun, in perfect order, took an oath of allegiance, and has returned to his house, where he will be permitted to remain so long as he continues to conduct himself properly, as he has most faithfully promised . . .

About this time the house of Robert Ievers, of Tullerboy, was attacked by an armed raider, who, when Ievers opened the door, fired two shots at him, the shots passing either side of him. A man from Athlacca parish, one Jeremiah Rourke, was charged with the shooting, was sentenced to death, and was hanged in Limerick on the 10th August, 1822. It is believed that Rourke was innocent, and that he was executed merely for the purpose of striking terror into the hearts of the local Rockites and Whiteboys . . .

In his very interesting book, *The Irish Faction Fighters*, Patrick D. O'Donnell tells us that in many areas from 1818 onwards the two well known factions, the Shanavests and Caravats, were known respectively as the Three Year Olds and the Four Year Olds. He says (p. 48) that on St Stephen's Day 1818 members of the Caravat faction, dressed as wrenboys, assembled in Guerin's public house in Kilteely, Co. Limerick, and pledged themselves to stand by one another for THREE YEARS. Members of the Shanavests, hearing of this, bound themselves for FOUR YEARS, 'for the purpose of remaining bound together until they saw whether their enemies would dissolve or renew their compact after the expiry of three years'. Another explanation of the names Three Year Olds and Four Year Olds was that they originated in an argument about the age of a heifer that was sold at the Fair of the Well at Ballyagran.

After the terrible events of the 23rd September 1825 the authorities obviously kept a close eye on the fair of Dromin. On the evening of the fair day of 14th December 1825, Captain Creagh of the Bruff Detachment of the 86th Regiment wrote to the Military Secretary, Royal Hospital, Dublin, saying:

> Sir, I have the honour to report that in obedience to the Requisition of Robert Ievers, Esq., magistrate, I repaired to the fair of Dromin, two miles distant, at 10 o'clock this morning, with one sergeant and 22 rank and file under my command, and 24 ditto from the detachments at Kilfinane and Glenosheen. During last night there had been some rioting between the factions which disturbed the neighbourhood, and a cask of porter was carried off from one of the tents by one of the factions, and some shots fired in the vicinity of the fair green . . .

Matthew Duhig, of Knockuregare, was baron of the fair of Dromin, and Tom Duhig, a descendant of his, now living in Ballinlee South, states that, in all, six men were killed in faction fights at the fair. Tom used to hear old people repeating one of the 'battle cries' of one of the factions, which went:

> Hayes, Capeless and Malone
> Again(st) Halligan, Galligan and the Dummy,
> And here we are!

From *Dromin Athlacca: The Story of a Rural Parish in Co. Limerick*, Glór na nGael, 1978

Castle Connell
Julius Rodenberg

In the midst of the wretchedness and discomfort my surroundings produced in me, a letter came across me. It dated from happier days; it had been given me by Mr Farquhar, on the evening I took leave of him, with strict orders to deliver it as speedily as possible. I took it up and gazed at the address: 'Miss Norah O'Keane, Castle Connell, Limerick'. This name twinkled before me like a star in a gloomy night. We poor earth-pilgrims believe in stars; oft in foreign lands, in pathless deserts, they have guided us. I had formed the acquaintance and learned to like Norah's brother, the student with the sweet sad eye and the soft sad heart, full of the sufferings of his country. I longed to see her and must do so this very day.

'Where is Castle Connell?' I asked the waiter who answered my bell.

'About six miles from here, sir, on the Killaloe-road. If you wish to visit the village, there will be an opportunity this afternoon. A railway has been made there, which will be opened today.'

I at once started, and the Limerick station was soon reached. It is a building which has stood for some years, and the new railway was only a branch, which was to be continued through the midland counties, and its opening must be the occasion for some festivity; so I expected, but was in every way deceived. A complete state of nature prevailed at the Limerick station; not a bench, not a waiting-room, nor any of the superfluous civilisation of the rest of Europe; only here and there a truck, on which you can sit, or a ladder against which you can lean. I had found a place on a quantity of boards; in the centre between the rails stood a wooden booth, on which was written in chalk, 'Booking-office', and in it sat a boy of about fourteen as clerk. There was not a sign of flags and garlands and merriment, as on the occasion of opening our railways. This people has no delight in what is new; it is not sensible of the progress of the age, and opposes to all events the gloomy feeling of distrust; the mob stood round with coarse, stupid faces, and the women I saw among them were also atrociously ugly.

I felt happier, though, when seated in the cushioned carriage and flying along to the well-known sound and inhaling the breeze, which blew damp but fresh across the wide, fog-hidden plain. The village was reached, and its Sunday quiet received the wayfarer. Hitherto it has had no dealings with strangers; and here for the first time the contradiction was explained, which I had borne in my breast so painfully since entering Limerick. Give me wretchedness, the whole sufferings of humanity, and I will endure them; but give them to me unveiled, and do not try to mask the painful necessity of their apparition in shabby garments. Do not call them by another name. Oh! misery has a powerful and world-convulsing voice, and it thunders its veto into your face if you dare to deny it. Here this voice was toned down to a soft, melancholy whisper; the trees rustled gently, the water murmured gently, and gently sang the wind through the laurel hedges of the wayside. The village is exquisitely situated at the foot of its hills, and the summit of the first of them is crowned by the ruins of an old castle. Come with me! We will weep for the fate of this country beneath ruins: when we are under ruins we are in Ireland. The broken genius of this land lives in ruins, and awaits the time when it will wave its drooping wings anew. It waits, and the time is already dimly visible.

On a conical rock in the centre of a blooming, pleasant plain, surrounded in the distance by bluish, moderately high mountain ranges, stand the ruins of the castle, lovingly preserved. A fine broad gravel-path leads up to it from the village, and at the top all is clean and fresh. One half of the corner tower still stands, some walls also remain with windows and doors, broken it is true, but overgrown with pleasant ivy. This is all that is left of the castle in which the sons and grandsons of the great Brian Boroo once lived; nothing remains of the halls in which the red Earl of Ulster once held his court; nothing of the keep in which the Irish rebels defied to the last man the arms of the mighty Oranger. But scattered around lie huge fragments of stone, defying decay, which the Prince of Hesse blew up after capturing the mountain castle. In many other Irish ruins I found graves; but here all was filled up with pleasant flowerbeds, breathing reconciliation. They had been twined round the relics of the castle like garlands of recollection and hope. The whole ruin seemed blooming and fragrant; and in the dim glow of the pale afternoon sun, Ireland seemed to me a woman — young, lovely, of rare beauty, a widow, who with moist eyes, but smiling and with modest hand, strews flowers over the ruins of a national fortalice, destroyed in the struggle for her liberty and her honour, and over the resting-place of the beloved who fell for her sake.

The new event which connected the village with the world — ah, it was surely a sorrowful world — had brought some life to the quiet spot. The stranger was regarded as a wondrous apparition, and they endeavoured with modest readiness to show him the way to the place he sought. A tall avenue of trees at the end of the village received me, and at the other extremity I saw the pleasant house, with its white walls and shining windows, on which the late sun was glistening. The O'Keanes, as I now heard, are an old race of the Irish nobility. Their forefathers were princes in this land, but as they ever remained faithful to the cause of their people, they had their full share in every new misfortune by which it was constantly pursued; they suffered by every persecution, every defeat of the Irish, every victory of the English, and of the extensive estates they once possessed, they were restricted to this last outwork on the border of Castle Connell village.

A large court-yard joined the old venerable trees, under which I had been walking. Shrubs, still damp with rain, grew over the front of the house; the last of the hedge-roses was dying away on its stalk, and the green of the leaves was assuming the russet of late autumn. An old man-servant asked for my card, and he had not been gone long, ere an aged, venerable gentleman with snow-white hair and dark eyes, appeared in the passage.

'You are heartily welcome,' the old gentleman said; 'my son in Dublin has written about you several times, and we are glad to welcome a friend of his beneath our roof.'

The door of a pleasant room on the ground floor was opened, and, introduced by the hospitable host, the mother, and then Norah, the sister of my friend, came towards me with outstretched hand. A heavenly peace seemed to preside in this room; while the parting splendour of nature, sunning itself in the soft light of sinking day, greeted me through the windows outside, the warm reflection of the chimney fire played on the bright gay carpet. A blue paper covered the walls, and the sportive gleam of the afternoon threw a golden hue over it. A comfortable, fragrant atmosphere pervaded the room, and I did not feel myself a stranger long. I seated myself at once by the side of the ladies. I was pleased with the dear, suffering face of the mother, doubly ennobled by aristocratic regularity of feature and matronly dignity; and my soul inhaled fresh strengthening in looking at the daughter. The oval of her face was soft; but decision was marked in the firm lines round her mouth, and her dark eye was full of fire. I could have imagined this young lady a princess of her people, with golden threads woven in her dark luxuriant hair.

Visitors arrived — several neighbouring squires with their wives — and were kindly welcomed like old acquaintances. They collected round the oak-table in the centre of the room, and drew nearer the fire. The daughter led me to a window, and we talked. The view on this side commanded the high road, the hilly land with a few patches of forest, broad meadows, groups of cabins, and the glistening windings of the Shannon. When all was quiet, a hoarse murmur could be heard, growing louder and then softer, but never entirely ceasing.

'Come,' Miss O'Keane said, 'I will show you the rapids.'

Just behind the house we entered a path which led to a wood, that glistened wondrously in the beams of the departing sun. The murmur grew louder the further we proceeded; it overpowered every word we spoke, almost every thought we formed. The grass became damp, as did our faces, and a cloud of fine spray fell on us. The tall ferns bent back and forwards, and over them the mighty trees bowed, and sought to embrace each other, starting back so soon as they came in contact. Presently we stood before the waterfall. The whole body of the Shannon, now strongly illumined by the bright red glimmering of the setting sun, pours here over rugged rocks. Nothing can be more perplexing at first sight than a river, mighty as any in Britain, rolling and tumbling in wild confusion over a series of rugged, rude and waterworn rocks.

We walked up the hill and at length stood over the village in front of the chapel, which is charmingly situated, surrounded by laurel bushes. It stood in a deep solitude, and divine peace had settled upon it in the russet clouds of evening. The last sunbeams which poured forth through the black clouds rising in the west, fell through the windows and sought the image of the Madonna, round whose head they collected. On the outer walls twined a broad layer of ivy, so thick and full, that it heaved like a field of ripe corn when the evening breeze glided over it. One of the little towers was entirely overgrown with ivy, so that it looked like a tower of verdure.

The path led back past the house, but I would not enter, for the sun had already set and I must think about returning. She did not press me to stay longer.

'We shall meet again,' she said, as we shook hands. 'We must not part on the same day we met.' Then she disappeared in the portal of her house.

I walked through the village. The clouds rising in the west had covered the whole vault of the sky; the last beams of the sun had died out, and a splashing shower poured down on me ere I had passed through the village. I sought shelter in an inn which fortunately stood by the road-side, and went into the upper room, reserved for better class visitors, where I had something warming to drink.

The next morning there stood at the door of the Royal Hotel of Limerick a wondrously shaped vehicle. It was a long open cart on four wheels, drawn by two half-lame cripples. The centre of the conveyance was occupied by herring barrels, large chests and wooden poles; on both sides, however, longways, were the seats on which the unhappy forms, representing passengers, hung rather than sat. At the same time a cold rain poured piteously down, and the streets were half under water.

'So soon as the rain has held up a little, we shall start, sir,' a man with a long whip said, who walked into the room to seize my two carpet-bags, the white one and the red one. Good Heavens! One was no longer red, the other no longer white; they had lost the hues of love and innocence, and assumed that ashen grey colour which follows the loss of both.

'Then that is the conveyance for which I have taken a ticket?' I asked, sadly.

'That is it, sir,' the man with the whip answered, and walked off with my two companions under his arm. He mounted on the 'conveyance', and both were buried under herring-casks.

A pause came in the mighty shower, and the man with the whip proposed to take advantage of it. He gave the signal for getting up. My ticket was for a first class.

'First-class? Here!' the man said, and pointed to a seat on the left of the vehicle.

The advantages of the first class were great. It had a woollen leather-bound rug, not saturated with wet, for first-class legs; it had a long smooth leathern cushion for higher comfort, but which was rendered very illusory, as said cushion had a tendency for slipping off; finally, it gave us the exclusive right of leaning against the herring-casks and chests. The second-class passengers were seated on the right bench, and the man with the whip watched sharply that they did not have any of the first-class privileges, especially leaning against the barrels. The third class stood on the hind board of the conveyance, and the company there was considerably mixed. There was a red-haired girl without shoes, and a man in a tail-coat, the tails being tied on with string; there stood a boy of sixteen making love to the red-haired girl, and an old woman who could not speak English but cursed us very powerfully in Irish. Above all sat the man with the whip, and all the three classes had the following things in common: the roof of heaven, the shudderingly cold rain, and the two cripples, which stopped every quarter of an hour, and only proceeded on a hint from the man with the whip.

Here commenced the misery which I bravely endured, on whisky and mutton, almost into the winter, on Ireland's bogs, and in her mountain villages, until I at length became even Hibernis Hibernior, until my coat was torn like theirs, till I only consisted, body and soul, of fragments, and looked like a savage Norman settler of the fourteenth century. The day of Limerick is the great turning-point in my Irish romance of travel. Good humour and the whisky-bottle became henceforth my most faithful allies.

From A *Pilgrimage through Ireland or the Island of the Saints*, Charles Griffin and Company, 1860

'Tis, it is the Shannon's Stream
Gerald Griffin

'Tis, it is the Shannon's stream
Brightly glancing, brightly glancing,
See, oh, see the ruddy beam
Upon its waters dancing!
Thus returned from travel vain,
Years of exile, years of pain,
To see old Shannon's face again,
Oh, the bliss entrancing!
Hail our own majestic stream,
Flowing ever, flowing ever,
Silent in the morning beam,
Our own beloved river!

Fling thy rocky portals wide,
Western ocean, western ocean
Bend ye hills, on either side,
In solemn, deep devotion;

While before the rising gales
On his heaving surface sails,
Half the wealth of Erin's vales,
With undulating motion.
Hail, our own beloved stream,
Flowing ever, flowing ever
Silent in the morning beam,
Our own majestic river!

On thy bosom deep and wide,
Noble river, lordly river,
Royal navies safe might ride,
Green Erin's lovely river!
Proud upon thy banks to dwell,
Let me ring Ambition's knell,
Lured by Hope's illusive spell
Again to wander, never.
Hail, our own romantic stream,
Flowing ever, flowing ever,
Silent in the morning beam,
Our own majestic river!

Let me from thy placid course,
Gentle river, mighty river,
Draw such truth of silent force
As sophist uttered never.
Thus, like thee, unchanging still,
With tranquil breast and ordered will,
My heaven-appointed course fulfil,
Undeviating ever!
Hail, our own majestic stream,
Flowing ever, flowing ever,
Silent in the morning beam,
Our own delightful river!

From *The Poetical and Dramatic Works of Gerald Griffin*, James Duffy, 1891

'An Undulating Plain'
Maurice Lenihan

The county of Limerick is . . . bounded on the north by Clare, the estuary of the Shannon, and Tipperary; on the east by Tipperary, on the south by Cork, and on the west by Kerry. The surface is an undulating plain, but the boundary over a great part of the south, and part of the east and west, is mountainous. The chief rivers, besides the Shannon, which forms its great boundary line on the north, are the Maig, Deel, and Mulcair. The Mulcair river, flowing from the Slievephelim mountains in the north-east, is greatly increased by the Newport river, which pours a large volume of water into the Shannon, three miles of Limerick. The Feale traces much of the boundary with Kerry. Lakes or ponds are not numerous, those of chief interest and size being, Coolapish, in the barony of Coonah, and Gur in that of Small County. The soil is remarkably fertile, especially in the 'Corcasses' along the Shannon, and the Golden Vein, which extends from the borders of Tipperary westward, through the centre of the county, from the sources of the Mulcair to the Maig, forming an area of about 160,000 acres, equally suitable for tillage and grazing, but chiefly used for the latter. Its soil is a rich, mellow, crumbling, calcareous loam. The subsoil of the county, generally, is limestone, trap, and sandstone. The Corcasses extend fifteen miles long, from Limerick to the embouchure of the Deel, and have a soil of yellow or blue clay, thickly covered with a rich black mould. The coal, which has been observed in six beds, is soft and slaty, and was worked at Newcastle and Loughgill. Iron, copper, and lead ores occur in various parts of the county, but they have not as yet attracted the investment of capital. The occupations are chiefly agricultural; pasturage and dairy farming are most cultivated, tillage less attended to. Large quantities of produce are exported. The manufactures are coarse woollens, flour, meal, tanning, lace, linen, and flax, the latter having lately received an additional stimulus. A good cider is still made in various districts, particularly round Adare, Rathkeale, and Croom . . .

Statistics — The population in 1851 was 262,136; in 1861, 217,271. The greatest length, north and south, is 35 miles; greatest breadth, east and west, 54 miles, comprising 1,061 square miles, or 640,842 acres of which 526,876 are arable, 120,101 uncultivated, 11,575 in plantation, 2,759 in towns, and 18,531 under water.

Baronies — Owneybeg, Coonagh, Clanwilliam, Small County, Costlea, Coshma, Pubble Brien, Upper Connelloe, Lower Connelloe, Kenry, Glenquin, North Liberties of Limerick, Shanid, and liberties of Kilmallock.

Towns — The post towns are, Adare, Askeaton, Ballingarry, Bruff, Castleconnell, Croom, Glynn, Kilmallock, Limerick, Pallasgreen, Pallaskenry, Rathkeale, and Shanagolden. Post Office accommodation is further extended to many villages, etc. . . .

The population returns of County Limerick in 1821 was 59,045, and in 1831 according to the population returns printed by order of the House of Commons, it was 66,554 showing an increase in ten years of 7,509. The population of the parishes forming the city as built upon, was estimated in 1831, at 49,769. The number of inhabited houses in the county by the returns of 1831, was 7,820. The number building 138. The number uninhabited 427. The number of families 11,953 — of which there were chiefly employed in agriculture 2,798 — in trade, manufactures and handicraft 4,057 — all other families not comprised in the two preceding classes 5,098. The proportion of females to males as 6 to 5. The number of males over twenty years of age 15,663 — labourers employed in agriculture 2,561; ditto not employed in agriculture 3,618. Persons employed in retail trade or handicraft as masters or workmen 5,106 — capitalists, bankers, professional and other educated men 1,323 — occupiers and others not included in the foregoing 3,055.

From *Limerick; Its History and Antiquities, Ecclesiastical, Civil, and Military, from the Earliest Ages*, Hodges, Smith, and Co., 1866

Shanid Castle
Charlotte Grace O'Brien

In the year 1863, in the last autumn of life my father, William Smith O'Brien, ever saw, I stood with him one beautiful evening on top of the hill of Knockainey, in the east of the county of Limerick — that interesting Knockainey, the site of so much both of legend and history. The western sky was full of light, and even at that great distance — I suppose at least twenty-five miles — we were able to distinguish the strange artificial hill of Shanid, its outline cut clear against the sunset, dominating the whole western horizon. Two rough drawings will give an idea of its remarkable appearance. The first shows just the Keep and top of the hill on which it is built; the second shows it in relation to the surrounding country, and Shanagolden in the foreground. The great masses of masonry, nine feet in width, have to be remembered in estimating the size; for though the actual remaining buildings are not large, the whole thing, the artificially-shaped hill, the great mass of masonry standing like a black clenched fist thrust against the western heavens, makes it certainly one of the most impressive of our ancient remains. It is a thousand pities that the Board for preserving ancient buildings has overlooked it, for it is quite unique. It is also interesting as the original fortress of the Geraldines — 'Shanid aboo' being their war cry. The time of the construction of the castle is unknown, but to me it appears that these circular fortifications were the fashion in the period just preceding and during King John's reign.

For the first time for many long years I went up to the castle the other day, myself and two raven-locked children, and the Boss and his dad. The children ran up and scrambled about hatless, their black locks flying in the wind that for ever beats about this high-perched castle, and gave no thought to me, while I climbed slowly up the almost perpendicular grass side, and many a scene out of the far away times of Ireland came out before my fancy. Yes, and also something of today — a something that spoke human life, but would need Miss Barlow's delicate genius fully to interpret. On this wild and lonely hillside I noticed a flagstone lying. I went up to it. It was a miniature grave — a new grave-stone drawn from the castle walls, laid down on a bed of moss and flowers, evidently fresh. The castle towered over my head, at my feet lay this child's work. On the stone was written in blue chalk: 'The death of the little queen.' Then another hand had apparently written: 'We were very hard on them.' I lifted the stone, but saw only moss and flowers. What child tragedy (or perhaps it was the fairies) lay in those words? Surely it was a poetic nature that sought such a resting place for some dead love, and adorned it so carefully — 'the little queen'. Ah! It touched all the chords of thought to contrast that not fully comprehended child work with all the terrible and wild human life that had been, and had ended, and was also hinted at but not explained by the gloomy remains of stone and earth building around.

My especial mission this time to the castle was also suggestive. There is a certain very rare thistle, with large smooth leaves and great feathery heads, called the Milk Thistle, or, in Ireland, the 'Virgin Mary's Thistle'. The reason it is so called is because the leaves are all blotched and marbled with white stains, and legend made it a sacred plant, bearing for ever stains of the Blessed Virgin's milk. Now, I had it in my mind that thirty years ago I had seen this plant at the castle, and as my brother had told me it was also found at Askeaton, I wished to confirm my impression. Sure enough, I found a mass of it growing together, only on the southern exposure, under the great wall. Now, this plant is said to exist only as an introduced plant in the British Isles. To account for it, therefore, on this utterly lonely and desolate hill-top, we must look back through the centuries and see the sacred plant in the monastery garden at Askeaton (mind, Askeaton was the great Geraldine home in Desmond). We must think how the seed may — in fact, must — have been carried up to this watch tower, perhaps by some long-haired daughter of the Geraldines, sent for safety to the mountain fortress; we must imagine how its frail growth (only annual) took hold on the sheltered side; we must see generation after generation of men swept away, the monastery torn down and desecrated, the name of Desmond almost forgotten, the great Geraldine race broken and destroyed; we must see the almost impregnable castle blown to pieces and left as a trampling ground for the summer-heated cattle; more wonderful than all, we must realise that time has so gone by that no record is left us of that great downfall and destruction — nothing — nothing but a few pieces of nine-foot thick wall, a few earth mounds, and the sacred plant. Irishmen! What national history lies in one seed of that plant. Think of it! realise it!

From *Charlotte Grace O'Brien: Selections from her Writings and Correspondence with a Memoir by Stephen Gwynn*, Maunsel and Co., Ltd, 1909

Christmas Holidays
Aubrey de Vere

Our home life pursued the even tenor of its way. We, the three elder brothers, worked at our classics in the morning, and in the afternoon took a long walk or a long ride, for each of us boasted a horse, though we seldom rode together; and in the evening there was often music, especially when Lord Monteagle was with us, for he and his sister, my mother, had been used to play duets from Mozart in their youth, he on the flute, and she on the pianoforte, and they continued the habit in advanced life. At Christmas we used to visit at Adare Manor. It was a gay as well as a friendly and hospitable house; after dinner we had private theatricals, games of all sorts, dances, and, in the daytime, pleasant wanderings beside the beautiful Maigue, which mirrored, in waters that even when swiftest seldom lost their transparency, as stately a row of elms, ninety feet high, as England herself can boast, and the venerable ruins of a castle which belonged to the Kildares — though islanded, as it were, in a territory almost all the rest of which belonged to the Desmond branch of the same Geraldine race. Adare, then as now a singularly pretty village, had for centuries been a walled town. It had seen many battles, and had been more than once burned down; but it was famous chiefly for the number of its monastic institutions, still represented by the ruins of a Franciscan convent, as well as by one of the Trinitarian and one of the Augustinian order, the churches of which have been restored, and are now used, one for Catholic and the other for Protestant worship. The Knights Templars once possessed a house at Adare; but its site cannot now be discovered.

   Among our Christmas holidays at Adare there is one which I am not likely to forget. About eight miles from the village rises a hill eight hundred feet in elevation, with a singularly graceful outline, named 'Knockfierna', or the 'Hill of the Fairies', because in popular belief it abounded in the 'Good People', then universally believed in by the Gaelic race in Ireland. We set off to climb it one day soon after breakfast, we, meaning my two elder brothers and I, and the son of our host, Lord Adare, afterwards well known as Earl of Dunraven, the author of two valuable works, *Memorials of Adare* and an excellent book on Irish antiquities. Two other members of the exploring party were our tutor, and a friend

of Adare's several years older than he. It was hard walking, especially after the
ascent of the hill began, we had to climb many walls and ditches, and to force our
way through many a narrow lane. We had brought no luncheon with us, and
before we reached the summit the winter sun had sunk considerably.

We walked about the hill top for some time admiring the view, a very fine one,
though, like many Irish views, somewhat dreary, from the comparative absence of
trees, the amount of moorland intersected by winding streams, and the number of
ruins, many of them modern. All at once we discovered that we were faint with
hunger, and so much fatigued without refreshment we could hardly make our way
home. Halfway down the hill stood a farmhouse. The farmer was most courteous,
but, alas! there was not a morsel of food in his house. What he had he gave, and
that was cider, for which, like the Irish peasant of that day, he would take no
payment. Each of us drank only one cider glass of it, and we took our departure,
cheered, but by no means invigorated. After the lapse of some ten minutes one of
us became so sleepy that he could hardly walk, and his nearest neighbour at once
gave him an arm. A little later the same complaint was made by another of us,
and the same friendly aid was forced upon him. But in a few minutes more not
only were we unable to walk, but we were unable to stand, the only exceptions
being the two among us who were no longer boys — our tutor and Adare's friend.

Never shall I forget their astonishment first, and afterwards their vexation.
They were in some degree in charge of us, and the responsibility seemed to rest
upon them. The Christmas evening was closing around us; there was no help
near, and apparently no reason why our sleep should not last till sunrise. They
argued, they expostulated, they pushed us, and they pulled us; but all would not
do. I was the last to give way, and my latest recollection was that my second
brother had just succeeded in climbing to the top of a wooden gate, but could not
lift his leg over it, and lay upon his face along it. Our tutor stamped up and down
the road indulging largely in his favourite ejaculation 'Gracious patience!
Gracious patience!' to which my brother replied, with his last gleam of wakeful
intelligence, 'There is one very amiable trait about you, Mr Johnstone: you are
never tired of toasting your absent friends.' The next moment he rolled over and
slept beside us in the mud. The cider had affected our brains because our stomachs
were empty. In about a quarter of an hour the trance was dissolved almost as
suddenly as it fell on us; and we walked forward very mirthfully, reaching home
just in time to hear the dressing bell ring. Only one light shone through the
mullioned windows of the manor-house; and I remember Adare's remark as we
drew near: 'Beside that light my little sister sits weeping. She is sure that I am
dead.' At dinner we told the story of our adventures, and it excited much
laughter. Lord Dunraven 'moralised the tale'. 'You see, young gentlemen, each of
you undertook to support and guide his neighbour, though not one of you could
take care of himself. That is the way of Ireland. You will help your neighbour best
by taking care each of himself.' His advice was like that of another old Irish
gentleman, a relative of mine, whose 'good-night' to his grandchildren often

ended with this counsel, 'Take good care of yourself, child; and your friends will
love you all the better.'

From *Recollections of Aubrey de Vere*, Arnold, 1897

A Jog, Jog Journey
Charlotte Grace O'Brien

My perverse desire to see everything made us attempt a road 'direct to Newport
through the hills'.

Hour after hour, hour after hour from Borrisoleigh, on we drove, twisting round
one black-capped and round-headed hill after another . . . I took refuge behind
my aged umbrella, but as I still wanted to see, I poked long slits in the old silk till
I got a fine view of the pony's ears . . .

When at last, near 7 o'clock, we opened up the Limerick valley, the sun came
out to greet us, or rather I suspect we came out of the mountain mist into a glory
of grey and silver lights over the Shannon plain. Then out popped Boss to bark
at everything, the weary pony pricked up her ears smelling familiar smells, and we
rejoiced as those do who have seen and endured and escaped! Well, we have seen
it. This bit of Ireland so near home, of which I knew nothing, is now in my hands
to put into its place as part of the country. Do my readers — do you who fly all
over the world in trains — understand at all the pleasure of having a mental grip
of your own country foot by foot? For me, I like a jog, jog journey.

From *Charlotte Grace O'Brien: Selections from her Writings and Correspondence with a Memoir* by
Stephen Gwynn, Maunsel and Co., Ltd, 1909

The Shannon
Aubrey de Vere

River of billows! to whose mighty heart
The tide wave rushes to the Atlantic sea —
River of quiet depths by cultured lea,
Romantic wood or city's crowded mart —
River of old poetic founts! that start
From their old mountain cradles, wild and free,

Nursed with the fawns, lulled by the woodlark's glee,
And cushats' hymeneal song apart! —
River of chieftains whose baronial halls,
Like veteran warders, watch each wave worn steep,
Portumna's towers, Bunratty's regal walls,
Carrick's stern rock, the Geraldine's grey keep —
River of dark mementoes — must I close
My lips with Limerick's wrongs — with Aughrim's woes?

From *Limerick; Its History and Antiquities, Ecclesiastical, Civil, and Military, from the Earliest Ages* by Maurice Lenihan, Hodges, Smith, and Co., 1866

Glenstal
William T. Cosgrave

Sir Charles Barrington, Bart.
Harfield,
Botley, Hants.

A Letter to Sir Charles Barrington
from William T. Cosgrave*
29th July, 1925

My dear Sir Charles,

Mr Duggan has, I am sure, informed you that I was unable to pay my promised visit to Glenstal as early as I had expected owing to the fact that the Dáil was prolonged for a fortnight after the date on which it was expected to adjourn.

The Governor General offered to accompany me and we went down to Glenstal on yesterday fortnight. The party included the Governor General, his son Mr Joseph Healy, Mr O'Hegarty, Secretary to the Executive Council, Mr E. J. Duggan and myself. The Governor General brought luncheon baskets. We were met at Glenstal by your steward, Mr McBean, and he, with the housekeeper, very kindly helped to make our stay at the Castle most enjoyable.

After lunch we were shown over the Castle, the Castle grounds and gardens and despite the fact that it was raining very heavily we made an exhaustive survey of the whole place. Notwithstanding all that Mr Duggan had told us about the castle, we were astonished at its magnificence, which far exceeded our expectations.

It is with the greatest personal regret that we feel compelled to refuse your very generous offer. Our present economic position would not warrant the Ministry in applying to the Dáil to vote the necessary funds for the upkeep of Glenstal, especially in view of the fact that we have already on hands the Chief Secretary's and Under Secretary's Lodges in the Phoenix Park, both of which are unoccupied and are a heavy financial burden on the State.

I think you should know that before making this decision I approached the leaders of the different parties in the Dáil, all of whom, in common with the members of the Executive Council, were convinced of the difficulties, in the circumstances of the moment, of accepting your gift while they keenly regretted that it was necessary to decline so magnificent an offer made in a spirit so generous and patriotic.

May I therefore convey from the Executive Council to you, Sir Charles, this expression of sincere thanks for your magnificent offer.

Now, having lost Glenstal, may I say that I deeply regret that you are leaving us. Our acquaintance has been short but I have the most pleasant recollections of it and my pleasure is to a considerable extent saddened by the news that you have definitely decided to leave Ireland. I sincerely trust, however, that whenever you are in Dublin you will not fail to call on me so that I may renew an acquaintanceship of which I have many happy recollections.

With best wishes to you and Lady Barrington, and sincere thanks in which I am joined by each member of the Executive Council.

I am,
Sincerely yours,
William T. Cosgrave

* President of the Executive Council

From *The Old Limerick Journal*, Barrington's Edition, No. 24, Winter 1988

Rathkeale
Seán O'Faolain

My mother's maiden name was Bridget Murphy. She came from a twenty-five-acre farm called Loughill on the banks of the little River Deel, two or three miles from the town of Rathkeale, deep in the flat, flat lands of West Limerick. She was very tall, slim as a reed and quite beautiful, with liquid sapphire eyes shadowed by an inborn melancholy. She laughed a lot, and when she laughed she swayed over like a reed in the wind. I am always reminded of her when I see, or evoke, the little blue lochs of Limerick, its pale albino sky, its grey stone walls, its winding limestone roads, dust-deep or mud-greasy, its outcropping rocks, its soft meadows, its wind flowing over them as if they were water . . .

Every summer, when we used to leave Cork to spend at least a month in the country we did so because fresh air and country food were supposed to be good for us, especially the fresh air.

'Drink it in,' my mother used to say, as if it were some form of nourishment, and she, my brothers and myself would stand in a row in the fields of Limerick with our mouths like four O's drinking in the pure air, much as her own country folk used to go to Kilkee or Kilrush to walk into the wavelets up to the calves and drink cupfuls of health-giving seawater. In Limerick we stayed with my mother's sister, my Auntie Nan Cosgrave, who had lived all her life since she was married in a long low cottage, thatched and whitewashed, its mud walls bellying with layers upon layers of lime, on the edge of the market town of Rathkeale. It was a pretty cottage; it had Jacoby geraniums in the windows; it was a step lower than the road; it flanked a long neglected orchard surrounded by a very high wall . . .

We always left the city in July or August when the theatre closed and it was the harvesting season in the country . . . The train was there, its engine hissing madly, breasting the tape to be off; my father commended us to the guard, the conductor and to God. If we were lucky we had a carriage to ourselves, one in each corner, each loudly extolling his position above the others. Then, at the very last moment, my father pressed into each clutching fist a bright sixpence, our holiday pocket money, ordered us sternly to be good boys, kissed my mother, made us close the windows tightly, stood back with a little salute, and the train slowly chugged into the tunnel where the windows at once went grey and we heard an occasional drip of moisture on the roof.

Then there was the sudden blaze of the open country, cows and horses in fields, blue and pink donkey carts trundling by with bright churns to the morning creamery, countless other things that meant much rushing from one window to the other. There were the *Gem*, *Marvel* and *Magnet* to be read, the stations to be noted, the changes to be made, the waitings to be enjoyed, until at last we came to the last junction of all with the solitary porter calling out in his flat Limerick accent, 'Ballingraane, Ballingraane, chaange here for Askeaytin and Fynes' — and there were the lake and the spire of Rathkeale wheeling slowly about us while we excitedly grabbed our belongings to be ready to alight at the next station, mount Uncle Tom's car, drive through the straggling street of the town, turn into Roche's Road, and pull up at its last cottage, over whose half-door Auntie Nan would already be leaning out to greet us with peals of red-faced laughter, open arms, shouts of welcome and floods of happy tears at the sight of her favourite sister.

As for me, I was by then already away and gone. Immediately we had turned the corner of Roche's Road a tang of turfsmoke had fallen from the high roof of

Normoyle's pub like the swish of a headman's sword decapitating time. When
Auntie Nan — a slattern old woman, her hair streeling, her eyes filled with tears,
her hands speckled with the dried flecks of the meal she had just been feeding to
the hens — squashed me to her bosom I was with the ages. I was where nothing
ever changes, where everything recurs — the dull sheen of morning sifting
through the holland blind on the sacks of meal crouched in a corner of my
bedroom, or the last of the sun glinting on a bit of brass in a horse collar hanging
from its peg in the bellying wall, or the lighting of the lamp when the blue
twilight fell and the town was wrapped in veils of silence for the night. Only the
clouds would move, and they barely, and they were always the same clouds, the
same weather, like the same scenes going around and around in the wheel of a
magic lantern. Everything was as solid as the fields, common as a cow, yet timeless
and tenuous as a faraway, fluting cock-a-doodle-doo or a distant, milk-heavy
mooing. Habit and custom ruled here. It was a place breathing its own essence.
Nothing was imposed, nothing made, everything grew as softly as the morning
light through the blind. Here there was no up W. Road and down Saint L., no
watch-your-step, no for-God's-sake-mind-who-is-behind-you, nothing except
Nothing — the lake, a road, a path, a spring-well tasting of iron, the swish of a
scythe, a rock to lie on, a hillock to stand on with your mouth open like an O to
the wind over the clover fields or the bogland heavy with mint and thyme, and
over it all Limerick's westering sun as pale in the albino sky as if she had been
frozen to a moon.

What did I do in Rathkeale? Nothing. I once described Rathkeale in a travel
book as a dead, lousy, snoring, fleabitten pig of a town, adding that I can never
think of it without going as soft as a woman. Nobody ever came to Rathkeale
unless he came there from his mother's womb or for business: a banker, a dentist
(in my day maybe twice a week, or once a week, from Limerick), cattle-drovers,
cattle-buyers, the parish priest, a parson, the teacher, a midwife. We used to see
some of them pass sedately along the road for a walk, the chemist's wife, bank
clerks, the teacher, returning as sedately an hour or so later. I do not know what
else these exiles had to do to pass their free hours. Perhaps they played cards, had
a drink in one of the pubs, read a book occasionally. Maybe it was 'something to
do' to go to Benediction. I used to see Auntie Nan lean over the half-door a dozen
times a day to look up and down Roche's Road. Remembering this habit of hers,
years later, on my last visit there, I leaned over the half-door, looked sideways
down the road, and took a photograph. It came out as the empty road, the long
ten-foot-high wall of her orchard on the left, a tumble-down low wall of round
stones on the right, one telephone wire following the long perspective of the
limestone road, and on the single telephone wire a crow. If my picture had had a
sound track, I would have heard nothing but a humming in the wire, although if
I had held the sound track open for long enough it might also have picked up a
basso hen clucking somewhere, or the soft *croc-croc* of a donkey and cart passing

by the other end of the road on the Main Street. There was no cinema. Later they got some sort of library. Once a year a one-tent circus came, with, on one occasion, a small, sad elephant . . . Ask me that question again so that I may answer it simply and honestly. 'What *did* I do there?'

I answer: 'Nothing!' Nothing that can mean anything to anyone unless he grew up there, or unless all this land around the little River Deel is holy ground to him because it is his mother's country. Limerick is to the traveller who travels only with his eyes one of the most uninteresting regions in the whole of Ireland. Flat, monotonous, colourless, shaggy, half asleep, a sighing land, wet underfoot and often wet above, a land of crinkling alders, little grey-lichened walls, tiny lakes, brown haystacks wind-ruffled, streams willow-edged or reed-clanking, poorish land sometimes breaking into good heart and high meadows, sometimes declining into scrawny, reedy fields, and all of it canopied by that unmistakably pallid sky. *Splendeur et magnificence des pays plats!*

I did nothing. I sat by a well and saw a spider race with delicate legs across the cold water from out of his cold cavern. I did the rounds of a Pattern (that is, a place dedicated to a Patron Saint) at the Holy Well of Nantenan near Ballingrane, with scores of old women come from long distances in their pink carts to pray as they circled, and to hang when they finished a medal or a bit of cloth on the sacred thorn tree by the well until it looked as ragged as a servant's head in curling-papers in the morning. I saw a line of cows pass along a road, their udders dripping into the dust. I went with Uncle Tom, each of us seated on a shaft of the donkey cart, jolting out to his bits of fields in the Commons near Lough Doohyle, taking with us for the day a bottle of cold tea and great slices of wheel cake cooked in a bastable, plastered with country butter and cheap jam. While, all day, he went slowly up and down the ridges on one padded knee thinning his turnips, I wandered. I saw a row of twenty poplars whispering to the wind. I picked and chewed the seeds of the pink mallow. I saw how the branch of a thorn tree in the armpit of an alder had worn itself and its lover smooth from squeakingly rubbing against it for forty years. I saw an old ruined castle and a Big House with the iron gates hanging crookedly from its carved pillars. And all the time away across the saucer of the lake there was the distant church spire of Rathkeale, like a finger of silence rising from an absolutely level horizon.

You see? Nothing! A fairy tale, a child's memory, a cradle song, crumbs in a pocket, dust, a seed. I lay on my back among lone fields and wondered whether the cloudy sky was moving or stopped. Childhood, boyhood, nostalgia, tears. Things no traveller would notice or want to notice but things from which a boy of this region would never get free, things wrapping cataracts of love about his eyes, knotting tendrils of love about his heart.

What a boy does not think he stores up. It was not until twenty-five years had passed that I suddenly remembered that Uncle Tom had a wen as big as a billiard ball on the back of his neck, and something near to a hump on his back. Suddenly all that had been timeless and tenuous became timefull and tense. Auntie Nan was not Auntie Nan, she was Nancy Murphy, a young woman being married in the church of Rathkeale to a man with a hump and a wen. My mother Bid, her sister, would have been there. There were — I have forgotten the precise number: six or eight or was it ten? — other sisters. They also would have been there watching the wedding. They had no brother, and the father was dead. They would have considered that Tom Cosgrave had two sidecars, a small contract with the post office for carrying bags of mail to some nearby station; that he had the cottage, the orchard, those few bits of fields on the Commons. It was a good match — that would have been the judgment of her mother; of her sister Bid, then behind the counter of McDonnell's Hardware and Grocery shop in the Main Street, 'serving her time'; of all her sisters, fated to emigrate to Australia and America, for what else could my old grandmother Mag Murphy (born a Power) do, a widow without even one son, with so large and helpless a family of girls on twenty-five acres of land in this wide, flat, soggy riverbasin of the Deel, rank with streams and dikes that feed into one small river, and from the small river, with many others, into the great River Shannon beyond? Nancy was lucky. As my mother had been to have caught the eye of young Constable Dinny Whelan, then stationed in Rathkeale. The ones who had to take the emigrants' ship? I have no record of any of them but one, an aunt whom I met many years later in Brooklyn. All the rest have vanished. That was the pattern of our line. Of our race.

Our visits to the farm, three miles west of Rathkeale, always took place on Sundays, and then only on fine days. Uncle Tom had a neat little tub-trap, drawn by a donkey, into which my aunt, my mother, one of my brothers and I would crush. The third brother would cycle. The brave little donkey would trot off down Roche's Road, down Well Lane into the New Line, and then having shown his paces to the town walk at his ease past Ballyallinan Castle, west past the Knockaderry crossroads, and so on until we entered the long, narrow, rutted *boreen*, or side road leading to the stone-strewn yard of Loughill. The farmhouse had, visibly, once been a small thatched cottage, about twelve feet by thirty, no bigger than my present living-room, where ten or twelve people had once lived — my grandmother and grandfather and their fatal line of girls. The eldest of them, when the last of the others had been shipped off or married off, had brought in her husband, a man named John Hough. These two, my Aunt Maggie and my Uncle John, and their family had, over the years, added a room or two, outhouses and a good metal barn. They were my first and unforgettable close-up of farmer stock, and I have to say that I did not wholly warm to them. Uncle John was a tall, bearded man, wearing on Sundays a swallow-tailed coat, with a gentle voice and smile, in whom I felt a tireless animal strength, a certain smiling contempt for Uncle Tom and Auntie Nan with their comical bits of scattered fields, and I knew he could be cruel, because we were often told about his wild son whom he had once stripped and whipped with a horsewhip so pitilessly that the youth had run away and never been heard of since . . .

Over the summer things fell into place historically. That well where I saw a spider crawl over the cold surface of the water was (I gathered from my mother's memories) the well where her mother used to come late at night, under the stars, when her children were in bed, to drink cold water and worry over her debts. That castle I have mentioned was called Caislean Arandubh, or Blackbread Castle, which invoked the famine of 1847, of which Martin Ross once said that for generations after its snows melted its ice water still shivered in the veins of Ireland. At the Pattern of Nantenan the slowly circling, dark-shawled women would have had plenty to pray for and pray against. Those iron gates hung crookedly from the entrance pillars of the Big House where the landlords had lived. The thorn tree had rubbed the alder, and the poplars had fluttered in an Atlantic wind that could also lodge crops and bring brushes of rain down from the clouds to sweep the fields. I learned that the pretty pink mallow is the flower of marshlands and ruins. It is all over Limerick. When my own mother sighed, and then went to the press in her kitchen to look at her lean purse, and then went to the tap for a drink of cold water . . .

I loved those visits to the farm once I got over my first shyness and awe. We tumbled in the tall haybarn with the Hough children. We were put up on the mighty back of the working horse for rides. We chased the geese in the haggard. Once I stayed for a couple of nights on the farm, sleeping by the undying turf fire with my cousins John and Jer in the excitingly novel settle bed — by day a plain, long box of wood, at night its seat and side folding down flat on the floor — hearing the crickets whistling quietly behind the hearth, telling them about Cork City, and the theatre and my school, they telling me about the farm, and rabbit-catching and otter-hunting, waking in the dawn to see John in his dayshirt blowing the smoored ashes into flame under fresh turf. When they had milked the cows in the half dark I went rattling off in the cart with John to the creamery, there to join a line of other carts from the plain about. One night, for some reason, I went with Jer up to the hill of Knockaderry. Below me a lighthouse winked on the Shannon. Twenty miles away a glow under the clouds meant Limerick town, their gateway to the world.

From *Vive Moi!*, edited and with an Afterword by Julia O'Faolain, Sinclair-Stevenson, 1993

The Enchanted Lake
Mary Carbery

When I think of home I see first Lough Gur, lying in summer sunshine like a bright mirror in which are reflected blue sky, bare hills, precipitous grey rocks and green pastures dotted with cattle and sheep; then a small, white house, half-hiding the fine farm buildings behind it, and four little girls playing ring-o'-roses before the door of their home, or touch-wood on the lawn, darting from the old oak before the house to the copper-beech, from the weeping-ash to the two rings of trees planted by our mother when she came to the farm as a bride.

Lough Gur dominates the scene. It was to us a personality loved, but also feared. Every seven years, so it is said, Gur demands the heart of a human being. Drownings were not infrequent and, as the bodies of the drowned were sometimes not recovered, Gur was said by some to be a bottomless lough.

In the lake is Knockadoon hill, joined to the land by a causeway built on the isthmus, once guarded by two fortresses where now only one, the ruined Black Castle, remains. Sometimes we children climbed by a steep and stony way to the summit of Knockadoon, where, when father was a boy, eagles made their nests and flew about the hills searching for leverets and new-born lambs to feed their young. From the top of Knockadoon we could see Garret Island, interesting for its prehistoric remains which were visited from time to time by antiquaries who gave my mother curious implements of the stone age in return for her hospitality.

Lough Gur has been called the Enchanted Lake; some say that in ancient days there was a city where the lake is now, before an earthquake threw up the hills and filled the hollow with water so that the city was submerged. Even now, the peasants say, when the surface of the lake is smooth one may see from a boat, far down and down again, the drowned city, its walls and castle, houses and church, perfect and intact, waiting for the Day of Resurrection. And on Christmas eve, a dark night without moon and stars, if one looks down and down again, one may see lights in the windows, and listening with the ears of the mind, hear the muffled chiming of church bells . . .

My father's land came down to the lake on the slope of the hill called the Carrigeen, which lay at the foot of Knockfennel. The Carrigeen was well fenced to keep in the yearling bulls which grazed there. Within this enclosure was a smaller one with high stone walls on three sides where dwelt our great bull; on the fourth side was the lake. We were thankful that father kept him safely shut up, for at that time many farmers let their bulls range the fields with other cattle and many were the stories we heard of people being chased and gored.

Carrigeen Hill is said to be hollow like Tory Hill and so many more. The stream flowing from the lake which we called the eel-stream, disappears into Carrigeen close to the eel-weir where there is a large light cave with a small opening at the back of it. It was said that anyone who had the courage to squeeze through the hole would find himself in the hollow heart of the hill . . .

May-Eve

One of the happiest things about my home was the quiet way in which the days passed and the amount of time there seemed to be in the hours. It must have been due to mother's methodical ways for neither she nor the maids ever seemed to be hurried or flustered. The work in hand rolled smoothly on as regularly as the clock ticked. Perhaps the maids worked well and calmly because the monotony of life was interrupted by numerous holy days when all but necessary duties were excused and we flocked into the world of faith which, to Catholics, is almost as real as the earthen world in which we live. In the bright imagination of a child, the Paradise of saints and angels is a wonderful and beautiful country into which it goes, by way of the church, to keep a feast-day with the people of that land. When we were very young we did not think of the saints as spirits, because we could not imagine a spirit. We thought of them as people like father and mother, of whom we could ask favours in our prayers and to whom we could talk in our minds. We felt we could walk with them in safety in a heavenly sunshine; theirs was a place of no fear. In imagination we gathered and brought back with us, small flowers and scented leaves, golden feathers from the breasts of birds-of-paradise, a downy plume from Gabriel's wing. What matter if our treasures were invisible? We pressed them just the same in the pages of our prayer books, among the lace-edged pictures of the saints.

From *The Farm by Lough Gur: The Story of Mary Fogarty (Sissy O'Brien)*, Longmans, Green and Co., 1937

The Soul of Brackile
James Kennedy

Nicker church is painted yellow. It stands out against the hill of Knockseefinn like a light-house — keeping an eye on the flat half of Pallasgrean parish below. There the milestones of our lives — birth, marriage, and death — were celebrated and then documented in the parish register which goes back to 1811. For birth, read baptism, for common sense, read first confession and communion; and for puberty, confirmation.

The parish priest and his curate who had separate houses — grandiose compared with ours — supervised our performance on the virtues and commandments through confession and sermons. There were pride, covetousness, lust, anger, gluttony, envy and sloth to be monitored, particularly lust. Sometimes the men would be ashamed to confess this to our priests and would cycle the ten miles to the Benedictines in Glenstal to expunge their guilt. Not so Eddie Dwyer of the garage who went to the confession box in Nicker with some whopper, confident that he could remain anonymous by disguising his voice. When he had finished his act of contrition and was leaving the box, Fr Kinnane added: 'By the way, Eddie, can you do a service on my car, tomorrow?'

I don't remember much about the priests in my early days. I never remember any of them in our house. I didn't know of anyone who had a very public and explicit faith except Matt Connell, our neighbour and a postman, and Miss Coffey, my teacher up to second class. Matt went to Mass every day and said the rosary in the church after all the evening funerals.

I served Mass for a few years but was never any good at it — always going in the wrong direction. One Sunday, the canon who held me back after second Mass gave me the holy water bucket in the sacristy and signalled me to precede him back out to the sanctuary again. He never said for what. There were two women kneeling apart from one another at the altar rails and I figured the exercise had to do with one or the other. I headed for Miss Coffey who was sixty years old and a spinster. Then I heard: 'Come back, you eejit!'

It was a churching ceremony.

I had great difficulty in memorising Butler's *Catechism* with the 'black and white' questions. They were called black and white because the most important questions were printed in bold typeface and secondary questions in Roman typeface. I was the worst in catechism out of seventy-two pupils and was kept in after class regularly as punishment. My teacher never realised that I wasn't malingering. I had a great visual memory for things I saw and if something was illustrated on the blackboard I would never forget it, but I couldn't remember lines. I had the same problem later in memorising Shakespeare.

Sanctifying grace was a big problem for me then. People were so sure about it, yet I couldn't nail it down. It existed in me, yet I couldn't feel it and didn't even know if I had it. I thought of myself as being in some way sanctified without knowing it by all sorts of goodies that came from the sacramental table. That was so unlike the way we understood things happening to us and being good for us at home. For once, we had to deviate from our ordinary way of understanding things and either take it or leave it. We took it.

It was the beginning of a split-level approach to life for me which lasted until I was in my forties.

Sociologically we were then labelled as rural, agricultural, and Catholic which made us as a class, the butt of many a cartoon in the early *Punch*. Yet the only thing many families around us had in common in terms of personal philosophies was a thick accent and the air they breathed. Our family had little enough in common with many of the people who voted the same as us, who went to the same church and played the same games.

Many of our attitudes were at loggerheads with the perceived wisdom of the locality. My father and mother had instincts — they would have acknowledged them as residual — which resented the kind of rural dogma which dominated us, and in particular, discouraged the need to develop our natural sensitivities to people and nature.

The sensual was a bad word in rural dogma. It was associated with lewdness, self-gratification, men and women with their passions out of control. From my parents I learned that it was through the senses as well as the mind that I could feel the world and be able to evaluate it and all that was in it for myself. Words of pure logic never meant a great deal to us. Abstract principles neither. The man who absentmindedly rubbed his dog behind the ears showed a rapport with the animal kingdom and had a kind of communication with it which was not expressed in philosophy or theology books.

I was encouraged to feel a sensitivity to the bush, crag, the running river. There is a time in the month of May and early June when the grass is new and shiny and dark green. I've often felt not only like lying down on it but lying down with it. This, according to my parents, was where sensitivity to people started — not the other way round. Yet the rural dogma had it that nature and animals had to be dominated in order to gratify some vision of ourselves as the only beings on earth destined for immortality.

Like the church, my family was for things and against things. There was very little grey in our lives. Yet lust, hate, pride, gluttony and so on never got much of a public airing, in the churchy sense, in our house. We were for nature, instinct, self-reliance, wit and humour, ingenuity, dogs, books and traditional music. We were against boredom, risks, servility, pompousness, waste, greed, slyness, boasting, and spongers. We had no strong views about important things like money, organised religion, sex or third-level education. It seemed that the church's values as expounded by the priests were going in a similar direction to ours but on separate railway tracks. There's nothing new in that. The roots of our culture go back farther than fifth century Christianity in Ireland.

Homo sapiens (the natural man) from the butt-end of East Limerick could go through life without any experience of the supernatural and hang on to the belief that, all else failing, the experience will come to him at death when he sets out on some trip into eternity. This is faith. Some people have it, and they become *homo fidelis* (man of faith) on top of *homo sapiens*. Some people don't have it. Some pretend to themselves that they have it and carry on behind the scenes as *homo sapiens* but on Sundays and holy days become *homo fidelis*. It is quite easy to do so. Nobody can prove you are not a man of faith. Neither is there any obligation to prove you are.

I'm sure my father lived in this kind of twilight zone between God and the gods.

One day I was cutting rushes (to top the reek) with him in Hammersley's marsh. It must have been during the run up to first communion. As children, he always made us sit on his coat (which had a recognisable but comforting smell of sweat and Garryowen tobacco) if the grass was damp. I brought up the subject of the soul. I thought he might be able to identify what it was seeing that he killed pigs and had seen people die.

'One thing I'm sure of,' he said, 'It's not something like a spud or a pig's *bodlach*. The priests say the soul is immortal and no one can contradict them nor does anyone want to. They are educated men.'

'I don't know what it is,' he continued, 'but I know that my soul — although it may not be as sanctified as they would like — is much freer down here in the marsh than it is up in Nicker.'

He had problems with the Canon who asked him for £20 in 1933 when he was about to marry my mother. He refused and stood his ground because he didn't have £20 to spare. He disliked the way the Canon gutted the old church and its upstairs gallery and replaced it with a 'monstrosity with concrete pillars' across the nave to support pseudo-gothic arches thus obscuring the altar. He hated the class-distinction which the seating in the new church copperfastened. The side-aisles were the penny aisles for the poor people. The two centre rows of the nave which was very wide were known as the sixpenny aisles and reserved for the best-off. Outside them were the two threepenny aisles where we sat, being neither rich nor poor. The penny, threepence, and sixpence entrance fees were paid on the way in.

My father fell out too with the curate who was a brother of the Archbishop — all over a bag of stale bread. The curate kept greyhounds and one of the shopkeepers in the village used to give him any of the loaves that had aged a bit on the shelves. My father met him coming out of the shop carrying a bran bag of stale bread and suggested he give the bread to such and such a family instead of to the greyhounds. I never heard any of this from him because he would never bad-mouth the Church or the priests.

My mother who had two brothers priests kept at him to keep his mouth shut. It was a source of embarrassment to her that when the names of all the people who contributed to the Christmas or Easter collections were read out at Mass, ours would be way down near the end. I remember, though, when he jumped from three shillings and sixpence to four-and-six. That put us in a slightly different category to what was known as the labouring class.

My mother tried too to get the rosary going on some kind of permanent basis in our house. It would go fine for a few days. Then as we sat with our backs to the fire, kneeling on the cement floor and resting our elbows on the chairs, someone would give someone else a pinch in the bum and there would be laughter. We had no great consistency, and would drop it especially when someone would accidentally say the 'Holy Mary' instead of the 'Hail Mary' or begin to imitate the loud, trumpet tones of Matt Connell.

The priests who came to our place had grown up in rural areas too — in County Tipperary and in a small part of County Limerick. With one exception in the latter years and possibly two, I don't remember any of them being men of the people. *Homo sapiens* had been well and truly knocked out of them.

I don't think they had any great choice in the matter either. The Church trained them like that and wanted it that way.

So, as much as many priests disliked it, they stayed on the fringes of people's lives. Their lives were defined for them so that they didn't have to plough, cut hay with a scythe, carry a cow to the bull or watch a child of theirs sick with pleurisy.

They were educated mainly in the rules governing their own lives as priests (canon law), and in the rules governing the lives of lay people (moral theology) and they felt they had to stay apart like judges in courtrooms. There was a real danger that if they didn't they might become like us. On the other hand, not being like us gave them an objectivity which came in useful when they were called upon to settle domestic or townland squabbles.

From *The People Who Drank Water from the River*, Poolbeg Press, 1991

A Shannon Sabbath Evening
Charlotte Grace O'Brien

A cloud land on its bosom
Of grey and gold and rose,
The silent river dreaming
Lies in a deep repose.

But ever, ever filling,
Comes in the flowing tide,
And near at hand the ripples
Across the pictures glide.

And far away an inlet,
More perfect than before,
Reflects in tender shining
The green indented shore.

Then slowly, slowly bending,
The tints fade one by one,
For the calm day at ending
Bids farewell to the sun.

Yet o'er the silent river
The dusk, the red dusk glows —
And see! its mirrored stillness
Is grey and gold and rose.

From *Charlotte Grace O'Brien: Selections from her Writings and Correspondence with a Memoir* by *Stephen Gwynn*, Maunsel and Co., Ltd, 1909

Newcastle West
Michael Hartnett

Newcastle West and its countryside provided me with images. Its neighbourhood is not spectacular: the mountains are miniature, the woods are copses at best. But it is soft, beautiful inland country, very green and over-lush in the summer. It is easy to sit in a house with chrome and enamel, in a city with 'all mod cons' and (perhaps) with that essential anonymity found there, away from parent and priest. It is easy to laugh and criticise quaint ways and hypocrisy, but beneath these there is a great part of a 'hidden Ireland' preserved, and no amount of modernity, no television set, no pointed shoes will make up the loss of the last vestiges of an older Ireland.

'Church Street without a church, Bishop Street without a bishop and Maiden Street without a maiden' goes a Newcastle West saying; and Maiden Street alone was — and is — a microcosm of an Ireland that is dying. It was the Claddagh of the town. When I was about ten, I took a friend of mine home. 'Please don't tell my father I'm down here,' he said, meaning in 'Maiden Street'. He was ten years old. The town was small — and he had never been allowed to go there by his parents. The street was mainly a double row of mud houses, some thatched, a few slated, most covered in sheets of corrugated iron. This was 'Lower' Maiden Street; 'Upper' was given over to small shops and public houses.

Before the Corpus Christi procession every year, all walls were limewashed in bright yellow, red and white colours, windows were aglow with candles and garish statues, and any unsightly object, such as a telegraph pole, was garlanded in ivy or ash branches. Banners and buntings were spread across the houses, and on the day, with the ragged band blowing brass hymns, followed by all the townspeople who carried confraternity staffs, the Host under a gold canopy was carried through the town. It matched any Semana Santa procession in Spain.

Old customs survived for a long time. I played 'Skeilg' once a year, chasing unmarried girls with ropes through the street, threatening to take them to Skeilg Mhicil; I lit bonfires along the street on Bonfire Night; I put pebbles in a toisin (a twisted cone of paper in which shopkeepers served sweets) and threw it on the road. If anyone picked it up and opened it, I lost my warts, one for each pebble in the paper, and the person who picked up the paper took the warts from me of his own free will.

Then Maiden Street received a severe but necessary blow. The houses were small with no sanitation: one fountain served the whole street, most of the floors were mud, with large open hearths with cranes and pothooks to take the cast-iron pots and bastables. And, of course, families were large. In 1951 a new housing estate was opened on a hill overlooking Maiden Street and many of the families, including mine, moved there. Now we had toilets and taps (six I counted, overjoyed), electricity and upstairs bedrooms. But Skeilg was never played again.

Better standards of living may improve the health of people, but this price of abandoning poor people's customs must always be paid and the customless bourgeoisie come into existence. Yet the general spirit has still survived. When the oppressions of religion and work are forgotten, they find again their old joy and innocence. This innocence is not to be confused with stupidity: I mean wonderment, such as expressed by the old man in a story a friend told me. My friend went home to Newcastle West from UCD and met, a few miles away on Turn Hill, an old man on the road, a distant relation. The talk came round to Dublin. 'Where do you stay there?' asked the old man. The other explained about 'digs'. 'An' you pay four pounds a week for a room only?' He was surprised. No, my friend replied, that included food as well. The old man was amazed. 'Surely they wouldn't charge you for the bite that goes into your mouth?'

Our entertainment was innocent too, but not without a touch of cruelty at times; watching crawfish clawing their ways towards the river across the roadway, gambling with passing cars. And on hot dusty summer evenings (all the evenings of summers before adulthood seem hot and dusty) suddenly at the pub not far from our door, there would be the joyous sound of curses and breaking glass, joyous to us because we knew the tinkers were settling some family problem in their own way. We would sit on the windowsills, eating our rawked apples, while they fought. We never cheered, nor would any of those who appeared over the halfdoors up along the street. Someone would send for the Gardai, and then light carts and swift horses would rattle off down towards the Cork Road, all the fighters becoming friends before the common enemy. We sat on, waiting for the last act, when half-an-hour later, the fat amiable Garda would come strolling down to an outburst of non-malicious jeers. But we were poor too, and there was the misery of drink in many houses.

I often tried to read by the faint light of an old oil-lamp with a huge glass globe which was suspended from the rafters. The house seemed big at the time, but is really incredibly small, and one had to stoop to enter. I sat there in the small kitchen-cum-living room, innocently working out the problems my father set me. 'If it took a beetle a week to walk a fortnight, how long would it take two drunken soldiers, to swim out of a barrel of treacle?' I never worked it out. Or 'How would you get from the top of Church Street to the end of Bridge Street without passing a pub?' He did supply the answer to that which indeed is the logical answer for any Irishman: 'You don't pass any — you go into them all.'

Once a year the otherwise idyllic life of the town was ruined by the coming of the 'Mission'. It was as if the Grand Inquisitor himself had walked through the town pointing out heretics. I sat in the church on the long seats, sweating with fear at the Hell conjured up by the preaching father, as he roared all sorts of vile accusations at the people. They sat, silent and red-eared, until he told an ancient joke probably first told by Paul in Asia Minor, a joke that they had heard year in year out, for a long time. But they tittered hysterically, delighted at being able to make a human sound in church. Outside the 'Stall', with its cheap trinkets from Japan, was dutifully looked over by the congregation: phials of Lourdes water, miraculous medals, scapulars, prayer-books and all the tokens of religion bought and sold like 'fish and chips'. But they were not 'holy', then, not until the end of the Mission did the preacher bless the huckster's dross and only then did they become sacred.

Part of the old castle grounds were made public by an Earl of Devon in the last century. These overgrown acres were a retreat from the Mission for anyone daring enough to go there during a service. Getting to the Demesne from the town without being seen was an art in itself (which I cannot divulge lest some young person read this and be led astray), but once gained, it was a haven of quiet trees and overgrown paths and two rivers. I read much poetry on such nights, watching the shadowy figures of fellow-transgressors hiding in the bushes, a small cloud of blue cigarette-smoke over their heads. I even met a girl there once: easy enough, as the Mission had Men's Weeks and Women's Weeks; their sins, I then assumed, were different.

There are as many things to love in a town as there are to hate. Indeed the only things I disliked were class and priest-power, but if injustice is not seen to be done, such opinions are merely private prejudices. I remember, with pity for the man, a priest beating a child about a schoolroom for no good reason. I remember, with joy for myself, my grandmother coming into town on her asscart, her black, fringed shawl about her small fresh face, with her stories of pishogues and enchanted fairy forts; I remember her illness and her dying and my absence from this, being in London working or drunk in a Dublin pub. If you cannot mock a place you love, how can you love it fully?

From *The Old Limerick Journal*, No. 20, Winter 1986

Purity by Brown Paper
Frank O'Connor

Limerick is without exception the pleasantest town in Ireland. It consists of two towns, the old and the new, but as the new was built about the beginning of the last century, the old has grown almost reconciled to it. In the new town is the pretty Custom House, with its arcade cemented up by some genius from the Board of Works, and a fine long street of Late Georgian which ends, rather feebly, in a frightened double crescent. Shop fronts do less to spoil the street than the Renaissance church in Ruabon brick, and the neo-Clonmacnois one in limestone. Limerick as well as being the pleasantest is also the most pious town in Ireland. Why it should be I don't know, except that it was founded by Danish pirates, whose flaxen hair, blue eyes and bad consciences still walk the streets.

The old town is on an island in the river with the Clare shore joined to it by a bridge, and the wild Clare hills up the river behind it. The bridge is guarded by a great castle with drum towers, over which a row of modern workmen's houses peers with a slightly self-conscious air. On a little hill above it stands the cathedral, not very impressive from any angle, for its blue stone gives it a frosty, virginal air; its tower is skinny and looks as if it needed love, and its walls are decorated with battlements which distinctly resemble curling papers. When you get nearer, you see that it is almost as broad as it is long, and that no two windows in the fifteenth-century shell bear much resemblance to one another.

It is better inside. In the porch there is a shrine with characteristic Transitional ornament, and when you enter you find yourself in a typical Cistercian church of the twelfth century, with sullen, massive piers relieved at the corners by half-columns, plain exiguous capitals and bases, and plain arches without mouldings. It is a very small church; four bays below the crossing; but, even so, it seems to have presented its builders and restorers with insuperable obstacles. For some reason it was extended not in length but laterally, in a series of transepts, and, as the builders stuck to piers instead of columns, one's first impression is not of a void with solids in it but of a solid very inadequately provided with voids.

As in many of the English cathedrals, there are curious passages running through the walls, across the west window and up through the clerestory, as though the principal recreation of the chapter were 'Hide and Seek'. On the south side, the clerestory is relatively normal, but on the north the aisle and transepts have been built higher than the clerestory, which thus opens on either side into the church, and accordingly has had to be railed off in case an unsuspecting visitor might take a header into the nave by mistake. It is only when you have had a really good look at the church that you begin to discover half its peculiarities. For instance, in England the clerestory windows are placed above the head of the arch, where, if the church is vaulted, they do not get in the way of the columns supporting the roof. It wouldn't be Ireland if they were not placed above the piers. But the Limerick masons went one better, for they have put one window over the pier, another over the head of the arch, and very odd and very charming they look with their deep sun-filled splays broken by these black, tapering, Egyptian-looking passages.

The fact is that at Limerick we really struck without recognising it a very interesting architectural backwater. Munster had been the centre of the reform movement and the probable source from which Romanesque decoration spread up the Shannon into Connacht. For a hundred years after the Normans the O'Brien and O'Connor country west of the Shannon was little affected by the invasions, and while the Normans of the Pale were putting up regular Transitional and Early English buildings which have all the formal beauty of their kind in England, the masons in the west of Ireland erected churches which, though deeply influenced by what was happening in the east, are still full of character. They are usually plain, sometimes to the point of ugliness; they are nearly always, to use an Irishism, 'contrary', but often, too, they have great brilliance, and are decorative in an exciting way in which the churches of the east are not.

Half the charm of English church architecture is its peculiar individualism, but any charm these Irish churches may have is entirely due to it, and though Célimène and I began by being repelled, we found ourselves at last becoming attracted in the way one is attracted by characters one meets in out-of-the-way places, men who superficially are all angles and oddity, but who, as you get to know them, reveal their value . . .

In the evening we cycled up the river to Castleconnell . . . a delightful Georgian spa with its arcaded assembly rooms on the bank of the Shannon, its charming inn, its rows of demure little villas. Towards the end of the nineteenth century some patriot got at them and gave them wrought-iron gates, representing Irish round towers, harps, wolf-dogs, and the Treaty Stone by Thomond Bridge, but even these do little more than emphasise the quiet decorum of the houses behind.

Unfortunately, since then it has been visited by another type of patriot. During Mr de Valera's rebellion some of the great houses along the river perished; under his government the housebreakers have been gradually accounting for the rest. We returned from Castleconnell along the back road just at sunset. Miles of stone wall which guarded the estate on our right were humped and rent by great clumps of ivy which straddled them and broke their back. We opened a ruined gate and cycled down a shadowy land which had once been an avenue, and rounded a great mass of buildings which proved to be stables. Suddenly as we reached the stable yard, the sun went out over the wild Clare hills across the river, and we looked up and saw in the yellow light the green, paling stucco behind a great Ionic front, reflecting like water the last pale gleam of day. It would be impossible to paint that yellow light on the peeling stucco and the dull smouldering of the masses of brick in the gloomy cavern of the house behind, but it was tremendous;

as though the sun going down beyond the Clare hills had clenched his fist and shaken it at the porch, and the porch, like some great beast driven to bay, dug its columns deeper into the ground and snarled back at it. 'A man must be stronger than God to build to the west of his house' goes the Irish proverb, but a man must think himself stronger than Ireland to build that insolent classic front to face the wild hills of Clare.

It must have been an enormous house. Outside we could trace the remains of a sunk garden, but of that nothing remained except a clump of wild daisies among the briars. Behind were acres of magnificent walled garden going wild, wilder I think than anything I have seen elsewhere, or perhaps it was the light which made it seem that the earth was rising to swallow up what remained of the house.

Stumbling in the dusk along the length of the wall, we came on a peculiar mound, almost covered with briars, and now almost unnoticeable in the desolation. There was an opening into it, and in the opening a gate with sentimental shamrocks that dated it as of the same period as the patriotic embell-ishments of Castleconnell. The lock was broken; we opened the gate and looked in. Three steps led down into the darkness. I lit my lighter, and the flare showed us three discoloured coffins on a slab under broken glass wreaths. We didn't go further. We returned as we had come, under the great Ionic columns that lost themselves in the night sky. As we went back the little dark lane we came upon an old countryman on his way home.

'Whose house was that?' I asked.

'That was the house of Lord Clare,' he said, stopping. 'He was one time Lord Chancellor of Ireland. You might have heard of him?'

'I did,' said I . . .

'When I was a boy all this place was woodland. You might have noticed the wall? Three and a half miles round from the Castleconnell Road to Annacotty Bridge. The timber fetched six thousand; it worked out at about fourpence a tree.'

'And then, what happened?'

'It was burned by the boys during the Troubles. They thought the military might be going to take it over. I saw it burning. There was a marble staircase that stretched the whole width of the house. It melted in the fire, and the melting lead pouring down on to it from the roof. It was a terrible sight! That was the finest house in this part of Ireland. There was a walk all round the roof. Often and often I strolled up there in the evening after the house was left empty . . . '

We had our tea on the river-bank under the cathedral wall. We made peace. We recognised that in all the articles in dispute, what really ailed us was too much scenery . . . Nature, as I say, is all very well in its own way, but it produces a ravenous appetite for civilisation, and Killaloe, after all, was only thirteen or fourteen miles from Limerick. You could nearly smell it up the Shannon; the Georgian architecture, the lights, the hotels, the pubs, the picture-houses and the resiners in Géronte's. How long was it since we had seen Géronte last?

At O'Briensbridge, with its tiny sandstone tower lost under the airy blue side of Keeper, the big clouds, lit with gold, sailed massively up the river like granite boulders and tossed silver streamers of light into the fields and the canal. Away to our right were the long hills down which Octave and his companions had galloped in the family coach. We sang. We passed Georgian mansions, orchards and nursery gardens, and at last we came in the dusk to the familiar bridge guarded by its grey drum towers, and above it the skinny old cathedral tower stood up against the sky, bleak and blue-grey and all old-maidish in its curling papers of battlements. As we cycled by it Célimène suddenly jumped off her bicycle and shouted to me to stop. She stood before a hoarding with her eyes popping out.

'What is it?' I cried in alarm.

'Don't you see?' she cried in a frenzy of excitement.

'No,' I said.

'The poster!'

'What's wrong with the poster?' I asked.

'Her chest, man,' shouted Célimène. 'Can't you look at her chest!'

And there it was, with another poster beside it that said 'Every Poster Tells Its Story' — the picture of the Icilma lass, with a modesty vest of brown paper pasted across her pretty chest!

'Civilisation?' I thought, going cold all over. 'Did I say civilisation?'

From *Irish Miles*, Macmillan & Co. Ltd, 1947

Christmas in Newcastle West
Michael Hartnett

A shouting farmer with a shotgun, a few patch-trousered urchins, soaked, snotty and unrepentant, running across wet fields, arms full of holly. The long walk on the railway tracks, the sleepers treacherous and slimy, the dark stations, the lamp-posts with their glittering circular rainbows. We stopped at the shops' red windows, to admire toys we could never have. A few drunks waltzed by, happy and moronic. An open lorry went by to jeers and obscenities; the pluckers, shawled and snuff-nosed on the back, on their way to a flea-filled poultry-store to pluck turkeys at ninepence a head.

Candles and paraffin-lamps did not brighten the darkness in kitchens in Maiden Street — they only made the gloom amber. The purloined holly hung on holy pictures. There were no balloons, no paperchains, no Christmas trees. Coal was bought by the half-stone, butter by the quarter-pound and tea by the half-ounce. The country people trotted by on donkey-and-cart or pony-and-trap with 'The Christmas' stones of sugar, pounds of tea. Women in shawls and second-hand coats from America stood at half-doors, their credit exhausted, while the spectre of Santa Claus loomed malevolently over the slates and thatch. Members of charitable institutions distributed turf and boots, God-blessing the meagre kitchens, as hated as the rent-man. They stood well-dressed on the stone floors, were sirred and doffed at. They looked without pity at the nailed together chairs, the worn oilcloth-topped tables, the dead fires.

Outside, the rain fell and blew along the street. The tinkers fought. Bonfires died out in the drizzle. We were washed and put to bed, happy and undernourished. The oldest went to midnight mass. The Latin was magic, the organ, the big choir. It always seemed like a romantic time to die.

It was a Christmas of tin soldiers, tin aeroplanes and cardboard gimcracks. We were Cisco, Batman, Johnny Mack Brown all that day. Our presents — 'purties' we called them — seldom lasted longer than that day. It never snowed. There was no turkey, no plum-pudding, no mince-pies. The Victorian Christmas was not yet compulsory. The very poor managed roast meat, usually mutton. We often rose to two cocks. The goose was common. There was a fruit-cake, jelly and custard; the dinner of the year. I never remember drink being in the house. There were never visitors, nor were we encouraged to visit anyone. If the day had been anyway fine, we were to be found on the footpath or in the puddles, knuckles blue.

The Wren's Day always brought frost. Small warm heads came from under rough blankets to the sound of flutes and banjos and bodhrans far up the street. We donned boot polish and lipstick and old dresses and went out to follow the wren, tune-less chancers. We sang and giggled our way to a few bob and a glass of lemonade. The back kitchens of the pubs filled up with musicians, the musicians filled up with porter and their wives filled up with apprehension. In a few hours, winter took over again. There will never be Christmases like those again, I hope to God.

From *The Old Limerick Journal*, No. 17, Winter 1984

Sweet Adare
From: **Matt Hyland**
Gerald Griffin

Oh, sweet Adare! Oh, lovely vale!
Oh, soft retreat of sylvan splendour.

Nor summer sun, nor morning gale
E'er hailed a scene more softly tender.
How shall I tell the thousand charms,
Within thy verdant bosom dwelling,
When lulled in Nature's fostering arms,
Soft peace abides and joy excelling?

Ye morning airs, how sweet at dawn
The slumbering boughs your song awaken;
Or, lingering o'er the silent lawn,
With odour of the harebell taken.
Thou rising sun, how richly gleams
Thy smile from far Knockfierna's mountain
O'er waving woods and bounding streams,
And many a grove and glancing fountain.

Ye clouds of noon, how freshly there,
When summer heats the open meadows,
O'er parched hill and valley fair,
All coolly lie your veiling shadows.
Ye rolling shades and vapours gray,
Slow creeping o'er the golden heaven,
How soft ye seal the eye of day,
And wreathe the dusky brow of even.

*****

Where glides the Maigue as silver clear,
Among the elms so sweetly flowing,
There fragrant in the early year,
Wild roses on the banks are blowing,
There, wild ducks sport on rapid wing,
Beneath the alder's leafy awning,
And sweetly there the small birds sing,
When daylight on the hill is drawing.

*****

In sweet Adare, the jocund spring
His notes of odorous joy is breathing,
The wild birds in the woodland sing,
The wild flowers in the vale are breathing.

There winds the Maigue, as silver clear,
Among the elms so sweetly flowing —
There fragrant in the early year,
While roses on the banks are blowing.

The wild duck seeks the sedgy bank,
Or dives beneath the glistening billow,
Where graceful droop and clustering dank
The osier bright and rustling willow;
The hawthorn scents the leafy dale,
In thicket lone the stag is belling,
And sweet along the echoing vale
The sound of vernal joy is swelling.

*****

Ah, sweet Adare; ah, lovely vale!
Ah, pleasant haunt of sylvan splendour;
Nor summer sun, nor moonlight pale
E'er saw a scene more softly tender.
There through the wild woods echoing arms
Triumphant notes of joy were swelling,
When, safe returned from war's alarms,
Young Hyland reached his native dwelling.

From *The Poetical and Dramatic Works of Gerald Griffin*, James Duffy, 1891

SIX

SPORT

'I Doubt It, said Croker'
Colonel Wyndham-Quin

Foremost in supporting the new movement was Mr Edward Croker, of Ballinagarde, who, in addition to a handsome subscription, presented his fine pack of fox hounds for the use of the Hunt . . .

To inaugurate the new status of the Club, a dinner was held by the members at Rathkeale, with Mr Edward Croker in the chair who, in describing the advantages of making the County Limerick a fox-hunting county, mentioned what was then a fact, that the gentlemen of the county seldom met together except at Assizes time upon the Grand Jury, when every man's knowledge of the road was only local, and their acquaintance in general so slight with one another, that they were often the prey of the road jobbers from want of previous information on the subject. But he said that if the gentry of the county joined the Club, the contrary would be the case, as sportsmen from similar inclinations became quickly acquainted, and that although he was aware he was surrounded by as hard-riding a set of men as any in Ireland, yet as they should perforce go along the roads to the different Meets within the county, they would all have an opportunity of surveying them, and thus be able to check any attempt at extortion.

Mr Croker, we are glad to learn, lived to know that the words he had spoken were justified, and to see the Limerick Hunt Club one of the most flourishing and successful in Ireland. Although at this time in his sixty-first year, Mr Croker is said to have been for his age a wonderfully good man to hounds, especially when mounted on his rat-tailed Swordsman horse, and to have been as joyous at a day's sport as an emancipated schoolboy . . .

One day towards the end of March 1830, the hounds met at Ballinagarde. Mr Croker had been for some time indisposed, but his illness taking a turn for the worse, his second son, the Rev. Edward Croker, rector of Croom, was sent for to be with him. On coming downstairs on the morning of the Meet, the rector was somewhat astonished to find his father seated on a wheel chair in the hall, hunting-horn in hand, and attired in the full costume of the chase. 'I am determined', said he, in answer to his son's inquiries, 'both to see and hear the hounds once more, even though it be for the last time. Wheel me to the window.' Gazing on the assembled pack, he then essayed to blow his horn, but strength failing him, he sent a message desiring the huntsman to sound the familiar notes for him. After listening for some moments to the horn, and the answering music of the hounds, Mr Croker turned his head from the window, and raising his eyes, exclaimed, as it were to himself, 'Sweet Ballinagarde, must I leave you?' 'Father,' said the rector, 'fear not, for you may soon be going to an even brighter and better place than this.' 'I doubt it, Edward, I doubt it,' replied the old man mournfully, 'but now I am satisfied, and you may take me away.' The servants then bore him back to his bedroom, where, but a few hours later, he ceased to breathe.

Commenting on the above, an obituary notice says: 'Be that as it may, it is the united prayer of his brother sportsmen, friends and neighbours of all classes, that the Last Trump shall waken him to that state of happiness which (if humanity dare judge) he has nobly earned, by the benevolent exercise of a kindly disposition, and a willing hand to relieve the wants of his fellow men.'

From *The Fox Hound in County Limerick*, Maunsel & Company Limited, 1919

The Barringtons in America

The Cunard steamer, Scythia, which arrived at the Jersey City wharf at seven o'clock, last evening (August 15), had on board the gentlemen selected to represent Ireland and Trinity College, Dublin, in the coming international rowing races at Philadelphia.

The names of the crew are as follows — G. N. Ferguson, bow; G. H. Hickson, C. B. Barrington (captain), Croker Barrington, stroke, and M. M. Barrington, extra man. Mr E. D. Brickwood, accompanied them as coach.

The three Barringtons are brothers, and sons of Sir Croker Barrington, Baronet, Glenstal Castle, Co. Limerick.

The crew arrived in excellent health and overflowing spirits. 'Get ready for the Fenians' shouted one of them from the steamer as she drew into dock. This was answered by a party of gentlemen on the wharf, who were there to receive them . . .

Mr C. Barrington, captain and No. 3, is twenty-eight years old, five feet eleven inches tall, and weighs 182 pounds. He is the oldest graduate of the crew, having taken his degree in '72. For many years he has been prominent in the Irish University races and the English inter-collegiate contests. He was a member of the Dublin University crew which won the Visitors' Cup in Henley in the years 1870, '73, '74. He also rowed at the four and eight for the Grand Challenge Cup at Marlowe in 1876. His record is a very good one, and his reputation is almost world-wide.

Mr Croker Barrington, the stroke, is twenty-three years of age, five feet ten inches in height, and weighs 170 pounds. He obtained his degree in the year 1874. He rowed stroke in the victorious Trinity College crews which won the Visitors' Cup at Henley in 1873 and 1874. He was also a member of two winning crews for the Dublin Cup.

Altogether, they are, in appearance, a splendid crew, and their records are more than ordinary ones. Their broad shoulders, healthy complexions and entire fine physique, speak well for their training and their future performances.

The extra man, Mr W. M. Barrington, is the youngest of the party, but appears capable of doing good work if called upon . . .

The crew bring but one boat with them, which is forty feet, six inches in length. They are ready and anxious to participate in as many races as possible, while here, and expressed great gratification when informed that there would be twenty-four entries in two great amateur fours races.

From *The New York Herald*, 16 August 1876

The First All Ireland Senior Football Title
Seamus Ó Ceallaigh and Sean Murphy

Limerick's participation in the inaugural All Ireland Senior Football championship was completely successful, and they brought to the County the first Football Championship decided under Gaelic rules.

Their initial match was against Dowdstown, Meath, and was played at Elm Park, Dublin. In a nice scientific contest the Limerick men were victorious by 3-2 to 0-2. Star of this game was Malachi O'Brien, and he scored a magnificent goal from midfield. Lord de Frenche, in whose park the game was played, was so impressed by Malachi's performance that he invited him to dinner after the game.

It was another trip to Dublin — this time Clonturk Park, for their second round tie with Kilmacow, Kilkenny, and after a desperate struggle the game ended in a draw of 1-10 each. That day blew a storm and scientific play was out of the question. Three weeks later the replay took place at Bansha. In bright sunshine, in a beautifully equipped meadow close to the Glen of Aherlow, the teams toed the line. For a while the well nigh invincible Kilmacow seemed to be winning, but once the Commercials settled down there was no stopping them; their ground work and rushes carried everything and they emerged good winners.

In the semi-final, played at Bohermore, near Tipperary, on 11th March 1888 Commercials beat Templemore, Tipperary, 4-8 to 0-4. This was a replay, the first game being disputed and ordered to be refixed.

The final was played at Clonskeagh, Dublin on 29th April, on a field known as the 'Big Bank'. Clonskeagh was then a remote County Dublin village. Commercials travelled to the Metropolis the previous evening and on the Sunday took a horse tram to Ranelagh Angle, where they changed to another horse tram which brought them the remainder of the journey.

The opposition was provided by Young Irelands, Dundalk, representing Louth. It proved a wonderfully fast game, scientific and clever, and was fought in a fine sporting spirit. Louth displayed a good deal of clever hand work and the Limerick play was characterised by a fine defence and spirited rushes. Dundalk led at half time, 0-3 to 0-1, but Commercials finished strongly to win 1-4 to 0-3.

The Limerick players were: Denis Corbett, goal; Timothy Fitzgibbon, William Gunning, Richard Breen, John Hyland, Thomas McNamara, William J. Spain, Patrick J. Corbett, Michael Slattery, Jeremiah R. Kennedy, Michael Casey, James Mulqueen, Malachi O'Brien, Patrick Kelly, Timothy Kennedy, Philip Keating, William Cleary, Robert Normoyle, Patrick Reeves, Thomas Keating, Thomas McMahon. Others to participate in some of the above mentioned contests were Ned Nicholas, Edward Casey, Richard O'Brien, James Purcell, Thomas O'Loughlin and Thomas Lynch.

Limerick was a very excited city on the evening of Monday, April 30, 1888, and when the train from Dublin arrived at the local terminus, a group of young men took Malachi O'Brien out of the carriage in which he had travelled with the other members of the Limerick team, who had won the previous day the first All Ireland senior football championship in the annals of the GAA and carried him on their shoulders through the city and to the hotel for the first reception ever accorded a winning All-Ireland team.

Malachi's nickname was 'the little wonder' — a title he certainly earned — for no man of his size or weight put more into Gaelic football than he did.

Congratulations poured in from all sides on the manly way in which they fought out the championship and won with undisputed merit the first and one of the greatest championships of the GAA.

From *One Hundred Years of Glory: A History of Limerick GAA 1884–1984*, Limerick GAA Publications Committee, 1987

There is an Isle
Anonymous

There is an Isle, a bonnie Isle,
Stands proudly from, stands proudly from the sea.
And dearer far than all this world
Is that dear Isle, is that dear Isle to me.

It is not that alone it stands
Where all around is fresh and fair,

But because it is my native land,
And my home, my home is there.
But because it is my native land,
And my home, my home is there.

Farewell, farewell, though lands may meet,
May meet my gaze, my gaze where'er I roam.
I shall not find a spot so fair
As that dear Isle, as that dear Isle to me.

It is not that alone it stands
Where all around is fresh and fair,
But because it is my native land,
And my home, my home is there.
But because it is my native land,
And my home, my home is there.

From *Shannon Rugby Football Club Centenary 1884–1984*

Encounters with Sir Thomas Myles and Bertie Cussen
Dr E. F. St John Lyburn

I soon took an intense interest in surgery, which appeared to me the most effective way of curing the sick. Nothing can make me forget the awe with which I watched the first operation; it was being performed on a patient with a perforated ulcer; while he was asleep his stomach was being repaired, just as if a hole in a stocking was being darned. The opening of the abdomen appealed to me as being dramatic, especially when the entire stomach was pulled out with hot towels and held up by an assistant for stitching. Sir Thomas Myles was working with the ease and dexterity of a needle-woman, stitching and inverting the area where the ulcer had been. This done, he replaced the stomach and quickly stitched up the abdominal muscles and skin. The result was sufficiently encouraging, for that patient was up and well in three weeks' time, and extremely grateful. Every operation that I saw, or helped at, increased my interest in surgery . . .

Sir Thomas Myles, of whom I was now to see a great deal, was a man of great stature, with massive shoulders and determined features, and at this time must have been about sixty-eight years of age. Those who attended at the Richmond Hospital, Dublin, where he was senior surgeon, have every reason to bless his skilful teaching. Born in Limerick, he had no adventitious aids in the career in which he was to climb to the top. A great yachtsman, with several beautiful craft under his command, he had sailed perhaps more than any other Irishman in the waters of the United Kingdom. His last ship, the *Harbinger*, was the finest of her class afloat. I treasured the days that I spent with him, both when he was tending the sick, with his cheerful Irish smile, and when he was at the wheel of his seventy-ton ketch, *Sheila*, as she came up-channel with the square sails set and the spray covering his sou'wester. Often we went together to ringside seats for big fights, and he was at the London Stadium Club to watch me win my second British title. If asked his nationality, he would say he was a poor man used to hardships to which Irishmen are born. He was a devout son of the Church of England, but, if asked his religion, he would say that he was a poor sinner. Very many must be the doctors and students and patients, of every class and condition, who have sorrowed for his passing, and will agree with me that we shall not easily see his like again.

Medicine was by no means my only interest. Indeed, boxing ran it very close. Big, cold and funereally gloomy as the gymnasium was then, nothing could keep me from spending my evenings there. I think we may boast that in the Trinity College gymnasium we laid the foundations of Irish amateur boxing, which has since made such enormous headway and today produces some of the most famous amateur fighters in the world . . .

It was in 1924, when I was still studying anatomy and physiology, that my first contest in the ring took place. This was in a novices' competition held in the gymnasium, but, in spite of that fact, it proved one of the hardest I have ever fought. My opponent was Bertie Cussen, a brother of a famous Irish runner and rugby international, and was himself an athlete of no little distinction. We had to fight on the floor, as the club did not possess its present ring until I persuaded the Board to erect it in 1927.

At the start I kept out of harm's way, with my left jabbing my opponent's jaw, while he rushed in with deadly blows at my chest and stomach. A formidable right drove me to the ropes, and this was followed by a cracking blow to the face, which was taken by my glove, as I had by then learnt the art of defence, which has since carried me through over fifty contests without suffering any facial disfigurement. Now, in my turn, I opened fire, and with fast lefts I damaged my opponent's nose. The sight of the freely flowing blood served to spur me on, and by the time the gong went I could see that some of my blows had taken effect. In the second round I found I had gained confidence and was really enjoying myself. In his wild rushes he missed some beautiful swings which had been aimed to knock me out. My parrying blows I sent as often as possible at the already damaged nose. A particularly fierce rush I stopped with my left, and followed it with a straight right to the jaw which sent him to the floor. What a thrill! My first encounter; my opponent inert on the ground and the crowd behind in an uproar.

But at the count of seven he was on his feet, and, after the manner of Limerick men, came rushing at me with tell-tale swings aimed at the stomach, so that things did not seem altogether pleasant, and I was not sorry when the gong went.

In the third and last round we started in truly and desperately to knock each other out. My eye began to swell, and blood was again pouring from my opponent's nose, greatly to the joy of the spectators, who greeted with wild applause the spectacle of a Dublin man murdering one from Limerick. A left punch which would have knocked over a bull brought me sagging to my knees, but only for a count of two, and I was soon able to force him back helpless on to the ropes. The undergraduates were losing their heads in their excitement, and such was the din that it was almost impossible to hear the referee. But there was no knock-out before the bell clanged. The judges disagreed, and the referee decided we must fight another round. My opponent's rushes I countered with uppercuts to the jaw, which stemmed his enthusiasm. I had him on the ropes, a sorry sight, but was myself exhausted. After cracks, swings and much in-fighting, I was able to get in a right swing which sent him back helplessly to the ropes, where he lay when the bell went, with myself lying utterly exhausted on top of him. Right proud was I when I was announced the winner.

From *The Fighting Irish Doctor (An Autobiography)*, Morris & Co., *circa* 1930s

Mick Mackey
Donncha Ó Dúlaing

The first hurler I ever heard of was Mick Mackey. His was the name, loved by Limerick and feared and respected by all others in the days of my early boyhood in Doneraile.

All of us who as children hurled imaginary All-Irelands in our back gardens created our own mythology. A good goalkeeper became Paddy Scanlan, a back was always Batt Thornhill, the only barber in Buttevant, and a forward was always Mick Mackey . . .

In 1979, that splendid GAA Club, Na Piarsaigh, invited me to Caherdavin in Limerick to present medals to their young heroes of that year. I was delighted. There I met Seamus Ó Ceallaigh, the doyen of Limerick GAA historians, who whispered conspiratorially into my ear: 'He's outside. Mick is here. He'd like to meet you.' I was stunned. And Mick Mackey was there. He sat quietly and modestly in a corner. Without preamble he said quietly, as if we were continuing a conversation, 'I'm sorry I missed you that night in Castleconnell. My wife Kitty says if you're ever passing Ardnacrusha, drop in to see us.' I didn't know what to say. 'What can I do for you?' he asked, and then added, like the humble man he was, 'Maybe what I have to say wouldn't interest you!' I switched on the tape-recorder.

DONNCHA: When did you first play for an actual team?

MICK: 1928. I played with the Ahane junior team in 1928.

DONNCHA: In what position?

MICK: Right-half-forward. We won the championship. That was the first championship that Ahane won. It wasn't played until 1929. The final was played in Adare against Feenagh-Kilmeedy. We had a great following. We always took three or four buses. That was the beginning for Ahane. We had to play intermediate hurling the next year and we went senior in 1930.

DONNCHA: When did you first play on a Limerick team?

MICK: I was a sub in 1929 against Cork in the League. I made the Limerick junior team in 1930 and we drew with Tipperary in Clonmel. We came back here to Limerick for the replay and they beat us — Tipp won three All-Irelands that year, minor, junior and senior.

DONNCHA: Even with all that and Cork's victory in 1931, Limerick were really about to come into their own.

MICK: They were, and even in 1931, they gave Tipperary a good match in the Championship, in Cork. I really came on the senior team in 1932.

DONNCHA: That must have been a good year for you.

MICK: Well, '32 was fairly good. We were beaten by Cork. We were somewhat unlucky and fairly green. We had a few great veterans, but most of us were too young, too green. However, the next year we were a different team. We weren't green anymore. We got to the final against Kilkenny.

Then we had a great run, a terrific run. We improved and we went into the final again the next year, in 1934, when we played a draw with a fine Dublin team. We played the replay very late in October. We beat them. It was very tight. My brother John played on my right. Timmy Ryan was the captain. By the way, Jim Barry of Cork trained us for the replay. We beat Dublin 5-2 to 2-6. It was one of the greatest days in my life.

We swept through Munster in 1935. There was no one to hold us. But the final — well bad weather and a single point by Kilkenny beat us that day.

We went to America in 1936 in the month of May and everyone said, When they come back, they'll beat no one! We came and nothing could stop us! As a matter of fact, I believe that the 1936 men were as good a team as ever wore the green and white of Limerick.

Donncha: Which of the players do you remember?

Mick: All of them. I was privileged to be captain and to be with the greatest bunch of hurlers that ever went out from any county. Every one of them was a star, from the goalie to the left-full-forward. If I had a bad day, the fellow longside me was twice as good. That was how it worked. There was a tremendous comradeship. There was a great spirit and they were all strong fellows. There was no codding about them!

Donncha: They were hard hurlers?

Mick: They could play it any way you liked. If you wanted it nice, they could be nice, but, I'll tell you, they could be ruthless too. No one could mess that Limerick team around. They were a great team. 'Tis hard to name them all, but I love them all, I remember them. (*At this, Mick paused and there were tears in his eyes as he struggled with memory and emotion.*) You could say that in all the positions we had stars.

We gave Kilkenny a bad beating, really. Some said 'twas a bad All-Ireland, but not for us! No one could live with us that day. I'll never forget that team.

Donncha: When you look back over all the years, which, Mick, was your greatest game?

Mick: I think the best match I played was in Thurles in 1935 against Cork. Clohessy had been sent to the line after fifteen minutes and we had only fourteen men when we beat them. That was my best individually. As we were a man short, I played like two men between centre-field and centre-forward.

Donncha: Did you have any special training methods?

Mick: No. But we had a great trainer called Peter Brown. He was a great physical man. We trained very hard.

Donncha: People always talk about you and your skill as a solo runner. Was this a style, a skill that you cultivated?

Mick: I suppose they do. It really all began accidentally. I never planned it. It started in a Railway Cup match. Dan Canniffe was centre-half-back for Leinster, and I swerved around him at one stage in the game, saw an opening and started to run with the ball on my hurley. Nowadays they run with the ball resting on the stick, but I always ran hopping it on a hurley, which made it more difficult to control. I ran about thirty yards and when I threw up the ball to hit it, Peter Blanchfield of Kilkenny, who was left-full-back for Leinster, hit it for me! He sent it back up the field. That was my first real solo-run! And 'twas no success!

After that, I got into the habit of it. Whether it was good or bad, I can't say. You see, it was great if you scored, but if you didn't 'twas gone back over your head again and the loose opponent had it. There is no point in going on a solo-run unless you are going to score at the end of it!

DONNCHA: Was there any particular time in a game when you would go on a solo-run?

MICK: Well, you see, if things were going against you, that was the time to break through and score a point after a solo-run. That was a great boost to the rest of the lads.

DONNCHA: I suppose, too, that you were what people called 'a marked man'.

MICK: Oh no, not at all. At that time it was man marking man, very close and very tough. If you weren't good enough or strong enough, you had no business playing the game of hurling. Centre-forward now, where I played, that's a very hard place, the hardest place on the team.

DONNCHA: Why do you say that?

MICK: Well, you see, if you beat the centre-half, the other half-backs would not be too far away. More often than not, the centre-forward has two and maybe three men to cope with. At my time 'twas vital, because say with Scanlan pucking out, he'd drive it well past centre field and every ball would drop in my area. You'd be murdered from him, he was that good! He was so good, God forgive me, you'd pray he'd miss it now and again! But he never did.

DONNCHA: If you had life over again, would you go hurling?

MICK: I would indeed. I look back at all the fine people I've met. I'd have met no one if I hadn't gone hurling. I had four trips to America. I had a great life in hurling. I was lucky. Any of the other lads in our team would have been entitled to as much as I got. They were all stars. I was really only one-fifteenth of a team, like anyone else.

DONNCHA: Which medal do you cherish most?

MICK: The medal I cherish most, I haven't got. It was the 1934 Championship Jubilee Year. It was my first medal and I treasured it, but I gave it away to a great friend of mine in New York.

DONNCHA: I suppose, inevitably, we must talk of other famous players. Did Christy Ring impress you?

MICK: Oh yes. He was fierce dangerous. I played at least four years with him on Railway Cup teams. Jack Lynch, Jim Young, Paddy Donovan, John Quirke and Billy Murphy, I played with all of them. They were fantastic.

But we can't forget the Kilkenny fellows. I remember Peter Reilly and Eddie Doyle in the early days and, of course, the great Paddy Phelan. He was an attacking player, who often marked my brother John. Where would you leave Lory Meagher and Jimmy Walshe of Carrickshock, the 'Yank' Dunne and Mattie Power? They were comrades, great gentlemen. I don't think there was ever a strong word between Kilkenny and ourselves. It was hurling all the time.

The match I most enjoyed was when we beat Kilkenny at the end of April in 1935. It was an exhibition. Never more than two points between us. The score was 2-6 to 2-4 at the end. There were 25,000 spectators at it. You always know you're beaten when the crowd starts to leave — if you're in front you have won, if you're behind, you have lost. No one stirred that day. We were level with minutes to go and I scored a point and John scored another. I was never as glad to hear a final whistle blow. Winning in Kilkenny was it!

Biography

Mick Mackey was born on 12 July 1912 into a well-known Limerick hurling family from Castleconnell. He was one of the outstanding hurlers of the thirties, as shown by his playing record. He won All-Ireland medals in 1934, 1936 and 1940, and was captain of the Limerick team when he won the two last. He won fifteen hurling championships, five Munster championships and eight Railway Cup medals, as well as National League medals. He received the Texaco Hall of Fame award and the Bank of Ireland 'All-time Great' award.

He was noted for his great skill and physical strength. Jack Lynch of Cork said, 'Mick Mackey could go through a stone wall.' A prolific scorer and an inspiring leader, his best position was centre-forward.

He is credited with introducing the solo-run with the ball on the stick. However, an English traveller in Ireland in the seventeenth century, one John Dunton, describing a hurling match, wrote, 'On this broad part (of the stick), you may sometimes see one of the gamesters carry the ball, tossing it forty or fifty yards in spite of all the adverse players; and when he is like to lose it, he generally gives it a great stroke to drive it towards the goal.' It looks, then, as though Mick Mackey, an instinctive hurler, revived a technique which had fallen out of use, rather than introducing something entirely new.

Hurling is acclaimed as the fastest field game in the world. A distinctively Irish sport, it dates back to prehistoric Ireland and the heroic deeds of Cuchulainn who won victory single-handed with his bronze hurley against three fifties of the boy-troops of Ulster.

The colonists took to hurling after the Norman invasion, and in alarm at this yielding to native ways, their overlords banned hurling by the Statutes of Kilkenny in 1366. This edict seems to have had little effect, for it was found necessary to ban the game again by the Statutes of Galway in 1527.

When asked his opinion of the standard of hurling in his later days, Mick Mackey said, 'Hurling is too timid nowadays, and players do not practise enough. In my young days we practised every evening and Sunday morning, but then we had nothing else to do. There are too many distractions today.'

It is not strange that Mick Mackey became such a great hurler, coming as he did from a hurling family and a county steeped in hurling tradition. (Few counties shine at both football and hurling. A Kerry footballer once contemptuously described Kerry hurling as 'compulsory tillage'.) When hurling fans meet, the argument goes on: which was the best player ever, Mick Mackey or Christy Ring, a question difficult to decide as they reached their peak in different decades.

Mick Mackey spent his entire working life with the ESB at Ardnacrusha, first as a driver and then as supervisor, save for the years of World War II, when he served in the army. He became a coach and selector for Limerick after he retired from the playing field. He died on 13 September 1982 at the age of seventy.

From *Voices of Ireland*, O'Brien Press, 1984

Tom Clifford
Karl Johnston

The start of rugby in Limerick was slow enough. In 1867–68 Sir Charles Barrington of the family whose name is still indelibly linked with the city, was captain of Dublin University FC, founded in 1854 and generally regarded as the club where the game had its genesis in Ireland. He is acknowledged to have been one of the first to introduce the emergent game to the city, where the first club to be established was Limerick County, in 1876, Rathkeale (in west County Limerick) having two years earlier been represented at a meeting of what was then the Irish Football Union.

By the early 1880s the game was beginning to gain a foothold, and by 1886 Munster's premier competition, the Senior Cup, had begun. The Garryowen club was founded in 1884, and won the Munster Senior Cup for the first time in 1889, and retained it for the following six years. Garryowen is Limerick's oldest senior club. Shannon RFC also dates from 1884, but did not gain senior status until the season 1953/54. Of the other three Limerick clubs, Young Munster takes seniority, dating its foundation to 1895; Bohemians came into being in 1922; and Old Crescent in 1947 (being accorded senior ranking five years later) . . .

After the Second World War came a notable Limerick breakthrough. The Third Wallabies toured Britain and Ireland in 1947/48, under the captaincy of Bill McLean, and played matches against both Ireland and Munster. On 6 December, 1947, the tourists defeated Ireland by 16-3 at Lansdowne Road, a game in which Paddy Reid of Garryowen made his international debut, to become the first Limerick man to play against Australia. Reid, a centre, was a gifted player, who the next year went on to share in Ireland's first Triple Crown win since 1899 and the only Grand Slam ever achieved by the country.

Three days later, at the Mardyke in Cork, Reid was one of six Limerick players in a Munster team which came within a whisker of succeeding where Ireland had failed; the others were his Garryowen clubmates Jackie Staunton, Hugh de Lacy, Con Roche and his cousin Tom Reid, as well as Tom Clifford, the mighty prop from the Young Munster Club. That day Australia scored two tries to one to win 6-5 (the try then being worth three points), but only a late rally, when one of their forwards, P. A. Hardcastle, forced his way for the winning score, saved them. Earlier, wing J. W. T. McBride had scored the tourists' first try. But in between those scores Reid, as if celebrating his call to Ireland's colours three days earlier, scored a try for Munster and converted it himself. Munster seemed headed for a famous victory until Hardcastle's late, match-winning effort . . .

Tom Clifford became a living rugby legend in Limerick. Like Paddy Reid, he shared in an Irish Triple Crown victory, his turn coming in 1949 when Karl Mullen led the team to a second consecutive success, an achievement yet to be equalled. Mullen had the honour of leading the first post-War Lions in New Zealand and Australia, and to Clifford went the distinction of being the first Limerick Lion as he was chosen among the band of nine Irish players in the party.

By modern standards it was a very long tour; the party travelled by ship, and were away from home for nearly six months. Clifford loved every minute of it and had an excellent tour, playing in five of the six Tests, missing only the fourth in New Zealand. Thus, he played twice against Australia for the Lions — at Brisbane on 19th August, 1950, where the tourists won by 19-6, and at Sydney a week later on 26th August. This time the Lions won by 24-3; the five tries scored by the Lions that day still stands as their record number in an international game. Australian press reports of the day paid notable tributes to Clifford.

He was described as 'the virile Clifford' in a report of the Lions' victory (22-6) over New South Wales. A report of the Brisbane Test said: 'All the forwards played particularly well, and the best were Stephens (Rhys Stephens of Neath and Wales) and Clifford.' Another press report stated: 'there were few better men than the captain Karl Mullen, Doug Hayward, John Robins and Tom Clifford'. Yet another journalistic testimonial said: 'Tom Clifford proved himself a tremendous scrummager, with a rare ability for going through from a line-out. He fitted in perfectly with his hooker and was one of those iron men who could keep going hammer-and-tongs, from start to finish in the most gruelling of encounters. He and John Robins were the best props in the tourists' team.'

And a letter to the Limerick Weekly Echo from a compatriot also sang Clifford's praises. John McMahon, of Pondage, Via Upper Mount Beauty, Kiewa Valley, Victoria, and formerly of 4 Upper Catherine Street, Limerick wrote: ' . . . our old friend Tom Clifford of Young Munster fame caused quite a stir in rugby circles with his terrific touch-finding and kicking, also with his tough forward play. The first game between the Aussies and the British Isles took place in Brisbane. It was a very hard and tough forward battle and the brave Tom was in his element.

Evidently, he likes it like that. It was a grand sight for myself and a couple of Limerick friends . . . '

From *The Old Limerick Journal*, Australian Edition, No. 23, Spring 1988

Limerick Races
Sam Collins

I'm a simple Irish lad, I've resolved to see some fun, sirs,
So to satisfy my mind to Limerick town I came sir;
Oh, murther! what a precious place, and what a charming city,
Where the boys are all so free, and the girls are all so pretty.

It was on the first of May, when I began my rambles,
When everything was there, both jaunting cars and gambols;
I look'd along the road, what was lined with smiling faces,
And driving off ding-dong, to go and see the races.

So then I was resolved to go and see the race, sirs,
And on a coach and four I nately took my place, sirs,
When a chap bawls out behind and the coachman dealt a blow, sirs,
Faith, he hit me just as fair as if his eyes were in his poll, sirs.

So then I had to walk, and make no great delay, sirs,
Until I reached the course, where everything was gay, sirs,
It's then I spied a wooden house, and in the upper story,
The band struck up a tune, called Garryowen and Glory.

There was fiddlers playing jigs, there was lads and lasses dancing,
And the chaps upon their nags, round the course they were prancing,
Some was drinking whisky punch, while others bawled out gaily,
Hurrah, then for the shamrock green, and the splinter of shillelagh.

There was betters to and fro, to see who would win the race, sirs,
And one of the sporting chaps, of course came up to me, sirs,
Says he, 'I'll bet you fifty pounds, and I'll put it down this minute,'
'Ah, then, ten to one,' says I, 'the foremost horse will win it.'

When the players came to town, and a fancy set was they, sirs,
I paid my two thirteens, to go and see the play, sirs,
They acted kings and cobblers, queens and all so gaily,
But I found myself at home, when they struck up 'Paddy Carey'.

From *The Old Limerick Journal*, No. 17, Winter 1984

J. P. McManus
Raymond Smith

J. P. McManus, the man to whom they gave the name 'The Sundance Kid' in the seventies because of his awesome tilts at the ring, especially at Cheltenham, has on his own admission 'grown older' but that does not mean that the legend has diminished in any way. He is now more selective. The recklessness that marked his betting in his twenties is a thing of the past . . .

However, he prefers nowadays, if he can manage it, to avoid centre stage when planning and executing a stroke.

'What is the best stroke in racing?' is the rhetorical question he poses across the table . . .

'The best stroke is the one that no one knows anything about,' he asserts. 'It's not a properly organised coup if the whole world knows about it, and of course, you may need to use it again.

'I like to think I am now more controlled and have a better chance of surviving, as a result of the learning process that has extended over the past twenty years,' he went on . . .

He constantly keeps before him the piece of advice he got from an old English bookmaker friend some years back: 'Beware of the certainty.' A piece of advice this, he emphasises, that has saved him a lot of money . . .

'I went broke twice as a bookie shortly after I started and had to return home. The second time I went back, my mother lent me a few hundred pounds. I told her "if I take it and Father gets to know about it, he won't be too pleased," as the last thing he had wanted me to do was to become a bookmaker. She replied "he won't know a thing about it." So I took the money and I suppose I had more respect for it than for any money I ever had before or since in my pocket. Strangely enough, I have never been skint again. Granted, I was often very, very, short of money but there is a world of difference between having just a little in your pocket and being flat broke with nowhere to turn . . . Once you have been skint in life and come through it, you come to respect money and you certainly never want to be flat broke again.' . . .

'I consider myself a professional gambler whether I am punting or making a book,' he went on to explain, 'but I am not an addictive gambler. If I didn't have a bet at a particular race meeting, it wouldn't bother me. Gambling is a state of mind. The gambler who doesn't operate to strict ground rules, and who chases his losses and cannot shut up shop when his tank for the day is gone, is like an alcoholic who cannot control his drinking. Only that the gambler can destroy his whole life in a half a day while it can take years to destroy your life with drink.' . . .

The most successful punters, he contends, are those who believe in the form book and know how to interpret form. They are not swayed by tips from owners, jockeys, trainers or connections . . .

He also emphasised that he tends to think more of the future than the past. 'You can't alter the past. It's done with, finished. Even when I lose at gambling I stick to the principle that it is no use dwelling on it. You must look ahead to the next day and the next battle.'

From *The High Rollers of the Turf*, Sporting Books Publishers, 1992

The Defeat of the All-Blacks
John Scally

As dawn broke on Tuesday, 31 October 1978, the Irish sporting public had no idea of the momentous events that lay in store for them on that day. The build-up to the match between Munster and the All-Blacks had been overshadowed with forecasts of doom and gloom. The reasons for these dire predictions were twofold. The tourists had gone through the best of the Welsh and the English sides, like a knife through butter. The rugby cognoscenti on both sides of the Channel confidently proclaimed: 'They will go through the tour unbeaten.' For their part the Munster side had flopped dismally on their pre-season tour of London. It would be like sending lambs to the slaughter . . .

The day before the game was a bank holiday Monday and while a thousand people or more had watched the final All-Blacks preparation, only a handful had bothered to watch Munster train at St Munchin's College. Throughout the rugby world the general belief was that Munster would do well to hold the tourists to a ten point winning margin. Tony Ward attributes great significance to the day before the match:

'On the afternoon before we played the All-Blacks we went to Lough Derg . . . It must have been a strange sight but three boatloads of Munster rugby players descended on one of Ireland's quietest lakes and we were anything but quiet. Buckets of water and duckings were the order of the afternoon and, as they say, the craic was mighty . . .

'Something happened that afternoon that transformed a group of interprovincial players into a group of blood brothers almost with one common aim — the destruction of the mighty All-Blacks.' . . .

The Clare hills provided a scenic background for the New Zealanders as they performed their traditional 'haka' before the game. Somewhat against the run of play Munster took the lead in the 11th minute — a delicate chip from Ward was followed through and won by Jimmy Bowen, who made an incisive run and as he was caught from behind, he fed Christy Cantillon, who crossed the line beside the posts. The great surging roar from the crowd could be heard for miles around. Ward kicked the conversion with ease.

In the 17th minute the tourists were penalised for indiscriminate use of the boot. Ward's penalty attempt fell five metres short but was knocked on by Brian McKechie. From the ensuing scrum Donal Canniffe fed Ward and he dropped a goal.

The home side hung on to their 9-0 lead until half time but realised that a modern day siege of Limerick awaited them in the second half when the men from down under would do all in their formidable power to protect their unbeaten record. Their fears were justified as the All-Blacks exerted enormous pressure. Metaphorically, and literally, the tourists did not know what hit them as they were stopped in their tracks with a series of crunching tackles by such players as Seamus Dennison, Greg Barrett and most notably Colm Tucker. Jack Gleeson, the All-Blacks' manager, subsequently described them as 'Kamikaze tacklers'.

As the seconds ticked by agonisingly slowly in the second half the crowd became more and more frenzied, sensing that here lay history in the making. 'M-U-N-S-T-E-R! M-U-N-S-T-E-R!' rang out at deafening sound levels. Ward got the only score in the second half — a drop goal — and Munster held on to become the first side to beat the touring All-Blacks. Russ Thomas, the tourists' coach, generously saluted 'fifteen great players'. It was an extraordinary team performance.

The Munster team that day was: L. Moloney (Garryowen); M. Finn (UCC); S. Dennison (Garryowen); G. Barrett (Cork Constitution); J. Bowen (Cork Con); T. Ward (Garryowen/St Mary's); D. Canniffe (Lansdowne); captain; G. McLoughlin (Shannon); P. Whelan (Garryowen); L. White (London-Irish); M. Keane (Lansdowne); B. Foley (Shannon); C. Cantillon (Cork Con); D. Spring (Dublin University); C. Tucker (Shannon) . . .

Although Ward could not have foreseen at the time the moments of deep despair that would cloud his career, the memory of that feeling of exhilaration will linger forever.

'There is something special about putting on the red Munster jersey, and beating the All-Blacks was an historic achievement. Nobody who played that day will ever forget the feeling. The All-Blacks were god-like figures, with a reputation for invincibility. The atmosphere that day in Thomond Park was incredible. We had won convincingly and left the pitch in a state of bliss. However, the crowd demanded that we come out again. It was the only time that I've witnessed a sporting occasion when all around people were crying. To be able to say you were there was great, but to have been at the centre of the action was just fantastic.' . . .

The only biblical story which appears in all four gospels is that of the loaves and fishes. Munster's victory over the All-Blacks has spawned a similar miracle. Although official attendance at the match was only 12,000 — since then hundreds of thousands of people have said, often with the benefits of generous liquid refreshment: 'I was there the day Munster beat the All-Blacks.'

From *The Good, the Bad and the Rugby: The Official Biography of Tony Ward*, Blackwater Press, 1993

Game of the People
Mick Doyle

Officially the Insurance Corporation All Ireland League, in reality the Limerick City Championship. And yesterday at Dooradoyle you could see why, as pride and passion, the bedrocks of the game in a city that loves its rugby, were so much in evidence. Munsters were something else.

Yesterday said much about Irish rugby and where the power base has moved. Garryowen from Limerick playing Young Munster from Limerick for the AIL Division One title; Shannon from Limerick awaiting the outcome in Cork; Old Crescent from Limerick enjoying it all, knowing they would be mixing with the big boys next season . . .

It is a disquieting thought for the sport to realise that if all four Limerick teams had a home game on the same day, there would still be more supporters at each game than at any other clash in the metropolis . . . or anywhere else for that matter. Can you envisage an All Ireland League without Garryowen, Shannon, Young Munster, Constitution and now Old Crescent? Apart from St Mary's, what other Dublin side could realistically and consistently compete with a Limerick club? . . .

At the inception of the league, it was anticipated that Ulster rugby would prevail and that Limerick clubs would have a problem because of the perceived lack of serious back play. It was true then that Limerick clubs were more renowned for the strength and ferocity of their forwards, with Thomond Park the torture-chamber and graveyard of visitors . . .

When the League became a reality Limerick's top three clubs and Cork Con took up the challenge. Back play in Limerick took on a new dimension and it is now fair to say that each Limerick team is a more balanced fifteen-man side, capable of playing tight or open rugby, than most, if not all, Irish clubs . . .

While rugby in the rest of Ireland is a middle class game, in general, Limerick has a classless game: it is the game of Limerick City's men and women. You will see more women and more teenage boys at, say, Thomond Park than anywhere else . . .

The supporters in Limerick are different. It being their game, rugby is forever on the agenda, always the first, middle and last conversation piece. There is no crowd more knowledgeable about every phase of the game, more supportive of their team . . .

Gutsy play and good rugby receive appropriate recognition and approval . . . In this most competitive of cities, competitiveness counts; no game is over until it's over, as has been epitomised by Garryowen even this season . . .

Appreciation of the game's basic points is more acute. The ability to assess a player and deactivate mythology is a pastime, in which men, women and the younger generation excel . . .

The acute rivalry is, of course, a huge spur in a smallish city where everybody virtually knows everybody else. The AIL woke up Limerick. From the sleepy town of the 60s when some forlorn American described it as 'the only graveyard he ever visited that had buses running through it', Limerick bestirred itself and their clubs, noted and famed and feared on their home grounds, girded their loins, organised their sponsors and developed their teams to travel all over Ireland to conquer . . .

Unlike anywhere else, rugby in Limerick is about communities. Every player, no matter how exalted he may become in the game, knows exactly what door, in which street and from what area he came — and never forgets it. The bonds that exist between players and clubs are almost unbreakable, describing succinctly the unity of purpose and the common will of teams and supporters.

Matches against any Limerick team, home or away, are never an equal contest. It is never a case of 15 against 15; you must also play against the supporters. Anybody who was at Lansdowne Road last April when Young Munster had to put 30 points clear on Lansdowne to remain in Division 1 will never forget the unitary purpose and intent that bonded the team on the pitch with the supporters on the terraces as each spurred the other on to greater effort. 'Munsters' naturally scored their points and, in the process, destroyed Lansdowne.

Crescent, both the college and the club, had for so long been the nursery to the other three clubs. Mungret, Munchin's, Glenstal and Rockwell contributed their share also. Now Crescent join the big league and, in retaining its players, will certainly pressurise Young Munster, Shannon and Garryowen. Can you guess the response? . . .

Rugby is the Limerickman's game — like it used to be in Wales. This is reflected nowhere else in Ireland . . .

It was fitting that the final act of this year's league was played in Limerick and decided by the three Limerick clubs who have taken on all-comers and won . . .

Up Limerick! You're a lady with a difference.

From the *Sunday Independent*, 28 April 1996

SEVEN

HISTORY

Lough Gur: The First Inhabitants
M. J. and C. O'Kelly

The area around Lough Gur is famous for the number and variety of its field monuments which range in date from the neolithic (new stone age) up to medieval times. Numerous objects dating from these periods have been picked up in the past around the shores of the lake and its environs and are now in various museums in Ireland and elsewhere. Indeed it is true to say that there is scarcely a museum or a private collection in these islands which does not contain one or more of them. Visitors to the British Museum will see many an object with the Lough Gur label in the sections devoted to antiquities of the British Isles.

The antiquities were first brought to scientific attention by Sir Bertram Windle, former president of University College, Cork, and first professor of archaeology there. He made a survey of the monuments and designated them by letters of the alphabet (Windle 1912). Excavations began in 1936, conducted by the late Seán P. Ó Ríordáin, also professor of archaeology at University College, Cork. He worked at Lough Gur throughout most of the war years and spent a few seasons there after the war as well. His untimely death in 1957 was a serious blow not only for Irish archaeology, but for Lough Gur also, as many of his excavations were . . . unpublished.

He contributed a wealth of information and established not only the presence of beaker people at Lough Gur, c. 2000 BC, but also that the area was extensively inhabited in the neolithic period, c. 3000 BC. By reason of its rich pasturage, abundance of water and because of the animals, birds and fish which were readily available, it was eminently suitable for prehistoric man. Bones of mammals, such as the Giant Deer, which had become extinct in Ireland before the coming of man, have been found, as well as interesting flora of the period. Today, the lake is the haunt of many unusual species of birds and it has been declared a bird sanctuary . . .

Lough Gur is truly an 'antique land' and many visitors will be conscious of the aura of mystery and magic which pervades it, whether in the bad weather when the lake can become unbelievably wild and forbidding, or in the golden evenings of summer when one can almost believe that at any moment Gearóid, Earl of Desmond, will come cantering over the water on his milk-white horse with the silver shoes. The legend says that he must do so once every seven years until the shoes are worn out and that then he will be freed from the spell of Lough Gur. Not everyone, however, will wish to be released from this particular bondage. Those of us who worked there with the late Ó Ríordáin are still conscious of it and, like the earl, feel we must return again and again. Two of his students offer this booklet as a small tribute to their former professor, known to all as 'Seán P'.

* * * *

Lough Gur is a small lake set among limestone hills somewhat less than 20km from Limerick city and about 4km from the nearest town of Bruff. In early Irish literature it is called Loch Gair and its modern name is an anglicisation of this. The lake is roughly C-shaped, the rocky peninsula of Knockadoon (highest point c. 122m OD) is set within the arms of the 'C', the lake being to north, west, and south, and a marshy area to the east.

In the middle of the last century the level of the lake was lowered by drainage and its extent diminished, so that it is now 184 statute acres as compared with 232 before the drainage. The lake is fed mainly by a stream which rises through a crevice in the rock bottom between Knockfennell and Knockadoon and the original outflow is at the NE corner. After running along an open surface channel for a short distance, it disappears into a rock crevice called Pollawaddra. The stream emerges again beyond the NW side of Knockfennell. When Pollawaddra became blocked by floating debris, the lake level rose, falling again when water pressure forced a clearance. In the drainage scheme a surface channel was cut westward from the NW corner of the lake. This not only reduced the lake level by about 3m but now maintains it at a more or less constant level.

Two castles guarded the points of easiest access to Knockadoon, Bourchier's Castle at the north end of the marsh and the Black Castle at the south. At the time they were built, Knockadoon must have been virtually an island. At each end of the marsh there was a solid or nearly solid strip of land connecting with the hill and the castles were erected on these, converting the peninsula into a fairly secure fortress. A map of 1681 shows the lake completely surrounding Knockadoon and shows a fore-building and a drawbridge leading from Bourchier's across the lake to the mainland.

Throughout its long history the level of the lake must have altered many times, particularly having regard to the surrounding limestone terrain. Ó Ríordáin was of the opinion that in pre-historic times the level may have been even lower than at the present day. After the alteration in the lake level of a century ago numerous objects were picked up in and around its shores and in its immediate vicinity, e.g. in the marshy area. Among the finds were over 20 bronze axes, 12 bronze spearheads, two leafshaped swords, a rapier, three daggers and a halberd. A circular bronze shield, now in the National Museum of Ireland, is locally believed to have been found in the marsh. A gold-chased bronze spearhead, now in the British Museum, is regarded by some as a votive offering which was cast into the lake and this explanation is offered for many of the other finds also. Stone, flint and bone objects from the area are very numerous and at least 120 stone axes have been found. The excavations produced large quantities of prehistoric pottery as well as artifacts of later periods, so that, taken as a whole, Lough Gur is one of the richest sites in respect of artifacts in the country.

The number and variety of its field monuments are equally striking. More than 30 ancient sites and monuments can still be identified in the immediate neighbourhood of the lake and as many more may have been present originally, now either destroyed or still concealed in the ground. The identifiable sites consist of megalithic tombs, stone circles, hut sites, ancient fields and roads, standing stones, forts, crannogs (lake dwellings), caves and castles.

It is not so easy to identify the people who erected these monuments. The first settlers, who must have come about 3000 BC, are only known to us from their circular and rectangular houses on Knockadoon and from their domestic utensils, many of which were excellently made and which showed affinities with similar ware in the British Isles at the same period. At a somewhat later date, beaker ware made its appearance, again denoting contact with the British Isles and Europe. There does not appear to have been any hiatus between this stage and the earliest neolithic one so that settlement must have been continuous throughout the thousand or so years represented. The early bronze age remains consist in the main of the stone circles, perhaps also some of the standing stones, and new weapons and ornaments made their appearance. Perhaps by this time the lake had begun to be regarded as sacred and had become a focus of religious life. In the early iron age and in the early Christian period many of the forts and crannogs were erected.

In early historic times the chief people of the area were the Érainn, later to be superseded by a more powerful sept, the Eóganacht, who ruled Munster until the middle of the tenth century. The *Eóganacht Áine Cliach*, a branch of the parent sept, had their headquarters at Knockainey (**Cnoc Áine**) south-east of Lough Gur. Professor E. J. Byrne (1973) says of the Eóganacht that they probably came to power in the fifth century and that they owed their rapid rise to successful raids on Roman Britain and perhaps also to their early adoption of Christianity. Their mythological traditions seem to centre on Cnoc Áine and the goddess Áine herself and many legends are connected with the hill and its vicinity. Before the end of the tenth century the Eóganacht supremacy in Munster had passed away and the Dal Cais, of whom Brian Boru was the most distinguished member, were in the ascendant.

It is recorded in the Book of Rights (*Lebór na cert*) that Brian fortified sites at Lough Gur between 1002 and 1012 in order to protect the area from the Norse. Knockadoon was probably the place in question. After his death the Norse destroyed one of the reconditioned fortresses.

After the advent of the Anglo-Normans the area came into the possession of the Fitzgeralds, later to become earls of Desmond, and it is with them that the history of Lough Gur is bound up for the next 400 years. The two castles already mentioned were Desmond castles though the date of their erection is in some doubt. Some sources claim both castles as belonging to the thirteenth century but, while this may be true of the Black Castle, Bourchier's is a century or so later, perhaps a re-edification of an earlier castle, the likelihood being that a defensive structure of some kind or other must have been present at these two vital points as long as Knockadoon was in any danger from the outside world. At the height of their power the Desmonds were said to be the equal of any prince but finally they rebelled against the Queen and lost. Their leaders were killed or executed and the earl himself was proclaimed a traitor, his castles and great houses (of which he was said to have had at least 20) were taken one by one, and when the rebel force was reduced to a handful, he was tracked down and killed at Glenageenty in Co. Kerry in 1583. Munster was by this time a devastated land and the Desmond power was no more. Henceforth, confiscation and plantation were to be the order of the day, Lough Gur castle being granted to the Bourchier family.

Subsequently, the de Salis family became owners of Lough Gur and are remembered to the present day as benevolent landlords.

From *Illustrated Guide to Lough Gur, Co. Limerick*, Claire O'Kelly, 1978

The Norsemen
P. G. Meghen

From AD 500 to AD 800 there was a period of fairly peaceful conditions and in this time there was a big growth in Irish monastic centres . . .

Limerick took its part in this great movement and the monasteries of Mungret and Killeedy were major centres in those years. The fact that no remains of these buildings are now to be seen is sometimes a cause of surprise but the buildings of the time, even large churches and assembly halls, were of timber with boarded or thatched roofs. Naturally no portion of these could survive in the centuries of trouble that came after AD 850 . . .

The account of the monastery of Mungret at the greatest peak may well be believed. At this stage it was said to have six churches attached to the monastery and 1,500 monks in its cloister: of these one-third were preachers, one-third were constantly engaged in celebrating the Divine Office and the remaining third were employed in the schools or labouring for the community . . .

And although in this period there was no great development in stone building there was considerable development in artistic metal work. The Ardagh Chalice, one of Ireland's great treasures, was found in 1868 at Ardagh, County Limerick. It is generally considered to be eighth century work but shows that the skills were highly developed by this time . . .

These peaceful times must have also seen the development of agriculture, the extension of the area of tilled land and the making of roads. These peaceful times came to an end in AD 825 when the Viking raids into Limerick started. That the fame of the monastery of Mungret was known to them is obvious because it was the first place they attacked. Later the Vikings were defeated at Shanid in 834 by the army of Hy Fidhgente . . .

The first Viking settlement at Limerick was probably not unlike the Irish settlements of the same period. The outer defence was an earthen bank, with timber stockade, and inside rows of wooden houses. Here is Alice Stopford Green's view of it: ' "Limerick of the swift ships" looking out to the Atlantic and the Gaulish sea was a rival even to Dublin. The Norwegians first fortified this town by an earthen or wooden fence, but presently, by a wall of stone, "Limerick of the riveted stones" . . .

'United by kinship, the lords of the Isles and the lords of Limerick constantly aided one another and made joint expeditions. Once more the Gaulish trade was revived and vessels sailed out from the Shannon to fetch wine and silks from the harbours of the Loire and the Garonne . . . Thus it was that the Irish wrested some advantage out of the Danish wars. They profited by the material skill and knowledge of the invaders. They were willing to absorb the foreigners, to marry with them, and even at times to share their wars. They learned from them to build ships, organise naval forces, advance in trade and live in towns: they used Scandinavian words for the parts of a ship and the streets of a town.'

From *The Limerick Rural Survey 1958–1964*, edited by Rev. Jeremiah Newman, Muintir na Tíre Rural Publications, 1964

From: **Adare**
John Francis O'Donnell

The morn comes freshly from the East,
It strikes with fire the upland ridge,
And pours a shaft of gold between
The midmost shadows of the bridge,
Where late at eve shall dance the midge.
Flame fills the immemorial tree,
Which keeps its chestnuts for the time
When harvest banquets through the world,
And the hot breezes flow in rhyme.

Soft sleeps the village in the maze
Of dreamy elm and sycamore;

Soft slides the river's rosy tide
Through blossomed sedges by the shore,
Rushes, and pendent willows hoar.
The little boat moored in the cove
Takes no pulsation from the stream,
But shadowed on the water lies,
The lovely image of a dream.

I leave the village to its rest —
White walls with ivy diapered,
Brown roofs that in the Springtime give
Asylum to the happy bird,
Whose wing the southern air has stirred;
And wandering down the grassy marge
Of Maigue, amidst its Paradise,
Turn one green bend of lawn, and lo!
Three Hundred Years confront mine eyes.

Three Hundred Years in channelled stones,
Hewn in some quarry vast and fair,
But touched with melancholy gray —
That habit of our Irish air,
Which slays, but still knows when to spare.
Chancel, quadrangle, tower, are here;
Gaunt cloisters, roof and mullions riven;
With that clear interspace through which
Souls, tired of flesh, looked out to Heaven.

I see it all — the choir, the stalls,
The broad east window, smote with blood —
(Bright as six rainbows ribbonded) —
St Francis's brown-robed brotherhood,
Each with his crucifix of wood.
Slowly the instant pageant fades;
Ruin returns to leaf and stone;
A shadow rises from my brain,
And I am, with the sun, alone.

And who were these? By what access
Of patience did they find their way
To those cold penitential aisles
To stifle self, to bravely pray
Until their hairs grew scant and gray,

And some one plucked them by the sleeve
Some hour of interrupted breath?
They turned to find who touched them so,
And met the smiling face of Death.

They were not wasted hearts alone,
Craving forgiveness and the rod —
Whose hearts' best wine had spilled to earth,
And left the sediments to God;
They heard no outside world applaud.
Their daily boon companions were
The matin lark, the sunset rock;
And for excitement and repose,
The cloister, or the desk chained book.

* * * * *

Thus thought I, musing in Adare;
The little village slowly woke,
And from a heaven of purple cloud
The sun, a bright conclusion, broke
Clearly as if some prophet spoke.
O lark in either choiring loud
In that blue sanctuary's light!
Tell those I love in far-off streets
I shall see Limerick to-night.

From *Poems*, Ward and Downey, 1891

The Norman Settlement
P. G. Meghen

In 1168, Donal More O'Brien was recognised as King of Thomond . . . and cleared County Limerick of all opposition to his rule . . .

Nevertheless, the kingdom he built up did not survive. The Anglo-Norman invasion of Ireland started in 1169 and soon the invaders were driving south and west in search of new conquests. Donal More played a careful game. When Henry II visited the country in 1172, O'Brien sued for peace and became tributary to the

King whom he met at Cashel. But he soon changed his mind and in 1173, he is found attacking the Normans. In 1174, his army was victorious over Strongbow's army at Thurles. In 1175, his city of Limerick was captured by the Normans, but he recovered it the following year and held his kingdom until his death in 1194. There were many attempts to seize his territory. In 1177, Henry II granted the Kingdom of Limerick to Philip de Braose to be held for a service of sixty knights but the City of Limerick was reserved to the crown. But Limerick was too strongly held by O'Brien and de Braose never obtained possession. But Donal More thought it wiser to form alliances with the invaders and towards the end of his reign he gave his daughter in marriage to William de Burgo. De Burgo had been granted lands in east Limerick and Tipperary by John, Lord of Ireland, in 1185 and in 1194 after O'Brien's death, he was able to obtain possession of them. In fact, the Anglo-Normans seemed to have gained possession of most of the City and County of Limerick at this time. In 1197, Prince John granted Hamo de Valognes two cantreds of Connello in Limerick and this Hamo built a strong fortress in Askeaton. Hamo also granted lands in County Limerick to the first of the Geraldines, namely to Thomas son of Maurice Fitzgerald and Croom to Thomas's brother Gerald . . .

Fairly soon in the beginning of the thirteenth century, we begin to find mention of a county of Limerick. The formation of counties or shires was part of the Anglo-Norman scheme of conquest. When an area was conquered, the king granted to his feudal tenants certain lands which were to be held subject to certain rents and duties. To collect these rents and to see that orders were obeyed, a king's officer was appointed in each county. The appointment of this officer, the sheriff, was made each year and the holder of the office had to account for his receipts at the end of the year. It is thus possible to trace the beginning of county administration in Ireland. There is mention of a shire of Munster in 1210. The sheriff of Munster was returning his accounts until near 1254 at which year Limerick and Tipperary became separate units, with separate sheriffs. There is some difficulty in deciding how the boundary ran between these two counties in those years. Canon Burke states in his *History of Clonmel*: 'From the rolls therefore it appears that in the beginning of the thirteenth century the southern boundary of the county Tipperary was formed by the Suir as far as Cahir, and thence by the Galtees. East and north the boundaries were substantially as at present but westward the county included some three of the present baronies of Limerick and extended to within a few miles of that city.'

It is unlikely however that these areas remained long within the power of the Sheriff of Tipperary. Other later accounts seem to indicate that the County of Limerick soon included most of the diocese of Emly in which these areas stood. For about a hundred years from 1254, there are various mentions in the old records of the work of the Sheriffs of County Limerick and the visits of the king's justices to the area. Within the county, smaller administrative units known as cantreds were recognised and this framework was used for administration of the ordinary affairs.

From *The Limerick Rural Survey 1958–1964*, edited by Rev. Jeremiah Newman, Muintir na Tíre Rural Publications, 1964

The Name 'Limerick'
Larry Walsh

Much speculation has existed from early times as to the origin of the name of Limerick. The medieval Books of Lecan and Ballymote preserve a prehistoric legend describing the origin of the name: The men of Munster and Connaught met here for warlike sports, the king of each party bringing his champion. These were the two sons of Smucaille, son of Bacdbh, and their names were Rinn and Teabhar (i.e. Spear and Sword). Of these champions, one put himself under the protection of Bonhbh Dearg, the great Tuath De Danann chief of Magh Femen in Tipperary, and the other had taken the protection of Dehall, chief of the Hill of Cruachain in Roscommon. The champions eventually descended to the strand to compete in single combat for the championship of the two provinces. The crowds on both sides were dressed in grey-green cloaks (Luimne), and when the combat commenced and the crowds pressed down to see it, the heat became so great that they threw off their cloaks in heaps on the strand. So intensely was their attention engaged by the combatants that they did not notice the flowing of the tide until it had swept away the cloaks, upon which some of the spectators cried out 'Is Luimenochola in t-inbhear anossa' i.e. cloakful is the river now, hence the name Luimneach Liathghlas, Limerick of the Grey-Green.

Holinshed's *Irish Chronicle*, 1577, gives the following explanation: 'The town is planted in an Island, which plot, in old time, before the building of the city, was stored with grass. During which time it happened that one of the Irish potentates raising war against another of his peers, encamped in that Isle, having so great a troop of horsemen as the horses ate up the grass in 24 hours: whereupon for the notorious number of horses, the place is called Loum ne augh, that is, the horse bare, or a place made bare or eaten up by horses.'

Thomas Dineley, in the journal of his tour in Ireland in 1680, gives another explanation which was clearly current in the city at his time: 'Wherefore its name Limerick is said to take its Original from the Gelding's leap, being in the vulgar tongue Leame aneagh, in the proper character Leamh aneagh. Verbatim ye Leap of the Gelding, from a water which runs through the Town, part of the Shannon, where they have a persuasion that a Gelding made a leap over it, with a man mounted thereon; which word by corruption of time is speeched into Limerick.'

Maurice Lenihan, in a footnote to Dineley's *Journal*, published in the *Journal of the Royal Society of Antiquaries of Ireland*, Vol. 8, 1864–66, p. 425, quotes the interpretation of General Vallancey, the 18th century antiquarian, that the name derived from the Egyptian word 'Lemne', meaning a maritime port.

The official derivation given in the city guide translates it from Irish, meaning a bare or barren spot of land. This is based on P. W. Joyce's 'The Origin and History of Irish Names of Places', 4th edition, 1875, pages 49–50: 'The Irish name of Limerick is *Luimneach* [Liminegh: Book of Leinster &c.], which was originally applied to a portion of the river Shannon; as the following passage from an ancient poem on the death of St Cuimmin of Clonfert, quoted by the Four Masters at 561, will show:—

"The Luimneach did not bear on its bosom, of the race of Munster, into Leath Chuinn,
A corpse in a boat so precious as he Cummine son of Fiachna;"

and the modern name was derived from this, by a change of *n* to *r*, and by substituting *ck* for the guttural in the end.

'The root of the word is *lom*, bare, of which luimne is a diminutive form; and from this again was developed, by the addition of the adjective postfix *ach*, the full name *Luimneach*, which signifies a bare or barren spot of land, and which was applied to the place long before the foundation of the city.

'In connection with the name of Limerick, it may be remarked that *lom*, bare, is a usual component of local names. There is a place called Lumcloon near the village of Cloghan in King's County, which the Four Masters call *Lomchluain*, bare *cloon* or meadow . . .

'*Luimneach* itself is a name of frequent occurrence, but only in one other place is it anglicised Limerick, namely, in the parish of Kilcavan in Wexford. It takes the form Limnagh in Sligo; of Lumnagh near Ballyvourney in Cork; and of Luimnagh in Galway. Lomanagh, the name of some places in Kerry; Lomaunagh (-baun and -roe, whitish and reddish) in Galway; and Loumanagh in Cork, are slightly different in formation; but they have all the same meaning as *Luimneach*. The word is seen compounded in Cloonlumney in Mayo, and in Athlumney in Meath, the meadow and the ford, of the bare place.'

In Cogadh Gael re Gaill, the author of which was a contemporary of Brian Boru, and in the Book of Lismore, references to the name before AD 822 apply to the whole of the Shannon Estuary, and after the arrival of the Vikings, to the city.

Mainchín Seoighe, in his *Portrait of Limerick*, 1982, states that the name 'very likely comes from *Loimeanach*, meaning "Bare Marsh", a name that originally applied to part of the shoreland of the Shannon immediately below the present city.'

T. J. Westropp in 'Illustrated Guide to the City of Limerick', 1916, refers to Mr

Pryce Maunsell's view that the word is Norse Laemrich, rich land (loam), and this has been seized upon locally as an alternative to 'bare spot' in recent times since the popularisation of the Vikings by the Wood Quay excavations in Dublin. However, this fails to account for the earlier references to Luimneach as the name of the Shannon estuary, for the other places with the same or similar name in Irish, or for the recorded Norse form, Hlimrek.

Minutes of Limerick Corporation National Monuments Advisory Committee, 25 April 1986

The 1651 Siege
P. W. Joyce

Oliver Cromwell was appointed Lord Lieutenant and commander of the forces in Ireland, and landed at Dublin on the 14th August 1649, with 9,000 foot, 4,000 horse, a supply of military stores, and £20,000 in money, accompanied by his son-in-law Ireton as second in command. He issued a proclamation against plunder, ordering that all supplies taken from the natives should be paid for . . .

At the end of January 1650 he set out to traverse Munster. Most towns he came to were given up; and where there was serious resistance he usually executed the garrison. Kilkenny, where the plague was raging, was yielded in March . . .

After the surrender of Clonmel, Cromwell, seeing the country virtually subdued, sailed for England on the 29th May 1650, leaving Ireton to finish the war. In August Preston surrendered Waterford . . .

Limerick, the most important place in possession of the royalists, was next to be attacked. It was commanded by Hugh O'Neill, the defender of Clonmel. By forcing the passage of the Shannon at O'Brien's Bridge, Ireton got at the Clare side of the city, which was now invested on both sides. Meantime Lord Muskerry, coming from the south to its relief, was defeated by Lord Broghill, and his troops scattered.

O'Neill defended the city with great bravery; but there was disunion, and he was not supported by the magistrates; and the plague was raging among the citizens. At length colonel Fennell betrayed his trust by opening the gates to Ireton, who took possession on the 27th of October 1651. The garrison of 2,500 laid down their arms and were allowed to march away unmolested.

Ireton caused several of the prominent defenders to be executed, among them Dr O'Brien bishop of Emly; but he was himself killed by the plague within the same month. The traitor Fennell was hanged with the others, though for a different reason.

After Ireton's death, lieutenant-general Edmund Ludlow taking command, marched to the aid of Coote at Galway, which surrendered on the 12th May 1652, after a siege of nine months. The capture of a few detached castles completed the conquest of Ireland by the Parliamentarians.

Charles Fleetwood, Cromwell's son-in-law (he had married Ireton's widow) took command of the army in succession to Ludlow, and was afterwards appointed lord deputy. Under his direction a High Court of Justice was instituted in October 1652, to punish those who had been concerned in the rising of 1641; about 200 were sentenced and hanged, and among them Sir Phelim O'Neill.

From A Concise History of Ireland from the Earliest Times to 1837, M. H. Gill and Son, 1903

The Treaty of Limerick
Liam Irwin

The events in Limerick 300 years ago which form the basis for the Treaty 300 commemoration were a direct result of the 1688 Revolution in England. James II was forced to flee to France and his son-in-law and daughter, William and Mary, became joint rulers of his three kingdoms of England, Scotland and Ireland. The ensuing war in which James, with French help, tried to regain his thrones was conducted entirely in Ireland due to the support which Irish Catholics gave to the Jacobite cause. Irish Protestants sided with William, the acknowledged champion of Protestant Europe. This War of the Two Kings also had an important European dimension arising from the Grand Alliance which William had formed with Austria and the Holy Roman Empire against the expansionist policy of France. The outcome of the war in Ireland was of importance to all the major powers in Europe with many of the catholic states and the papacy sympathetic to William rather than the catholic James, because of their resentment to French policies under Louis XIV.

William landed in Ireland in June 1690 and inflicted a decisive defeat on James at the Battle of the Boyne in July. This battle, the most famous in Irish history, is still celebrated on the twelfth of July each year by Ulster Protestants as the basis of their political and religious liberty. After his defeat James returned to France leaving his Irish and French allies in disarray. The Jacobite forces retreated to Limerick where deep divisions arose on whether the war should be continued or a negotiated settlement sought. After much acrimonious debate the view of the flamboyant cavalry commander, Patrick Sarsfield, prevailed and it was decided to defend Limerick. Grave reservations were expressed about the ability of the city to withstand a siege most notably by the French commander, Lauzan, who felt that its old and decayed walls could be knocked down 'with roasted apples'. William and his army set up camp on Singland Hill, half a mile outside the city in early August. His forces then advanced along the marshy ground towards the south-east corner of the Irishtown walls near the present day St John's Hospital. The heavy guns required for a siege together with ammunition and supplies, were proceeding slowly from Dublin to Limerick and had reached Ballyneety, fourteen miles south-east of the city on August 11th. Patrick Sarsfield in a daring manoeuvre decided to intercept the siege train. Taking a force of cavalry and dragoons and guided by a famous rapparee, Galloping Hogan, Sarsfield crossed the Shannon at Killaloe, followed an old road through the Silvermines and arrived undetected at the spot where the Williamite cavalcade was camped for the night. Having discovered that the password was his own name, he reputedly launched the attack by proclaiming 'Sarsfield is the word and Sarsfield is the man.' Two of the eight siege guns were destroyed as well as the ammunition and wagons. It was a severe, though not a crushing, blow for the Williamites but its daring and skilful execution has given it an enduring fame.

After a short delay, William began the siege of the city and after five days of bombardment, a breach was opened in the walls on August 25th. Two days later a full assault was launched and during many hours of heavy fighting the city was heroically defended. The women of Limerick played a major role in the repulse of the attackers. In the words of a contemporary observer, they stood boldly in the breach, fighting with broken bottles and went nearer to the enemy than the soldiers. This unexpectedly strong resistance coupled with the lateness of the season, shortage of ammunition and bad weather led to the decision on 30th August to abandon the siege. Limerick had proved to be a major stumbling block to William's plans to capitalise on his victory at the Boyne and quickly crush the Jacobite resistance. Both sides then withdrew behind frontier lines and William left Ireland, never to return.

Hostilities were resumed the following summer with the Dutch general, Ginkel, in command of the Williamite army. The Jacobites suffered major defeats at his hands. Athlone was captured and the loss of the critical battle at Aughrim was exacerbated by the death of the French commander St Ruth. This was followed by the surrender of Galway and a retreat to the last surviving stronghold of Limerick. Ginkel began his assault of the city on September 8th, 1691. He concentrated his attack from across the Abbey river on the walls of the Englishtown. A large breach was made in the walls followed by major fires and great destruction of houses within the city. The citizens and defenders fought back resolutely, as they had in 1690, and no attempt was made to storm the town. The siege dragged on until the 22nd September when the Williamites crossed the Shannon and attacked the city from the Thomond bridge side. Great casualties were suffered by the Irish especially when the drawbridge was raised prematurely by the French inside the walls. On the following day, with great recriminations between the French and the Irish, it was decided to seek terms for surrender. This culminated with the signing of the Treaty of Limerick on October 3rd 1691. Much debate has occurred about the controversial decision to surrender, the terms of the treaty itself and its subsequent dishonouring. In purely military terms the surrender was surprising: the Jacobites should have been able to hold Limerick and continue the war. It would appear that the explanation for the surrender is largely psychological, low morale leading to a loss of nerve. Having made that decision it is arguable that they should have held out for better terms, both in regard to religious liberty and restoration of landed estates though it must be remembered that contemporary Protestant opinion held that the treaty was far too generous to Catholics. In the event the Protestant Irish parliament prevented the limited concessions from being implemented and Limerick acquired the sobriquet 'the city of the broken treaty'. The stone on which this symbol of betrayal and broken promises was reputedly signed became, and remains, the symbol of the city itself.

From A *Brief History of the Sieges and Treaty of Limerick*, Treaty 300 Committee, Limerick, 1990

Sarsfield's Ride
A. M. Sullivan

Early on the 9th of August, 1690, William drew from his encampment at Caherconlish, and, confident of an easy victory, sat down before Limerick. That day he occupied himself in selecting favourable sites for batteries to command the city, and in truth, owing to the formation of the ground, the city was at nearly every point nakedly exposed to his guns. He next sent in a summons to surrender, but De Boisseleau courteously replied that 'he hoped he should merit his opinion more by a vigorous defence than a shameful surrender of a fortress which he had been entrusted with.'

The siege now began. William's bombardment, however, proceeded slowly; and the Limerick gunners, on the other hand, were much more active and vigorous than he had expected. On Monday, the 11th, their fire compelled him to shift his field train entirely out of range; and on the next day, as if intent on following up such practice, their balls fell so thickly about his own tent, killing several persons, that he had to shift his own quarters also. But in a day or two he meant to be in position to pay back these attentions with heavy interest, and to reduce those old walls despite all resistance. In fine, there was coming up to him from Waterford a magnificent battering train, together with immense stores of ammunition, and, what was nearly as effective for him as the siege train, a number of pontoon boats of tin or sheet copper, which would soon enable him to pass the Shannon where he pleased. So he took very coolly the resistance so far offered from the city. For in a day more Limerick would be absolutely at his mercy!

So thought William; and so seemed the inevitable fact. But there was a bold heart and an active brain at work at that very moment, planning a deed destined to immortalise its author for all time, and to baffle William's now all-but-accomplished designs on Limerick!

On Sunday, the 10th, the battering train and its convoy had reached Cashel. On Monday, the 11th, they reached a place called Ballyneety, within nine or ten miles of the Williamite camp. The country through which they had passed was all in the hands of their own garrisons or patrols; yet they had so important and precious a charge that they had watched it jealously so far; but now they were virtually at the camp — only a few miles in its rear; and so the convoy, when night fell, drew the siege train and the vast line of ammunition waggons, the pontoon boats and store-loads into a field close to an old ruined castle, and, duly posting night sentries, gave themselves to repose.

That day an Anglicised Irishman, one Manus O'Brien, a Protestant landholder in the neighbourhood of Limerick, came into the Williamite camp with a piece of news. Sarsfield, at the head of five hundred picked men, had ridden off the night before on some mysterious enterprise in the direction of Killaloe; and the informer, from Sarsfield's character, judged rightly that something important was afoot, and earnestly assured the Williamites that nothing was too desperate for that commander to accomplish.

The Williamite officers made little of this. They thought the fellow was only anxious to make much of a trifle, by way of securing favour for himself. Besides, they knew of nothing in the direction of Killaloe that could affect them. William, at length, was informed of the story. He, too, failed to discern what Sarsfield could be at; but his mind anxiously reverting to his grand battering train — albeit it was now but a few miles off — he, to make safety doubly sure, ordered Sir John Lanier to proceed at once with five hundred horse to meet the convoy. By some curious chance, Sir John — perhaps deeming his night ride quite needless — did not greatly hurry to set forth. At two o'clock, Tuesday morning, instead of nine o'clock on Monday evening, he rode leisurely off. His delay of five hours made all the difference in the world, as we shall see.

It was indeed true that Sarsfield, on Sunday night, had secretly quitted his camp on the Clare side, at the head of a chosen body of his best horsemen; and true enough also that it was upon an enterprise worthy of his reputation he had set forth. In fine, he had heard of the approach of the siege train, and had planned nothing less than its surprise, capture, and destruction!

On Sunday night he rode to Killaloe, distant twelve miles above Limerick on the river. The bridge here was guarded by a party of the enemy; but, favoured by the darkness, he proceeded further up the river, until he came to a ford near

Ballyvally, where he crossed the Shannon, and passed into Tipperary county. The country around him now was all in the enemy's hands; but he had one with him as a guide on this eventful occasion, whose familiarity with the locality enabled Sarsfield to evade all the Williamite patrols, and but for whose services it may be doubted if his ride this night had not been his last. This was Hogan, the Rapparee chief, immortalised in local traditions as 'Galloping Hogan'. By paths and passes known only to riders 'native to the sod', he turned into the deep gorges of Silver Mines, and ere day had dawned was bivouacked in a wild ravine of the Keeper mountains. Here he lay *perdu* all day on Monday. When night fell there was anxious tightening of horsegirths and girding of swords with Sarsfield's five hundred. They knew the siege train was at Cashel on the previous day, and must by this time have reached near to the Williamite lines. The midnight ride before them was long, devious, difficult, and perilous; the task at the end of it was crucial and momentous indeed. Led by their trusty guide, they set out southward, still keeping in by-ways and mountain roads. Meanwhile, as already mentioned, the siege train and convoy had that evening reached Ballyneety, where the guns were parked and the convoy bivouacked. It was three o'clock in the morning when Sarsfield, reaching within a mile or two of the spot, learnt from a peasant that the prize was now not far off ahead of him. And here we encounter a fact which gives the touch of true romance to the whole story! It happened, by one of those coincidences that often startle us with their singularity, that the pass-word with the Williamite convoy on that night was '*Sarsfield*'! That Sarsfield obtained the pass-word before he reached the halted convoy is also unquestionable, though how he came by this information is variously stated. The painstaking historian of Limerick states that from a woman, wife of a sergeant in the Williamite convoy, unfeelingly left behind on the road by her party in the evening, but most humanely and kindly treated by Sarsfield's men, the word was obtained. Riding softly to within a short distance of the place indicated, he halted, and sent out a few trusted scouts to scan the whole position narrowly. They returned reporting that besides the sentries there were only a few score troopers drowsing beside the watch fires on guard; the rest of the convoy being sleeping in all the immunity of fancied safety. Sarsfield now gave his final orders — silence or death, till they were in upon the sentries; then, forward like a lightning flash upon the guards. One of the Williamite sentries fancied he heard the beat of horse-hoofs approaching him; he never dreamt of foes; he thought it must be one of their own patrols. And, truly enough, through the gloom he saw the figure of an officer, evidently at the head of a body of cavalry, whether phantom or reality he could not tell. The sentry challenged, and, still imagining he had friends, demanded the 'word'. Suddenly, as if from the spirit land, and with a wild, weird shout that startled all the sleepers, the 'phantom troop' shot past like a thunderbolt; the leader crying, as he drew his sword, '*Sarsfield* is the word, *and Sarsfield is the man!*' The guards dashed forward, the bugles screamed the alarm, the sleepers rushed to arms, but theirs was scarcely an effort. The broadswords of Sarsfield's five hundred were in their midst; and to the affrighted gaze of the panic-stricken victims that five hundred seemed thousands! Short, desperate, and bloody, was that scene — so short, so sudden, so fearful, that it seemed like the work of incantation. In a few minutes the whole of the convoy were cut down or dispersed; and William's splendid siege train was in Sarsfield's hands! But his task was as yet only half accomplished. Morning was approaching; and William's camp was barely eight or ten miles distant, and thither some of the escaped had hurriedly fled. There was scant time for the important work yet to be done. The siege guns and mortars were filled with powder, and each muzzle buried in the earth; upon and around the guns were piled the pontoon boats, the contents of the ammunition waggons, and all the stores of various kinds, of which there was a vast quantity. A train of powder was laid to this huge pyre, and Sarsfield, removing all the wounded Williamites to a safe distance, drew off his men, halting them while the train was being fired. There was a flash that lighted all the heavens, and showed with dazzling brightness the country for miles around. Then the ground rocked and heaved beneath the gazers' feet, as with a deafening roar that seemed to rend the firmament that vast mass burst into the sky; and as suddenly all was gloom again! The sentinels on Limerick walls heard the awful peal. It rolled like a thunderstorm away by the heights of Cratloe, and wakened sleepers amidst the hills of Clare. William heard it too; and he at least needed no interpreter of that fearful sound. He knew in that moment that his splendid siege train had perished, destroyed by a feat that only one man could have so planned and executed; an achievement destined to surround with unfading glory the name of Patrick Sarsfield!

Sir John Lanier's party, coming up in no wise rapidly, saw the flash, that, as they said, gave broad daylight for a second, and felt the ground shake beneath them as if by an earthquake, and then their leader found he was just in time to be too late. Rushing on, he sighted Sarsfield's rear-guard; but there were memories of the Irish cavalry at the Boyne in no way encouraging him to force an encounter. From the Williamite camp two other powerful bodies of horse were sent out instantly on the explosion being heard, to surround Sarsfield and cut him off from the Shannon. But all was vain.

From *The Story of Ireland*, M. H. Gill and Son Ltd, 1870/1926

The Siege of Lock Mills
Jim Kemmy

An important but forgotten chapter in the lives of the people of Limerick is to be found in a few lines of Maurice Lenihan's *History of Limerick*.

The years 1771 and '72 were a bleak period in the city. Unemployment, poverty and famine were widespread among the working classes. In 1771 the Pery Charitable Loan Fund was established for the relief of tradesmen through loans of three guineas to each, to be paid in instalments of 1s. 4d. per week.

Though this fund helped to alleviate the distress of a large number of tradesmen, it did not prevent the hardship and misery from biting deep into the poor. A number of schemes were started to provide work for the unemployed, but by May 1772 work, money and food were still as scarce as ever.

Matters came to a head on 12 May, 1772, when a starving crowd gathered outside the Lock Mills seeking food. The people believed that a quantity of corn was hoarded in the building. The Mayor, Christopher Carr, called out the soldiers, and the mill was occupied by a sergeant's guard. The hunger-maddened crowd refused to disperse and were fired on by the guard. Three men on the opposite side of the canal were killed.

The killing of the three men did nothing to assuage the anger or hunger of the people. On the following day another large crowd assembled in the Irishtown to again seek out bread or corn at the mill. The military was once again sent for and the 24th regiment was marched against the starving men and women. Three more people were killed, including a poor Park woman who was selling milk in Broad Street at the time.

No further attempts were made to seek food at the mill. Charity, that ancient stand-by for all the social ills of the world, was again called into service. The Honourable Dean Crosbie revived a neglected charity in the same year of 1772. This charity, known as the Widow Virgin Charity, was provided from a fund left by a widow named Mrs Virgin in her will dated 30 August, 1732. She bequeathed to the Dean of Limerick, in trust to the poor of St Mary's parish, a sum of 40 shillings per annum to purchase bread, to be distributed on every Christmas Day and Whit Sunday.

Forty shillings' worth of bread hardly went far among the famished poor but the widow's dying thought was a generous one. Apart from the fact that the Widow Virgin left a house in Quay Lane, held by Simon Holland at forty shillings a year, little else is known about this woman. More is the pity. One would like to know much more about this charitable woman.

From the *Labour Party Conference Magazine*, 1995

Newspapers
Maurice Lenihan

The *Munster Journal* [was] a venerable broad sheet, with which, and its immediate successors, several curious associations are connected, that throw light on the journalistic and dramatic history of the day. The *Munster Journal* was said to be the oldest journal in the province of Munster. The proprietor was Mr Andrew Welsh, ancestor of the respectable family of Welsh of Newtown House, County Clare, and a gentleman of enterprise and ability. Mr Welsh also published the *Magazine of Magazines*, which appears to have been a reprint of Exshaw's *London and Dublin Magazine*, with a Limerick title-page. The *Munster Journal* was succeeded, about 1787, by the *Limerick Journal*, of which Mr Edward Flinn was the proprietor; this Journal enjoyed the patronage of Lord Clare, to whom the owner of it was agent, and reaped a harvest by the publication of the Castle Proclamations. Mr Flinn who was a Catholic, resided in Mary-street, opposite Quay-lane; Athlunkard-street not having been made for many years afterwards. His fellow-citizens and neighbours in Mary-street were Mr William Goggin, the great Chap Book and Ballad Printer, whose shop at the corner of Quay-lane, was known by the sign of Shakespear. Alderman Andrew Watson, the successor of Mr John Ferrar, in the proprietorship of the *Limerick Chronicle*, had his office and residence near the office of the *Limerick Journal*, whilst 'Charley Keating', as he was familiarly called, who rejoiced in the dignity of 'Seneschal of Parteen' — had a small ware shop at the opposite corner. Andrew Cherry, the comedian, and author of the 'Soldier's Daughter', and the 'Travellers', to which Dibdin wrote the songs, &c., served his time as an apprentice in the printing-office of the *Limerick Journal*. Cherry often printed the play bills for his own poor strolling company; and underwent many trials, having been reduced to the verge of starvation on some occasions . . . It is related of Cherry, that, having been offered an engagement by a manager who had previously forgotten to pay him, he wrote:—

'Sir, — You have bitten me once, and I am resolved you shall not *make two bites of* A. Cherry.'

Cherry was one of the leading comedians at Covent Garden Theatre for several years; his portrait was painted by De Wylde, and printed in the *Monthly Memoir*. Mr John Gubbins, a successful portrait painter, also served his time in the *Limerick Journal* office . . .

In newspapers Limerick took an early lead in the last century. In the present century there have been several newspapers projected and launched, many of which were destined to meet with almost immediate shipwreck; some of which, however, flourish. Among the journals that existed in the earlier portion of the century, were the *Limerick Evening Post and Clare Sentinel*, of which Daniel Geary, Esq., was the proprietor; the *Limerick Star*, of which his son, William D. Geary, Esq., and Joseph

Hayden, Esq., were the proprietors; the *Limerick Times*, of which the above Joseph Hayden, author of the *Dictionary of Dates*, was the proprietor; the *Limerick Herald*, of which William R. Yielding, Esq., was the proprietor; the *Limerick Guardian*, which was published for a short time in 1833, and the *Munster Journal* in 1832; the *Limerick Standard* in 1840–41, of which G. W. Dartnell, Esq., was the proprietor; the *Limerick and Clare Examiner* in 1845, of which Messrs Lynch and Co., were proprietors, and afterwards Messrs McCarthy and Mr J. R. Browne; the *Limerick Observer*, in 1856, of which Patrick Lynch, Esq., solicitor, was the proprietor; the *Limerick Herald*, by Messrs Purdon, of Dublin, in 1853. Mr William Glover started the *Munster Telegraph* in 1819, but it did not survive long. Mr Alexander McDonnell published the *Limerick Advertiser* in Rutland Street. There are at present in the city the *Limerick Chronicle*, established in 1766, of which William Hosford, Esq., and Mrs Sarah Bassett, are the proprietors. The *Limerick Reporter and Tipperary Vindicator*, the first named established on the 12th of July, 1839; the latter in Nenagh on the 21st January, 1844; both incorporated on the 1st of January, 1850, of which Maurice Lenihan, Esq., the author of this History, is the proprietor. The *Munster News*, established in 1852, of which F. Counihan, Esq., is the proprietor; and the *Limerick Southern Chronicle*, established in 1863, of which G. W. Bassett, Esq., is the proprietor.

From *Limerick; Its History and Antiquities, Ecclesiastical, Civil, and Military, from the Earliest Ages,* Hodges, Smith, and Co., 1866

Freemasonry in Limerick
Fred L. Pick and G. Norman Knight

The Origins of Irish Masonry

One of the traditional heroes of Celtic mythology was the Gobhan Saor, the 'free smith', of whom many legends are told. It is perhaps significant, as Lepper and Crossle point out in *History of the Grand Lodge of Free and Accepted Masons of Ireland*, Vol. 1, that 'Saor' in the Irish tongue denotes both 'free' and 'a mason'.

That the ancient Irish possessed able masons is proved by their famous round towers, some of which still stand after existing for well over a thousand years . . .

Pre-Grand Lodge Freemasonry

In Limerick a still more ancient relic exists and now forms one of the treasures of the Union Lodge, No. 13 (IC). This is the nearly 460-year-old Baal's Bridge Square, which was discovered in excavating the foundations of the bridge of that name over the River Shannon.

The wording on it runs:

> Upon the Level, By the Square
> I will strive to live, With love and care.

This shows that Freemasonry was established in Ireland in the early part of the sixteenth century, and while we cannot be certain that it was then partly Speculative, yet it had already an ethical symbolism for its working tools . . .

Daniel O'Connell

This famous Irish Statesman was not only Master of Lodge No. 189, Dublin, in which he had been initiated in 1799, and affiliated to the well-known No. 13, Limerick, but also acted as Counsel for Grand Lodge in the litigation over Seton.

At this time the Papal Bulls of 1738 and 1751 were ignored in Ireland, in which at the beginning of the nineteenth century the Roman Catholic Freemasons far outnumbered the Protestant. The tightening up of the ban, however, by the priests resulted in a great decline in the number of lodges and accounted for the resignation of Daniel O'Connell.

In 1837, when taunted by political opponents with still being a member of the Order, he stated in *The Pilot* that many years before he had unequivocally renounced Freemasonry, urging as his objections to it the tendency to counteract the exertions of the temperance societies and 'the wanton and multiplied taking of oaths'.

From *The Pocket History of Freemasonry*, Frederick Muller Limited, 1953

The Jackets Green
Michael Scanlan

When I was a maiden, fair and young,
On the pleasant homes of Lee,
No bird that in the greenwood sung
Was half so blithe and free.
My heart ne'er beat with flying feet,
No love sang me his queen,
'Till down the glen rode Sarsfield's men,
And they wore the jackets green.

Young Donal sat on his gallant gray,
Like a king on a royal seat,

And my heart leaped out on his regal way
To worship at his feet.
Oh, love, had you come, in these colours dressed,
And wooed with a soldier's mien,
I'd have laid my head on your throbbing breast,
For the sake of your jacket green.

No hoarded wealth did my love own,
Save that good sword that he bore;
But I loved him for himself alone,
And the colour bright he wore.
For had he come in England's red,
To make me England's queen
I'd rove the high green hills instead,
For the sake of Irish green.

When William stormed with shot and shell
At the walls of Garryowen,
In the breach of death my Donal fell
And he sleeps near the Treaty Stone.
That breach the foeman never crossed
While he swung his broad sword keen;
But I do not weep my darling lost,
For he fell in his jacket green.

When Sarsfield sailed away, I wept,
As I heard the wind ochone,
I felt, then, dead as the men who slept
'Neath the fields of Garryowen.
While Ireland held my Donal blessed,
No wild seas rolled between,
Till I could fold him to my breast
All robed in his Irish green.

My sould has sobbed, like waves of woe,
That, sad, over tombstones break;
For I buried my heart in his grave below
For his and for Ireland's sake,
And I cry: 'Make way for the soldier's bride
In your halls of death, sad queen;
For I long to rest by my true love's side,
And wrapped in the folds of green.'

I saw the Shannon's purple tide
Roll by the Irish Town,
As I stood in the breach by Donal's side
When England's flag went down,
And now it lowers when I seek the skies,
Like the blood-red curse between!
I weep, but 'tis not women's sighs
Will raise our Irish green.

Oh, Ireland, sad is thy lonely soul,
And loud, beats the winter sea,
But sadder and higher the wild waves roll
O'er the hearts that break for thee.
Yet grief shall come to our heartless foes,
And their thrones in the dust be seen,
So, Irish maids, love none but those
Who wear the jackets green.

From *The First Book of Irish Ballads* by Daniel D. O'Keeffe, The Mercier Press, 1955

The Colleen Bawn
Maurice Lenihan

In the spring of the year 1820, a trial as remarkable as any that has since taken place, occupied the attention of the public. Romances have been written and dramas enacted on the groundwork furnished by this terribly tragic event, which became the subject of judicial enquiry before the Right Hon. Richard Jebb (fourth Justice of the King's Bench), who, with the Hon. Henry Joy (first Sergeant), went the Munster Circuit at that assizes. A fearful murder had been perpetrated on the 4th, of the previous July, in the River Shannon, within the jurisdiction of the city, and under circumstances of the most revolting atrocity — circumstances which have awakened the indignation of every individual to whom they have become known in all parts of the world. The principal in that murder was a person who had served in the Royal Navy as an officer, and who had moved in the highest ranks of society; the victim was his wife. The wife, no doubt, belonged to a grade much lower than that which the murderer had occupied, and hence he was inclined to get rid of her. Search had been ineffectually made for a long time for the murderer; but it was not till the following November, (1819) that he was arrested whilst enjoying himself in the house of a friend in the west of the county, conducted to the city gaol on the warrant of the Mayor, and brought to trial at the City of Limerick Spring assizes, which were opened on the 11th of March, 1820, before the Judges above named.

Probably no murder ever committed has excited more attention than that of Ellen Scanlan, a fact which is chiefly owing to the treatment her melancholy story has met with at the hands of the authors of 'The Poor Man's Daughter', a narrative in a serial entitled 'Tales of Irish Life', another in the *New Monthly*, the beautiful novel of the truly gifted Gerald Griffin, the *Collegians*, and the extraordinarily successful drama of Mr Boucicault, the *Colleen Bawn* . . . She was living with her uncle, one John Connery, a ropemaker, others say a shoemaker, in a small town in the County Limerick, who had adopted her, when she contracted her ill-omened marriage. Scanlan was defended by Daniel O'Connell, the Liberator, and Mr George Bennett. Messrs Pennefather and Quin were Counsel for the prosecution. Scanlan . . . was a Protestant, and attended by the Rev. Henry Gubbins, who raised the cap from his face just before he was turned off, imploring him to make his peace with God by telling the truth. His answer was, 'I suffer for a crime in which I did not participate. If Sullivan be found my innocence will appear.' He thus died with a lie in his mouth. Scanlan's family were connected with some of the highest names in the county and city of Limerick. One of his relatives rode from the Court House, immediately on his conviction, through the country with a memorial for a respite to the judge. The memorial was influentially signed, and presented by a number of influential persons; but the judge inflexibly refused its prayer, stating that he had left for execution a poor man who was found guilty of a minor offence, and asking, how could he interfere in a case of such undoubted magnitude as Scanlan's. Scanlan was about 23 years of age, and of fair and prepossessing appearance.

From *Limerick; Its History and Antiquities, Ecclesiastical, Civil, and Military, from the Earliest Ages*, Hodges, Smith, and Co., 1866

Throwing the Dart
Fr James White

To soothe the wounded feelings of . . . litigants and to restore peace and good-fellowship among the citizens, the mayor, Thomas Smyth, on the 5th September, 1764, invited all the populace to ride round the franchises of the city and the Liberties of Limerick. The procession is thus described by Father James White . . . the accomplished annalist of the diocese:—

Servants, bailiffs, and mayor's sergeants proceeded on horseback with blue cockades in their hats, the bands of music belonging to the army, the sword-bearer and water-bailiff with their proper ensigns, the two sheriffs with their rods, the mayor richly dressed, with the rod in his hand, rode; after them followed the rest of the corporation, John Quinn, Esq., carrying the blue corporation standard; and then followed numbers of other gentlemen well mounted, all having blue cockades in their hats. Then fourteen of the trades or corporations rode after them, each trade according to the antiquity of their charters, and each was headed by their respective masters and wardens. Each trade had a standard according to the colour of their trade, with the arms of the trade in the centre, and cockades peculiar to the trade, and after their masters and wardens followed the principal of each trade well dressed, well mounted, and accompanied with drums and music. On Thursday they rode from the King's Island through the city and visited the south-east of the Liberties of the city. On Friday in like manner visited the south-west Liberties, returned through the city and visited the north Liberties but never broke down any walls or regulated any encroachments. On Saturday the corporation and the aforesaid trades with their standards and cockades in their hats walked with the mayor from the square behind St John's Church to St Mary's Church, and returned with him in the same order to the said square, where he treated them with wine and had the masters and wardens of each trade to dine with him that day. The Thursday of the following week the mayor, sheriffs and the rest of the corporation in the King's yachts went down the river in order to assert and make good his right of being admiral of the River Shannon. When they arrived at Scattery Island the mayor held a court of Admiralty, and the next day set sail for the mouth of the Shannon, where he threw a dart into the sea to point out the limits of his jurisdiction; at the same time it happened that a sloop of war entered the river, whom the mayor compelled to lower her colours and her fore top-sail in acknowledgement of his power of Admiralty in the said River Shannon. The mayor and corporation returned to Limerick on Saturday with the ringing of bells, etc.

From *The Diocese of Limerick: From 1691 to the Present Time* by John Archdeacon Begley, Browne and Nolan Limited, 1938

Manners and Customs
Rev. P. Fitzgerald and J. J. McGregor

The higher and middle classes are in general polite, hospitable, and public spirited, and exceedingly attached to social parties. On such a subject we would prefer the opinion of an impartial intelligent stranger to our own. Speaking of Limerick fifty years since, Dr Campbell states in his Political Survey, 'The old Milesian manners prevail more here than in any place I have yet visited. At night as you pass along, you may hear music in every ale-house; and from the number of backgammon tables to be seen at the coffee houses, one may conjecture what are the amusements of these good citizens.' We are not aware, however, that at present there is any extraordinary rage for gambling in Limerick. The gentry indulge much, in the season, in field-sports: horse-races are annually held at Newcastle, within two miles of the city, where also the large garrison generally stationed here, sometimes exhibit military reviews, and sham-fights.

The passion for music still continues in full force among all classes; but the love of the drama has so much declined for some time back, that no regular theatre now exists in the city. Whether this arises from a fastidiousness of the public taste, or the increase of religious feeling, we are not able to decide. Not many years back a very elegant theatre was erected in George's-street, by subscription, at the expense of four or five thousand pounds, but for want of encouragement it was sold to the monks of the Augustinian order, for about a tenth of the original cost. There are various agreeable rides about the town, but no public walk, though no city in Ireland is more favourably circumstanced for a promenade on either side of the river. Except, therefore, an occasional lounge at the Club-house, or the Commercial Coffee-room, or a ball at Swinburne's, the amusements of the citizens of Limerick are purely domestic. Half a century ago, Doctor Campbell acknowledged that the ladies of Limerick deserved their celebrated character for beauty: more modern travellers confess that their daughters have not deteriorated, and the streets are still enlivened by handsome and well dressed females.

Many of the customs and amusements of the lower classes have become obsolete, though others are still retained. Bull-baiting, and cock-fighting being scarcely known among them, tippling, dancing, and the music of the fiddle or bag-pipe are their chief enjoyments at fair-time, or on festival days. Amongst the airs selected upon these occasions, 'Patrick's Day', and 'Garryowen' always hold a distinguished place. Though the magistrates are as attentive to enforce the proper observance of the Sabbath as in most of the great towns in Ireland, yet it is to be lamented that the sacredness of the day is too often profaned in this city and its suburbs. The tradesmen have laid aside the custom of marching on Midsummer-day, when, arranged under their respective leaders, decorated with sashes, ribbons, and flowers, and accompanied with a band of musicians, and the shouts of the delighted populace, they proceeded through the principal streets of the city, while their merry-men played a thousand antic tricks and the day generally ended in a terrible fight between the Garryowen and Thomond-gate boys (the tradesmen of the north and south suburbs). Bonfires are still lighted on May-eve, and St John's-eve; and Patrick's-day commences with numerous acts of devotion at a well dedicated to the patron saint in the neighbourhood of the city, and ends with copious libations to his memory. On Sundays and holidays, scarlet cloaks are the prevalent costume of the humbler classes of females . . . The Irish language is rarely spoken by the inhabitants, except when they have to transact business with the neighbouring peasantry; and it is necessary for the occupiers of those shops which the latter frequent to be able to speak the native tongue. Among the lower classes, marriages and christenings are celebrated with more or less joviality according to the circumstances of the parties, and the unseemly custom of drinking and carousing at the wakes of deceased friends is still practised, though the hullulloo, or Irish-cry, is now rarely heard in the streets at funerals.

From *The History, Topography, and Antiquities of the County and City of Limerick; with Preliminary View of the History and Antiquities of Ireland*, George McKern, 1827

The Big Wind
Peter Carr

At half-past eight the storm set in, blowing a rough gale from the West-north-west, which increased in fury every hour, until between eleven and twelve o'clock when it raged with all the horrors of a perfect hurricane, sweeping in violent gusts through the streets, and extinguishing all the gas lamps. The watchmen took refuge, in terror of their lives, under hall-door porticos, and archways, no living creature being able to stand in the streets, while the spirit of the tempest was careering in all his might through the air, streaks of lightning, at intervals, illuminating the midnight darkness, and a shower of slates at every angle which were exposed to the blast, strewing the ground with broken particles, and flying before the tempest, literally, we may add, like shreds of paper.

Not a public edifice or institution in the City escaped the ravages of the storm, all suffering material damage in the fierce encounter. The best built houses of the New Town . . . trembled in the rude embrace of their imperious visitor, and were sadly dismantled in the upper stories. House tops and flues fell prostrate, the crash of window glass was general and incessant, while, to crown the panic . . . a whole stack of chimneys would occasionally tumble down, after struggling with the blast like a drunken man . . .

The English and Irish towns, which constitute the abode of the less affluent and labouring classes, at every turn, manifest the devastating progress of the storm, by scenes of ruin and dilapidation . . .

A crowd of people gladly took refuge in the hall of the Exchange [where] they remained until daylight, many of them with only a blanket or sheet, for in their anxiety to escape . . . they never bethought of clothes.

Imagination will convey to the sympathising mind a better picture of the wild and dreary spectacle than description can render . . . (LC)

The demesnes of Adare, Curragh, Castletown, Shannon Grove, Tervoe, Doonas, Hermitage, Tinerana, Kilballyowen and Ballinaguard, have suffered severely, many hundreds of the oldest and finest trees torn up by the roots. The chapels of Stone Hall and Cappa, complete wrecks, not a vestige of a roof on either. (DJ)

The Club House roof was thrown down, Wellesley bridge greatly injured, owing to the vessels in the river being driven against it. The old Town suffered severely; some say there was over £36,000 worth of property destroyed . . . The mortality by the storm . . . for the port of Limerick, already comprises sixteen deaths. (DJ)

There is a complete wreck of small boats in the river. Thirty sail boats left the quays on Sunday, after discharging turf and oats . . . We fear not half of them could survive . . . and already we have ascertained the loss of four down the river, three at Grass Island. A large sail boat, named the *Daniel O'Connell*, is also lost. John Hartigan, of the *Richmond Lass*, was killed . . . by a stroke of the jib-boom, which nearly severed his head from the body. At the Customs-house a capacious lighter, of forty tons burden, was thrown high and dry out of the water. (LC)

Sir, Amidst the awful devastations, any suggestion for future benefit is valuable. One great cause of loss of life and property is the height and weight of the house chimneys, and for both of which . . . is Limerick conspicuous . . . if the tops of those damaged and those to be built, were formed by short pipes of zinc, instead of heavy brickwork . . . [such] accidents could not occur. What is here recommended [is] in London . . . almost universal, *yours obediently, A Subscriber*. (LC)

LC Limerick Chronicle
DJ Derry Journal

From *The Big Wind*, White Row Press Ltd, 1991

A May March

Sinn Fein Volunteer Parade
Scenes in the City
Volunteers Stoned

A series of remarkable scenes was associated with the parade of about 1,000 Sinn Fein Volunteers and Boy Scouts who visited the city on Sunday. In connection with the parade excursions were run from Dublin, Cork and Charleville and the

Sinn Feiners from these centres were supplemented by about 150 of the local body. The Volunteers wore uniform, were fully equipped, and were accompanied by a Mr P. Pearse of Dublin and other prominent members connected with the movement. They formed up in Pery Square and marched through the city to the accompaniment of the music of two bands. Everything went well until passing through Mungret Street, where they got a hostile reception. In this locality the Volunteers were groaned and booed and stones were freely thrown. For a time things looked threatening. Some blank shots were discharged in the endeavour to check the violence of the women, girls and boys who assailed the Sinn Feiners with all sorts of missiles. Having escaped through this thoroughfare with a few injuries, the parade was continued along by Broad Street where things were extremely lively. A shower of stones was fired into the ranks of the Volunteers, who, however, kept their temper, and the march continued without further incident. When the men paraded through the Irishtown hearty cheers were raised by the crowds on the sidewalks for the Munster Fusiliers and other Irish Regiments at the Front. In other parts of the city things were pretty quiet, having regard to what occurred in the old town, but there were isolated attacks on the Volunteers, some of whom drew revolvers but did not use them. Several had to seek police protection and gain shelter from the crowds, who became more demonstrative as the day wore on. In Nelson Street, a lady wearing Sinn Fein colours was obliged to enter a house from the more excitable elements of the crowd, and in the attempt by a party of Volunteers to afford her a safe exit, they were subjected to rough treatment.

Long before the departure of the Cork and Dublin trains a large mass of people had congregated in front of the railway station, the approaches to which were barred and held by a number of officials, who denied admission to anyone not in possession of a ticket. Some short time before 7 o'clock the Cork Volunteers marched up, and were received with groans and jeers. An observation by one of the Volunteers nettled the crowd, which became almost unmanageable. Stones and bottles were thrown at the Volunteers, who managed to get into the station yard after a tremendous struggle. Shots were fired and the butts of rifles used by some of them to beat off the hostile attentions of the attackers. But it was only when the Dublin Volunteers arrived that the disturbances reached their zenith. In making their way through the railway gate the Sinn Feiners, who indulged in 'Hochs', were set upon. A free fight occurred and in the melee a number of people were injured, but not seriously. Shots were again discharged and in the scrimmage seven rifles were wrested from the Volunteers. It was a serious affair while it lasted, but the presence of a number of Roman Catholic clergy, notably Fr J. M. O'Connor, Administrator, Rev. Fr Mangan CSSR, and Rev. Fr Bernard OFM, and some fifty police did valuable work in mollifying the crowd and in checking the attacks on the Volunteers. Before the mail train departed at 11 o'clock some Volunteers who travelled on it came in for attention by a knot of people, but nothing untoward happened. In the Irish Town district, where a few Sinn Feiners reside, some of their windows were broken but there was nothing like a combined or organised attack upon them. About half a dozen people were treated at Barrington's Hospital for minor injuries and one man from Mitchelstown was detained overnight. The proceedings, it must be conceded, were regrettable, but it was unwise of the Volunteers, having regard to the number of men from the Irish Town serving in the war, to march through that area.

From *The Limerick Chronicle*, 25 May 1915

How the Mid-West was Won
J. M. MacCarthy

When boyhood's fire was in our blood we read of the defence by Limerick men and women of their ancient city against the Williamite army; of Sarsfield's ride to Ballyneety, under the guidance of the Rapparee Galloping O'Hogan, to take and break the cannon of the Dutch invaders; of the powerful blacksmith who smashed the foemen's heads with his ponderous hammer. We thrilled to the password 'Sarsfield is the word and Sarsfield is the man,' and our spirits sank when the Treaty was broken ere the ink on it was dry and the fighting men of the Ireland of the time passed into service with continental armies.

Why did they go to fight and die on the battlefields of Europe, from Dunkirk to Belgrade? 'Oh that this was for Ireland,' said the dying Sarsfield as his life-blood flowed on the plain at Landen. He was echoing the death sigh of thousands of Irish men of lesser rank who had marched with the armies of France, Spain, Austria, Russia and, lastly and most numerous of all, with the armies of England in her wars of conquest, subjugation and empire-building.

Why not stay at home, indeed, and fight and die for the freedom of Ireland. Who would do so when Irish men in tens of thousands were fighting for the Empire, for Little Belgium, for the Freedom of Small Nations, for Home Rule, for Self-Determination, for any cause that the British choose to invent and hang a slogan on it. Twelve hundred men in Dublin dared to do so. Among the leaders were Edward Daly of Limerick City, and Con Colbert of Athea, who fell before British firing squads. Before them into eternity went Donal Sheehan of Ballytubrid, Monagea, drowned in the River Laune on his way to Caherciveen to seize a wireless transmitting set. Other Limerick men were in the fight in Dublin and, like Cork and Kerry, Limerick mobilised its Volunteers who were ready for the local actions that did not eventuate.

Limerick and its Bishop and its two patriotic priests heartened the Ireland that was sickened by General Maxwell's blood-letting before it reacted with spirit. Thereafter Limerick was in the van of the struggle for the assertion of Ireland's independence and paid the price in blood and tears for its adherence to the cause. Young and old suffered death at the brutal hands of British hirelings in city and county. The Mayor of Limerick, George Clancy, and the ex-Mayor, Michael O'Callaghan, were murdered in the presence of their wives, as were other men less prominent.

Meanwhile the active service units, the first of which was formed in the East Limerick Brigade area by Donnacha O'Hannigan, were repaying the score to the best of their limited armaments and, backed by the men and women in and out of the IRA and Cumann na mBan, they fought with courage and initiative against heavy odds. A unique claim that Limerick can make is that one of its fighting units captured a British military plane which had made a forced landing.

A county of dairy farms, of rich pastures, of quiet, peace-loving people, Limerick, when it was roused to action, when blood was shed in foul night murders and daylight brutalities were commonplace, when the IRA marched from billet to billet across its flat countryside or lay in ambush inside its hedges and walls, did not wilt under the pressure that was exerted so heavily on it by the Occupation Forces.

The three brigade areas, west, mid and east, into which the county was divided, caused the IRA to fight over three different kinds of terrain. Sandwiched between the rural areas and small towns and villages of west and east Limerick was the Shannonside city where different methods had to be adopted in the face of closer and more sustained enemy pressure. How the British regarded the opposition it was meeting in County Limerick can be judged from the county's inclusion in the martial law area, with counties Cork, Kerry and Tipperary, in December 1920, when the terror was mounting in the vain hope that the Irish people would break under it. Flying columns of the three Limerick brigades were in the field when the Truce came, on July 11, 1921.

Limerick's Fighting Story takes us back to the days and nights of fear in city and countryside, but it also turns a strong light on the bravery and resource of men who refused to yield to superior numbers and to terror tactics.

From the cover of *Limerick's Fighting Story*, edited by J. M. MacCarthy, Anvil Books, 1966

The Shelling of the Strand Barracks
P. J. Ryan

On the King's Island, the Staters held the Courthouse, St Mary's Cathedral and the pub at the corner of Nicholas and Athlunkard Streets. They also held Mary Street Police Barracks and Pa Healy's house at Park Bridge. In each of those posts they had up to twenty men. Four bridges connect the Island with the City and the Staters held three of them. The fourth, Thomond Bridge, connected the King John's Castle with the Clare bank of the river.

The Diehards held the Castle and St Munchin's Protestant Church with a splendid sniping position on its square tower. There were nearly one hundred men in the Castle. This was a ridiculously small number of men to maintain a minimum of five sentry posts with daily reliefs under conditions of potential massed attack.

Day by day and slowly but surely the Staters leisurely approached the Castle, their nearness being indicated by the rifle fire of the snipers. The Staters were in no hurry. Their purpose was attrition, to wear down the garrison by keeping them continuously on the alert. They had no intention of a massed attack, as they had not enough men for this purpose. They hoped that the Diehards would evacuate the Castle without bloodshed.

It became clear to the officer in command of the Castle that his position was untenable. A line of retreat lay open to him at night, across Thomond Bridge to the Clare side of the river. A Lewis gun on St Mary's Cathedral tower would deter even the most foolhardy from crossing by day, and the nights are short in July.

A speedy evacuation of the Castle was vital to avoid surrender or death. The O/C could not escape from the Island except by boat. The fast-flowing river could not be crossed by boats except when the tide was almost in and ere it ebbed. This was a period of almost three hours. These were the hours of watchfulness by the Staters. As the Staters had a post on the Metal Railway Bridge across the Shannon above the Castle, it was seen that the Island, besides being surrounded by water, was also surrounded by Staters — a geographical precaution employed by the Staters.

It was decided to remove all sick men from the castle in a Red Cross van. The plan was put into action and in a short time the van made several journeys to the Strand Barracks. The route from the Castle to the Strand is downhill, so that a laden van would have little difficulty in making the short journey.

The speedy movement of the van attracted considerable attention. It seemed to indicate that the van was being loaded at the Castle with dead or wounded men. The dreadful thought arose that the garrison had indulged in mutual slaughter, or that some explosion or accident had occurred and that the ambulance was removing the men to the Strand for medical treatment. As the nearest hospital was at the Workhouse, it was considered odd that the van did not take that uphill journey.

As the van moved along the Strand for what proved to be its last journey, it stalled. Two men got down and, by pushing, managed to get it in motion again. It was then seen that these were not sick men needing medical attention but militant men needing militant attention. These things being noted, fire was opened on the ambulance. There were no casualties.

The story of the Staters firing on the Red Cross ambulance quickly spread throughout the city. In plaintive tones the infamous deed was condemned by the Diehards. The citizens were assured that the few men in the ambulance were in for a joy-ride only. The whole affair was explained away as a mere boyish prank carried out by youngsters who as soldiers of the Republic would do nothing mean or low.

In ringing tones and with flashing eyes the question was asked: To what depths of depravity would the Staters sink? In voices appalled with horror it was even suggested that the Staters might bring down the Big Gun from Dublin and start shelling the brave defenders of the Republic. As everything which went on in the rival camps was known to each side and to the citizens, the various events of the day were discussed with homely and spirited candour. As the city prepared to bed down for the night, the possibility that the Staters might bring down the Big Gun was freely discussed.

In the four military barracks there was quiet and confident calm amongst the garrisons. The possibility of the Big Gun being used against them was also freely discussed. It was felt that the gun would come in by the Dublin Road and that its progress would be resisted and halted. It was felt that Patrick Sarsfield of glorious memory looking down from celestial orbit would smile approval on their noble efforts and bless their brave hearts.

While some discussed and others mused and some lay quietly dreaming, the gun came south over O'Brien's Bridge. It crossed the Shannon again at Corbally Bridge and continued on by the Corbally Road. It crossed over the Abbey river by Park Bridge and entered the city before ten at night.

The gun was towed by a covered heavy motor lorry and travelled at about nine miles per hour. If it travelled any faster, the iron-shod wooden wheels would fall to pieces. The gun slowed down to a crawl to pass the barrier at the humped-back, narrow Park Bridge. The gun was called Sean McKeon's 18-Pounder. It entered the city on the evening of Wednesday, the nineteenth of July, 1922.

The gun was taken to Arthur's Quay that night. Next morning July 20th, the gun was set up alongside the Curragour Mills and forty feet from the quay wall. The gun was manned by three Limerick city men, Jim Leddin, John and Michael McNamara, all from the Island. These three men had been in Artillery regiments of the British Army and had been demobilised in 1919 and 1920 at the end of the First World War. The officer in charge of the gun was Colonel Fraher, an ex-officer of Artillery and also a Limerick man. By 10 a.m. in the morning, the whole city was aware of the arrival of the gun and that the Strand Barracks was to be shelled. Crowds of citizens flocked to every vantage point to view the scene of impending horror. The Staters were unable to stop the onrush of spectators except at Arthur's Quay where masses of barbed wire prevented entry. Almost dead on 10.30 a.m. the gun was ready. The range across the river was about 150 yards. At such short range aim is always taken through the barrel of the gun. Colonel Fraher and each of the gunners in turn looked through the barrel of the gun. Some few privileged officers also had a look through the barrel of the gun . . . The view through the barrel was true; it gave a telescopic view of the Strand Barracks' gate. The shell was then inserted in the breech in correct military manner; the gunners then saluted their officers and the officer returned the salute.

This gun was one of a pair left behind in Athlone Barracks by the British when they evacuated and the Barracks was handed over to General Sean McKeon. They were old 1912 vintage guns, and were badly worn. With the guns was a supply of solid shells. The shells did not contain an explosive charge and so did not explode; in fact, like the guns, the shells were obsolete. It was a solid shell that was inserted in the breech of the eighteen-pounder. Now that everything was ready a great hush fell upon the military and spectators and a last consultation was held between the officers. Everyone realised that this was an historic occasion, a momentous event. Not since the siege of 1691 had a siege-gun been fired in Limerick City. Standing twenty feet from the gun, Colonel Fraher waved his arm. Michael McNamara then pulled the lanyard and fired the gun. It was 10.30 a.m. With the roar of the explosion the gun jumped eighteen inches in the air and recoiled backwards, the 'trail' of the gun narrowly missing the gunners. The shell travelled forward and struck a telegraph pole, thirty feet to the left of the Strand Barracks' gate, cutting down the pole. The shell ricocheted and then struck the second window to the right of the gate. It skidded along the road and later was picked up near the Treaty Stone.

The spectators were happy with the spectacle and the loud bang which was heard for miles away. They were unhappy with the result and expressed disapproval of the gunners until it was pointed out that this first shot was a trial shot to get the feel of the gun. Better results would follow the next shot. A consultation was held between the colonel and the gunners; it was agreed that the soft mud and stone of the roadway at Arthur's Quay was not the best surface for the spade of the gun. A deeper hole was then dug for the trail. Once more the gun was mounted and aim was taken through the barrel of the gun. From the first shot it was realised that the gun was shooting thirty-five feet to the left at one hundred and fifty yards range. This represented a lateral deviation of about fifteen degrees. To allow for this deviation the gun was aimed at the window near the red brick house on the right of the Strand Barracks. Once more into the breech was slammed a solid shell. Once more the gunners saluted and the colonel returned the salute. The colonel's hand dropped the signal and McNamara fired the gun. The gun belched smoke and flame as it again jumped almost two feet in the air. It then moved forward, swung round and a wheel became embedded in the hole dug for the 'trail'. The gun was now pointing at Strand House.

After this odd behaviour of the gun, no further shells were fired, as it was feared the gun might swing around and shoot the gunners. The tenants in the tenement houses on Arthur's Quay complained loudly saying — take that damned yoke away before the houses are knocked down on top of us.

The second shell struck the barracks' gate knocking it down. It bounced off the barrack square and disappeared over the roof at the back of the barracks, and thus ended the shelling in the Fourth Siege of Limerick.

From the *Limerick Socialist*, August 1976

'A Turning-Point in the Civil War'
Helen Litton

The struggle for Limerick was a turning-point in the Civil War. The republican forces held most of the Limerick barracks at the start, with at least 700 troops. [Liam] Lynch set up his HQ there, and engaged in truce talks with Michael Brennan, commander of the Free State army in the area, but [Eoin] O'Duffy soon stopped this. He had heard that Brennan was anxious for an agreement, and was afraid he would resign his command, taking most of his troops with him. However, a truce agreement was reached on 7 July.

Brennan said he agreed to this to prevent the Irregulars marching on Dublin. Lynch felt that the truce would help him to consolidate Republican control of Munster, but most of his officers were annoyed by the truce, wanting a more aggressive policy. Free State reinforcements began to arrive, and the Limerick truce was later seen as demoralising to the Irregulars.

The Provisional Government, breaking the truce, attacked Limerick and won it after two days of fierce fighting and destruction in the city centre. The Republican troops managed to escape, and the fight moved on to the surrounding counties. The fighting at Kilmallock was one of the few 'proper' battles in the Civil War.

From *The Irish Civil War: An Illustrated History*, Wolfhound Press, 1995

The Shannon Scheme
D. L. Kelleher

Here is Ardnacrusha, three miles north of Limerick, hitherto for all the years of recorded time a green, glancing, fertile place, with cattle lowing and birds smiling over it with a song. A house here and there, white and tidy, hardly bigger-looking than a milestone, a herd following his cattle, a milkmaid in the tradition of the ballads, as poetical and, perhaps, as unreal — that was all the *hitherto*. The *now* of Ardnacrusha is different; Diesel engines are the deities, kilowatts the acolytes, the servers are volts. This is absurd metaphor. But, even so, at Ardnacrusha, where once King Brian Boru was a neighbour, the natives can talk in terms of modern magic today. The scheme that made a new and bloodless revolution in Ireland begins here. That is to say, the people have begun from Ardnacrusha to exploit their greatest river economically at last.

The following three paragraphs, timely when this book was first published in 1930, have now gone somewhat out of date, but they may stand as a period-piece written after a first survey of the local scene in that year:—

'At Ardnacrusha, in 1928, the cow, like the earlier dwellers, has departed to the near foothills towards Clare, the larks have retired to the safer blue of Tipperary. Little German children play on the old road beside the foundry where once the untidy, timeless Irish fairies owned the thornbush. One may rejoice with the lark, or lament with the cows, but the steam-hammer and the drill, inventing new landscape and energy here, have no care for such heartfelt, old-fashioned emotions. In their disciplined truculence, they are eloquent of the new spirit in Ireland, or, rather, the old spirit, for Ireland always was truculent, as the wars prove.

'The Shannon Scheme is evolution-revolution, more subtle than any before it. It is partially, a psychological move, a diversion from the battles of the baser, if more idealistic order. It may, by this finesse, drive some of the despair out of the new country. It will certainly give the people a new stimulus by freeing them from the long compulsion of foreign coal.

'Every village and cow-house can now clean itself up under the urge of a bright light. Old oils, and tallow candles and the dreary mess of lamps will go on to the shelf with broken things. The electricity may for a year or two fail to finance itself in terms of the auditor's balance sheets. But a million, or more, people, at the least, will have a new sensation of comfort and efficiency. Darkness and half-lights are an enemy to all except poets. Ireland has been, insufferably long, a twilight place. It is a good thing that a daring, young government has been rash and young enough to invent the Shannon scheme. They will be justified for ever ultimately though, for a brief while, the bailiff may sit in their parlour.'

The Shannon at its rise, in north-west Cavan, is three hundred feet above sea-

level. It falls rapidly to Lough Allen, 160 feet above sea-level. After Lough Allen
the fall is slow, only fifty feet to Lough Derg by Killaloe. There is thus from Lough
Derg to the estuary at Limerick, a distance of fifteen miles, a fall of only 110 feet.
It will be seen that at no point is there sufficient power in the natural decline of
level to work turbines for the production of electricity. The problem was to trap
the Shannon into a canal at some point, and, by carrying it for some distance, to
achieve an artificial fall at the point where the canal was led again into the main
stream. A weir was therefore constructed across the river four miles south of
Killaloe. Here, at the intake building, the flow of water into the canal is
controlled. This canal is the head-race familiar in all accounts of the undertaking.
The head-race canal, 300 feet wide and 42 feet deep, runs for seven and a half
miles to Ardnacrusha. At Ardnacrusha the water falls 90 feet through steel tubes
at the rate of ninety tons per second. This fall rotates the turbines which, in turn,
drive the dynamos that produce the power. The water then runs for a little way
along the lower tail-race canal, and joins the Shannon one and a half miles from
Ardnacrusha.

From *Ireland of the Welcomes*, The Irish Tourist Association, Inc., 1943

In Blueshirt Battle
Maurice Manning

On 9 October 1932 there occurred what were probably the most serious disturbances to date. Shortly before a Cumann na nGaedheal meeting in Kilmallock,
Co. Limerick, was due to start, a crowd of about three hundred young men
gathered in a different part of the town and, led by a group carrying banners,
formed up four deep and marched in the direction of the Cumann na nGaedheal
meeting, shouting anti-Cumann na nGaedheal slogans. The dozen police present
moved into line across the road to meet them. When it looked as if this police
cordon would be broken, about fifty members of the Army Comrades Association
under Commandant Cronin rushed to the Guards' assistance. However, the
crowd broke through this cordon and soon there was general turmoil. In the
pitched battle which followed, broken poles were used as weapons in addition to
sticks, hurleys and stones. Then suddenly, two shots rang out as Commandant
Cronin fired over the heads of the crowd. The shots had the effect of causing
many of those involved to run for shelter. Thus the first stage of the Kilmallock
riots ended. All this time the opening speaker, Mr G. Bennett, had been making
his speech.

Later during the meeting, further scuffles broke out and many shop windows were shattered by flying stones. After a while, comparative quiet was again restored with the 'opposition' grouped at one end of the street, the cordon of police a few yards away and the ACA halfway between the police and the meeting. As Michael Hayes, TD, the former Ceann Comhairle, began to speak, a renewed spate of stone-throwing began. A large jagged flint narrowly missed his head but struck one of General Mulcahy's bodyguards full in the face. By this stage, many of those at the meeting were bleeding or swathed in bandages.

The next speaker was General Mulcahy, and as he rose to speak, the disorder intensified. The General, according to the *Limerick Leader* reporter, 'not satisfied with speaking from the floor of the lorry, chose the higher elevation of the driver's canopy whereon he stood silhouetted against the sky and completely ignoring his opponents'.

Shortly after this, a rival meeting was begun fifty yards from where Mulcahy was speaking. The main speaker at this meeting was the Chairman of the East Limerick executive of Fianna Fáil, Mr Michael Hayes.

The Cumann na nGaedheal meeting ended at half-past four in the afternoon, and at five fifteen, the battle broke out again and lasted for over an hour. The fighting was even more fierce this time, with hurleys, sticks and stones being freely used. Although it subsided round about half-past six, the lorry load of ACA members from Limerick were unable to leave the town until a military escort — the members of which were armed with rifles — arrived at nine o'clock. The departing ACA lorry was followed for about two miles out of the town by a hooting and jeering crowd.

From *The Blueshirts*, Gill & Macmillan, 1971

The First Radio Pirate

The first prosecution in the Irish Free State for the unlawful possession of wireless transmitting apparatus took place in the City District Court today.

When it was stated that there was 'another pirate on the air' using very offensive language, Mr J. J. Power, State Solicitor, said: 'Yes, but by degrees we will eliminate them all.'

Michael Madden junior, Wolfe Tone Street, Limerick, was fined £1 and two guineas costs, District Justice Flood stating that he believed the defendant was only experimenting for his own amusement and had not been guilty of offensive language.

Walter Dain, General Post Office Broadcasting Engineer, Dublin, said that when he visited Madden's house with Guard Lenihan on the 31st October last he found a very crude transmitting apparatus, as well as a megaphone, a gramophone pick-up and short wave and medium wave coils. The apparatus was removed, and a test revealed that it was capable of transmitting.

Replying to Mr Power, the witness said that the defendant maintained that the apparatus was not used for broadcasting. He admitted, however, that he had attempted to transmit on the short wave band.

Answering Mr Collins, solicitor for the defence, the witness said that the machine was made up of parts of a very old type of receiving set.

Guard Lenihan stated that some of the pirate broadcasting was very offensive. Names were mentioned, and scandalous remarks used.

The defendant said that while experimenting with a crystal set he found that he could transmit, and only tried to broadcast gramophone records, which he did for a month.

Mr Power said that great annoyance was caused to ordinary listeners by interference with the legitimate broadcast programmes. If the justice had decided to convict he was instructed to ask for an exemplary penalty in view of the scandalous remarks which had been heard recently from a 'pirate' wireless station. Some of these remarks were libellous and caused considerable pain to the families mentioned.

District Justice Flood said that it was an outrageous thing that people had been subjected to annoyance of the kind alluded to, but he did not believe that the defendant was guilty in this respect.

From *The Irish Times*, 29 February 1936

The Foynes Flying Boat

1988 sees the 50th anniversary of the first commercial crossing of the Atlantic by air and the community of Foynes, Co. Limerick have reason to be proud. The idea of commercial transatlantic flights had been on the minds of commercial airlines for many years. In 1937 many test flights took place at Foynes but it was the following year, 1938, that saw progress being made. Following an important North Atlantic Air Route conference in Dublin in March 1938, the weather reports, radio and ground support details were put in train. Imperial Airways, a British company, planned to use an ingenious but somewhat far-fetched device known as the Short-Mayo composite aircraft. The Short-Mayo, designed by Major Mayo, Assistant General Manager (Technical) of Imperial Airways, consisted of a lower component in the form of a modified Short C Class flying boat named 'Maia' and upper component comprising of a Short S.20 four engined seaplane named 'Mercury' which for take-off was mounted on top of 'Maia' and later released at a suitable height.

During 1938 only three aircraft visited Foynes. The first of these was a French flying boat on a survey flight. A few hours after this plane had departed 'Mercury' came into view, flown by Capt. Donald Bennett. No sooner had 'Mercury' moored when its mother craft 'Maia' arrived into Foynes. The 'Mercury' seaplane was defuelled to make it lighter and a crane used to place it on top of 'Maia'. The cargo on the flight was to be the first commercial load ever carried by seaplane across the North Atlantic. Throughout the following day, Wednesday 20 July, preparations went ahead for the departure that evening. Messages of good luck poured into the post office at Foynes. The crew of the 'Mercury' was Capt. Donald Bennett and his radio operator, A. J. Coster. A final weather briefing was held at 1 p.m. at which the decision was made to go. The crews went on board at 7 p.m. and at ten minutes to 8 p.m. 'Maia's' engines were started and as it moved away 'Mercury's' four engines also started up and the composite aircraft disappeared behind the island. Suddenly there was a tremendous deep roar as all eight engines were fully opened up and as the aircraft came into view again, it climbed slowly, circling away to the left around Monument Hill and was soon over the main channel of the Shannon and heading westwards.

As soon as it was opposite the pier, on which thousands of people had gathered to watch, the two aircraft broke apart, 'Maia' dipping slightly to glide away as 'Mercury' began to climb away. The separation was perfectly executed and was watched by Major Mayo and his wife from a launch. The combined power of the two four-engined units made it possible for the upper component to be put into the air with a load which it was quite incapable of taking off the water itself.

Having left Foynes at 8 p.m. on the Wednesday evening, 'Mercury' made good time across the Atlantic. Such was its speed across the ocean that a planned stop was dispensed with and the aircraft continued on directly to Montreal. It made its landfall over the Canadian coast at 9.31 a.m. the following morning (Irish time), having crossed the Atlantic in 13 hours 29 minutes, a new east–west record. The total time from Foynes to Montreal was 20 hours 20 minutes, 'Mercury' arriving at Montreal at 4.20 p.m. on Thursday afternoon (Irish time). After a quick turnaround it continued on, departing Montreal at 7 p.m. and landing in New York at 9.08 p.m. (Irish time) on Thursday evening 21 July. The total time for the 3,042 mile journey from Foynes to New York was 22 hours 31 minutes, giving an average speed of 130 mph. 'Maia' left Foynes at 12.30 p.m. on Thursday and returned to Southampton. Thus ended an exciting but commercially unacceptable exercise.

From the *Irish Philatelic Bulletin*, 12 May 1988

Mount Shannon House
Constantine FitzGibbon

The road to Mount Shannon, by which I mean the house that had once belonged to my family and not the village of that name some twenty miles away on Lough Derg, starts badly, for Clare Street in Limerick is an unattractive thoroughfare flanked by ugly, seedy buildings. When it was being built the Earl of Clare, driving in from Mount Shannon, stopped his carriage and had a word with the man in charge. He inquired what the new street would be called, and the man in charge, who presumably had no idea, replied promptly if somewhat sycophantically: 'Clare Street, in honour of your lordship.' No doubt this story was not known to the authorities who changed Wellesley Bridge to Sarsfield Bridge and George Street to O'Connell Street a generation or two ago. Certainly they would not willingly have left any public monument, even as insignificant as a street name, to a man who was the object of such historic hatred. Perhaps they thought the street had some connection with the County Clare which starts on the far side of the Shannon. No doubt it did not occur to them that it runs, in fact, in the opposite direction. But then even mayors and aldermen are occasionally capable of error or oversight. At least the name of this street, like all others in Limerick, is written in Gaelic characters which would no doubt have been as incomprehensible to Lord Clare as they are to most of Limerick's citizens today.

The demesne walls stretch for miles and miles, though here and there a gap has been cut that a farm track might be driven through, and almost everywhere they are crumbling away from the top. Those walls, seven or eight foot high, which enclose so many of the larger Irish estates, are a depressing feature, shutting off the view to the pedestrian, bicyclist and motorist alike, though a man on a horse can see over many of them. Some were built from a public-spirited point of view, to give employment during the hard times, but most, I fear, were put up with the simple selfish motive of preventing those outside seeing what went on within. They sometimes fulfilled a less satisfactory purpose in preventing those from within from noticing what was happening without. There were periods in Irish history when the rich were as ignorant as they were uninterested in the condition of the country from which they derived their wealth.

This is rolling, quite hilly country, with the river out of sight down below and a half circle of distant mountains in Clare, Tipperary, and Limerick closing the inland horizon. Between the road and the river, behind the demesne walls, are a number of large or largish estates. Almost all were burned during the troubles, in theory lest the British military move in, in practice because here the struggle was in many cases a class struggle too. These burnings were systematically and, on the whole, not unkindly carried out. Many of the houses were empty at the time, but where they were occupied the owner was notified of what was to happen and, unless he was particularly unpopular, was usually given time to remove at least his more valuable possessions. And then, when the troubles were over, he was quite handsomely compensated for the damage done to his property. In at least one case of which I know, the compensation was sufficient to enable the owner to build a more comfortable and commodious house than the one which had been burned.

Some of the estates, then, were rebuilt and the estates are still well-wooded. Others stand, gaunt shells in their parks where all the timber has been sold. Mount Shannon is one of these. What was once a front drive is now not even a cow path and the approach to the house is from the back, past the ruined stables, past the ruined bakery, the laundry, the place where in the old days they made their own gas, the servants' quarters, past the ruined coach houses, and out onto the front lawn to come suddenly upon the gaping facade of the ruined house. It is almost a small village that was here destroyed, and only one house still stands intact, the former steward's house in which there now lives the farmer who owns and farms this part of the estate.

I found him outside this house, a pleasant man in early middle age, and he most obligingly walked around to the front with me, but he had not much to tell me about the place or about my family. He had only been a boy when the house was burned and even then the family had been gone from here for forty years. Yet somehow, obscurely, I felt that perhaps he resented my appearance. Resented is not quite the right word and his manner towards me was civil in the extreme, but for centuries there was a firm Irish belief that land does not really belong to the people who took it or even who bought it: the land, it was felt, really belongs to the heirs of those to whom it used to belong. A soldier or a financier might rename his house Castlesmith or Jones House; for many people it remained the O'Gorman Castle or the O'Shaughnessy place. That, of course, was many years ago, but still FitzGibbons had lived on and about this land for a very long time and had built the ruin through which the farmer and I now picked our way. He knew, of course, that the ruin was his as was the land on which it stood. The roofless library into which we walked while the cows moved away into the Earl of Clare's roofless study, was his by every law. I had no claim to it whatever, not even the remotest, emotional shadow of a claim. I had never even been there before and, who knows? perhaps I shall never go there again. He pointed out a hole in the ground, the way to the wine cellar, choked with dockweed. Last week a calf had fallen into the wine cellar and they had had the devil of a time getting the beast out again. My presence made him slightly uncomfortable. I offered him a cigarette, that pathetic gesture of goodwill, and we walked together through the rusty framework of the conservatory. He showed me the stumps of what had once been a double avenue of beeches. They must have been large trees. No, he knew nothing about Lady Louisa, nothing at all except that she had spent a great deal of money. But, he said, as he accompanied me back to my car, there was an old man who was always talking about the old days at Mount Shannon. I might be able to find him in a pub at O'Briensbridge and he might have something to tell me. On the other hand he might not. He had worked there as a boy, but he was very old now. It might be worth my while to see if I could find him, though there was no telling where he might be. He had a nomadic job, catching rabbits on the banks of the canal built in connection with the Shannon scheme. They might know his whereabouts in O'Briensbridge. Or they might not. I thanked the farmer and got into my car. As I drove off past the ruined buildings I glanced back. He was standing there looking at me.

From *Miss Finnigan's Fault*, Cassells & Co. Ltd, 1953

On the Rampart: Limerick
John Francis O'Donnell

Cheerily rings the boatman's song
Across the dark-brown water;
His mast is slant, his sail is strong,
His hold is red with slaughter —
With beeves that cropped the fields of Glynn,
And sheep that pricked their meadows,
Until the sunset-cry trooped in
The cattle from the shadows.
He holds the foam-washed tiller loose,
And hums a country ditty;
For, under clouds of gold turned puce,
Gleam harbour, mole, and city.
O town of manhood! Maidenhood!
By thee the Shannon flashes —
There Freedom's seed was sown in blood,
To blossom into ashes.

St Mary's, in the evening air,
Springs up austere and olden;
Two sides its steeple gray and bare,
Two sides with sunset golden.
The bells roll out, the bells roll back,
For lusty knaves are ringing;

Deep in the chancel, red and black,
The white-robed boys are singing.
The sexton loiters by the gate
With eyes more blue than hyssop,
A black-green skull-cap on his pate,
And all his mouth a-gossip.
This is the town beside the flood —
The walls the Shannon washes —
Where Freedom's seed was sown in blood,
To blossom into ashes.

The streets are quaint, red-bricked, antique,
The topmost storeys curving,
With, here and there, a slated leak,
Through which the light falls swerving.
The angry sudden light falls down
On path and middle parquet,
On shapes weird as the ancient town,
And faces fresh for market.
They shout, they chatter, disappear,
Like imps that shake the valance
At midnight, when the clock ticks queer,
And time has lost its balance,
This is the town beside the flood
Which past its bastions dashes,
Where Freedom's seed was sown in blood,
To blossom into ashes.

Oh, how they talk, brown country folk,
Their chatter many-mooded,
With eyes that laugh for equivoque,
And heads in kerchiefs snooded!
Such jests, such jokes, whose plastic mirth
But Heine could determine —
The portents of the latest birth,
The point of Sunday's sermon,
The late rains and the previous drouth,
How oats were growing stunted,
How keels fetched higher prices South,
And Captain Watson hunted.
This is the town beside the flood
Whose waves with memories flashes,
Where Freedom's seed was sown in blood,
To blossom into ashes.

How thick with life the Irish town!
Dear gay and battered portress,
That laid all save her honour down,
To save the fire-ringed fortress.
Here Sarsfield stood, here lowered the flag
That symbolised the people —
A riddled rag, a bloody rag,
Plucked from St Mary's steeple.
Thick are the walls the women lined
With courage worthy Roman,
When, armed with hate sublime, if blind,
They scourged the headlong foeman.
This is the town beside the flood
That round its ramparts flashes,
Where Freedom's seed was sown in blood,
To blossom into ashes.

This part is mine: to live divorced
Where foul November gathers,
With other sons of thine dispersed,
Brave city of my fathers —
To gaze on rivers not mine own,
And nurse a wasting longing,
Where Babylon, with trumpets blown,
South, North, East, West, comes thronging —
To hear distinctly, if afar,
The voices of thy people —
To hear through crepitating jar
The sweet bells of thy steeple —
To love the town, the hill, the wood,
The Shannon's stormful flashes,
Where Freedom's seed was sown in blood,
To blossom into ashes.

From *Poems*, Ward and Downey, 1891

EIGHT

THE STAGE

Playhouses and Players, 1736–1800
William Smith Clark

From 1736 onwards Dublin troupes, while on their summer tours to the south of Ireland, often stopped to perform at Limerick. Thither in 1754 a veteran stroller, James Love, migrated from Edinburgh to manage a summer company . . .

In 1760, when Spranger Barry, manager of the Dublin Crow Street Theatre, opened the fine new theatre at Cork, he instituted regular summer seasons at Limerick as a supplementary undertaking. For the next decade the Dublin Theatre Royal company played almost every year at the small inconvenient structure called 'the Theatre in Peter's Cell' . . .

Some ingenious theatrical entrepreneur transformed the refectory of the one-time nunnery into a playhouse containing boxes, pit, one gallery, stage, and a few dressing rooms. Seats in the 1760s sold at 3s. in the boxes, 2s. in the pit, and 1s. in the gallery. The refreshments served at the Peter's Cell performances constituted the theatre's one distinction: they were not oranges, as in London and Dublin, but peaches. The fruit sellers circulated with baskets of luscious four-inch specimens at a halfpenny each.

In September and October of 1767 the Crow Street actors were performing at Limerick under the leadership of William Dawson, Barry's deputy . . . The mean and cramped interior of the playhouse made for very informal and prankish behaviour. On one occasion the Badgers Club, composed of the county's first gentlemen, sponsored *Romeo and Juliet*. The club members as privileged spectators sat on the stage and imbibed freely from the contents of a nearby sideboard. Towards the close of the play, at the moment of Juliet's death, the Grand Badger, an old man dressed in a high cap of badger's skin, could not contain himself. Crying out, 'Oh, my poor pretty little soul! Don't be lying there,' he stepped forward, lifted Juliet up in spite of her remonstrances, and took her to the sideboard for refreshments. On the day Shakespeare's tragedy ended in laughter!

At another performance a Limerick buck, familiarly called 'the Grand Bugle', mounted to the stage in order to show himself off after the prevailing fashion, discovered too many of his kind ahead of him between the scene wings at the sides, and therefore walked behind the scene at the back. Then in the nicely painted and valuable flat he cut with his penknife a hole large enough to show his face. There he stood at his ease, boldly looking out at the audience. The Grand Bugle had a worthy rival for public attention in a personage known as 'the Child' because 'Frolic was his whole affair in this world.' One evening at Peter's Cell 'the Child' was sitting in the gallery with a crowd of fellow roisterers, bottles in hand, leading the crowd in shouting toasts. 'A clap for Mahon the player on the stage' was followed by hearty clapping from the gallery bucks. 'A groan for my aunt in the side-boxes' brought a loud response. The whole house got into an uproar. The sheriff, 'Hero' Jackson, left his box, climbed to the gallery, grasped 'the Child' by the scruff of the neck and shoved him down the gallery stairs into the street. After the sheriff had reached his seat again, he looked across the stage and there he saw 'the Child' sober and quiet beside his aunt in the side-box opposite.

The boisterous interruptions from the Peter's Cell audiences infected the manners of the actors. In a performance of *The Beggar's Opera*, West Digges as Captain Macheath had just put on his fetters at Newgate prison. He found himself unpleasantly bound with chains that were not the customary set. Turning in irritation to 'the Grand Bugle' who was seated near by, he complained in a loud voice about the property-man: 'Look here, sir, what a pair of fetters he has brought me — they've cut through my ankles! Instead of giving me proper light tin ones, he has got them out of gaol, and they have been on some murderer!' Such persistent goings-on caused the playhouse in Peter's Cell to be remembered with unusual vividness by John P. O'Keeffe, the far-strolling Dublin comedian.

From *The Irish Stage in the County Towns 1720 to 1800*, Oxford at the Clarendon Press, 1965

Catherine Hayes
Gus Smith

Limerick-born soprano, Catherine Hayes, was to achieve international acclaim; in fact, the year 1846 saw her at her peak, a firm favourite with La Scala audiences for her unfailing beauty of tone and resplendent coloratura. During the season she sang the title roles in Donizetti's *Lucia di Lammermoor* and his *Linda di Chamounix* and Desdemona in Rossini's *Otello* as well as Violetta in Mercadante's *Il Braco*.

During the 1840s and 1850s she was greatly in demand in European opera houses, and in April 1849 made an immediate impression at Covent Garden in *Linda di Chamounix*. In July of the same year she partnered the renowned Italian tenor, Giovanni Mario, in Meyerbeer's *Le Prophète*. Years afterwards Margaret Burke Sheridan would pay tribute to Catherine Hayes' achievements: 'She paved the way for me in Italy. Italian audiences adored her.'

She was born at 4 Patrick Street, Limerick in October, 1818, the third daughter of Arthur Hayes, who was Bandmaster in the Limerick City Militia. He deserted his family and left them in very poor circumstances with the burden of bringing up the family falling on their mother, Mary Hayes, who eked out a living by making straw hats.

The story of young Catherine's discovery is reminiscent of Cinderella. She was in the habit of accompanying her cousin, a Mrs Carroll, to Lord Limerick's house in Henry Street where she worked as a char. On one occasion, Dr Knox, the Church of Ireland Bishop of Limerick, who lived next door, was enjoying a siesta in his garden when he was awakened by the traditional air *Jemmy, mo mhíle stór*, sung by the 'most beautiful voice he had ever heard'. Looking over some shrubs, he spied the frail-looking girl 'thrilling the air with the sweetest of melody'.

After making enquiries, the bishop with the assistance of friends in the local commercial and musical life of the city, had Catherine sent to Dublin for voice training with Antonio Sapio. She gave her first public concert in Dublin at the Rotunda in May, 1839 and at a recital in the Theatre Royal Limerick she thrilled the audience with her pure, sweet-toned soprano voice although she was still inexperienced as a stage performer. Within a few years she would become known as the 'Swan of Erin' and the 'Irish Nightingale'.

Catherine later went to Milan where she studied with Signor Roncono, an authority in the Italian school of singing. She made her continental debut at Marseilles in May, 1845 in a performance of Bellini's *I Puritani*, and toured the continent as 'La Hayes', winning growing acclaim. She was soon engaged as *prima donna* at La Scala, Milan, where her performance in Don Donizetti's *Linda di Chamounix* established her supremacy as an interpreter of Italian opera, and she appeared in works by Ricci, Mercadante, Rossini and Verdi in Venice, Vienna and London where she sang in April, 1849 with the Royal Italian Opera. Mile-long queues formed to hear her and she was invited to Buckingham Palace by Queen Victoria. By the time she returned to Limerick, she was an international celebrity.

News of her success at Covent Garden in *Linda di Chamounix* had already reached Limerick, so that when it was announced that she would sing in opera there in March, 1850 there was a clamour for tickets. The Theatre Royal was filled to capacity on the opening night of Bellini's *La Sonnambula* with Catherine Hayes singing the role of Amina. Next day, the *Limerick Chronicle* reported: 'Limerick has rarely seen a more splendid display of rank, fashion and beauty as that assembled for the occasion. It must indeed have been a gratifying moment for Miss Hayes when every hand, voice and heart present united in one of the most enthusiastic welcomes that ever our theatre has witnessed.'

The newspaper described her singing as 'the perfection of vocalism' and her acting as 'charmingly natural'. The excited audience made the diva encore Amina's romance, 'Ah, non credea mirarti' and at the final curtain the stage was showered with flowers. During the same week she sang the title role in *Norma* and again her radiant voice thrilled the audience. 'Another glorious triumph for Miss Hayes' stated the *Limerick Chronicle*. 'Never have we heard her in better voice, never was her acting more convincing.' Catherine also sang . . . a song especially composed for her by Harvey:

> *When roaming on a foreign strand*
> *I fancy still my steps were here:*
> *Home of my heart, my native land.*

Later, she undertook arduous tours of North and South America, as well as Australia. Catherine was particularly taken by the warmth of the reception accorded her in San Francisco. A local newspaper reported: 'A most enthusiastic audience threw necklaces, gold trinkets and other gifts at her feet on stage.' Her agent in the USA was William Avery Bushnell who had also acted for Jenny Lind on her American tours. Tickets for Catherine's recitals sometimes cost $1,150 and in San Francisco, from November 1852 to May, 1853, her fees averaged £650 per month.

Her arrival in Sydney aroused 'an excitement wholly unparalleled in the theatrical annals of the colony'. Audiences were impressed by her bravura operatic arias but were more affected by her singing of such ballads as 'Home Sweet Home' and Irish airs. Her repertoire on these tours consisted primarily of the great Italian operas by Bellini and Donizetti with their unsurpassed opportunities for virtuoso coloratura singing.

Shortly after her return to Britain, she unwisely undertook an exhaustive concert tour but on medical advice was persuaded to cut her engagements. Constant travel and overwork had exhausted her and impaired her health, which was never robust. In 1857 she decided to settle in London where she married her manager, William Bushnell. She continued to sing in London and on provincial tours, but restricted her performances after her husband's death in France in July, 1858, aged thirty-five. She died in August, 1861 in London and was buried in Kensal Green cemetery, leaving an estate of £16,000. There is a small plaque erected on the house in Limerick where she was born, but the great soprano is worthy of a more impressive memorial.

From *Irish Stars of the Opera*, Madison Publishers Ltd, 1994

Memories of the Old Theatre Royal
J. F. Walsh

The older generation of Limerick people remembers with affection the Theatre Royal in Henry Street. It was the second theatre in the city to bear the name. The first Theatre Royal was built in 1770 by one Tottenham Heaphy in Cornwallis Street, now Lower Gerald Griffin Street, and was destroyed by fire in 1818. In 1810 another theatre was built in George's Street, now O'Connell Street, but after a brief career of some twelve years was purchased by the Augustinian Fathers and converted into a church. Limerick remained without a theatre until in 1841 Joseph Fogerty purchased a plot of ground in Henry Street and on it erected a new

Theatre Royal, a dwelling-house for himself and a row of houses in the lane off Lower Mallow Street, known as Fogerty's Range or Theatre Lane.

The theatre was a one-storey building, with the main entrance in the centre of the Henry Street frontage. At first this was a columned portico fitted with double doors, somewhat similar to the entrance to the Country Club, but following damage by storm about the year 1900, the portico was removed and at a later date a veranda was built to replace it. At the left was the entrance to the stalls, and on the right, around the corner of the lane, was the entrance to the gallery. On the parapet over the main entrance was the Royal Coat of Arms; on the roof a louvered ventilator, surmounted by a weather vane. The building was compact and could accommodate 1,300 persons. For some years after the destruction by fire of Dublin's Theatre Royal, the Limerick theatre was the largest in Ireland.

Classical figures in chalk on pedestals ornamented the vestibule, and its walls, as well as those of the lobby leading to the stalls were adorned with pictures of famous actors and actresses, including one of Catherine Hayes. At the end of the stairway leading to the Circle stood two wooden figures of soldiers in armour, which had at one time adorned the band wagon of Thady Cooney's Circus. To the right was the foyer leading to the Pit. Inside the floor sloped towards the stage, the Pit being divided from the Stalls by a barrier, and while the seats in the latter were padded and had back-rests, those in the pit were merely hard wooden forms. Round the sides of the building above the Pit ran the Circle, terminating in two stage boxes at each end. High above was the usual gallery, or rather 'Gods', as it was familiarly called, and here, as in all theatres, the habitués were wont to voice their approval, and on occasion their disapproval of the show.

Obtaining entrance to the theatre during the run of a popular show was, in those pre-queue days, a feat in itself. Might was right. One joined the elbowing jostling crowd where possible, and took part in the pushing and shoving until at last, breathless but happy, one was forced through the entrance. All the while an attendant at a side door enticed the more wary with his call of 'Early doors, sixpence extra.' The usual prices of admission were, circle, 3/0; stalls, 2/6; pit, 1/-; gallery, 6d.

Up to the advent of electricity, the house was lighted by gasaliers suspended from the gallery balcony, over the circle. The stage was spacious and the theatre was so constructed that no matter what part of the house one was in, the stage never appeared far away. The drop-screen — a work of art in itself — had been painted by Henry O'Shea, a well-known artist in those days. In the centre Shakespeare stood, under a pillared cupola, scroll in hand and leaning on a low column. Seated on steps, one at either side, were two female figures, one representing Music and Comedy, with a lyre and a mask, and the other, Tragedy, with a poison-cup and dagger. Underneath ran the caption, 'All the World's a Stage.' There was another curtain of heavy dark material that fell to indicate the conclusion of a performance and time and time again great actors and actresses had to come on in front of this to make their final bows. Running right across the top was a long canvas panel with the Royal Coat of Arms in the centre. This panel had been over the stage of the theatre in George's Street originally.

Touring companies, often direct from London, on tour to Dublin and Cork, came to Limerick with operas, musical comedies, plays and dramas, so that the patrons of the old Royal were well catered for. In addition there were local amateur productions, comic operas, plays, pantomimes, concerts and school entertainments, as well as balls, political meetings and other functions . . .

Musical productions were always the most popular and the music-loving Limerick people gave pride of place to opera. Who can forget those companies, great in their day, Arthur Rousby's, Carl Rosa, Moody Manners, O'Mara, D'Oyly Carte, and last, but not least, the Elster-Grime, recalling, as it does, memories of the ever popular Frank Land? The early appearance of John McCormack here was an event. Madame Clara Butt enthralled Limerick, but the scenes of enthusiasm when our own Joe O'Mara came excelled them all. The thunderous applause of his townsmen shook the very rafters of the building as they encored him again and again. Surely he never sang so well as in the old Royal.

Musical comedies were always in demand and the music of 'The Belle of New York', 'San Toy', 'The Flying Dutchman', 'The Messenger Boy', and the splendidly staged 'Gay Gordons', with Stanley Brett and Mai Ashe, will long be remembered. Many people famous in the world of music appeared here, as did many famous bands, among the latter Sousa's being outstanding.

Some of the greatest Shakespearean actors faced the footlights of the Royal and held the audience spell-bound; F. R. Benson (afterwards Knighted), one of the greatest actors of his time and a true sportsman; Norman V. Norman, Osmonde Tearle, Ian McClarne, Madame Bandom Palmer, Alexander Marsh and Carrie Bayly, are some who come to mind.

The Victorian melodramas were real thrillers, and of these, the most memorable was 'East Lynne'. This usually moved the ladies in the audience to tears, and made even the men find it difficult to suppress their emotions. 'The Nugget of Gold' was another thriller, recalling to mind S. F. ('William') Cody, who attired as Buffalo Bill, used to ride about the town accompanied by his troop of 'Red Indians'. He was an excellent marksman and could shoot a glass ball off a man's head, or a clay pipe to pieces. One of the most spectacular scenes in his play was that in which a horse fell from a broken bridge on to the stage below. In the light of his later interest in aeronautics it is interesting to recall that while on a visit to Limerick, the 'Colonel' had a pleasure boat towed up the river by a large kite.

Kennedy Millar specialised in Irish dramas, such as 'Seamus O'Brien', 'Michael Dwyer', 'Conn, The Shaughraun', and 'The Colleen Bawn'. His plays were well staged and never failed to arouse the patriotic feelings of the audience. The scenes depicting the capture of Lord Edward in 'Lord Edward Fitzgerald', the escape of Seamus O'Brien from the gallows, and the shooting of Danny Mann and rescue of the Colleen Bawn were most realistic.

To omit, what was an annual event, 'Pool's Myriorama', would be unforgivable. As a vivid and interesting entertainment it was unsurpassed and was looked forward to by young and old each year. This entertainment took the form of a conducted tour of many lands. Large pictures of famous places, painted on canvas and worked on rollers, passed across the stage, sometimes with beautiful lighting effects. There were also pictures of topical interest. One picture that always created a sensation was the blowing up in Havana Harbour of the USS Maine, complete with sound effects. In contrast to this was a picture of Milan Cathedral, beautifully illuminated by night. In addition Pool's always had a good orchestra and a programme of variety turns. Pool's first introduced 'Living Pictures', as they were then called, to Limerick, and I can remember some Boer War pictures meeting with such a hostile reception that the gallery was closed for several nights.

Even in those days Limerick was not lacking in amateur talent. The Limerick Operatic Society produced the Gilbert and Sullivan operas for several seasons under the baton of Joseph P. Bellens, and from time to time the late Paul Bernard and Kendal Irwin produced some beautiful pantomimes. Saint Michael's Temperance Society specialised in Irish dramas, in which that veteran amateur actor, Tom Duggan, invariably filled a leading part . . .

The audience, while there to be entertained, were keen critics, but it was in the 'Gods' that the real 'critics' arrayed themselves. They seldom left any performer in doubt as to what they thought of his merits or demerits as an actor, and indeed amongst themselves, frequently displayed no mean talents as popular entertainers. The better known 'Gods' artists were often called upon to render songs or mouth-organ solos during stage intervals. At all times they displayed a wit that, if at times a little forceful, was generally shrewd and penetrating, but on the whole their humour was without malice. Prominent patrons of the stalls came in for the usual quota of good-natured banter, and many a prominent local personage had his dignity impaired by a chorus of 'Good night, Jim. Come in and take off your hat.' Many a youthful swain who brought his young lady to the stalls was importuned by the 'Gods' to 'Buy her a box of chocolates,' and he generally did, to their mutual embarrassment and the delight of the 'Gods'.

Hunt balls, too, were held in the Royal. For these the seats and floor boards were removed, making available the excellent dance floor beneath. The decorations usual for such events were put up, and the scene during the dance was a gay and colourful one. Less picturesque, but on occasion not less exciting, the political meetings which were held in the old theatre. Of these I remember well the Unionist meeting in October, 1912, which led to three nights of rioting in the city and the boycotting of the theatre for over a week.

With the coming of the films, plays became less frequent, and, except for concert-parties and variety shows, there were few stage productions. Actors and actresses, wagons of scenery and costumes were replaced by a few tin cases of films . . .

On the afternoon of Monday, 23rd January, 1922, the alarm of 'Fire' at the old theatre was given, and within a few hours, despite every effort to save it, Limerick's Theatre Royal was burned to the ground. The curtain had come down for the last time on the old Royal of happy memories.

From *Journal of the Old Limerick Society*, Vol. 1, No. 1, December 1946

Garryowen
Anonymous

Let Bacchus's sons be not dismayed,
But join with me each jovial blade;
Come booze and sing, and lend your aid
To help me with the chorus:—

Instead of Spa we'll drink brown ale,
And pay the reckoning on the nail;
No man for debt shall go to gaol
From Garryowen in glory!

We are the boys that take delight in
Smashing the Limerick lamps when lighting,
Through the streets like sporters fighting,
And tearing all before us.

We'll break windows, we'll break doors,
The watch knock down by threes and fours;
Then let the doctors work their cures,
And tinker up our bruises.

We'll beat the bailiffs, out of fun,
We'll make the mayor and sheriffs run:
We are the boys no man dares dun,
If he regards a whole skin.

Our hearts, so stout, have got us fame,
For soon 'tis known from whence we came;
Where'er we go they dread the name
Of Garryowen in glory.

Johnny Connell's tall and straight,
And in his limbs he is complete;
He'll pitch a bar of any weight,
From Garryowen to Thomond Gate.

Garryowen is gone to wrack
Since Johnny Connell went to Cork,
Though Darby O'Brien leapt over the dock
In spite of all the soldiers.

From *The Lyrics of Ireland*, edited by Samuel Lover, Houlston and Wright, 1858

Joseph O'Mara
Gus Smith

'My early life was wild, harum-scarum. A devil-may-care was I, and I fear the passing years have not materially changed me but, after all, I come from Limerick.'

Years ago, famous tenor, Joseph O'Mara, made this frank admission when asked by T. P. O'Connor, his London-Irish parliamentary friend, to contribute to his paper. And in the same vein, O'Mara added, 'I was convinced that a life on the ocean wave was the only life for me, so I shipped as an apprentice on board a liner sailing from Dundee to Calcutta. I saw myself as captain of a Cunarder in a year or two. I will not dwell on all I endured on that voyage, suffice to say I returned home totally cured.'

James O'Mara, his father, was the owner of a prosperous bacon factory in Limerick and had hoped that his son would join it, but early on he became only too aware of Joseph's restless disposition.

The O'Mara home was a happy one. 'I was born with a great love of music,' the boy would say later on in life. 'I remember my mother's voice which though untrained, was full of purity and sweetness. Hearing her sing folk songs was a delightful treat that never failed to lure me away from the nefarious pursuits upon which I was usually engaged.'

He was born on 16 July 1864, the second youngest of a family of 13 and became a pupil of the local Jesuit College. Despite his wild escapades, he found time to sing in a church choir and was encouraged by his teachers who recognised the potential in his voice.

Joseph was only 14 when his mother died. It was a cruel blow and he took time to get over the trauma. After his short-lived sea voyage, he accepted his father's offer to join the family bacon factory and also resumed singing with St Michael's Choir . . .

At this time, Joseph fell in for a small legacy, so feeling very independent — and with his father's blessing — set off for Milan on New Year's Day, 1889. He soon found an able voice coach in Signor Moretti . . .

After two years in Milan, O'Mara returned to Limerick more determined than ever to get on with his career. Hearing of a new opera being put on by the D'Oyly Carte in London he applied for an audition . . . and was successful. He was engaged to share the title role in Gilbert & Sullivan's new opera, *Ivanhoe* with Ben Davies — then Britain's finest tenor. It was the breakthrough he needed and soon his voice attracted wide notice and he received many concert engagements. He decided, however, to return to Milan to complete his training in Italian opera and took lessons from Signor Perini.

In 1893 while on holiday in Limerick he received a telegram from Sir Augustus Harris asking him to contact him at once. O'Mara lost no time and was told he was wanted for productions of *Cavalleria Rusticana*, *Pagliacci* and *Faust*, apparently having to go on without rehearsals. On tour with the company he also sang in *Carmen*, *Lohengrin* and *Meistersinger*. In October 1893 the company crossed the Channel to present a season at Dublin's Gaiety Theatre . . .

As a company member, O'Mara was popular with his colleagues who enjoyed his puckish sense of humour and warm, if forceful, character . . .

In that same year 1896 he married a Miss Power from Waterford, of whom little is known . . . A year later they set sail together for America where O'Mara was engaged to sing the tenor lead in *The Highwayman*. From all accounts his fine voice and acting ability so impressed impresarios that he was offered attractive concert and operatic work but turned the offers down; he longed to be nearer Ireland.

Back in Britain he was not short of engagements. It was the age of oratorios, concerts and musical 'at homes' and he soon sang in houses of note . . .

But opera was really the tenor's first love and in 1902 he joined the Moody-Manners Company, one of the most respected in Britain and toured with them for some years . . . Always a firm favourite with Irish audiences, he went on to achieve a number of operatic 'firsts' in Ireland. He was the first tenor to sing Enzo in *La Gioconda* and in 1908 the first Rodolfo in *La Bohème*. Later he was the first to sing Cavaradossi in Ireland and in the same season was in the Irish premiere of *Samson et Dalila*.

Ever on the move, O'Mara, accompanied by his wife, returned to New York to take the tenor lead in a musical *Peggy Machree* and received such enthusiastic notices in the press that two Dublin papers quoted from them at length.

Under the heading, IRISH TENOR'S TRIUMPH, Ashton Stevens in the *New York Journal* wrote:

There is an Irish Caruso at the Broadway Theatre and his name is Joseph O'Mara and in a ballad he can sing a sure straight note that hits the heart; he is a real tenor, something of the reedy sweetness of the clarinet, sweetness without cloying his treble voice. He is a virile singer and most of his music in *Peggy Machree* is recruited from the good old virile love songs of Ireland . . .

Apart from the nostalgia the musical evoked among the Irish in particular, there was no mistaking the splendid impression O'Mara had made. 'A voice full of feeling', wrote one music critic, and a colleague added, 'A voice rare in its appeal'. There is no doubt that if the tenor had cared to stay in America for a year or more, he would have become a wealthy man. He agreed to sing in the musical at the Park Theatre in Boston and during his stay in the city he and his wife were special guests of the Gerald Griffin Club which was composed of Limerick men and women.

On his return to London, he joined the Thomas Beecham Company in 1909 and a few months later was back on the Covent Garden stage singing in *The Tales of Hoffmann* . . . and *Faust* . . .

The year 1912 was to be a highlight in Joseph O'Mara's career. Limerick people rejoiced when he was accorded the Freedom of the City, an honour they felt he richly deserved, for in their eyes he was their ambassador of song. Bands played at the railway station to greet his arrival and he and his wife were conveyed in an open, horse-drawn carriage through the city streets. The tenor counted the experience as one of the proudest moments of his life . . .

For his first Dublin season, October 1913 he opened singing Raoul in *The Huguenots*. The company missed Dublin in 1914 because of the outbreak of war. In February 1915, however, he returned for two weeks . . .

By 1919 the O'Mara Company was so popular in Dublin that it was engaged for four weeks in February and another four in June and this continued for several years, despite the fact that the Carl Rosa Company also gave three weeks opera in the autumn. From this period onwards O'Mara produced many interesting works, notably Puccini's *Manon Lescaut* in which he also sang; *Mignon, A Masked Ball, La Wally* (Catalani), *Tristan and Isolde, Orpheus* (Gluck) and Mozart's *Seraglio*. Another revival was Balfe's *The Rose of Castile* which proved quite a hit. During these years the O'Mara Company appeared with great success at the Opera House, Cork and the Theatre Royal, Limerick. Usually on arrival at the railway station in Limerick he and the company were welcomed by a brass band and the tenor himself sometimes sang an aria from *The Bohemian Girl* or *Maritana* to the waiting crowd . . .

By now he was acknowledged as an outstanding actor-singer. His Canio was unforgettable. As one critic wrote, 'With his heart-broken sobs, he could tear passion to tatters and at the same time never exaggerate the character.' Like many artists who excelled in tragic parts, the tenor could also extract the last ounce of humour from roles that lent themselves to mirth, such as Myles na-gCopaleen in *The Lily of Killarney* and Mike Murphy in Stanford's *Shamus O'Brien*. Sir Charles Stanford told of one occasion when he was conducting his opera and O'Mara was in exuberant form and so funny were his antics that Sir Charles became quite doubled up with laughter and unable to conduct. He had to lay down his baton, the orchestra ceased playing and also commenced to roar with laughter along with the entire audience; and only when all had recovered and the uproar ceased could the opera proceed . . .

Altogether he sang in 67 operas. A prodigious worker, he was blessed with an exceptional musical memory. He could prompt either soprano, contralto, baritone or bass in any one of the operas in which he sang. Because of his innate acting ability it was agreed that if he ever lost his voice he could have earned a good living as an actor . . .

When he died in Dublin on 5 August 1927 the newspapers stated, 'Death has removed the greatest figure in the Irish musical world, a great singer and the greatest force behind grand opera in Ireland.' . . .

In Limerick his name is not entirely forgotten, though he is surely worthy of greater recognition. A small plaque on the facade of the house where he was born, and which today is known as Ozanam House, the headquarters of the local St Vincent de Paul Society, is the only reminder of one of Limerick's most famous sons.

Would not a bursary in his name, awarded, say, annually to a talented young Limerick singer or instrumentalist, be more lasting and appropriate?

From *Irish Stars of the Opera*, Madison Publishers Ltd, 1994

A Limerick Apprenticeship
Harry Bailey and Tom O'Shea

I [Harry Bailey] was born in Limerick on Christmas Day 1909 . . . The Shannon River flowed directly under my birth place, Nolan's Cottages . . . My schooling started at the local Presentation Convent. In no time, I was chosen to play the title role in *Goldilocks* at the Christmas Pantomime, mostly, I hope, because of my long, blond, curly hair. At this time, of course, boys up to the ages of five or six, used to wear velvet suits and had their hair in ringlets . . . A year later, I was sent to Sexton Street Christian Brothers . . .

My mother was a wonderful actress and very popular at the turn of the century. Carrie Ferguson is still fondly remembered in Limerick today. She was leading lady in most of the shows of her day. She relished playing in *East Lynne* and the musical comedy *Indian Prince*. In *Napoleon and Josephine*, she played Josephine. She used to dress up as an officer of the Connaught Rangers and in her military uniform gave a tear-filled rendering of *Only a Piece of Khaki your Daddy wore at Mons*.

Limerick was a famous winter-quarters for many shows. At any one time you could have Transfields, Battys, Hannafords, John Duffys, Buff Bills, Chipperfields, Fossetts, Scotts, Corvenios and more, all hibernating in Limerick. When my mother's six month touring stint finished each year she always returned to the theatre in Limerick. The circus and show business worlds are very closely inter-related through marriage, so it came as no surprise when my father and mother met up together in Limerick . . .

When my father married my mother, he was involved in cinematography. This was after the unfortunate collapse of the Lloyd Circus . . . My father's first venture into the area of cinema was through the magic lantern. He travelled Ireland showing his slides and accompanied them with a running commentary . . . When animated pictures came on the scene, my father and his brother Bracey introduced the first gas-operated movie machine to Ireland. Later my father bought a steam-engine, with a dynamo mounted on front and became one of the first men in Ireland to travel and show electric pictures. In the development of cinematography, the big step from gas to electric movies was a step of major significance.

In some of the areas visited, the locals had never before seen an electric bulb and when the engine arrived in the village, it was greeted with awe and amazement. Once the engine was started up, the coloured lights on the canopy illuminated the whole area and the numerous on-lookers loudly applauded. My uncle Bob always took a bow at this early stage of the proceedings. The Wallace and Stephens steam-engine was a beautiful job and the joy and pride of my father. It had eight rolled brass pillars holding up the canopy and was envied by all who viewed it. He also bought a Pullman caravan at this time, so things must have been good. So good, in fact, that he changed his name from Daniels to Baily, his mother's name.

Bob, my uncle, used to drive the engine and operate the machine for showing the pictures. After her marriage mother sang to song slides, while father took the money at the door. One must remember that there were no cinemas in most Irish towns or villages at that time, or, indeed, no electric light, unless privately owned. So the arrival of *Bailey's Electric Pictures*, with the name lit up in coloured bulbs on the canopy, was an event of major importance to many a country town. The local kids would follow the engine to the local river to collect water and then stand in sheer amazement as Uncle Bob switched on the lights . . .

Remember that at this early age the films shown by my father were silent films. It was becoming more and more necessary to supplement them with music, and, as well, film-showing only occupied approximately six months of the year, while the other six were devoted to putting on plays, up and down the country. Father decided I was academically qualified to leave school. He needed somebody to play child parts. I wholeheartedly agreed with him in the former. The latter I wasn't too sure about. In those days, children were born to serve their parents. At any rate, my schoolmaster presented me with a one-string fiddle and told me that when I had learnt to play it, my father could buy me a bow . . . Limerick would serve as base-camp for my travels.

I now started my theatrical career in earnest. I played Little Willie in *East Lynne*, Stephanus in the *Sign of the Cross* and any other child's part, as required. Contrary to my earlier doubts, I loved it. The show usually started with variety acts, then on to a drama and finished with a comedy sketch. I had to do a song nightly. I wasn't too keen on this at times and had to be pushed onto the stage . . .

I remember the time my father bought an old carrier lorry, in the town of Hospital, Co. Limerick. We were playing nearby Emly at the time. This lorry had solid tyres and was chain-driven. There was no cab or body on it, so Uncle Bob built a driving seat, a temporary affair and put a flat body on the chassis. He gave me a couple of driving lessons on the Saturday and Sunday and then told me that I had passed my driving test. I had never driven anything before in my life. The piano was used as a back rest and, on travelling day, a few baskets were placed behind to steady the piano. Talk about Kamikaze. Uncle Bob started the engine, put it into second gear, handed the steering wheel to me and jumped off. He was required to drive another lorry. To say I was frightened would be a total understatement. I was panic-stricken. It was OK to practise in a field, but out on the open road! That was a different situation altogether. While 'driving' to Knocklong, I was told that the railway bridge had been blown up the night before by the IRA. I was warned not to attempt to cross the railway sleepers that had been installed as a temporary measure. The warnings were totally unnecessary because I never reached the bridge or what was left of it. A hair-pin bend laid prior claims to me. This bend was a left-hander and the lorry only had a forty per cent left-hand lock. I jammed on the brakes, but nothing happened. I hit the ditch an unmerciful wallop and the piano went over my head into the adjoining field. Luckily, the piano was a Kramer Yacht iron-framed job, with a folding keyboard and the only damage done was that it was knocked out of tune. So was I, need I add.

One day I visited Castleconnell, with my father, and while he discussed fishing with Charles Enright, who was champion dry-fly caster of Ireland, I wandered along the riverside. Suddenly, a little boy fell into the river, and being a strong swimmer, I dived in and pulled him out . . . His parents gave me a pound . . .

Around this time an event happened which brought about major changes in the travelling-show business. It was a most tragic fire in Drumcollogher, Co. Limerick. A film show was in progress in an upstairs loft when the projector went on fire. In the rush to escape dozens of young people were trampled and burned to death. As a direct result of this horrible happening, the authorities insisted that all travelling cinemas should have an iron box surrounding the projector. Also at hand would be required buckets of water and sand, as well as a wet blanket. Each hall should now possess two exit doors, opening outwards and two illuminated exit signs. All those regulations were stringently enforced by the Gardai and no show opened until the requirements were met.

When I was seventeen, I decided to leave home. I had an argument with my mother, as many a seventeen year old does, and my grandmother advised me to try another show. In typical showbusiness dramatic fashion, I picked up my violin, left home and started walking.

From *Encore! The Harry Bailey Story*, Dublin, 1990

Anew McMaster at the Ritz
Harold Pinter

I toured Ireland with Mac for about two years in the early 1950s. He advertised in *The Stage* for actors for a Shakespearean tour of the country. I sent him a photograph and went to see him . . . He offered me six pounds a week, said I could get digs for twenty-five shillings at the most, told me how cheap cigarettes were and that I could play Horatio, Bassanio and Cassio. It was my first job proper on the stage . . .

Joe Nolan, the business manager, came in one day and said: Mac, all the cinemas in Limerick are on strike. What shall I do? Book Limerick! Mac said. At once! We'll open on Monday. There was no theatre in the town. We opened on the Monday in a two thousand seater cinema, with Othello. There was no stage and no wingspace. It was St Patrick's night. The curtain was supposed to rise at nine o'clock. But the house wasn't full until eleven thirty, so the play didn't begin until then. It was well past two in the morning before the curtain came down. Everyone of the two thousand people in the audience was drunk. Apart from that, they weren't accustomed to Shakespeare. For the first half of the play, up to 'I am your own for ever,' we could not hear ourselves speak, could not hear our cues. The cast was alarmed. We expected the audience on stage at any moment. We kept our hands on our swords. I was playing Iago at the time. I came offstage with Mac at the interval and gasped. Don't worry, Mac said, don't worry. After the interval he began to move. When he walked onto the stage for the 'Naked in bed, Iago, and not mean harm' scene (his great body hunched, his voice low with grit), they silenced. He tore into the fit. He made the play his and the place his. By the time he had reached 'It is the very error of the moon; She comes more near the earth than she was wont, And makes men mad.', (the word 'mad' suddenly cauterised, ugly, shocking) the audience was quite still. And sober. I congratulated Mac. Not bad, he said, was it? Not bad . . .

Mac gave about half a dozen magnificent performances of Othello while I was with him. Even when, on the other occasions, he conserved his energies in the role, he always gave the patrons their moneysworth. At his best his was the finest Othello I have seen. His age was always a mystery, but I would think he was in his sixties at the time. Sometimes, late at night, after the show, he looked very old. But on stage in Othello he stood, well over six foot, naked to the waist, his gestures complete, final, nothing jagged, his movement of the utmost fluidity and yet of the utmost precision: stood there, dead in the centre of the role, and the great sweeping symphonic playing would begin, the rare tension and release within him, the arrest, the savagery, the majesty and repose. His voice was unique: in my experience of an unequalled range. A bass of extraordinary echo, resonance and gut, and remarkable sweep up into tenor, when the note would hit the back of the gallery and come straight back, a brilliant, stunning sound. I remember his delivery of this line: 'Methinks (bass) it should be now a huge (bass) eclipse (tenor) of sun and moon (baritone) and that th'affrighted glove (bass) Should yawn (very deep, the abyss) at alteration.' We all watched him from the wings . . .

His wife, Marjorie, was his structure and support. She organised the tours, supervised all business arrangements, sat in the box office, kept the cast in order, ran the wardrobe, sewed, looked after Mac, was his dresser, gave him his whiskey. She was tough, critical, cultivated, devoted. Her spirit and belief constituted the backbone of the company. There would have been no company without her.

Ireland wasn't golden always, but it was golden sometimes and in 1950 it was, all in all, a golden age for me and for others.

From *Poems and Prose 1949–1977*, Eyre Methuen Ltd, 1978

Those Old Sweet Songs
David Hanly

'I stand in a land of roses, but I dream of a land of snow,
Where you and I were happy in days of long ago,
Nightingales in the branches, stars in the magic sky,
I only hear you whisper, I only hear you sigh . . . '

Or words to that effect, I hurriedly add, in mortal fear of the pedants. Do you know that verse? If you do, you must be — what shall I say — of mature years and/or come from a certain town or city. No 28-year-old from Ferns, say, would have a clue what it was. On the other hand, the chances are that anyone over 35 from Limerick or Cork would know the verse well, and would know it to be the opening lines of a Victorian song called 'Thora'.

A friend of mine now, alas, an emigrant, was a founder member of that great Limerick rock band, Granny's Intentions. He was, and is, a brilliant bass guitarist, a passionate expert on music, and the perfect man to have at a party, because he has a nicely understated way of taking over and orchestrating things so that the best people sing the best songs. But what does he sing himself? 'Barefoot Days' as God is my judge. It does seem incongruous, doesn't it? But the secret is that he was born and reared in Limerick, a city which — aside from producing the highest per capita percentage of superb tenors in Ireland — also has a wonderfully rich tradition of the sing-song, and — perhaps for garrison reasons — a goodly number of the verses sung are among the finest Victorian love songs.

There is a body of opinion, I know, which would hold that the phrase 'fine Victorian love songs' is a contradiction in terms, and scoff at the sentimentality and oft times gothic phraseology. I can't deny that some dreadful aberrations have come down to us from earnest 19th century penmen . . . there are hundreds of 19th century love songs whose graciously poetic lyrics perfectly complement beautiful melodies, and I can think of no better way to get from Dublin to Limerick than in the taped company of that amiable and generous-spirited Welshman, Stuart Burrowes, while he sings his *Songs of Love and Sentiment*.

And it all has to do, I'm sure, with my Limerick background, heightened by the fact that my father had a glorious tenor voice and sang every night from a thick black book of songs: 'Bonnie Mary of Argyle', 'Thora', 'Cherie', 'Parted', 'Macushla', 'Mandalay', 'Catari', 'Roses of Picardy'. Another member of the household was a Ceolta Tíre addict and hoped, perhaps, that the fiddle and the uilleann pipes would gain ascendancy in the minds of the children, but it didn't happen: for reasons which I have never properly scrutinised, it took me years to overcome an intense youthful dislike of the best of traditional Irish music (and sean-nós singing still gives me aural piles).

It was the English songs that won me, and not just those sung by my father and others who would come to our house from time to time: Sunday morning was Kathleen Ferrier singing 'What is Life to me without Thee' and the smell of Science shoe polish (and of course it was the Science sponsored programme that introduced me to *La Traviata*).

A very musical home then? Not necessarily, but a very *Limerick* one. Classical music got very short shrift in the city, and a good Haydn was something you got when you were caught stealing apples from the neighbour's orchard. But great singers were revered: Gobbi, Di Stefano, Bjorling and Nash were familiar names and talked about with informed and unaffected ease in the pubs. This is still true today: I doubt if a symphony has ever been played on Radio Luimni, and probably few concertos, but at any time, any day of the week, you are likely to hear a great singer singing a great song. (It occurs to me, too, that tenors are more admired than sopranos, but that may just be my imagination.)

Is this, then, why I've never been to a symphony concert? . . .

Grand, grand. But when night falls and friends are about me in this red tartan room, and the need is felt to celebrate, inanimate, inadequate vinyl is ignored: up step Vincent, and Bob, and Mick, and Dolly, and Jack, and out roll the songs of passion, and sentiment, and humour. I'm at home again.

From *The Sunday Tribune*, 22 May 1988

Richard Harris Bids Adieu to the Alickadoos
Michael Feeney Callan

Sick of Limerick and home, [Richard] Harris conspired to emigrate. With his cousin Niall Quaid he applied for a Canadian visa. But the application called for a medical and Harris knew he was in trouble. A few years earlier, at nineteen, he had been diagnosed as having a tubercular spot on his lungs, but had taken medication and ignored the risk. During the 1952 Munster Senior Cup campaign he felt ill, but a chemist pal gave him benzedrine to keep him going. At six foot three inches, he was losing weight throughout 1952, and was down to twelve stone before the Cork cup match. Now, in mid-1953, his GP, Dr Corboy, confirmed that he had tuberculosis and must be confined to bed. Treatment and recuperation might take up to three years.

Harris was shattered. His Canadian escape was gone, his rugby life was over: 'I never played again. And I have often thought that it was rather ridiculous getting a Munster Cup medal and TB all at the same time.' His life went into crash-reverse. He had been strategically loosening the bonds to Overdale; now he was housebound. The night life ended: there would be no more women at Cruise's, no more treason talk at Charlie St George's, no more Kilkee play-acting, no more movies. He took to his bed, at first in anger and fear, finally prostrate with boredom. Looking back, he later reflected, his confinement had been inevitable. After the first diagnosis he should have rested for a few months. Instead: 'I got up when I should have been lying down and to break the monotony I began to drink. First to forget. Then to remember.' . . .

Harris was inconsolable. So often the soul of the party, he had only the house pet — a dog — to entertain. 'Time became of great importance to me. Whenever I asked the doctors when I would be cured and begin doing something with my life they would reply, "In six months." It was always six months. Never any more, never any less. And like two dots on a circle, the two dates never drew any nearer . . . I was dribbling away my youth, identified with nothing, achieving nothing.'

Harris remained housebound for nearly two years, for six months of which he lay inert in bed, staring at the damp Irish walls that, he reckons, caused his TB in the first place. It was this period of silence and reflection that forged the direction of his career. At last he was sitting still long enough to unscramble the threads of his life and make decisions. 'From the beginning Dickie lived life at the gallop,' said Dermot Foley. Now the running was over. 'In illness you are a great burden to your friends,' said Harris. 'In the first week they all come and say you'll be up in a month, you'll be up in a week. After a couple of months you have fifteen friends, and a couple of months later you have six. And then you've got three, and then you have one, and then you are on your own. They come only at Christmas and birthdays, either looking for or giving presents. So I was put on my own, and I invented people out of light bulbs. I had conversations with people in light bulbs, and I invented hundreds of people coming to talk to me. I was King of England, or I was the Pope. That is how my acting career started.'

Throughout Harris's life the variety of story-telling in his interviews is dizzying . . . His imagination was . . . exceptional. During his confined period he wrote copiously, filling copybooks with surreal notes that were the first lucid indications of artistic potential. Though he was never successful at art (his constant doodles are basic matchstick men with balloon heads), his mature writing, removed from self-pitying love hymns, was often remarkable, boomeranging from Nietzschean *vers libre* to elegiac Dylan Thomas and back. It was all the more remarkable because he was not widely read, and had often experienced difficulty reading. Only now did he seek out books to while away the time, showing a preference for buccaneering yarns and, obsessively, the letters of Vincent Van Gogh to his brother. But still he kept his dreamer side to himself. Almost none of the jottings of his bedridden years remain, and just one nineteen-line piece was published in his eventual book of poems. It is called 'My Blood Reflects Nothing of Me' and speaks about the double life of a hard-drinking hard man, and the Catholic suppression of passion.

'During this period of incarceration,' Harris told a women's magazine in 1965, 'I lived my life at second-hand through the adventures of others, in books. And I decided that, when I was cured, I would like to direct my own scenarios, to bring to life the whole world of my creation, to look at my life through the telescope of truth. I wanted to bring a little shock, a little disease into middle-class drawing rooms, to lift up the carpets and shake up the dust a bit.' This bold calculation wasn't evident in the sternly run Overdale, nor beyond. The local pubs that knew his business were only vaguely aware that he was seriously ill. 'He just disappeared,' says Charlie St George. 'It was a time when a few of us wondered if we'd seen the last of him.'

Dickie Harris was well familiar with the Limerick expression 'alickadoo'. It describes the rugby man who knows all, but stands forever on the wings. The world of Crescent and Garryowen was full of alickadoos. He knew many of them personally, but disliked them. Always a man of movement, and one who liked to see things through, he had no sympathies with back-scratchers and idlers. In the autumn of 1955, as his condition improved, he dodged out of the house seeking only one nourishment — the ether of the theatre. His mind was made up: he wanted no future in the family business, even if Ivan forgave him and dragged him back. Instead he would go abroad and study theatre . . . Harris later said, 'My parents couldn't understand what drew me to the make-believe world of acting. I didn't know myself.' He had not consulted Dermot Foley . . . nor Kevin Dinneen. He had made his enquiries in secrecy and sent applications to two London drama schools . . . he had a small shares inheritance from an aunt who had recently passed away: it was enough money for the Holyhead mailboat and survival for a few months in the Smoke . . .

His brothers didn't debate the issue too long. Dickie had been in prison for countless months. His strength was back and he had living to catch up on. He loved action, laughter, daring — and all his old sparring cronies had flown. It was, in the end, inevitable that he would bolt.

From *Richard Harris: A Sporting Life*, Sidgwick & Jackson, 1990

In Festival Mood
Kieran Sheedy

The Clare Drama Festival at Scariff gained added prestige when playwright and producer, Lennox Robinson, was engaged as adjudicator for the third festival which was set to run from 19–28 March 1949 . . .

All of the three entries for the open competition came from Limerick City groups; the Catholic Institute Players, an offshoot of the well-known city club whose members included Jack O'Donoghue, Joe O'Sullivan (an uncle of stage manager Des O'Sullivan) and May Hartney, entered 'Margaret Gillan' by Brinsley McNamara while the College Players, a group founded in St Munchin's College in the late 1920s, and whose prime mover was Jack Leahy, chose 'Mourn the Ivy Leaf', a new play about Charles Stewart Parnell which was written by the young playwright Gerry Gallivan, who was working in Shannon Airport at the time.

And his two brothers Cyril and Eddie were also leading members of the group as was Madge Dinneen. The third entry came from the Poetry Circle, Limerick, a group originally founded to read poetry and verse plays, and whose members included poet Ger Ryan, assistant librarian Paddy Madden, county librarian Dan Doyle and his wife Kitty, Breda and Annette Larkin, Arthur O'Leary, Christine (Chris) Robinson, Terry Rowlands, Maisie Cooper and the inimitable Kitty Bredin, who, over the coming years, would become an indispensable part of the Clare Drama Festival scene as she held court in McMahon's Royal Hotel, complete with cigarette holder, and with the inevitable pint of Guinness in her hand. And the Poetry Circle would create their own particular piece of festival history as their production of 'Hamlet' would prove to be the only occasion in its fifty-year-old history when a play by William Shakespeare would be performed. On the night, however, their production would be remembered for a very different reason . . .

On the evening before the festival was due to open, secretary John Ryan was slightly apprehensive as he awaited the arrival by car of Lennox Robinson who was due to be dropped off by Radio Eireann broadcaster Norris Davidson. His apprehension grew as time slipped by, but finally a car hove into view, and he was relieved to see the famed adjudicator emerge. It transpired, however, that Lennox had indulged in a substantial liquid luncheon, and as he was assisted in the direction of the Royal Hotel, he asked John Ryan to name the various plays which had been entered. John duly obliged but when he mentioned 'Hamlet' he was interrupted by Lennox who asked: 'Did I write that?' . . .

But Lennox soon became the star of the festival, and his unfortunate mannerism of scratching his posterior each night as he commenced his adjudication became one of its great folk memories. In addition, the fact that he was invariably tipsy only served to enhance his reputation, although one group were entitled to feel confused when at the conclusion of his adjudication he remarked that they would receive a total of seventy-five marks for their efforts, but before they had an opportunity to savour the moment, he casually added: 'Of course, when I wake up in the morning I might only give them twenty-five marks!' . . .

The Limerick Poetry Circle's production of 'Hamlet' was scheduled for Monday 21 March, and the cast included Paddy Portley (Hamlet), Chris Robinson (Hamlet's mother), Eoin O'Moore (Claudius) — who had acted in the Gate Theatre — Paddy Mullins (Laertes), George Eggleston (Osric), Terry Rowlands (Ophelia), Arthur Griffith (Polonius), Dan Doyle (Gravedigger). The music for the play-scene which was played by flautist Gus McNamara was composed by Maisie Cooper, who also took the role of the Player Queen, while the producer was Kitty Bredin. But in common with other groups at the time, a lack of motor cars among its members meant that it was still often difficult to arrange transport to Scariff, and festival committee members Dan Hegarty, John Ryan and Padraig Vaughan occasionally had to make time-consuming return trips to and from

Limerick on the night of a performance to ensure their participation.

Arthur O'Leary (Horatio) was then working as a young assistant in O'Mahony's Bookshop, and during the day of the performance he received a number of phone calls, some of a contradictory nature, indicating various travel plans, with the result that by the time he finished work that evening he was even more confused about individual travel plans. Padraig Vaughan duly arrived outside O'Mahony's to collect the remaining members of the cast and he waited until almost seven o'clock to ensure that no-one was left behind. But they were totally unaware that Arthur Griffith was waiting to be picked up at home and it was only when Padraig Vaughan arrived back in Scariff close to curtain-up time that it was realised that Polonius was missing.

One of the group's members who was not in the cast read the part on stage, but in a lounge suit (possibly the first modern-dress Polonius) and there was another scare during the performance when Michael Sheridan, who was doubling up as Rosencranz and Guildenstern, tripped on leaving the stage and fell headlong into the nearby dressingroom. But when Arthur O'Leary anxiously inquired if he was hurt, he gravely replied: 'Arthur, we are both hurt' and when Maisie Cooper, who was also acting as prompter, whispered the same question he gave a more pessimistic prognosis: 'Rosencranz is dead and Guildenstern is dying.' Meanwhile, according to Maisie Cooper, 'Lennox was above in the balcony with the lank hair falling over his eyes, and his hands trembling and the cigarette ash spilling into the gallery.' But when he commenced his adjudication Lennox rose to the occasion by commenting airily: 'Pity that poor Polonius missed the bus. Doesn't matter. He was a tiresome fellow.' But for the producer, Kitty Bredin, and the devastated members of the Poetry Circle it was a case of 'Alas poor Polonius! I knew him well,' as the opportunity of defeating their two rival city groups in Scariff had disappeared.

On the final night, in the course of a lively speech, Lennox Robinson claimed to have made many friends during his first visit to Scariff, but ruefully added (to general laughter) that on leaving he might have only four or five — the winners of the various trophies. He confessed that he loved watching plays — even badly-acted ones; he even admitted to having had a losing bet on the Grand National, but added that it was more exciting to have a bet on the awards: 'Who will win the local cup and will the College Players beat the Catholic Institute?' . . .

The Catholic Institute Players won the first open competition with 'Margaret Gillan', ahead of the College Players in 'Mourn the Ivy Leaf' and the Poetry Circle's 'Hamlet', and interestingly, at the same time at Feile Luimni, adjudicator Micheal O hAodha placed the College Players ahead of the other two groups. The Kilfinane Players won the first rural competition with 'The Big Sweep' . . .

It was the custom of the time for members of casts to line up behind the adjudicator on stage (they had nowhere to hide) and for Eamonn Hayes of the Portumna Players it became an even more harrowing experience. He was playing the part of an old man and, in the course of the adjudication, Lennox suddenly rushed over to him, took hold of the wig he was wearing and, holding it aloft, exclaimed: 'Look at that! Look at that! You would think that it was a rat!' . . .

In 1950 Limerick City groups monopolised the entries for the Gaelic League (1-Act) competition; the Catholic Institute Players with 'Spreading the News' by Lady Gregory; the Singers Group in 'Riders to the Sea' by J. M. Synge and the Stella Maris Players, 'Kathleen Ni Houlihan' by W. B. Yeats . . . The adjudicator was H. L. (Larry) Morrow, Head of Productions in Radio Eireann; more serious in outlook and lacking the charisma of his immediate predecessor. Some of the participating groups found it difficult to grasp the relevance of his remarks as they gathered around him on stage for the dreaded adjudication . . .

In the course of his overall adjudication on the final night, Larry Morrow, unwittingly, entered into dangerous terrain when he stated that one of the most enjoyable features of drama festivals was the contrast in the methods of production between plays from the country and the towns. And he added that he was 'delighted, and indeed astonished with the marked superiority shown by most of the country groups over most of those from the towns, especially their vigour, without which any production was about as appetising as a railway station sandwich'. His comments evoked loud laughter but Kitty Bredin signally failed to appreciate the humour of his remarks and when he compounded the situation by adding that he did not wish it to be understood that he was running down the Limerick players, but that the time had come when 'city groups would have to pull up their socks' an enraged Kitty rushed onto the stage to take issue with him publicly . . .

In the 1951 Festival Challenge Cup competition Stella Maris Players, Limerick, won the battle of the 'Maurice Hartes's' . . . The Singers, Limerick (producer Kitty Bredin) were the convincing winners of the 1-Act competition with 'Lost Light' . . .

The Stella Maris Players . . . went on to win the main award also at the Kerry Drama Festival in Killarney when the adjudicator was Micheal MacLiammoir. Some weeks later when Babs Shanahan was cycling home from her work in Limerick Corporation she was stopped in the street by the ubiquitous Micheal, who was accompanied by Hilton Edwards, with the cry of: 'As I live and breathe, Mrs Harte on a bicycle!'

From *The Clare Drama Festival at Scariff (1947–1996)*, Clare Drama Festival Committee, 1996

Limerick, You're a Lady
Denis Allen

Limerick, you're a lady,
Your Shannon waters, tears of joy that flow,
The beauty that surrounds you,
I'll take it with me love where e'er I go.
While waking in the arms of distant waters,
A new day finds me far away from home,
And Limerick you're a lady,
The one true love that I have ever known.

As children you and I spent endless days of fun,
In winter's snow or summer's golden sun,
We fished in silver streams,
The fabric of my dreams
Was fashioned by your loveliness,
And so I have to say:

Chorus

A gift that time has made to travellers on their way,
Seeking out the beauty of our land,
A shrine where children pray,
And bells ring out to say,
Thank God we're living just to feel
The freedom of each day . . .

Chorus

From Denis Allen's song collection

Suzanne Murphy
Gus Smith

From an early age, Suzanne Murphy had fallen in love with music. She suspected that her parents must have thought her strange to be 'so mad about music'. Her father was in the hardware business and the family lived in the Limerick suburbs.

Sometimes she wondered where she inherited her love of music and concluded that it was hearing her grandparents singing parlour songs around the piano. Her parents had met at a concert in Bruff Convent, where her grandmother had also been a pupil. She was sent with her sister, Noelle, to the same convent, and Noelle turned out to be a good singer.

School plays were her big moments, and today she thinks that even then the stage was calling her. Learning the piano also provided her with much satisfaction. But music and acting were, she thought, only for people abroad. 'I never thought it could be for the likes of me. I suppose, however, I had it in me and it had to come out.'

Eventually, when she moved to Dublin to take up a secretarial post she took up singing with the folk group WE 4 . . .

Later, she met Veronica Dunne at a dinner and they talked briefly about music and other current topics. It would be months before she plucked up enough courage to ask her to take her on as a pupil. 'When Suzanne first came to me,' recalled Veronica Dunne, 'I thought the voice had a fine quality, but I quickly pointed out to her what I'd expect if I took her on . . . She went away and didn't come back for a whole year.'

One day, however, she rang up and said, 'Will you take me back, Ronnie?' Veronica Dunne agreed. 'I knew that Suzanne had stayed away because she hadn't realised her own potential. She lacked self-confidence as far as singing was concerned. I understood her reaction. I intimated to her that if lessons went well she would have to think about leaving the WE 4 and becoming a full-time singer. I left her in no doubt that training for a singing career required sacrifices.' . . .

To Veronica Dunne, the soprano's voice was by now more secure and better focused and had fine agility. And she was a most dedicated worker. 'I had no doubt that in time Suzanne would make it. I have an instinct about these things. Every week, I could see her voice developing; it had a lovely quality and good range and an improving coloratura. Her confidence had grown and I knew she was ambitious enough to become a professional singer.' . . .

Suzanne Murphy joined the Irish National Opera Company in the seventies and sang the title role in Rossini's *La Cenerentola*, in which she displayed operatic potential, and in 1975 Elisetta in Cimarosa's *Secret Marriage* . . .

Hearing that Welsh National Opera were looking for someone for the chorus, she applied and was accepted . . .

Her first role was Constanze in Mozart's *The Seraglio*, which because of the disastrous fire, had to be performed in make-shift sets. She would have to wait, however, until the spring of 1977 for her first starring part and it was as Amalia in Verdi's *I Masnadieri* . . .

In that same year, she got an opportunity to sing her first Gilda in *Rigoletto* . . .

It was a most encouraging start for her and she was prepared to learn as she went along. Her versatility as a singer paid dividends when she switched successfully from Verdi to Britten; her Helena in A *Midsummer Night's Dream* did not go unnoticed. She was also heard as Leonora in *Il Trovatore*, a role that at the time seemed too heavy for her voice.

Elisabetta in Verdi's *Don Carlos* is a role admired and loved by sopranos, not only because of its beautiful music, but the moral strength of the heroine herself . . . Was Welsh National Opera wise then in casting a newcomer like Suzanne Murphy in the role? To find out, I flew to Bristol where I was joined by a number of London newspaper critics . . . all of them, without exception, noted Suzanne Murphy's convincing portrayal and her ability to sustain the role . . .

Next, she sang the Queen of the Night in *The Magic Flute*, followed by her first Violetta in *La Traviata*, a role that had long attracted her. Although the cast as a whole did not please the critics, she emerged as a star; indeed, Tom Sutcliffe, who can be an acerbic critic, penned the kind of notice in the *Guardian* every singer dreams about:

> Miss Murphy exceeded the expectations whetted by her virile, passionate Queen of the Night and emerged as an operatic star who will make her mark on the international market. It may be rash to base such a prediction on one beautifully sung Violetta . . . But Miss Murphy is not just a pretty voice. She possesses an instrument of great tonal character. She commands the vocal heights with strength, excitement and a ravishing quality of sound. The individuality of the voice lies in a quality she shares with the late Callas — a kind of wedge-shaped hollowness in the tone of each note that, with a slight upping of the pressure, fills generously and thrillingly with colour, vitality and piercing resonance . . .

Verdi continued to take up much of her time. In the autumn of 1979 she was cast as Elvira in *Ernani* . . .

Handel was not a composer associated with WNO, but in 1981 it was decided to present his *Rodelinda* and Suzanne was cast in the title role. She welcomed the opportunity to extend her repertoire and though a newcomer to Handel, performed convincingly . . .

Veronica Dunne had always felt that Suzanne Murphy's agile voice was ideal for bel canto and she was to be proved correct, when in 1982 the soprano was handed a plum role in the shape of Elvira in Bellini's *I Puritani*. In fact the company was mounting the opera especially for her, which was a sure indication of the enormous esteem in which she was by now regarded . . . The opening night in Cardiff was a remarkable success . . . 'Miss Murphy's performance was little short of magnificent,' stated William Davies in the *Classical Times*. 'It's an impersonation that will long remain in the mind's eye.' . . .

In 1983, she was cast as Amelia in *Un Ballo in Maschera* with Dennis O'Neill as Gustav and Donald Maxwell as Anckarstrom. The Cardiff audience received the production enthusiastically. If O'Neill stole the honours with some thrilling singing, Suzanne Murphy brought typical commitment to her role and together they were worthy protagonists. As a Verdi heroine she was by now one of the most respected in Britain.

It was hard to imagine that in six short years she had achieved so much with the company. It was inevitable that one day she would sing the title role in Bellini's masterpiece, *Norma*. After the enthusiastic reception for *Puritani* Welsh National Company decided in 1985 to do *Norma* . . .

While the critics expressed reservations about Serban's production . . . John Higgins in the *Times* summed up: 'Suzanne Murphy had one or two cloudy moments vocally, but for most of the evening it was a thrillingly full-throated performance, lacking neither stamina nor the control for the start of "Casta Diva".' . . .

Suzanne was by now a freelance artist and much in demand. She sang Norma at the New York City Opera, with Richard Bonynge conducting, Amelia in *Maschera* and Elvira in *Puritani* in Vancouver, and Ophelia in *Hamlet* in Pittsburgh. She began also to get engagements in Germany . . . she guested with Welsh National Opera in its new production of Puccini's *La Fanciulla del West* and scored one of the biggest triumphs of her career.

Hugh Canning wrote in *Opera*: 'Suzanne Murphy's Minnie surely ranks with the finest interpretations of the role anywhere: she sang her music tirelessly and with unusual delicacy — her bel canto training — in the lyrical moments. She gave a touching and convincing portrait of the improbable gun-toting hostess who has never kissed a man. This fanciulla is a huge success and deserves to be seen and heard throughout the world.' . . .

She had sung the title role in *Tosca* for Welsh National Opera in October 1992. She stood in for the injured Marion Vernette Moore and showed that her singing and acting were ideal for the part. Hugh Canning was to make the comment in *Opera*: 'Toscas as good as Miss Murphy's do not grow on trees these days and hearing her in Cardiff made one wonder again why the Royal Opera had to go trawling the operatic outback of the United States to come up with the unremarkable Elizabeth Holleque in their most recent revival?' . . .

She has remained as busy as ever. She sang Alice Ford in Peter Stein's much acclaimed new production of Verdi's *Falstaff* for Welsh National Opera, Abigaille in *Nabucco* in Modena and Piacenza, and . . . the world premiere in Washington in 1994 of Dominic Argento's new opera, *The Dream of Valentino*, in which she was cast as Valentino's secretary and was praised by the critics.

Strangely, she had neglected the recording side of the business, but in 1992 made amends with an album of Puccini and Verdi arias. Suzanne would have to wait, however, until the autumn of 1993 for commercial success in this sphere, and this came about in an unusual way. Her brother, Michael Murphy — he is manager of Limerick's magnificent new University Concert Hall — suggested that for her next album she include the popular Limerick song 'There is an Isle', and she agreed; not only that but it formed the title of the album. She would also include other favourites such as 'Galway Bay', 'Kathleen Mavourneen' and 'I Dreamt I Dwelt in Marble Halls'.

Before long, it proved a chart-topper in Ireland, mainly because of the technical quality of the album, the sympathetic musical backing by the Welsh National Opera Orchestra and Suzanne's judicious choice of songs, a number of which were classically arranged by Julian Smith, who also conducted the orchestra.

In September 1993 she was in Limerick for the gala celebrations to mark the opening of the new concert hall.

Limerick, her native place, had waited a long time for its new hall; fittingly, its greatest soprano since Catherine Hayes had given her own welcome in song.

From *Irish Stars of the Opera*, Madison Publishers Ltd, 1994

The Cranberries
Aidan Corr

Sharing the bill with Bono and The Edge of U2, Dolores O'Riordan of Ballybricken, has been invited to perform with Luciano Pavarotti in the charity concert for Bosnia in Modena on September 12. She will be accompanied by Mike Hogan on guitar . . .

Just two years after springing to international fame from the obscurity of Limerick's young band scene, the Cranberries must now accept the often unwelcome public tag of millionaires. That four youngsters, all under the age of 25, could amass such wealth from their music in such a short time is not alone a tribute to their undoubted talent, but a phenomenon that at times is difficult to grasp.

While Limerick is proud to claim them as its own, the band enjoyed only limited recognition in the city during their formative years. Thirty-nine paying customers came through the doors of Seamus Flynn's Theatre Royal on Saturday, December 21, 1991 for their last pre-fame Limerick performance . . .

By the end of 1993 the Cranberries were big business and their triumphant return home at the end of November to play a concert in the Theatre Royal is now legendary.

A lot can happen in two years and for the Cranberries all of it has been good. Their success has increased beyond all expectations. Record sales of their two albums, 'Everybody Else Is Doing It So Why Can't We' and the follow-up 'No Need to Argue', have already grossed millions; their world-wide concert tours have been a succession of sell-outs and every note sung and chord struck registers extra digits on a bulging bank balance.

While the Cranberries' relationship with the press in these islands has lacked warmth they cannot be blamed for feeling aggrieved by some of the negative columns directed against them in the past two years. The fact that they have succeeded in the States . . . may not have pleased many in the pop production corridors of power in these islands but nothing can justify some of the low grade column-fillers that have been directed towards the band over the past two years.

It speaks volumes for the strong character of the band that they have remained unaffected by both success and criticism . . .

Reviewing their appearance at the NEC in Birmingham, pop reviewer Emma Forrest of the British newspaper, *The Independent*, is quoted as saying:

Fergal Lawler's drumming is so good it seems almost to have its own melody. Mike Hogan's bass sets a voodooesque mood of expectancy, Noel Hogan's exquisite guitar gives the song (Zombie) more depth and shading than it ever had on record . . .

The individual talent of Fergal Lawler and the Hogan brothers has always been exceptional and the arrival of Dolores to replace Niall Quinn as lead singer provided the leadership as well as the singing talent that the band needed in 1990. Since then Dolores has been encouraged to lead, encouraged to take centre stage, encouraged to provide the focal point of the band. It is a role that she initially took on reluctantly being more noted for her extreme shyness before the band came to fame during their American summer tours of 1993 with Suede and Duran Duran. Early Limerick fans of the then Cranberry Saw Us recall Dolores singing a full set with her back to the audience.

From the *Limerick Leader*, 26 August 1995

Kitty Bredin
Desmond O'Grady

Both aware of it
we put no words
nor rash act on it.

Especially you —
part of my straight start
in Arthur's sitting room with blue

wallpaper and stuffed birds
on the table in their flower
glass bower

size of a high hat.
Haughty as a model gilly, flat
witted as a winkle, I tried to stuff

light into each feathered eye,
flowers into each winged fly-
bitten blossom while

you looked on from behind
your chewed, cocked fag-holder —
clouty in brown tweed. Older,

knowing Father
before Mother, you saw
me as a grown-up, a glass dobber

More than any other
you watched my growth, like a tumour,
whorl its bole. Later —

over that one —
we killed our time drinking Eamon
Gleeson's black pints. No change! I

think one fight in all
we've had between us —
and that a natural need for crisis.

Otherwise fastidiously
wherewithals, we side
off lefty lefty.

Since then — whether the far
side of tin whistles and banjos,
the time spent watching what goes;

or the image at alien airports waiting,
waiting at bars nor a brass farthing
to drink your name;

or sleeping it off
on the bench of some station
and never a train getting in —

it's all the same fierce fire
for the pair of us
banked down in our common ash;

the same old raw
wound won't knit
and both of us surviving it.

You well see — beyond the mouth
of it, as from the other
side of our mad minds' mirror,

under the skin and the rogue
ninny nights in Gillogue —
the dark serpentine

thing, like a poisoned vein,
heading straight for the target area.
You've got its measure.

We're all from the same scrapiron shop,
and it's a regular downhill run
to the final, full, stop.

From *Castle Poets* (I), The Treaty Press, 1970

NINE

THE CITY

The Legends of Limerick
A. J. O'Halloran

Limerick's main artery, O'Connell Street, has always been regarded as one of the finest thoroughfares in Ireland. Its length, its division into blocks of regular size, and the uniformity of its buildings combine to create this impression. A stranger entering it for the first time can be excused for thinking, with Thackeray, that he is in a second Liverpool. This effect is intensified towards its lower end, where, between warehouses of which any city need not feel ashamed, surges to and fro a ceaseless stream of traffic. As the visitor reaches the junction of O'Connell and Patrick Streets, he looks involuntarily to his left, expecting to see the inevitable side-street, and then must needs stand spell-bound. Before him spreads a majestic sheet of water, broken at low tides by the jagged Rocks of Curraghgower, spanned in the distance by the low sweeping arches of Thomond Bridge, flanked on one side by King John's stately castle and St Mary's, on the other by St Munchin's Church and the picturesquely grouped houses on the Strand; in the background the Hills of Clare, tinted according to the weather's mood — green, mauve, or grey — the whole blending into a panorama of old-time beauty. And lo! his thoughts are whirled out from the rush of the twentieth century, and he is back in the distant ages listening to the shrill war-cry of the Celt, the guttural defence of the Dane, and the strident challenge of the Norman. Above the din of modern traffic sounds the hiss of the arrow, the whirr of the javelin, and the crash of the battle-axe.

This typifies Limerick . . . It has never divorced itself from the past; and the songs and stories of its olden glories for ever vibrate through the air. Thus it is that, under the light that glows softly from a porcelain bowl and sitting at a gasfire, the citizen of today tells his children the same old charming legends that were told by his ancestors a thousand years ago in the smoky glare of a bog-wood fire. Unhappy indeed is the man who cannot sometimes laugh at himself, and lost is the community that may not wither its follies with the God-given gift of humour. Whatever else it may lack, Limerick is richly endowed with this saving grace.

Witness its oldest legend, which, bubbling with laughter, relates that fifteen hundred years ago its earliest bishop and patron saint roundly cursed all who would first see the light of day therein, because his contemporary fellow-citizens would not help him to build a church. So it is that, to this day, on account of St Munchin's curse, no Limerickman ever prospers in his native city.

The insolence of a jack-in-office, the arrogance of an upstart, the ignorance of a boor are laughed to tatters by the story of Shawn-a-Scoob, the immortal broom-maker, who, dazed by his rapid transition from the humble toil of heather-gathering to the dignity of Limerick's mayoral chair, grew so overbearingly forgetful of his past that he failed to recognise his own mother . . .

Listen to the Limerickman laugh as he explains why it is that for a thousand years the ladies of Mungret have enjoyed a proverbial reputation for wisdom. How the band of foreign scholars who had established their theses in every other one of Eire's famous schools, worsting in debate the most learned doctors, light-heartedly faced for the University of Mungret fully anticipating a crowning victory. How the finesse of the Limerick monks countered their assurance, and the pseudo-women beetling linen at the wayside brook sent them to the right-about in abject confusion. And that is why — apart from compliments to her good looks — the most acceptable praise one can bestow on a lady is to tell her that she is as wise as the Women of Mungret.

Nor is the eerie or supernatural forgotten in these legends. Where is the Limerickman worthy of the name who, having occasion to cross the Thomond Bridge late at night, does not shiver with apprehension as, passing from under the protection of the Castle walls, he beholds in every patch of shade the floating mantle and grasping hands of the Bishop's Lady, and hears in every fugitive sound the swish of her garments as she prepares to hurl him over the battlements of the bridge.

What though, in the snug security of his own fireside, he stoutly asserts that the unruly dame was long-since banished to the Red Sea. Little comfort is that to him as, in the awesome midnight gloom and with the night-winds from the Clare hills sobbing around him, he fancies it is just possible that the Lady is allowed to pay a flying visit to her old haunts now and again. Does he not sigh his relief as, reaching Thomondgate, he beholds the sturdy old Treaty Stone on his left, and feels that he is under the blessed shadow of Saint Munchin's Church?

On the same bridge but at another time — when the summer sunset is tinting the Shannon waters to a ruby glow and the chimes of St Mary's or Mount St Alphonsus are filling the air with music — his thoughts would have winged back to another story, to the legend of the poor Italian wanderer, who, having searched the world for the bells which he had made and which had been stolen from him, heard them once again as his ship sailed up the river on such an evening — heard them but to die of joy.

In this old city the very stones echo stories from the past — stories in which one may hear the rustling wings of the twin spirits of tears and laughter.

From *The Glamour of Limerick*, The Talbot Press Limited, 1928

Shawn-a-Scoob
Desmond O'Grady

When a child I associated my maternal grandfather, whom I never knew, with a story my uncle Feathereye told me of a Limerickman by the name of Shawn-a-Scoob. This was an old story also celebrated in verse by the Limerick poet Michael Hogan, the Bard of Thomond. The story has foundation in fact and the characters really lived and breathed the local fresh air, but after it got into the Bard's hands and he had done with it, his version became the one generally accepted by local storytellers.

It appears the City of Limerick was in crisis. The City Fathers had failed to elect a new Mayor. Session after session resulted in a deadlock. The Fathers could not settle on any one of themselves and no citizen would take on the responsibilities of so badgerable an office.

The crisis bulged as the deadlock held. Finally one worthy Father came up with a suggestion: the first man to cross Thomond Bridge — which led out of town to the county Clare and the western seaboard — at dawn on the following Saturday morning, whether he liked it or not, wanted, willed or wished it; would be appointed Mayor of the city. Everybody agreed that this was an astonishingly simple and acceptable solution and for the first time in a long time the weighty and wide-waisted City Fathers were of one mind.

There lived in those far off days a man who went by the nickname of Shawn-a-Scoob to all who knew or saluted him. He lived with his good wife in a wattle hut out in Cratloe Woods. His profession, if humble, was an honest one. He was a maker of brooms and brushes. All week long he toiled at cutting twigs and gathering heather, gorse and bushes which he bound to long and short wooden shafts — depending on whether he was making a broom or a brush. Early every Saturday morning — lark and linnet high in the sky, early curlew, rooking crow — he would carry strapped to his back, the week's brooms to the marketplace in Limerick city where he stood over them, his fists in his pockets, and sold them for an honest price. This is why he was called Shawn-a-Scoob, or John of the Brooms, for *scoob* means broom or brush in the Gaelic.

And so it was Shawn was the first man to cross the river Shannon by way of Thomond Bridge that Saturday morning when the City Fathers were waiting on the alert.

Shawn was hardly the length of his big toe across the Bridge, innocently dreaming his way to market and thinking his early morning thoughts when he was accosted by the entire Council of City Fathers.

This was no small surprise for Shawn.

Before he could draw breath and give voice to his amazement — for he knew them well enough by the rich robes of office they wore — they informed him there and then, on that infamous but historical spot, that he was the first male human to cross Thomond Bridge that morning, and as such was therefore, as of this most solemn moment, Mayor of the City. All that remained was the official ceremony of swearing in and taking office. And this, they assured him, would be put into effect, carried out and dispatched forthwith and without further delay.

They transported him immediately, voiceless and bewildered, to their great, neoclassical granite Town Hall with its towering columns, formal facade, and carriage arcade. Once there, crowded into the regality of the robing room they vested him in the official robes of scarlet and ermine, hung the historic gold chain about his rough neck and shoved the symbolic silver mace into the palm of his country paw.

That night, in his befuddled honour, they held celebrations all over the town with lights and coloured bulbs, luminosities and brightly foreign fireworks. Meanwhile, in the offices the lesser clerical cast made arrangements for Shawn's Mayoral Parade through the streets of his city on the following morning, the Sabbath, before the entire population.

Back in Cratloe Woods, in his husbandman's wattle hut, Shawn's healthy and honourable wife began to wonder what in the world had happened to Shawn that he had not shown his face home the Saturday night. She came to the crestfallen conclusion that he must have fallen foul of drinking company in the town and that they had got him so boneless drunk he could not make the road home. Or maybe he met a young thing, flighty and easy, who had turned his head and led him heedlessly astray against his awareness. He might well, even at this very mortal moment, be lying prone and punctured in pride and pocket in a common gutter of the town or somewhere in the ditch by the side of the open road under the indifferent moon.

So, Sunday morning, when Shawn didn't show, she threw her long black shawl about her shoulders and started down the road for Limerick.

When she reached and crossed Thomond Bridge, she found the entire populace abroad in the streets in festive mood and the town's entirety decorated like a dandy for a great parade.

And then the parade swung into sight.

There were marching soldiers and soldiers on jogging horseback all spit and polish, buckles, buttons and brass. There was a brass band with whirling drumsticks and stomping band major with moustaches. There was the easy stride of the high ecclesiastical orders about the plain purpose of their own purple and gold-embroidered authority, and in the middle of all, the centre and cause of attraction, rolled the delicately sprung, open Mayoral Coach, drawn by snow white prancing horses with the Mayor himself, no less, seated within, smiling benignly and waving graciously to the cheering, flag-waving people of his City.

The poor woman could hardly believe the two eyes in her head. There, regally enthroned in the upholstered amplitude of the Mayoral Carriage, a dazzling smile of surprised success and well-being as broad as a shark's on his porkchop, country face, benignly waving, almost Papally blessing the delirious throng, rigged out in scarlet silk and ermine fur, with gold chain entangle and weighty mace in the crook of his arm, sat her one and only, larger than life, honest husband . . . Shawn-a-Scoob.

Certainly the sight gave her pause. But not for long. When reality reasserted itself, she moved. She rushed forward and out. Blind and senseless to all else about her, eyes wide and fixed on the image of himself before her, as in a trance or ecstatic transportation, she broke through the cheering throng calling 'Shawn!, Shawn!'

Then she was at his side. One hand grasped at the french-polished carriagework, the other stretched forward in supplication.

'Shawn,' she cried, 'Don't you know me? Don't you know me at all?'

His attention caught by her shrill voice, his head turned a moment away from the applauding populace, his celebrating people. He looked down at her from his mayoral height. He looked deeply into her pleading eyes. His own eyes smoked. His brows arched. He raised his Mayoral hand as if in benediction and the scarlet stuff of his robe fell silkily back from his rough wrist. His features set gravely. His gaze had the penetration of some powerful prince of the Church.

'Shawn, Shawn. Don't you know me at all?' she cried again in her desperation.

'Get away home out of that woman,' said Shawn grandly in one breath. 'Can't you see I don't even know myself?'

From *ERA 1*, Spring 1974, The Goldsmith Press

'What a Respectable Figure this City Makes'
J. Ferrar

Whatever may be the motives to induce a man to compile a History, the task is an arduous one, and if executed with a just portion of accuracy, and diligence, will be entitled to some degree of praise. To the love of literary pursuits the world is indebted for the preservation of its antiquities, so pleasing to an enlightened mind. The honest desire of rescuing our History from oblivion, of transmitting remarkable events to posterity, supports the historian in his undertaking, renders him superior to every difficulty, and repays the toil of reading and collating a number of manuscripts and old books.

It is near twenty years since the Author published a sketch of the History of Limerick. He was then little acquainted, what a respectable figure this city makes in the History of Ireland. Unwearied diligence has increased his knowledge, and finding the work has not been undertaken by an abler pen, he has endeavoured to complete one more worthy the perusal of his fellow-citizens, to whom he will be ever happy to acknowledge himself connected, by every tie of affection and gratitude.

The materials for the book published in 1767, were taken from a manuscript, preserved with great care for a long series of years, in the family of the Rev. Mr White, a clergyman of the Church of Rome, who died in the year 1768. The manuscript is now in the possession of Dr MacMahon, the present Roman Catholic bishop of Killaloe. Another manuscript of some antiquity, relating chiefly to Limerick, was found in the possession of the late Mr Robert Davis, burgess. It is written in verse, and brought down no farther than the year 1680; it confirms Mr White's in many places, and on the whole was deemed so curious, that several passages of it have been brought into the annals of this History . . . To these and other respectable authorities, the Author has added anecdotes of several ancient families, and the History of Limerick within his own memory.

Controversy in religious matters, is of all others, the most unedifying, most unentertaining, if not handled with charity and politeness. The heaps of books on this subject, published on the continent in the last century, which contributed to deluge several parts of Europe with blood, were a disgrace to humanity. What! Shall we quarrel with an honest man, because he differs from us in his manner of worshipping the Supreme Being? No, the divine Author of the Christian religion has taught us love, meekness, and charity, even to our enemies; and the great Mr Locke has proved from reason and scripture, that religion is at all times, a matter between each individual and his God. The Author therefore, in writing the following Pages, was extremely anxious to unite his fellow-citizens, and, as far as lay in his power, to lessen the little jealousies which have divided men living on the same land, under the same roof — men, who thank God, have now the means of being united and happy. Toleration is the basis of all public peace.

It has been remarked by a celebrated writer, that 'All History, so far as it is not supported by contemporary evidence, is romance.' How far the Author has kept this remark impressed on his mind; how far he has faithfully collated his books, and quoted his authorities, must be left to the judicious reader. He confesses to have studied a concise and perspicuous language; therefore hopes the book will prove an entertaining one. To his countrymen abroad, who have not seen Limerick for many years, it will be acceptable. He submits it to the Public, with that deference to which they are always entitled, in an humble, but well grounded confidence, that posterity will prove its utility, and applaud the industry of a man, who, amidst the avocations of a laborious employment, and the duties of a citizen, has been diligent in finding, and exact in stating facts; collecting into one point of view, every remarkable transaction relative to Limerick.

It was a pleasing and glorious task to render his native city respectable to distant nations, to give new traits of our national character; — and his satisfaction has been great indeed, that it has fallen to his lot, to record the names of his learned and illustrious countrymen.

> Hail, happy city! With fair freedom blest,
> At thought of thee, how throbs the anxious breast!
> When distant far, the heart impatient burns,
> And all our country on our souls returns!

All the materials of this book are Irish; many of our manufactures have been brought to perfection. (The Author was desirous to promote the manufactures of his country; the paper, except a few copies on Royal, was made in Dublin, but not equal to the sample sent down to him. The Irish will never rival the French in this great article of commerce, until they are enabled to give age to the paper, and until they lay aside the shameful practice of putting too much blue in it.) When Ireland has burst all her fetters! When the spirit of the nation is called forth to industry, as it was to arms, then will it shine with equal splendor! At this moment Ireland is the most rising country in Europe, considering what freedom of trade, and toleration she has lately obtained . . .

In such a variety of matter, as this book contains, some errors will be found, for which he intreats the indulgence of his readers. And as he intends to persevere in the study of this subject, he will thankfully receive any correction or addition.

J. Ferrar, Citizen of Limerick
Sir Harry's Mall,
Limerick
December 25, 1786.

From *The History of Limerick*, A. Watson, & Co., 1787

New Town Pery
Rev. P. Fitzgerald and J. J. McGregor

A stronger contrast can scarcely be imagined than between the appearance of the city fifty years ago, and at the present time. When Doctor Campbell wrote his Survey of the South of Ireland in 1775, the number of its streets was 27, and of its houses 3,859, with a population of probably less than 30,000: there are now near seventy streets besides innumerable lanes, and by the Census of 1821, the houses were enumerated at 8,268, and the inhabitants at 66,042. The city is watered in its whole length by the Queen of British rivers, which flows to the sea in a majestic volume, and returns, frequently wafting on its bosom to the quays (a distance of sixty Irish miles) vessels of five hundred tons burthen. It is composed of the English Town, the Irish Town, and New Town Pery. The first stands on the Northern side of the river, being separated from the two latter by a narrow arm of the Shannon, which embraces the English Town in its entire circumference: and on the NW side of the great branch of the river, in the county of Clare, is the extensive and populous suburb of Thomond-gate. The English Town has all the antiquated appearance of a close built fortress of the latter part of the seventeenth century: its venerable cathedral, narrow streets, and lofty houses, chiefly built in the Dutch or Flemish fashion, are said to give it a considerable resemblance to Rouen in Normandy. This gloom is however relieved at various openings by a view of the cheering waters of the Shannon, while the vicinity of the canal, and the verdant fields and gardens which skirt the borders of the Abbey-river, afford a pleasant promenade to its dense population. The projected erection of a bridge at Athlunkard, in contemplation of which a new and spacious street is laid out through the centre of the English Town, promises to be of material service to the interests of the Old Town. Baal's-bridge which is still disgraced by a row of houses on its western side, leads from this part of the city to the Irish Town, the chief emporium of the country trade, where the streets are wider than in the English Town, and the houses of a more modern construction. This quarter is now nearly united with New Town Pery, by various connecting streets and avenues, so that we may anticipate that it will progressively partake in all the advantages and improvements of its more modern neighbour.

The ground on which the New Town is built, is rather elevated, and the soil in general gravelly and dry. The streets are spacious, cut each other at right angles, and are occupied by elegant houses and merchant's-stores, constructed of brick and lime stone, for which the neighbouring district supplies the finest materials. A more superb city-view can hardly be presented to the eye, than the range of buildings from the New Bridge to the Crescent, a distance little short of an English mile, including Rutland-street, Patrick-street, George's-street, and the Tontine; and its interest will be greatly heightened, when the line of buildings is continued from the Crescent along the Military Road, and the projected Square built on its left. Shops tastefully laid out and richly furnished line these streets, while others diverge to right and left, which are chiefly occupied by the residences of the gentry. At every opening to the westward, salubrious breezes from the Shannon, inspire health and vigour, and a walk to the quays is amply compensated by the scenes of busy traffic there presented, and the various enlivening prospects which meet the eye. Here the packet boat from Kilrush is landing her joyous passengers, whose nerves have been braced, and spirits exhilarated, by some weeks residence on the shores of the Atlantic at Kilkee or Malbay. There turf and fish-boats are discharging their cargoes, which are rapidly conveyed by Herculean porters to the dwellings of the consumers, amidst various specimens of Munster wit, sometimes delivered in the native language, and sometimes in Anglo-Irish. Seamen of different nations, and merchants engaged in the important business of import or export, enliven by their activity, this busy scene, the interest of which is much enhanced at present, by the number of workmen employed in constructing the docks, and building Wellesley-bridge at the end of Brunswick-street. Wearied with this tumult, should the mind wish to contemplate more tranquil objects, retired situations, and gratifying prospects, are not wanted. On the West are seen, the distant towers of Carrigogunnel Castle; and the Pool, where the larger ships ride at anchor in perfect security, while many a skiff cuts the blue wave: on the East, appear the mill of Curragour, built in 1672, and its rapid current, which roars and eddies amidst rocks of various shapes and sizes — the bridge of Thomond, hoary with age, and the ivy-mantled turrets of King John's Castle, backed by the mountains of Clare and Tipperary. The view of the North Strand, though not devoid of interest, is less striking than might be expected from its commanding situation, in the vicinity of a rich and populous city. Its only ornaments are a few country-seats, thinly decorated with trees, and the House of Industry, a plain substantial building. But it is likely that the completion of Wellesley Bridge will remedy this defect, and that the fine acclivity which runs along the North side of the river will soon be covered with picturesque cottages, and handsome plantations. The city contains nearly fifty public edifices, about one half of which stand on the south-west side of the river. At night the streets of the New Town are splendidly lighted with gas, while those of the English Town are left with unaccountable negligence in total darkness, except where the brilliancy of some public-house illumines the gloomy scene. Yet the commission of crime is rare in the streets, from the caution with which the wealthy and respectable part of the community approach this part of the city after the close of night, and the vigilance of a truly efficient City Police.

From *The History, Topography, and Antiquities of the County and City of Limerick; with Preliminary View of the History and Antiquities of Ireland*, George McKern, 1827

Garryowen
Gerald Griffin

The little ruined outlet, which gives its name to one of the most popular national songs of Erin, is situate on the acclivity of a hill near the city of Limerick, commanding a not uninteresting view of that fine old town, with the noble stream that washes its battered towers, and a richly cultivated surrounding country. Tradition has preserved the occasion of its celebrity, and the origin of its name, which appears to be compounded of two Irish words signifying 'Owen's garden'. — A person so called was the owner, about half a century since, of a cottage and plot of ground on this spot, which from its contiguity to the town, became a favourite holiday resort with the young citizens of both sexes — a lounge presenting accommodations somewhat similar to those which are offered to the London mechanic by the Battersea tea-gardens. Owen's garden was the general rendezvous for those who sought for simple amusement or for dissipation. The old people drank together under the shade of trees — the young played at ball, goal, or other athletic exercises on the green; while a few lingering by the hedge-rows with their fair acquaintances, cheated the time with sounds less boisterous, indeed, but yet possessing their fascination also.

The festivities of our fathers, however, were frequently distinguished by so fierce a character of mirth, that, for any difference in the result of their convivial meetings, they might as well have been pitched encounters. Owen's garden was soon as famous for scenes of strife, as it was for mirth and humour; and broken heads became a staple article of manufacture in the neighbourhood.

This new feature in the diversions of the place, was encouraged by a number of young persons of a rank somewhat superior to that of the usual frequenters of the garden. They were the sons of the more respectable citizens, the merchants and wholesale traders of the city, just turned loose from school with a greater supply of animal spirits than they had wisdom to govern. Those young gentlemen being fond of wit, amused themselves by forming parties at night, to wring the heads off all the geese, and the knockers off all the hall doors in the neighbourhood. They sometimes suffered their genius to soar as high as the breaking of a lamp, and even the demolition of a watchman; but, perhaps, this species of joking was found a little too serious to be repeated over frequently, for few achievements of so daring a violence are found amongst their records. They were obliged to content themselves with the less ambitious distinction of destroying the knockers and store-locks, annoying the peaceable inmates of the neighbouring houses, with long continued assaults on the front doors, terrifying the quiet passengers with every species of insult and provocation, and indulging their fratricidal propensities against all the geese in Garryowen.

The fame of the 'Garryowen boys' soon spread far and wide. Their deeds were celebrated by some inglorious minstrel of the day in that air which has since resounded over every quarter of the world; and even disputed the palm of national popularity with 'Patrick's day'. A string of jolly verses were appended to the tune which soon enjoyed a notoriety similar to that of the famous 'Lilli-burlero, bullen-a-la' which sung King James out of his three kingdoms. The name of Garryowen was as well known as that of the Irish Numantium, Limerick, itself, and Owen's little garden became almost a synonym for Ireland.

But that principle of existence which assigns to the life of man its period of youth, maturity, and decay, has its analogy in the fate of villages, as in that of empires. Assyria fell, and so did Garryowen! Rome had its decline, and Garryowen was not immortal. Both are now an idle sound, with nothing but the recollections of old tradition to invest them with an interest. The still notorious suburb is little better than a heap of rubbish, where a number of smoked and mouldering walls, standing out from the masses of stone and mortar, indicate the position of a once populous row of dwelling houses. A few roofs yet remain unshaken, under which some impoverished families endeavour to work out a wretched subsistence by maintaining a species of huxter trade, by cobbling old shoes, and manufacturing ropes. A small rookery wearies the ears of the inhabitants at one end of the outlet, and a rope-walk which extends along the adjacent slope of Gallows-green, (so called for certain reasons) brings to the mind of the conscious spectator, associations that are not calculated to enliven the prospect. Neither is he thrown into a more jocular frame of mind as he picks his steps over the insulated paving stones that appear amid the green slough with which the street is deluged, and encounters at the other end, an alley of coffin-makers' shops, with a fever hospital on one side, and a church-yard on the other. A person who was bent on a journey to the other world, could not desire a more expeditious outfit than Garryowen could now afford him: nor a more commodious choice of conveyances, from the machine on the slope above glanced at, to the pest-house at the farther end.

But it is ill talking lightly on a serious subject. The days of Garryowen are gone, like those of ancient Erin; and the feats of her once formidable heroes are nothing more than a winter's evening tale. Owen is in his grave, and his garden looks dreary as a ruined church-yard. The greater number of his merry customers have followed him to a narrower play-ground, which, though not less crowded, affords less room for fun, and less opportunity for contention. The worm is here the reveller, the owl whoops out his defiance without an answer, (save the echo's,) the best whiskey in Munster would not now 'drive the cold out of their hearts'; and the withered old sexton is able to knock the bravest of them over the pate with impunity. A few perhaps may still remain to look back with a fond shame to the scene of their early follies, and to smile at the page in which those follies are recorded.

Still, however, there is something to keep the memory alive of those unruly days, and to preserve the name of Garryowen from utter extinction. The annual fair which is held on the spot presents a spectacle of gaiety and uproar which might rival its most boisterous days; and strangers still enquire for the place with a curiosity which its appearance seldom fails to disappoint. Our national lyrist has immortalised the air by adapting to it one of the liveliest of his melodies; — the adventures, of which it was once the scene, constitute a fund of standing joke and anecdote which are not neglected by the neighbouring story-tellers; — and a rough voice may still occasionally be heard by the traveller who passes near its ruined dwellings at evening, to chaunt a stanza of the chorus which was once in the mouth of every individual in the kingdom:—

> 'Tis there we'll drink the nut-brown ale
> An pay the reck'nin' on the nail
> No man for debt shall go to jail
> From Garryowen a gloria.'

From *The Collegians*, Appletree Press, 1992/Saunders and Otley, 1829

Our Green House
Richard Harris

1942

Our green house
was where Beau Geste
ran to
deep in the desert

Our gooseberry bushes
was where
I ambushed all the Wells Fargo's

Our apple trees
was where
I played Tarzan
with my neighbour (Sally)
(She wasn't as pretty as a Maureen O'Sullivan
but I forgave her when she rescued
me from the hungry crocodiles)

The plum tree
was where
(it wasn't our plum tree but the branches
hung over the wall into our garden)
I boarded the Spanish ship
and saved the British Empire

Our pear tree
was where
I saved Sally from the giant

The pole
that kept the Monday washing up
was my
brother's own surrender flagpole
(Mum was angry when
he used my sister's knickers as a white flag)

The garage
without the car
was where
I judged the bad
and was judged when bad

The garage
with the car
was the plane
I bombed the Germans from
the ship I captained
the tanks I drove
the stagecoach I killed
Geronimo from
he died five times
(My brother said I was a lousy shot
the truth was that he was a bad loser)

The outside toilet
was the electric chair
(I didn't like that game
although I got to play James Cagney)

Our lane
was where I captained Ireland
against England at Rugby
kicked endless goals
was carried off the field
shoulder high
by my thousands of fans
and called the greatest ever

I
won everything my heroes won
in our lane
I was the greatest ever
until I took a bath
then I was me again
the middle son in a family of eight
wearing my elder brothers'
hand-me-downs

Our house
was where
my mum and dad lived
and at night
it was the happiest place
I'd travelled all day

From *I, in the Membership of my Days*, Michael Joseph, 1975

'The Fairest City of Munster'
Maurice Lenihan

It has been observed that there are few cities in Europe more delightfully situated than Limerick. In the midst of a country teeming with agricultural and mineral riches, and surrounded by one of the most abundant salmon fisheries in the world, with all the advantages of navigation, etc., it requires only the hand of industry and enterprise, to constitute it all that it was intended by Providence it should be. Seen from the towers of St Mary's cathedral, it presents a view that cannot be surpassed for picturesque beauty and antiquarian interest. North and south, east and west, the country about it, bounded in the distance by ranges of lofty mountains, is fertile to a proverb, constituting a portion of the 'golden vein'. The broad Shannon winds its course above the city, and expands into an estuary below on its way to the Atlantic Ocean, after traversing 240 miles from its source in Leitrim, where, flowing out of Lough Allen — imbedded in lofty hills abounding in iron and coal — it washes the county of Roscommon, expands into the great Lough Ree, twenty miles long and four broad; going on by the counties of Tipperary and Galway to Portumna, in a more confined channel for thirty-seven miles; then through Lough Derg to Killaloe, and thence by the Doonas, with a fall of ninety-seven feet to Limerick — the scenes of ancient battles, and of more modern sieges: the old castles, the bridges — the quaint streets of the Englishtown, with their fading and falling Dutch gables — the Irishtown, with its historic places — the handsome and regular streets of the new town, with its churches, public buildings, shops, private residences, etc. — these objects all group together into a panorama on which the eye loves to dwell, suggesting the thought that a city so well circumstanced, must eventually rise superior to any combination of adverse circumstances by which it may be encumbered, and that as it has been 'the fairest city of Munster', so it will not only preserve its reputation in that respect, but become the busy seat of manufacturing and commercial enterprise — the home of prosperity — as it has always been the pride of Irishmen in whatever part of the world they may dwell . . .

The picturesque village of Kilkee, romantically situated upon the Clare coast, is the favourite bathing place of the citizens of Limerick, who generally repair thither in considerable numbers when the season arrives. There are many other places within a few miles distance, which will well repay a visit, from the beauty of their scenery and their antiquarian and historical interest. Such are Carrig-o'-Gunnell, Adare, Castleconnell, Bunratty, Killaloe, Lough Gur, etc. For those, indeed, who are fond of exploring Druidic, military, and ecclesiastical antiquities, there is no county in Ireland which supplies more ample materials than Limerick, which possess likewise numerous attractions for the lovers of sporting.

From *Limerick; Its History and Antiquities, Ecclesiastical, Civil, and Military, from the Earliest Ages*, Hodges, Smith, and Co., 1866

From: **Limerick**
John Francis O'Donnell

Dear city of the tributary wave,
Rolled past thy bastions by the warring tide,
From fields where fortune fell, and sleep the brave,
Buried with trampled flag, and broken glaive,
Under rent canopies which, waved aside,
Show thee, as once thou wast, the citadel
Within whose walls a nation dared to hope —
Within whose walls a nation's soul found scope
For conflict's farthest issue, good or ill.

Thy towers upon the midmost torrent cast
The lightnings, darknesses, of centuries, —

War's pitiless and trebly-breasted blast,
Heroic figures, shapen of the past,
And counsellings of foreign lands and seas;
There rallied Ireland round her final stake,
Ringed by alliances that grudged no cost;
'Twas thrown, 'twas doubly chanced, and it was lost,
As one drop bosomed in the league-long lake.

Slain was the cause, but thou remainest still,
Gray, by the white hem of the refluent flood,
Having in thee what years can never kill,
Strong courage, and inexorable will,
Challenge of sacrifice, and scorn of blood.
The storm dissolved, yet still St Mary's threw
Her latticed splendours through the southern air, —
A lance of iron-stone austerely bare —
Yet kindly kindled by the wind and dew.

And, as I pace each still and storied street,
The pageants of forgotten days arise;
I feel the tumult and the gathering heat,
I hear the measured fall of warrior feet,
I see the banners in the narrow skies.
Cries and rejoicings burthen the warm air —
Some foe has perished, some good deed been done,
Some toil has borrowed comfort of the sun,
And poured a moment's light upon despair.

*****

Still thou, brave city! hadst to fight the fight
Of desperate valour, when, outside thy girth,
Leaders, from apprehension weak and white,
Beheld the baffled cause of battling Right
Fade, or become the mockery of earth.
Above thy walls, Right's ensigns latest flew,
Nailed to thy bastions rent with racking fire,
Until thy streets became a flaming pyre,
Where perished liberty, and honour, too.

I see O'Brien in the thickest press —
Pale are his lips, exhortive are his eyes;

'Tis his to scorn death's hail, encourage, bless,
Whilst the defender's ranks grow less and less
And nearer roll the foemen's thirsty cries.
His gallant heart is worth a hundred guns,
And Ireton knows it as he pales to see
The headlong, surging Irish chivalry
Led by the bravest of St Dominic's sons.

Spilt blood and sacrifice availed thee not,
Dear city of the tributary wave!
Shattered and blackened by destroying shot,
Thy very shape became a smoking blot,
Thy bastions, charnels; and thy moat, a grave.
Let Ireton sound his trumpets long and loud —
He has achieved his stubborn purpose well;
Put out the lights and toll the passing bell —
The head of valiant Limerick is bowed!

O'Brien dies, and with his latest word
Comforts his people — blesses the great town.
Now shall the sparkling brand assist the sword,
And Shannon, with its freight of shame abhorred,
Run red to where the sun goes redly down.
But brief, O Ireton! was thy victory:
A prophet's voice had summoned thee to meet
Thy just requital at God's awful feet,
Whose soles are limits of the jasper sea.

So flashed thy story by me, city mine,
As leaning over Thomond's memoried bridge,
I saw, gold-fired, upon the peaceful ridge,
The banners and the spears of autumn shine,
And heard behind me the town's murmurous tune,
And watched afar, all violet, or bare,
The sea-declining hills of breezy Clare,
And deep in heaven, the shadow of the moon.

From *Memories of the Irish Franciscans*, James Duffy, 1871

The Sewers
P. J. Ryan

The Shannon played another important role in the lives of the people. A city prospers or perishes by its sanitary services. From the refuse dump of the earliest known age to today's more elaborate systems, they help to reveal the living conditions of the age. In the newer part of the city, Newtown Pery, the sewers were eight feet high, over five feet wide and arch roofed. The walls were two feet thick and built of bricks made in the many brickworks on the perimeter of the city. From the sewers two arches led to the basement area of the houses, laid out when a block of houses was built. The gorgeously periwigged and beribboned staffs of the houses entered those with the sanitation buckets and emptied them through openings into the sewer. A heavy shower of rain would cause a foot high flood of water to rush through the sewers and clear them; on this account the Corporation workers examining the sewers could walk the length and breadth of the city in safety and purity of thought without coming above ground. The Grand Master of this development was Edmond Sexten Pery.

The sewers followed the plan of the streets and were named after the streets above them. The principal street of the city, George Street was called after George IV and the sewer underneath was named King George. Queen Street was called after Queen Victoria; Her Majesty's generous donation of five pounds towards Famine relief in 1848 was thus gratefully remembered. The sewer beneath was called Queen Victoria as a further gesture of the esteem of the Famine Queen. Cornwallis Street was named after Lord Cornwallis; the sewers below also commemorated the Viceroy.

The names of the streets were later changed to those of other honoured people but the sewer names were not changed; and so, though they are dead and gone, the names of those Imperial British personalities are immortalised in the sewers of Limerick city. Each day the citizens, with long drawn sighs, shed their tears and donate their tributes to the memory of those long departed but not forgotten regal rulers.

From 'The Fourth Siege of Limerick', *The Old Limerick Journal*, No. 13, Autumn 1982

Housing Conditions in 1909
Thomas Johnson

As I have observed quite a few extraordinary things pertaining to the affairs of this city, I thought it might be interesting to the citizens hereof to have copies of a few of my notes.

The first thing I noticed while travelling through the air in the direction of the city was that, while in open country there seemed to be very few houses, in the small area called 'Limerick City' there were very many huddled together in all sorts of peculiar alleys and lanes. I could not help but wonder what strange notions of comfort the inhabitants of that city must have had to crowd their homes together in such a fashion while so many square miles of open country lay all round about!

But, when I took a walk along those lanes and alleys, my wonder was turned to disgust when I found that these houses were not only crowded into congested areas but many of them were insanitary and unfit for human habitation and, to my unpractised eye, did not appear to have ever been otherwise even when originally built. In the course of my walk I saw that in some of the streets there were large airy houses with plenty of space at the front and rear and presumably with efficient sanitary conveniences within. I naturally assumed that these would be occupied by the families of the people who did the work of the city; who unloaded the ships, built the houses, cleaned the streets, and generally spent their strength ministering to the needs of the population; and that the other houses (or 'kennels' as they may more appropriately be called) were the dwelling places of people who were under punishment for refusing to work, or who preferred to live on what might remain over after the workers' needs had all been supplied. But judge of my astonishment when I elicited the fact from a local worthy that the workers lived and appeared content to live in these kennels and even went so far as to pay a weekly or monthly sum of money called *rent* to the owner for the 'privilege' of living therein.

When I asked how many house-owners had been hanged within the past twelve months he showed me with evident pride a newspaper account of the presentation of a pair of white gloves to the judge of assize! Evidently on this planet it is not a crime to take advantage of a man's poverty and make a profit out of a death trap.

But strangest of all to me was that, while scores of men, women and children every year suffered preventable disease and death and while the causes of this were apparent to the simplest, no fuss was made about it. High rates, water, gas, the Irish language, the mayor's trip to Belfast, some old women named Molly Maguire, these topics monopolised public interest. I enquired in vain for any organised body whose object was to abolish this deplorable state of affairs.

Merchants, professional men, clergy, artisans, labourers, even tender-hearted women — all seemed too familiar with the sights that had appalled me — a stranger from another world — to feel any indignation.

Taking a trip over the neighbouring country I noticed many cottages of the unsanitary type which I saw in the city but most of these were unoccupied and derelict while nearby had been built tidy, cheerful cottages with a considerable piece of ground attached suitable for a garden. Upon asking for an explanation I was informed that these new cottages had been built for the farm labourers by the public authorities and were let at rents sufficiently low to meet the income of labourers.

The questions which arose in my mind on hearing this were: Why is not the same plan adopted to re-house the labourers in the city? Have the City Fathers no paternal care for the city's children? Have they done their utmost to enforce the laws dealing with these matters? Are there any owners of insanitary property inside or outside the corporation whose influence is great enough to prevent the enforcement of the law? Have all working men and women councillors, with practical experience of the lives of the poor, done their duty to their constituents on such vital matters as these? Are there no public-spirited men and women outside the council with sufficient energy and civic patriotism to take up these questions of the health of the people and not rest until Limerick has become a city of which the citizens need not be ashamed?

From *Thomas Johnson, 1872–1963*, J. Anthony Gaughan, Kingdom Books, 1980

Warmest Love
Kate O'Brien

Bunratty Castle is a limestone fortress to be seen, and nowadays to be visited, in Co. Clare, on the main road between Limerick City and Shannon Airport . . .

For all of my life and for many generations before me the castle stood desolate, a slowly crumbling ruin, above the bridge on the turn of the familiar road to Ennis. It was the property of the Studdart family, a forsaken old relic. And then a few years ago came John Hunt — that learned, impassioned student of the past and of forgotten arts, forsaken skills and beauties, a man of pure and scholarly devotion, a lover and servant of Ireland if ever there was one. He decided, studied, plotted, planned, implored, begged and everyway thought and importuned — to restore Bunratty Castle to what it was when Barnaby, 6th Earl, was a child there at the beginning of the seventeenth century. He loved the neglected structure that he found, and as an expert he knew how to read its indications; and he formed the wish to return it to Ireland, and to Europe, as an accurate example, as accurate as love, learning and money could make, of its own kind of aristocratic house at its own best time.

He had the love, he had the learning. He had a few friends whose taste and judgment were with him. He got erratic, vague 'Yes, yes'es' from uncomprehending patriots, and I believe that he got real attention from the Tourist Board. Also, some anxious, vague words from the Government.

But then he found Lord Gort. This generous peer, landlord of Cutra nearby, in the Coole and Gregory country . . . came to examine Bunratty Castle with John Hunt, listened to what he had to say, agreed with it, was fired by it. He bought Bunratty from the Studdart heir and entered into John Hunt's dream, open-handed and determined.

One may leave the ups-and-downs of their undertaking to the imagination of any experienced person. The point is that — with the eventual help of the Government of Ireland these two men did what they desired — and so on a day of May 1960 a great number of us were invited to celebrate in the Hall of the Earls the restoration of Bunratty Castle to its former estate, and as a national possession in perpetuity.

The event was in itself a triumph — but the achievement, as we saw that day and as any passer-by now can see, is beyond praise, a work of gentle and exacting knowledge, perfected by that patience, that insistence that only knowledge has, and that only love can sustain.

The occasion was celebrated most fittingly. The world was there at noon in the Hall of the Earls — princes of the Church, peers of Ireland, a Minister of the Government, officers of state, ambassadors and visiting foreigners of high-sounding style: some splendid figures of our *haute bourgeoisie*; some priests and nuns, and an observant riff-raff of writers and journalists, in the cloud of which I came, my parchment in my hand. Mass was sung in the Earl's beautiful chapel and afterwards speeches were made, sherry was drunk, there was much talk, and great admiring of the treasures gathered with such care — tables, cupboards, tapestries, goblets, pots and pans; and nothing allowed throughout the house that had not been in existence before 1640. Then we swept off, 500 of us, to a sixteenth-century luncheon in the restaurant of one of the most forward-looking airports in the world. Derelict Bunratty had become a lovely museum of Irish sixteenth-century life; and we were all delighted with our day's work . . .

Yet, that said and whilst I always rejoice in conservation of old beauty (and am slow alas, to welcome conceptions of tomorrow), it is not Bunratty Castle that is dear to me, but the road and land and water that lie about it. For these moved and changed with the weathers of my own childhood, they were alive with me, whereas a pile of forgotten stone above the little bridge was dull: there seemed no movement on its face, only a set pronouncement of dead soldierliness and pride

— characteristics which have never attracted me. I did not know when I was young that this harsh-faced monument had been so much humanised by a man of the sixteenth-century: I did not dream that it was so richly spaced within for the arts of living. I took it for a rude keep, where soldiers crammed themselves together and thought only of killing passers-by.

But the fields that lay about Limerick, and these flattish western ones among them, were dear to my musing eye when I was young; and I had always a great love for roads. I liked very much the ordinary roads, with hedges and footpaths, that led in and out of my town. Much happened that was interesting on these; and we were often on them, in pony-traps or walking. The footpaths are gone — and how lovely they were, with low grassy ridges keeping them defined — and with gates here and there breaking the hawthorn — gates on which to sit and consider the fields, for mushrooms or fairy grass, or bulls. From behind Bunratty it is not far up to the Windy Gap or to old, crumbling Six-Mile-Bridge, and to go home by Delmege's Glens was interesting. 'When up through Cratloe Woods I went, Nutting with thee — And we plucked the brown and clustering fruit from many a bending tree . . . ' Samuel Ferguson's happy girl and boy would have to mind where they were going now with their love-making, for on a cleared slope of Cratloe there is a spectacular Lourdes Grotto, with steps up and down, and much ancillary pious ornamentation — and this is a place of prayer and pilgrimage. When I was young the woods were pagan and innocent . . .

Walking into Limerick from the west, from Cratloe or Bunratty, used to be rustic progression not very long ago, between wide fields and past glimpses of the chimneys or kitchen gardens of secluded residences, until one came to the Workhouse Cross where the wide Ennis Road became a respectable, flowery avenue of terraced villas. An orthodox and short lead in to the river and the Georgian town. But now that self-conscious avenue and south of it those embosqued and tennis-courted mansions of the upper *bourgeoisie*, though still in fact there, are all but engulfed in new Limerick, which has rushed and is rushing out westward very fast — though not as untidily as might be feared. A sports stadium, some gleaming petrol stations, a furniture factory, a pleasant modern church, uncountable bright villas, and of course no workhouse any more but in its place an alert-looking City Hospital — all these blur out the clear, remembered lines of the town one learnt by heart on pony-drives and in school crocodile-walks. And the fields which used to melt away beyond the Workhouse to Long Pavement and the edge of the Clare Hills, are housing estates now — which God knows, as does anyone who remembers Limerick's fabulous eighteenth-century slums, were badly needed, and now alarmingly and happily swarm, ring and clamour, day in day out, with the child-life of the vanishing Irish . . .

At the inner end of the Ennis Road on this slow walk we are taking, we come to Limerick itself, and as we stand to admire it beyond the river and over the bridge we will find ourselves at a wide, tree-shaded *carrefour*. The riverside roads to left and right of us here are called O'Callaghan's Strand and Clancy's Strand. Quiet roads, in which a few Victorian-style villas stand back in long gardens, in sound of the Shannon, and with fine views of the city.

Strangers may pick up nothing from the two name-plates; but like Cork, Limerick had its First Citizens murdered by Black and Tans — only with a difference. They walked coolly about their city in defiance of the new, inexclusable enemy, as in Cork Terence McSwiney had done until they jailed him.

Michael O'Callaghan who was Mayor in 1920 was said to have been the one who gave those 'Auxiliaries' their nickname. He by chance saw somewhere a first lorryload of them just landed, with Lloyd George's terrible instructions and in their untidy uniform, half policeman's black, half soldier's khaki — and described them as like a famous Tipperary pack of hounds, Black and Tan.

George Clancy, who took mayoral office in 1921, had been a friend of James Joyce in University College, Dublin — and had tried to interest him (a) in the Irish language and (b) in Irish patriotism. He is called *Davin* in *A Portrait of the Artist as a Young Man*. Richard Ellmann says that according to Joyce, George Clancy was the only one among his friends at university who called him James; and there appears to have been a special vein of gentleness and respect in Stephen Hero's feeling for this young dreamer from Limerick.

Clancy had, it is recorded, sometimes said in Joyce's hearing that twelve men with resolution could save Ireland. Such foolishness suggests almost a death-wish. And anyway, the Black and Tans came to his door, in masks, on a spring morning, at 1 a.m. in 1921, and waking him from his bed, shot him dead, in the presence of his wife.

They had just come from the southern end of the Strand. There they had roused Michael O'Callaghan also from sleep, and in his hallway as he stood beside his wife, they had shot him dead . . .

And oddly enough, in a tree-surrounded house that stood midway between those two outraged houses, there lived a man the friend and colleague of the two dead — who also was 'wanted' by the Tans. He was not at home on that night, Stephen O'Mara — but for the 'Auxiliaries' there were plenty of other nights . . . And it was only by the thinnest chance that it did not come to him also, masked and in the night . . .

So across Sarsfield Bridge, between the two boat clubs — and taking my time. I always like to go slowly, either way, across this bridge, for from it there is everything to see — all of life and one's own regrets and sentimentalities, of course; but also much better things, detached and, in terms which human imagination will allow, everlasting — the sky, in unchanging changefulness, high, wide and handsome indeed, as always from this vantage; the marvellous river, strongest and most impatient, most contemptuous, if we admit the pathetic fallacy, and least sentimental of Irish waters — and the ancient and so eagerly progressive town itself, its lovely and sad and repetitious human life pouring back and over for centuries gone and unborn between these simple parapets. St Mary's; the Courthouse lighting up above the water; prams in collision. Seagulls tearing a filthy fish apart; a Boeing Jet streaking across the blue, making its own pure line of cloud.

I am home from my meander — and I find I am out of step again. For the deep wound made by burnt-out Todd's is filling up — concrete, glass and steel are the new graft; and, shockingly Cannock's 1822 façade has vanished behind scaffoldings, though they say we are to be given back the clock. Let us indeed hope so! But, almost worse than the death of Cannock's is that one of our two beautiful medical halls is suddenly gone — and gone forever: to give place to Aer Lingus's proud needs. I suppose no one could be expected to book a Polar Route flight to Tokio — and that is now a major Limerick pastime — behind a stucco, Dieu-et-mon-Droit frontage of 1835 (William IV!), or standing on early nineteenth-century mosaic? There is, one notices, a sympathy, a need of sympathy, between action and the scene of proposed action. But we still have that other medical hall which once was a music shop, and carries plastic emblems and symbolic figures of music on its exterior — a house where young Catherine Hayes, the washerwoman's child who was to sing in La Scala and in Covent Garden, gave a first concert to her patrons and backers of the city, before they decided to send her on to Italy. We still have that medical hall. But beside it we had until now the Royal George Hotel, in the same pleasant mid-nineteenth-century idiom. And that is coming down in dust and rubble all about O'Connell Street, to make room for an objectionably named sign of our progress — a luxury hotel.

All this in a few months.

Will Limerick stay? Can it hold out and hold its character much longer? I, for one, do not know — but hope to find it mine for the time left to me. St John's still points its holy finger to a recognisable sky. And as I walk away from it, thinking to take an evening bus to Castleconnell I do not feel inordinately sad. Limerick is a well-proportioned place, and from its established layout, its old look of good manners and good sense I take repose. And that blessed word reminds me perversely of the motto on the city's coat of arms, which I have never liked. '*Urbs antiqua fuit, studiisque asperrima belli*'. It was an ancient city, and fierce (most fierce) in the skills of war. I am instructed that this unattractive slogan or commendation is taken, in two bits made into one, from the Aeneid. But I find it neither Virgilian nor at all to my Limerick-conditioned mind . . .

It was, by the way, a distinguished son of Limerick, William Moloney of Reuter's, who gave me the provenance of our patched-up motto. He learnt his Greek and Latin in Limerick; in the hard way of scholarship, from 'The Holy Fathers'; and now, with Horace always in his left-hand pocket or on his ready tongue, I think he would say that he owes to those stern instructors uncountable hours of pure delight among pagan poets, whose felicities first surprised him in boyhood in a school which might have been described as *asperrima*.

But it is not a good word for Limerick. Circumstances did sometimes demand of us the virtue, or attribute, it claims — but mercifully the accompanying expression did not stick — for the features of the place are humanistic. There is a certain austerity, or rather decorum, underlying the civic character, perhaps — an addiction to form and self-control, which we must hope will stay with us, even now when Shannon Airport with new and strange devices for weather and progress brings daily so much threat and glitter to our doors: novelties, exotics, ambitions that are not to be stemmed, since everywhere now we are in 1961, and nowhere can be called a hiding place. Nowhere anymore is there silence — though there used to be in the winter days in Roundstone. And still there is in Castleconnell. So I will get off the bus, and walk past the Tontines as far as the pier at the World's End.

From My Ireland, B. T. Batsford Ltd, 1962

The Carnegie Library
P. J. Ryan

Due to the benevolence of Andrew Carnegie, the Scottish millionaire philan-thropist, a Carnegie Free Library was established in the city. Other Carnegie Libraries were also set up in many cities and towns throughout the country. The library building was sited in Pery Square. With indecent haste the name of the library was changed to Limerick Free Library. The only part of the library open to the public was a small reading room in which the literate poor could read the daily papers and secure refuge in the warmth of the room from the freezing temperatures in winter. A corridor, flanked by a counter, was presided over by the Librarian and Assistant Librarian.

In winter, the library was a dark, dismal gas-lit ghetto of dog-eared volumes. In summer the place was almost deserted. Books could only be borrowed by first perusing a catalogue and then giving the title and number of the selected volume as well as a brass plate with the borrower's number. The borrower was then closely questioned in order to establish his *bona fides* in the library.

Some of the books in the library dated back to 1836 and earlier. Included in the stock were a half-dozen Irish-English dictionaries and Bedel's Bible in Irish (1827). The tenor of many of the books extolled the gloom and horror of the dead past.

The Origin and Use of the Round Towers by George Petrie (1847), Vol. No. 2654, sought to prove a Christian origin for those graceful spires . . . *The Towers and*

Temples of Ancient Ireland by Marcus Keane (1867), Vol. No. 4780, claimed that those erect conical-capped towers were pre-Christian temples of phallic worship . . .

The Congregated Trades sent two men who, with the president and secretary of the Pork Butchers' Society, gave their honest labour in the furtherance of literary endeavour. The Town Clerk, the Secretary of the Library Committee and the Hon. Treasurer, helped by the City Librarian, with the assistance of the Assistant Librarian, made this Library Committee a formidable barrier to progressive thought and inspired writing.

Because of the fame of Gerald Griffin, as a poet, playwright and novelist, and Aubrey de Vere, Curraghchase, as a poet, it was felt that the city might possess some rare literary talent which, if discovered, could be developed into the creation of a literary masterpiece, to enhance the fame of the city. To this end, the Catholic Literary Institute was founded.

The common workman who worked for twelve or more hours each day had little time or energy for literary pursuits. The Bard of Thomond, Michael Hogan, got no grace or papal blessing from that literary institute, with its thousand volume library of dogma and doggerel.

From *The Old Limerick Journal*, No. 13, 1982

Mikey Raleigh's Band
Bob Hamilton

One evening in the early 'thirties, when I was about eleven years of age, a group of Thomondgate lads picked up some tin cans and sticks and set off on a long and colourful musical journey. The story of that journey, like so many other stories of the lives of ordinary Limerick people, has never been written.

But if one knew that these young tin-pot players were to be moulded into music-makers by a one-legged man who had fought in First World War trenches, then surely some fitting record would have been kept. We started out on an unsure, uncharted road together, but the pieces fell into place without conscious design, nor indeed, the realisation that we were part of anything special. For on that night when we caused bedlam and headaches in Thomondgate, one man listened to the jarry symphony of sound, and an idea formed in his mind. He was Mikey Raleigh, and we were to be his band . . .

The Thomondgate of that time was almost a rural community, pushed outside the walls of an expanding city, yet nestling close to green fields and golden hay under the Clare hills . . .

Within a few days Mikey Raleigh had us across at his house, near Villiers Square, in the shadow of King John's Castle and the St Munchin Churchyard. After a while, he secured a meeting and practice place, an old shed near the Water Passage on the front Island Road . . .

As the only tune known to the instrumentalists was 'Clare's Dragoons' soon the people of Thomondgate put their own words to the music and often I heard the refrain wafting out on to the moonlit New Road from the crowded pubs:

> 'Only two more flutes . . .
> for Mikey Raleigh's band . . .
> and that's all we want . . . '

When we were adjudged worthy of public display, Mikey Raleigh had another problem — uniforms. We wore short black pants and white blouses. A jaunty touch was the headgear — green tams. These were acquired by rather dubious means . . . More than a few girls in Limerick missed their tams in the days before the band was launched . . . So we hit the road . . . bearing the name of the man who had lived for the day.

It is my recollection that Mikey Raleigh and his wife did not have children. He had been invalided out of the First World War and he lived on a disability pension because of losing the leg. He had fought with the British and probably got his love of music from their military bands. He had put so much time and effort into teaching us that I suppose we were an extended family to him. He had an 'ear' for the music and a 'knack' for teaching it. With his one leg, it always amazed me how he kept up with the band, marching at brisk pace through the streets of Limerick . . .

The early 'fifties were the beginning of a decade of despair for the city. One night I came home and sad lonely notes of a fragile flute floated up to our room. I went out and traced the music to a small shack down Francis Mews where a young lad practised, watched by a few more, and all under the encouraging gaze of the man who limped around on the fringe.

Yes . . . he was Mikey Raleigh . . . endeavouring to recapture old glory of former marching days. He said he was re-organising the band — Mikey Raleigh's Band — to march again through the city to mould music from another generation of Limerick boys.

'You could always teach the youngsters,' he said to me.

But by then the close-knit fabric of the life of the community was beginning to break up. The movement of younger married people to newly-built houses in Ballynanty marked the end of the old Thomondgate we knew so well.

That night I left Francis Mews and returned by Polly Carr's shop to our cramped room . . . with nostalgic memories of pots and pans . . . of girl's tams . . . of 'Clare's Dragoons' . . . of clear New Road moons . . . of flutes and drums . . . of young boys' dreams . . . of marching music . . . salute and stand . . . of being a boy once again in Mikey Raleigh's Band.

From *The Old Limerick Journal*, No. 12, 1982

'My Dear Native Place'
Kate O'Brien

As my life began at Limerick and has often brought me back there, so these memories and reflections about Irish travel seem naturally to start there too and to weave and wind from that first focus. And now from Shannon Airport it must often be the first Irish city that a stranger will set foot in. It may not be a radiant starting point; but first impressions need not dazzle; and a slow approach is wise where true acquaintance is expected . . . Limerick should prove a good place for that exercise. Its aspect is grave and maybe surprising; it could be corrective of literary fancies . . . But Limerick's aspect, Limerick's first manner — which is sceptical, quiet and deprecatory, I think — might well affect a newcomer, proportionately and with all modesty, as could Santander, or, let us say, Düsseldorf. It seems to me that a sensitive stranger, crossing one of Limerick's bridges, having looked up and down the Shannon and along any one of the wide, grey streets, might feel detached awhile from the mood of coloured folders, and inclined to postpone the sending-off of first-impression postcards. Not merely because the first impression came to him as if sedatively; but also because he would feel that he was going to have to pause over this town, and begin again on his Irish notions.

Mind you, I said a *sensitive* stranger. And as to that, let me confess that I have had one or two, and maybe more than one or two, of that very kind tell me to my face, most politely and even with pain, that they disliked Limerick, found it prim, or boring, or empty. They had complained of its food, of the poor quality of the amusements, and the dullness of its surrounding country. I have heard that there are too many churches and chapels, and that the Limerick people are cold and suspicious in manner; that they lack style and that the women are not pretty.

Sad fault-findings indeed. But as a man finds so he must speak, and only a fool will try to contradict expressed dislike. Yet one soft and sometimes effective answer to these objections to Limerick is to agree — as truly one must — that some of them may be in a measure true. And why not? There is dull food to be eaten in Limerick, and that city can no more than any other command the quality of the movies of this decade, or hush away the Top Twenty noises that issue night and day from juke boxes and radio sets uniformly now throughout the world. On wet days in Limerick the wind can be brutal, the great river a mere stretch of sulky flood, and beyond the subtle fields the unemphatic, lovely hills can simply disappear. As for the churches and chapels, there are indeed many and some of them dull and boring to the eye. But they ring their bells and cause a stir — and there is one new set of chimes which is a terror when it strikes too close; and anyway these places of worship — Limerick has most of the Christian kinds, and one small synagogue — are the very life and expression of the place, often for comedy, for anger, for conviction, for pride, for music and formality and ceremony — and always for prayer. And I believe that the citizens will not apologise for them to any captious visitor. As for manners: in Limerick people tend somewhat to mind their own business, if that is to be cold? But one *might* describe the inclination, or disinclination if you will, as a form of politeness, a courtesy — even a way of charity? About suspiciousness, well, perhaps a hint of it here and there against exuberance. For what we do lack, markedly, in Limerick is the 'come hither' approach, the sunburst technique . . .

The spire of St John's — let us take bearings from there, since it is easy to see from anywhere across the plain, and is beautiful and gentle. It is infinitely younger than Limerick, it and the cathedral church of which it is the constant praying voice — for they are not yet a hundred years old; and Pugin was already more than ten years in his grave when a modest local character, an architect called Hardwick, ventured to thrust this piece of brand-new Gothic into an unsuspecting Georgian skyline. But there was no quarrel at all; there could not be with such a fluke-felicity. And St Mary, good grey thirteenth-century tower could do no less than welcome the accent, the stress of reminder, the pointing-up of her age and importance, which the new-old neighbour in the sky bestowed as it were fortuitously upon her.

So St John's, in a shabby north-east corner between Garryowen and the slums of Irishtown, took its place as late as the eighteen-sixties in a rather tired and history-tattered town, and as if it was indeed itself a part of the long, uneasy record.

Marcel Proust's family party, or rather the family of the Narrator, always knew Combray from the train by the spire of St Hilaire, for the church epitomised the town; and once they saw it they knew exactly where they were and made haste to fold their rugs. So strangers, travelling Munster, when they see a greyish blur on the blue and green and out of it rising a spire that makes them think of Salisbury will know that they have arrived, whether they want to or not, at Limerick.

The Shannon is a formidable water; nothing parochial about it, nothing of prattle or girlish dream. It sweeps in and out of the ocean and the world according to the rules of far-out tides, and in association with dangerous distances. So its harbour has been long accustomed to news and trouble in and out, and in the general movement of time Limerick has been shaped as much by invasions and sieges as by acts of God and the usual weatherings. It is for Ireland therefore a representative city: whatever happened to Ireland happened also here — and some things happened to Ireland because of things that happened here . . .

Walking back . . . along the North Strand which is leafy and residential and in County Clare, one can take a good stare at Limerick's best façade. The river is wide and, joined under the Court House by its little tributary, it runs fast under two good bridges towards the docks and the deepening estuary. The old town rises mainly in grey from here, its dominant being the stained and shadowed limestone of St Mary's Cathedral and King John's Castle on their dark lichened rocks: Limerick's chief Norman remains, and specimens with merit. But as for the still grim and strong Castle, now made to look silly by the ugly tops of little mean cement houses built within and staring stupidly over its parapets — I for one am allergic to fortifications, and find them boring wherever I go.

City walls, for instance — and we have a few remnants of such in Limerick — do not attract my interest . . . City walls, in short, displease the eye; as do Norman forts and keeps, and nineteenth-century gaols, and twentieth-century barracks, oil tankers, hotels, spaceships, garages, warheads and space-war emplacements. All are conceived in defensiveness and ruthlessly; egotism and 'I'm All Right, Jack' always come out on their strong features . . .

I have gone a long way round merely to say that I care not at all for King John's Castle in Limerick, while always gratefully admiring of gentle St Mary's. Square-towered and grey, never of first-flight inspiration, and often patchily restored, it is nevertheless of stalwart Norman bearing and the city's only extant reminder now of the saints and scholars.

The stranger should visit St Mary's. If he climbs the tower on a summer's day, as I did long ago, he may think himself rewarded, for the view thence on any side is at once lively and tranquillising; beyond the intricacies of roofs, trees, streets and people, the landscape spreads, if the sun is shining, in a Persian weave of colours broken by serpentine flashes of waters, to blue hills, mainly blue, and a high, transparent sky.

The traveller may well undergo, unsuspecting on this parapet, a first injection, or infection, from Ireland's beauty. As he looks south over Limerick's Georgian part and past the lonely great warehouses of the docks, as, smelling brackishness in the fresh air, he seeks towards where the Atlantic must be, his sensibility may pick up a kind of rarity, a foreign, new element — new to him — in what he looks at. Austerity? A kind of cold restraint, an underflow of silence, a bony, throwaway grace?

It is here, I think, to be found. I have always found it about the Limerick lands — the hard essence, the deep limestone indestructibility of Ireland's puzzling and eternal good looks. Good looks as indisputable, as unpredictable and indeed at their most native as much a special taste as is, say, that delicate yet uncompromising beauty which their painters once found in the women of Siena.

A troublesome claim. Down from the tower, the newcomer should walk about the nave and transepts, to look at a few good tombs, and the misericords in the stalls; and consider the sad silk of battle flags. On the tombs he will find the once dominant local names — O'Brien, for one — as everywhere in the churchyards, mansions, pubs and cottages of Limerick and Clare. The princes of Thomond — the O'Briens, a wild and treacherous and touchy people left a bad record at the end, in the seventeenth century. But they left noble ruins too — Bunratty and Leimnigh Castles; and such great abbeys as Holy Cross and Corcomroe — gifts to his people, as was the cathedral of St Mary, of the pious prince Donal O'Brien. A few of his less virtuous descendants rest under these cathedral stones — peaceably neighboured by later arrivals, for instance, Roches, Perys, Arthurs, Russells, Sextons — upstarts of the eighteenth century who built the modern city in its Georgian order, and merit their memorials in this place . . .

Were it not so tricky nowadays about printing what one has in mind, I could offer flesh-and-blood introductions in my own city to persons who could make a foreigner's passage through it far more vivid and entertaining than ever can I from between the covers of a mere book — persons more integrally engaged with Limerick too than by, say, selling rosary beads outside the Augustinians. (But that is something no one does in Ireland any more, as far as I can see.) It was all very well in the eighteenth century, when a few bored subscribers might or might not dip into the calf-bound folio of memoirs that an indebted author pressed upon them with flourishes of flattery. In such a happy and illiterate time Arthur Young, for instance, could coolly record in print: 'To Limerick. Laid at Bennis's, the first inn we had slept in since Dublin. God preserve us this journey from another!' He can slap out like that, most helpfully to other travellers — and not a word out of Bennis! Or out of any kind of *Turismo* Authority. Happy Arthur Young! How intelligently and graciously he travelled! One has, of course, to skip about in his pages, and accept his maniacal interest in rape cake and 'turneps' . . .

Young's scientific purpose apart — though you cannot separate him from his ruling passion — he is a wonderfully humane, observant and mannerly traveller, and a man impossible to fool, I should say. He comes into mind as we leave St Mary's Gate, and stroll towards modern, eighteenth-century Limerick, leaving the old quarters of sieges, wars and destruction at our backs, because he liked Limerick well and was about when its fine new streets were going up in Georgian order, tall and well-spaced houses of brown brick, and Custom House, Court House, Savings Bank. He found it a very lively place, with many carriages and sedan chairs on the move; an assembly house, and plays and concerts, he reports. And a responsible citizen informed him in 1776, that a gentleman commanding £500 a year in Limerick could keep a carriage and four horses, 3 menservants, 3 maids, a good table, a wife, a nurse and 3 children. A design of living which even then, one suspects, must have meant some strain about keeping up with the Joneses; still, it does sound very nice — and with the wife well down the catalogue of comforts, in a place which suggests that she is not expected to be any way vocal or burdensome. The serious expenses will be, one would guess, the carriage and 4 horses.

Then at Limerick this cultivated Englishman salutes the great Shannon with reverence and admiration. ' . . . A most noble river, deserving regal navies for her ornament, or what are better, fleets of merchantmen . . . '

' . . . Upon the whole, Limerick must be a very gay place,' says Young, 'but when the usual number of troops were in town much more so . . . '

Yes it was a gay town, within memory, when the troops were in; at least, that was one aspect of gaiety that Limerick wore, up to 1914. It was a garrison town, and did not deny itself the glitter and spangle of such. Troops are no longer gay, in any part of the world; 'gay' will never again be an appropriate adjective for soldiery; the decorative, thin notion died around 1914, and a long way from Tipperary. All to the good. But the women of Limerick have often been brilliantly beautiful — *pace* those one or two observers who have declared themselves cheated of glamour hereabout — and English regiments flirted and courted among them with traditional allure — my memory tells me — and often effectively, and even respectably. They must indeed have been an answer to life very often, those enemy troops, if not literally an answer to a prayer. And one of them, come to think of it, fathered Lola Montez here, in some gay hovel near the docks.

The married women of Limerick — and we had some singularly beautiful ones around at the time I am remembering — were often very gay and gentle with the fairhaired lieutenants and trim captains from 'across'. And one well-instructed school-child watching the comedy, in skating-rinks, on tennis-courts, on river picnics and around demure pianos, used to wonder about the rules, about confession and temptation and continence and the queer phrase 'taking pleasure'. She was often troubled for favourite beautiful ladies who probably did not know her at all and certainly were unaware of her sneaky and precocious watchfulness. And if the ageing, dimming eyes of any matron of the Limerick *bourgeoisie* should fall on these lines, let no such reader protest in virtuous forgetfulness that it was only the loose beauties of the Protestant ascendancy who enjoyed a military gallop — for she will not be telling the truth. There was a chiel amang ye.

No: Limerick was and is gay — as well as grave. A measure of gaiety is essential to normal life, and that life is quick here the wide streets proclaim. For they are packed and restless, and quite monotonously now have all the usual shops of all the world, with the usual tediously celebrated packaged goods. No glossy cosmopolitan need go short of his customary fads in Limerick. A mink stole could probably be bought as soon as wept for; diamonds are certainly on sale, and there is no way at all of flustering our wine or spirit importers. There can be no known make of car that would surprise our younger citizens, the cosmetics of the world are on the girls' shopping lists and faces, and we have elegant teddy boys to give any visiting critic a cool once-over. We can easily ask four-and-sixpence for a single rose — and in jazz can be as far out as you've ever heard.

That is what is ordinary about us — that is what seems inevitable and is sad. The unavoidable mass supply-and-demand thing which has long ago made most of the cities of America unidentifiable, interchangeable. There is no use crying out against it. That is the way the future intends its world to be — in uniform. But we are not really into the future yet, thank God. And when I ramble about Ireland I evoke indeed all the efficient, day-after-tomorrow things that are being done, and the lifts and changes that are being worked, for all our benefits, upon the beautiful old face. But the beautiful old face stays old, is still itself. And so in Limerick, while I admire now prosperous handsome O'Connell Street, admire and wonder, I can identify it; I can find Limerick, the private town I was a child in.

Todd's is gone, of course — fine, Victorian Todd's where every stitch that everyone wore was always bought — and charged! And where an old man in a top hat opened the doors. The burning down of it is a loss which no town of character can easily bear. It will come back, and we can suppose in splendour, but there is an important sense in which it is gone forever. Yet Cannock's clock is still above our heads and still keeps time and chimes. Lloyd's is ended — all untidy mahogany within, with grapes standing round in barrels of bran, and the air sedative with smells of spilt port and brandy; but a little up the street where once there was a tea merchant's the life-size Chinese mandarin still stands against the old façade. There is a long-shaped kiosk near Tait's Clock that hasn't been repainted since I was twelve years old and where comics are still called *Tiger Tim* and *The Magnet*. And the coachmen on the carriage boxes when the funerals cross the bridge from St Munchin's are the same coachmen of all the generations, as are their horses and their very high top hats. Also Limerick still has, dominating proudly all the new drugstore-style chemists' shops, lofty marbled mahogany-ed medical halls that inspired awe in children and still in Victorian calm can do the same through evocation. How peculiar, how delicate the smell of a medical hall!

But let us leave Limerick for a bit. The place grows too much my own.

From *My Ireland*, B. T. Batsford, 1962

City of Pigs
Frank Corr

Not every historic community would want to call its home The City of Pigs . . .

Yet it is not so long ago since King Pig ruled over this ancient city providing employment for literally thousands of people, food for every table and a symphony of tastes, sounds and aromas which gave Limerick something of the ambience of a bustling city of the East.

I was born among pigs and lived happily with them until changing economics hunted them from backyards, organised farmers stopped bringing them to fairs and markets and finally 'industrial progress' brought about the closure of each and every one of Limerick's great bacon factories.

Pigs tended to be raised in the more historic areas of Limerick . . . on The Island and in Thomondgate and were few and far between where we lived at the top of Henry Street opposite the Holy Fathers church. But our relative remoteness did not cut us off entirely from the local bacon and pork industry. Far from it indeed. Every day a woman would call to our house pushing a handcart on which was precariously balanced a milk-churn. We would contribute all of our kitchen waste (apart from scraps fed to the household pets) to this aromatic vessel and its contents would then go to feed pigs which were being fattened in the area of Vizes Field . . .

While live pigs were, alas, absent from our house, they were not entirely absent from the family. My maternal grandfather bought thousands of pigs on behalf of Denny's factory, rising daily at 4 a.m. to travel through the darkness to early morning pig fairs in Kilrush, Kilmihill, Doonbeg and up into Galway. He had died before I was born, but among my early adventures was visiting a pig fair in Kilkee with my father. From the crack of dawn creels of squealing pigs, hauled by asses and horses trundled into the Market Square. Farmers huddled in groups talking between their teeth as their animals deposited mounds of fresh dung on the cobbled square. Soon big men in big overcoats began to arrive, strolling casually between the creels, poking a pig with their thorn sticks to feel the depth of its hams. For a long time there would be no contact between the buyers and sellers until quietly the first offer was made and rejected and the buyer walked away towards another creel. Gradually the pace of bargaining would accelerate and before long we were in the middle of a Square of Babel as offer and counter-offer was made in a dialect known only to the participants in the ritual. A deal was struck when the farmer accepted a 'pig docket' written by the buyer and these were used as a kind of currency. The buyer would write a price on the docket and thrust it into the farmer's hand. It would immediately be thrown back with contempt only to be amended and offered again. Eventually of course market forces would prevail and the pig docket would be accepted, to be exchanged later in the pub for crisp pound notes. My somewhat tenuous connection with the ritual . . . was that my father printed the pig dockets for a number of Limerick buyers and I remember proudly showing a Clare farmer over a glass of lemonade in a Kilkee pub at 7 a.m. on a fair day the imprint 'Frank Corr and Sons, Crescent Printing Works, Limerick' on the docket which he was about to exchange for a month's income . . .

City pigs sold at a premium and were delivered directly to their executioners in Shaw's, Matterson's, O'Mara's and Denny's. These great bustling bacon factories were locations of feverish activity from early morning and anyone who lived in their vicinity had to grow accustomed to cacophonous squealing of pigs, the rattle of carts and a curious sickly smell from the singeing hair and the smoking process.

These factories produced the famous Limerick bacon and ham which was exported to Britain and many other countries and which had a deserved place on every Irish table, be it in the home or the most expensive restaurant. The tradition of Limerick ham indeed lives on in the catering industry and the appellation can be found on many a restaurant menu alongside the Dublin Bay prawn, Slaney salmon and Galway oyster . . .

Limerick ham was produced by a body of men who were members of the Limerick Pork Butchers' Society . . . In its heyday it was a powerful organisation in Limerick and even had its own annual holiday during which members would attend a special Mass.

The pork butchers I first met worked at Shaw's. We sometimes stayed at the house of a friend in Mulgrave Street and during such visits I was considered to be exempt from attending Modh Scoil na Buachalai in O'Connell Avenue. So I would lean out the window of the house watching the less fortunate young boys of the family scurry in the direction of the dreaded Sexton Street CBS, their eyes always glancing upwards to check the time on the large Shaw's clock which hung outside the factory entrance. In later years that same clock would provide valuable intelligence on our chances of making it to the Markets Field before kick-off.

From Shaw's, Matterson's and O'Mara's there flowed a cornucopia of delicacies of which only ham and bacon were sold outside of the city. The multitude of other pig products were reserved for the citizens of Limerick who appreciated them greatly. Crubeens (which I knew as pig's toes) were perhaps the most popular and could be bought ready cooked and steaming in some shops . . . They were but one limb of the pig whose many bodily parts provided us with gourmet meals. My mother would buy salted pig's head (a magnificent piece of pig meat) . . . gammons, spare ribs, skirts and kidneys, 'lots' and of course the famous Shaw's and Matterson's pork sausages and puddings.

A lesser known porcine product however had closer connections with our family. A great-uncle owned O'Hallorans (later Treacy's) packet and tripe emporium off Athlunkard Street and while the stock in trade of this specialist shop originated largely from the sheep, it did a unique and thriving Sunday morning trade selling fresh pig's trotters. The manner of shopping for this delicacy was that each customer would bring a plate into the shop on Saturday and pay in advance for the Sunday morning order. They were largely 'standing orders', so that James would automatically dispense change from a huge drawer under the counter which contained rows of metal bowls reserved for half-crowns, florins, shillings, sixpences, thruppences, pennies, ha'pennies and farthings.

By Saturday evening the counter was laden with a colourful mound of crockery ready for the Great Trotter Sale on Sunday morning. In a tremendous feat of memory James would not only know who owned each of the several hundred plates and how many trotters they had ordered — but also the Mass they attended at nearby St Mary's. As the final 'amen' of the prayers after Mass died away a stream of the faithful would wend its way down the lane to O'Hallorans and there waiting for them would be their own individual plates, each laden with their precise order of freshly cooked trotters which in a few moments would grace the tables of the houses of The Parish.

Even the greatest dynasties are temporary and as I grew towards manhood, the Kingdom of the Pig was beginning to crumble in Limerick. As I pushed a pen in my first job in the office of the Limerick Steamship Company more of the bacon being shipped through the port was coming from Castlebar and Tralee. The famous Limerick bacon factories began . . . to decline. Within the next decade, as a reporter with the *Limerick Weekly Echo*, it was my sad lot to chronicle the closures and job losses which marked the end of a golden age of bacon-curing in Limerick City.

Now when I see those magic words 'Limerick Ham' on a menu, I pretend that what I am about to eat is the product of the great Limerick pig and the craftsmen of the now defunct Pork Butcher's Society. But deep down I know that it isn't true, that I might search Limerick shops in vain for pig's toes and that a whole generation has grown up which has never savoured the special aroma and taste of James O'Halloran's trotters.

From the *Limerick Association Yearbook 1991*

Homecoming
Desmond O'Grady

The familiar pull of the slow train
trundling after a sinking sun on shadowed fields.
White light splicing the broad span of the sky.
Evening deepens grass, the breeze,
like purple smoke, ruffles its surface.
Straight into herring-dark skies the great cathedral spire
is sheer Gothic; slender and singular,
grey as the slate at school when a child looking up —
a bottle of raspberry in one hand, a brown bag of biscuits in t'other —

Feathereye Mykie my uncle told me a man
shot down a hawk dead from the cross
with a telescope fixed to his rifle.

Pulling home now into the station. Cunneen waving
a goatskin of wine from the Spain he has never seen
like an acolyte swinging a thurible.
My father, behind him, as ever in clerical grey,
white hair shining, his hand raised,
preaching away to the Poet Ryan.
And after a drink at the White House — out home.

The house in bedlam. He's here says my father.
Sober? my mother. She's looking me over.
Brings out the bottle. Pull round the fire.
Talk of the journey, living abroad.
Paris, and London, Rome and New York.
What is it like in an airplane? my sister.
Glad you could make it — my brother.
Everything here the same tuppence ha'penny — the neighbours;
just as you left it; the same old roast chestnut.
After the songs, the one for the road,
the last caller gone — up to my room.

As I used find it home for the Christmas from school.
The great brass bed. The box still under it full
of old prayerbooks, assorted mementos,
the untouched bundle of letters mottled with mould.
Now it's a house of doorways and walls
and no laughter. A place for two old people
who speak to each other but rarely. And that only
when children return. Old people mumbling
low in the night of change and of ageing
when they think you asleep and not listening —
and we wide awake in the dark,
as when we were children.

From *The Dark Edge of Europe*, MacGibbon & Kee, 1967

Return to Bengal Terrace
Seán Bourke

By the end of the week I was still without a hideout. I decided that I would go home to Limerick on the Monday, spend a week there, and try again when I got back. On the Saturday I spoke to Blake and told him I would contact him again on Tuesday, the 18th, four days before the escape.

On Monday I flew to Shannon Airport, buying a one-way ticket at the Aer Lingus office in Regent Street. I gave my correct name.

I was so glad to be going home. I had not seen my mother for five years, and there was no telling how long it would be before I was in a position to visit Limerick again. The hostess made a number of announcements in Irish, which none of the Irish people on board could understand, and then she made them in English, which they could. I paid special attention to the ease with which people could enter the Irish Republic from Great Britain. There were no immigration formalities. It was like flying to Scotland, except for the Customs check.

I caught a bus from Shannon Airport to Limerick, and got off at O'Connell Street. I would not catch a taxi: after five years I wanted to see if there were any changes.

Limerick had always been a dump, but now it was dirtier and more dismal than ever. I walked up William Street and went into the red-brick public lavatory in the middle of the road. The doors were hanging off the cubicles, and the plumbing was out of action but people went on using them and they were piled high with excrement. I went to the urinal. The same glass-fronted panel that was there when I was going to school was still fixed to the wall at eye level. In it, printed in an immaculate copperplate, there was a prayer to God beseeching Him to protect the beholder from all temptation. Years before, some anonymous ecclesiastic in an inspired moment had hit on the idea that a man's immortal soul was in greatest danger when he held his penis in his hand. At the top of the panel, painted in large letters, were the words: *Not for ourselves but for our country*. The panel and the neatly printed prayer seemed incongruous in the surrounding squalor. I found this difference of approach between the Irish lavatory authorities and the English rather interesting. The Irish exhorted you to avoid sin, whilst the English assumed that you had already sinned and gave you the address of the place where you could get treatment. But both tried to make you feel guilty for having a piss.

Outside the lavatory I was accosted by one of the gypsies who always hung around there. He wanted the price of a pint, and I gave it to him.

I walked up Mulgrave Street, passing the jail on the right and then the lunatic asylum, which is separated from the jail by a narrow road called the Jail Boreen. At the entrance to the asylum Mulgrave Street ends and the Pike begins. At the end of the Pike the road forks: to the left, the Ballysimon Road; to the right, the Cork Road with Bengal Terrace just a little way along. To the right, also, is Mount St Laurence's cemetery, separated from the asylum by a low wall. At the point of the V where the fork in the road begins there is a public house called the Munster Fair Tavern. It is one of the few pubs in Ireland which do not sell Guinness; it sells Murphy's instead. It has an entrance both in the Ballysimon Road and in the Cork Road, the latter being almost directly opposite the entrance to the cemetery. In Ireland you will always find a pub not far from a cemetery.

As I approached the Munster Fair Tavern I saw a man standing there facing down the Pike. He seemed to be waiting for someone. A few minutes later I discovered that he was waiting for me. At first I did not recognise him. But when he shook hands and spoke I remembered. It was Ger Casey, a man I had gone to school with.

'Hello Seán,' he said. 'Your mother told me you were coming home today. God, 'tis a long time since I saw you, now. It must be fifteen years.'

'Will you come in for a pint, Ger?'

'Indeed I will.' . . .

We started to talk about our schooldays . . .

'Old Ma Murphy is dead too, the Lord have mercy on her soul,' he said presently.

'Who's Old Ma Murphy?'

'Don't you remember?' Ger was surprised.

'I'm sorry, Ger, I don't. I've been away a long time.'

'She's the old woman with the shawl,' he said, 'who used to come in the road with a donkey and cart selling sour milk at a penny a quart an' we going to school. Don't you remember her, Seán?'

'Oh, of course,' I said. 'Isn't that the woman who was passing underneath when a gang of us were up on the railway bridge that day?'

'That's her,' said Ger, draining his second pint. 'And didn't my brother Fonsy destroy the poor woman.'

I ordered another couple of pints. 'Destroy' was putting it very politely, but then Ger had never been one for vulgarity or bad language. He was a better Christian than any of the rest of us in the gang could ever hope to be. I remembered the incident as if it had happened only yesterday. The gang of us had been up on the railway bridge just beyond Bengal Terrace, where the countryside abruptly begins. Old Ma Murphy was coming in from the country where she had a cottage and half an acre near Ballyneety village. She was sitting up on the little cart next to the tank of sour milk and the jaded donkey was pulling her towards the town at the rate of about two miles an hour.

We all saw her coming. There was a hurried conference, as there usually is when there are a few very young boys on a bridge and a likely target comes into view. But we had no missiles handy. Stones were out of the question and there was no water near by. 'I have it!' said Fonsy, Ger's brother. 'I have it!' He dropped his trousers, placed one foot on either side of a wide gap in the boards and squatted down. His rectum was poised with precision over the centre of the opening. 'Give me the signal, Seán,' he said, looking up at me with a grin. 'And you better allow a couple of yards because 'tis a high bridge.' I took up a strategic position and raised my hand in the manner of a battery commander, like I had seen it in the films. Ma Murphy came closer, her eyes fixed permanently about half-way along the donkey's burdened back, completely oblivious to the impending danger. The rest of the boys were all down on their hands and knees peering through other gaps in the boards. She was under the bridge. A couple of yards to go. 'Now!' I said, dropping my hand suddenly. The first one, tapered just like a bomb, landed dead centre between the donkey's ears, exploding on impact to splash all over the animal's neck. Ma Murphy stared disbelievingly for a moment at the brown mess. She was sixty years of age and had never before seen shit falling from the sky. Hail, rain and snow, yes; but shit, never. She looked up, her eyes and her mouth wide open in an expression of shocked incredibility. But the second one was already on its way. It might have missed her, if it weren't for the donkey. Even that docile creature was so taken aback it stopped dead in its tracks. And by now Ma Murphy was staring straight up at Fonsy's bare arse. She saw it coming but couldn't believe it. She just stared at it, mesmerised. Then it landed, right on her forehead, and splashed smoothly all over her face. 'Jesus, Mary and Joseph,' she screamed, 'I'm destroyed! Holy Mother of God, what's happening at all!' A dozen pairs of eyes, like cats in the night, were staring down at her through the gaps in the boards and Fonsy's arse was still poised there menacingly. 'Ye dirty blaggards!' she screamed. 'Ye dirty blaggards! May God forgive ye!' And her face was brown all over.

'My God, Ger,' I said, 'that was a long time ago. We were only ten or eleven then, weren't we?'

'That's all sure.'

'And how's life treating you in Birmingham, Ger?' I asked.

'Ah, not too bad, Seán. The digs are all right, that's the main thing. So long as a man has enough for a pint, what more does he want?'

'You're not married, then?'

'Indeed, I'm not,' he said. 'I don't think I'll ever get married. And I'll never commit adultery, either.' For a brief moment I was taken aback by this expression. It was straight from the children's catechism that we had to learn by heart at school and was meant to imply *all* sex outside of the bonds of holy matrimony, whether between married or single people. Since leaving school this was the first time I had heard the term used in this context. But it was characteristic of Ger. He could never use any other mode of speech . . .

I ordered another couple of pints. There were half a dozen or so other men at the far end of the bar. Some I recognised immediately, and Ger reminded me of who the others were. These were men about the same age as ourselves who had not emigrated to England. They had found work in Limerick, usually alongside their fathers who had put in a good word for them.

They had all said hello to Ger as we came into the bar, but they ignored me completely. They were hard-working, law-abiding citizens. They knew I was a criminal, and they would no more be seen drinking with me than they would be seen with a leper. It is an interesting sociological fact that an Irishman who has been in an English jail is more readily acceptable afterwards to the English themselves than he is to his fellow countrymen. I couldn't bring myself to resent this, for I knew that if Ireland were to become as sophisticated as England it would lose a lot of its Irishness in the process.

Ger and I finished our pints and made for the door . . .

I walked up the road. Bengal Terrace is a row of fifty houses at the side of the main road built by the British Government for ex-soldiers of the First World War. Now most of the soldiers were dead and their children emigrated, and only the elderly widows remained. At the near end on the right was a grotto to the Blessed Virgin built on subscriptions from the residents of the terrace. It was by now a firmly established practice in Limerick that every outlying district should have a grotto to the Blessed Virgin. As I passed the grotto I noticed that there was an abundance of fresh flowers at the foot of the statue inside the wrought-iron railing. A number of people gathered there to say the rosary at seven o'clock every night . . .

At no. 32, I opened the gate and walked in . . . I looked across the room. In a corner there was a table which had been made into an altar. Standing in the centre of it was a two-foot-high statue of the Blessed Virgin. The statue was surrounded by pictures of the Sacred Heart, the Madonna and Child, and various saints. There were at least four rosaries scattered about the table-top. In this household, as in nearly every household in Ireland, Communism was the ultimate evil, the final sin. *Communist* was synonymous with *Devil*. When I was going to school I had actually seen a house in Limerick stoned because the family within were suspected of having Communist sympathies. The Irish found it difficult to accept fellow Christians of a different faith, let alone non-Christians or anti-Christians. Jehovah's Witnesses had been beaten up in Limerick more than once, sometimes by a mob led by a priest. Hanging on the wall to the left of the altar was a picture of the late President Kennedy: the personification of the Western, Christian, Catholic, Irish struggle against the evil of Communist atheism.

My mother was poking the fire and singing something like, 'I see diamonds in Amsterdam'. She had been singing this since before I was born. It was the first song I had ever heard. I looked at her intently. She was seventy years of age and her sight was nearly gone. Her eyes were glazed. Despite her age her hair was still mainly black with just a few streaks of grey. Her face was deeply lined. For the first time in my life, at the age of thirty-two, I found myself loving her as a son should love a mother. Love was so easily stifled in youth. The poverty and degradation of those days provided a soil far too barren for the survival of anything more than a somewhat tenuous family loyalty. Who or what are you supposed to love as you walk to school barefooted through the snow on a breakfast of tea and bread and margarine? In the sermons we are told that it was God's divine will and that far from complaining, which was sinful anyway, we should actually give thanks to God for our poverty. 'Blessed are the poor,' they reminded us, 'for theirs is the Kingdom of Heaven.' But the man up in the pulpit was well fed, wore a good pair of shoes, and lived in a big house next to the church. He was fed and clothed by the poor of the parish who were bound under the Precepts of the Church to support their pastors. But, of course, it wasn't the priests who made us poor. Their fault lay in telling us that poverty was a virtue, a blessing from God, a means to sanctifying grace. We should emulate Our Lord and Saviour Jesus Christ. But then Jesus had never been very badly off. He was never short of a few shillings, and he didn't have to work hard, either . . .

I knew as I looked at my mother that my love had come too late. It was born of the knowledge that the final parting was at hand. Could I ever step over this threshold again? Even if one day I were free to do so, would I be welcome? Indeed, most important of all, would there be anyone here? She was seventy. No matter what happened next week, a long time was going to pass before I set foot in Limerick again.

From *The Springing of George Blake*, Cassell, 1970

A Foot in the Door
Michael O'Toole

The first newsroom I ever set foot in was that of the *Limerick Weekly Echo and District Advertiser*. Newsroom is perhaps too grandiose a term for that section of what was essentially a large lean-to clinging to the gaunt limestone frontage of the former Presbyterian church that houses McKern's Printing Works. The chief — and only — reporter was a man called Christy Bannon who drank large quantities of black rum washed down with bottles of stout. Christy had been a barber and he had drifted into journalism through bringing in snippets of news that he picked up in his shop. He wore a soft brown hat, *Front Page* style, and an expression of intense woe. Pat Finn, the photographer, said that in a previous incarnation Christy must have been covering the Agony in the Garden and that the face stuck. Christy spoke sparingly and cynically. He was one of those people who had known practically everyone he knew before any of them had an arse to their trousers.

T. P. (Tommy) Morris, the editor, was the brother of the *Echo*'s proprietor, Ivan Morris, who had a printing business in Dublin, and they had known Christy when they were youngsters and they all played soccer together. Tommy frequently complained about his protégé. 'There was a time when Christy would do the "wall of death" for a story,' the editor would say, shaking his head in resignation and pointing through the window to the slight and apathetic figure huddled over the two-bar electric fire in the corner of the lean-to.

According to Tommy, Christy's transition from barbering to news-gathering came one busy afternoon when Christy, who had been drinking tea in the office, was asked if he would mind running down to Cruise's to pick up a press release from the Irish Creamery Milk Suppliers Association. 'The next thing was I had a delegation from the NUJ complaining that their member wasn't getting a living wage,' Tommy said.

Although lively and voluble when on a licensed premises (Christy would never call it a pub) in the office he had the true detachment of the mystic. Threats and entreaties wafted over him with as much effect as the smoke from his eternal Gold Flake. It was claimed that he had been fired six times but on each occasion turned up for work in the lean-to on the following Monday, explaining to the embarrassed clerk in the front office that 'Tommy was only joking.'

The story went that when he turned up for work on the Monday after being sacked for the sixth time, Tommy called him into his office on the other side of the lean-to and had a serious talk with him. 'How many times have you been sacked, Christy?' the editor asked.

'Several times, Tommy,' said Christy.

'And were you given notice on all these occasions?' asked Tommy.

'Indeed I was,' Christy said.

'And on this last occasion were you given notice by the firm's solicitors?'

'I was, Tommy.'

'Were your cards sent to you by registered post?'

'They were, Tommy.'

'And was everything explained to you?'

'Yes,' replied Christy, showing signs of boredom.

There was a pause, broken eventually by Morris. 'What have you to say to all this, Christy?' he asked solemnly.

'All I have to say, Tommy,' said Christy rather tartly, 'is that this ball-hopping will have to stop.'

I learned a great deal about journalism in the lean-to. Like Christy, I was a blow-in, an interloper in this crazy world of journalism who hoped that if I hung around long enough I too might be called upon to do the 'wall of death' for a story.

At this time I was working as a kitchen clerk in Shannon Airport . . . More and more I found myself drawn to the lean-to beside the Dominican Church in Baker Place . . .

Limerick had three local newspapers then. The *Limerick Leader*, owned by the Buckley family and edited by the aged and autocratic Con Cregan, was the biggest. Next — in status though not in circulation — came the *Limerick Chronicle*, soon to merge with the *Leader* but at this stage still under the control of the diminutive Paddy Fitzgibbon in its Dickensian office in O'Connell Street. *The Limerick Weekly Echo and District Advertiser* (known locally as the *Weekly Echo*) was controlled by the Morris brothers, who were Protestants, but its appeal was almost exclusively to working-class Roman Catholics. In a city where at that time a large section of the population regarded snobbishness as a civic duty it suffered because of its down-market image. For the sophisticates of Ballinacurra and the Ennis Road, to be seen with a copy of the *Weekly Echo* would be a social solecism as grievous as being caught using margarine instead of butter. Although it battled valiantly for years, it never succeeded in overtaking the *Leader* and eventually succumbed in the eighties.

I look back on it and the lean-to with the greatest affection. Here I made my first friends in journalism: Frank Corr, the youthful advertising manager who soon changed over to journalism; Pat and John Finn, philosophers who took photographs and ran the Echo Photo Service; and the ebullient editor, who opened a door in journalism to me.

T. P. Morris, though he never had a formal training in journalism, was an excellent editor. Impervious to flattery, devoid of cant and humbug, he revelled in a show of philistinism in which everything had to be reduced to pence, shillings and pounds — and in that order. He was a Thatcherite before the lady from Grantham was even heard of, railing against the extravagances of local councils and the iniquities of bureaucracies and trade unions. He had a good eye for a story and an even better one for the till. He was constantly urging economies such as sending postcards rather than making trunk phone calls. 'A postcard costs only tuppence,' he always said . . .

By the time I got to know him he had more or less given up his fight to outsell the *Leader* and the paper was already in decline. He used to boast sometimes that when he and Ivan took over the *Echo* it had a circulation of minus six. 'You can understand the plight of a man taking over a paper with a circulation of plus six,' he would say stabbing the air with his pipe, 'but weren't we two brave men to take one over with a circulation of minus six?' That peculiar situation came about because for a few weeks the previous proprietor printed only six copies which he sent out as voucher copies to contract advertisers.

Like many local papers in Ireland, the *Echo* was of secondary importance to the printing business that was carried out alongside. In some cases these papers existed solely to keep printers occupied in between jobbing business and the proprietors regarded the editorial matter as something to flush out the advertisements. In many cases journalistic standards were non-existent, the journalists concentrating on the reiteration of local myths and the production of cheap, safe copy most of which came from either the local courts or the county council . . .

But the notion of implanting the liberal journalistic ideals of C. P. Scott on the Limerick of the 1960s was, at the very least, naive. The Limerick of those days was a different world from the city of today. There was no university; unemployment was high and an inordinate proportion of the jobs were in low-paid service industries. Artistic endeavour, such as it was, was largely amateurish and desultory, and an overpowering sense of Jansenistic religiosity permeated the entire city. Brendan Behan, on a brief visit, had inelegantly described the place as 'the city of piety and shiety'. The all-powerful Redemptorist arch-confraternity — then the largest body of its kind in the world — was still a huge influence with its members, their sashes and medals gleaming, marching Orange-Order style to church behind brass bands and banners. In those days the confraternity members gave the straight-hand fascist salute to their spiritual director. No one has ever been able to explain to me how this salute came to be adopted by a religious body.

The Redemptorist confraternity had a huge influence over the Limerick Leader, as did the Knights of St Columbanus, whose two local councils (CK 39 and 90) had a direct entrée to the paper through the then general manager, Jimmy Kelly, a leading member of the organisation. In addition to being general manager, Kelly took a keen interest in the editorial affairs of the paper and contributed a weekly comment column under the pseudonym 'Spartacus' . . .

As underdogs are wont to do, the Redemptorists had eagerly set themselves to the task of establishing themselves as the dominant men in their field — in their case the hell, fire and brimstone business. And they succeeded most brilliantly.

The Redemptorists concentrated their Methodist-style evangelism largely on the working class, leaving the salvation of the bourgeoisie to the Jesuits down the road at The Crescent . . .

In journalism the Redemptorists exercised a subtle influence through individual reporters who were in awe of them and whom they skilfully manipulated. Gerry Ryan, then chief reporter of the Leader, would automatically phone the director of the confraternity on press day respectfully asking whether there was anything he wanted put into the paper. This privilege didn't stretch to the other denominations. On my first day in the Leader Gerry handed me the current issue of the Church of Ireland Gazette saying with obvious distaste: 'Have a look at this ould Protestant thing and see if there's anything in it.'

And it wasn't only in the local press that the Redemptorists were given sway over what the citizens might or might not read or view. The local repertory company, the College Players, employed the Redemptorists as unofficial censors on the understanding that it was open to them to excise any line or lines that might be considered unsuitable. A number of Redemptorists would attend each dress rehearsal and afterwards confer with the producer of the play.

When I joined the Limerick Leader in 1963 the confraternity was enjoying the last years of its mass popularity and was still capable of mounting campaigns to preserve local morality. In these it found an enthusiastic partner in the *Leader*. One of the last of these campaigns, in the mid-1950s, was against alleged immorality in Limerick city cinemas. Like the other campaigns it was based on either imaginary or totally inflated notions of what was going on. It attracted international publicity and helped reinforce the image of Limerick as a city of religious bigots and fanatics.

With its high population of young and poorly paid workers, Limerick always had a big cinema trade. The cinema, along with the weekend hop, was the only cheap form of public entertainment which embraced both sexes. Despite the existence of an official censor, the confraternity had always been suspicious of the cinema and, on at least one occasion, had organised the public burning of a film which it considered unsuitable for Limerick minds and consciences. The mid-fifties was a time of extreme religious fanaticism in Ireland, particularly in regard to entertainment . . .

Now the word went round that 'immoral practices' were taking place in the back seats of city cinemas and the confraternity soon became engulfed in an imaginary sea of illicit sex. Vigilantes were appointed to patrol the cinemas and to report back to the director. The story travelled round the world — even *The Spectator* commented on the imaginary depravities of the youth of Limerick.

The last great public morality campaign of the confraternity was fought in 1963, the year I joined the staff of the *Limerick Leader*. It started with the pseudonym 'Terrified' and it was followed by several others in similar vein, practically all of them under pseudonyms. Several letters suggested that vigilantes should be appointed to inspect bookshops and newsagents. The confraternity was immediately involved and its director assisted the vigilantes in calling on bookshops, newsagents and libraries. An attempt was made to revive the cinemas campaign and weary cinema workers were called to a series of late-night meetings at Connolly Hall where they were lectured on their responsibilities to the upkeep of a proper standard of public morality. A poem (in Italian) found in a public library was denounced as lewd, and a dealer in second-hand books appeared in the District Court accused of having four banned books on his premises. (The titles were: *Cabbage Holiday*, *The Wind that Shakes the Barley*, *Arctic Village* and *Mr Stimpson and Mr Gorse*.) Justice de Burca accepted the defence that the dealer having bought his stock in lots of 500 was unaware that the books had been banned, and he applied the Probation of Offenders Act.

On Saturday, 2 February, 1963, the *Limerick Chronicle* (sister paper of the *Leader*) carried the banner headline: 'Adults Not Immune to Evil Books — Preacher Outlines Church Attitude'. Alongside a three-column picture of the confraternity director, Fr Gerard Mahon, was the text of his sermon. The Church, Fr Mahon said, was wiser in her judgements than the so-called children of light . . .

The *Leader* was even harder on the 'so-called children of light' than Fr Mahon

. . . There was, of course, no organised trade in pornography in Limerick in 1963 any more than there was widespread promiscuity in the back seats at the Savoy or Lyric. The confraternity was having one of its periodic bouts of hysteria and it was being aided and abetted by a large section of the local press. But, unlike the earlier and more notorious campaign of violence and vilification against the city's tiny Jewish community, no bones were broken on this occasion. In fact, to most of those under fifty the 1963 campaign was a bit of a joke. Not long afterwards Fr Mahon left the Redemptorists and the priesthood . . .

Limerick has changed completely since my brief spell there as a reporter. It has always had a bad press but the charges of coldness and unfriendliness have been exaggerated. As so often happens in journalism, certain clichés become fashionable and in the case of Limerick whole generations of journalists have approached it with preconceived notions and never gave it a fair chance. Even in my time there was always more to laugh about than to cry about; true there were bigots aplenty but there was never a shortage of decent warmhearted souls always ready to burst into chat or into song. And you didn't have to be a rugby *aficionado* to share in that camaraderie although if you were it certainly helped. Limerick has at last come of age . . . Its university and urban restoration programme have given it new confidence, the kind of confidence that Kate O'Brien would have wished for. She regarded Limerick as a 'representative' city for Ireland and she took her bearings for life from it.

From *More Kicks than Pence: A Life in Irish Journalism*, Poolbeg Press, 1992

Afternoon
Desmond O'Grady

Afternoon, and the houses are quiet as dust at the foot of a wall.
The tea and the coffee things cleared away from the talk and the thinking,
The magazines flicked through, the telephone tempting, the sand in the hourglass
    sinking,
The waiting — knowing nothing will happen at all.

Afternoon, and just for the want of something more daring to do
Lunch is being seriously digested in the serious bowels of the town.
The buses are empty, the taxis unwanted and lorries are caught in a brown
Study of idleness. Business is slow.

In the parks and the playgrounds, shifty-eyed watchers in colourless clothes
Are hanging around like agents of death, while professional loungers,
In soft hats and silence, disinterestedly wait for the next observation; and
    scroungers
And tricksters are nervously watching what goes.

Down by the shipless, motionless docks; abandoned by all
Except for a stray indefinable blur of what must be a man
And the inevitable rake of a pigeon scratching for corn; the cranes
Are struck dead — unable even to fall.

The voice on the radio — remote, unmelodic — gives news of events
And things that are happening — urban expansion, rural improvements,
Revolutions and riots, social reforms and new intellectual movements —
In lands with more future than this one presents.

In the lanes and the archways the children are few, the lovers fewer still
And those who are left have plans and intentions of joining the rest
On emigrant tickets. In the streets there is no one but old men and widows,
    cursed
With sorry separation and a broken will.

Crack, and the shouts of men go up as a rat breaks cover
To die by the stones and the longhandled sticks of exasperation
Back of the wagons in the stopped yards of the black, uneventful station —
And just for a moment the waiting is over.

From *The Dark Edge of Europe*, MacGibbon & Kee, 1967

TEN
─────────
TRAVELLERS

Some Profligate Women
M. de la Boullaye Le Gouz

From Solohoye, we arrived at Limmerick, the strongest fortress in Ireland. It has a castle, and a harbour, where large vessels can anchor; the quay is very fine . . . There is a house of Jesuits, and convents of Dominicans and Soccolantes. In this city there are great numbers of profligate women; which I could not have believed, on account of the climate. Tam Neuel [*Tom Neville*] with whom I had joined in company at Doublin to perform this journey, was caught by the artifice of these damsels, who robbed him one night of his money. In the morning he came to throw himself at my feet, saying, 'O my good French gentleman, until now I have not made myself known to you; I implore you to credit what I assert, and not to abandon me. Know then that I am a native of Korq [*Cork*], that by travelling in France, Spain, and England, for the last ten or twelve years I had been enabled to accumulate sufficient from my industry in trade, to make an honourable retreat from business; when unfortunately I embarked again in the same pursuits, and having taken ship for England, fell into the hands of the Parliamentarians, who took from me all I had. With difficulty was I able to save some rings, by the sale of which I have got as far as this City, and as misfortune never comes alone, I have again been robbed last night of the little remaining to me; so that I have no hope except in your kindness, and though I am distant but three days journey from my native place, I find myself in a state of destitution. For the remainder, fear not to trust me, as my father is one of the richest merchants in Korq; his dwelling resembles rather a palace than a private house. If you pass that way, you would see how he would receive you; he, and all my relations. You must have seen by my conduct since I have had the honour of being in your company that I am no sharper.'

I told him that he should want nothing to enable him to return to his native place. 'While I have any money you shall share it with me; we must look on the misfortune we are visited by from above, as sent for our correction. You ought to have made this reflection, and your first misfortune would have shielded you from your subsequent calamity.'

We left Limmerik, and came to breakfast at Chamdelesse [ ] eight miles off. Half a league from this estate is the birth place of Mr Dulée [*Daly?*] Doctor of Sorbonne, and Professor in the University of Paris. Many worthy persons made enquiry after him. Then we dined at Malagué [*Kilmallock*] and slept in a castle; distant sixteen miles from Limmerik.

From *The Tour of the French Traveller: M. de la Boullaye Le Gouz in Ireland, AD 1644*, edited by T. Crofton Croker, T. and W. Boone, 1837

City of Beautiful Churches and Spires
Anonymous

City of beautiful churches and spires,
City of pubs and lowly desires,
City of gossips that tell what they're told,
City of youth that just waits to grow old.

Society's city, home of the snob,
Show me your penny before you hob-nob,
Do have some coffee, Oh, do have a bun,
Do what the others do, do 'cause it's done.

Conventional city, Victorian smug,
Peas in their little pods, bugs in their rugs,
Here is no night life, no stygian fun,
They withstand temptation because there is none.

Resenting the outsider's critical speech,
Playing a part they are frightened to cease,
Professing a culture that they never knew,
Living their lives out with nothing to do.

From the *Limerick Socialist*, April 1972

A German Wayfarer
Julius Rodenberg

The street that was before me is called George-street. It is the main street of the city, broad, massive, not without some degree of grandeur, but at the same time so naked, so bare, so cold! . . . The Ireland of the future rises before me, and I do not complain because I have it in my power only to present a picture of its sad present, which is, however, rich in the seeds of development. I looked at things without prejudice, I am striving to drown the voice of my heart as I write, and I hope for the time when my happier successor, on comparing the description of the German wayfarer with reality, can exclaim, 'It is better now!' . . .

I was about to survey at one glance the utter corruption, filth, and rottenness of Irish life. It was Saturday afternoon, and the Irish town was full of marketers of the lower classes. The main and business street, Irish Town Ward, full of people and costermongers, sent to meet me the hoarse cries and the indescribable stench which the lowest misery is wont to produce. The houses that stand here are filthy dens, on whose ground floors are shops for the sale of the most disgusting articles of food. Herring tubs, covered with a dirty brine, are put up at the doors, slices of rusty bacon are spread out on shelves, greasy dishes with pig's-fry and trotters stand near them, fusty hare-skins and goose-wings hang around. Donkey-carts occupy the centre of the street, and half-naked men surround them. The ground floor of nearly all the houses is occupied by clothes-dealers; every third house is a pawnbroker's; and, as if poverty extended even to the smallest details, while this noble guild of money-dealers usually display their trade by three golden balls, here only one is hung out. And what articles are seen under it! Coats whose sleeves scarce hang by a thread, uniforms which whole generations of soldiers seemed to have worn, slit up trousers, boots without soles, caps full of filth, sheets full of vermin. And then, too, the customers who buy these wares — men with crushed hats and ragged tail-coats, women with faces never washed and hair never combed. The street is crowded with frightful objects; the whole wretchedness of humanity has collected here in its most shudder-arousing specimens, and becomes more terrible through the dirt and every possible sign of neglect which it displays. Here a man without legs, walking on his hands; there a woman crawling across the street on hands and knees, like an animal. In a doorway sat two bagpipers playing in turns. A band of ragged fellows were collected and listening to the well-known strains; but no one sang to the melodies, which died away mournfully in the gloom of the arch; and where I stood with the rest, an old woman standing behind a herring-tub sprinkled me with the unsavoury brine . . .

On a stone close by sat a man who had taken off his boots, and by him on a low wooden stool a cobbler, who was mending them. Every ten paces in the open street, a cobbler could be seen in full work, and round him on the ground were the 'brogues', those peculiar shoes of the Irish peasants, fastened by leather bands over the feet like sandals. This trade has come out of the houses into the open air; hence it gives the aspect of southern life, which, however, formed a very wretched contrast with the damp fog with which the stones were dripping, and the frozen, miserable forms in the street. Nevertheless, all were immensely busy with their trade, and I was stopped at least a hundred times. There were girls who offered me 'the celebrated Limerick lace', and boys who insisted on selling me waist-belts. A woman came too, who offered me a freshly-caught salmon . . .

Gloves, however, were not to be met with on the Saturday market of Irish Town; they are only carried about in the better class streets of English Town, where the things you catch hold of are a trifle cleaner. On the other hand, crowds of boys went about offering yards of songs for sale. Here is the market for street ballads; here is the people that buys and passionately loves them. I do not know whether they sing these songs — I fancy not; but not a peasant returns from market to his mud cabin, without adding a new leaf to the others that occupy a place by his hymn-book and catechism. A very considerable trade is done in these productions of the street music; a class of men live in the towns by writing, printing, and selling them; and it is affecting to see how this people, while sinking in the great current of English predominance, strives to cling to the extreme branch of that tree, whose splendid crown in past times was its pride and glory.

The ballad boys were not choked off by the conversation I held with the fishwoman; and thanks to their zeal, I took home with me a perfect collection of the popular songs of the day as a reminiscence of Limerick market. They are all printed on large dirty yellow sheets, and in their external appearance, do not deny their origin or their purpose. They bear in one corner the name of the printer; but the poet is nowhere mentioned. In another corner, remarks such as these may be read: 'Country dealers, please notice that S. B. Goggin, the printer, is continually supplied with a perfect collection of pictures and ballads, which are all produced under his own supervision.' This remark may produce a smile, but it may make the reader very sad too. It is evident from it that the poetical wants of the people have remained as they were; but it is, perhaps, a new sign of its misery, though no reproach to it, that these wants can be satisfied machine-wise. As regards the 'pictures' which Mr Goggin recommends, they mostly represent the male and female saints, of whom Ireland possesses several thousands, and which form the sole ornament of Irish cabins. The father, the mother, and each of the children, have their special patron saint fastened on the clay wall, or over the poor straw bed, and which is renewed at regular intervals. The rest of the pictures are of a very inartistic nature, and it is rare to find a street ballad which is not adorned with one or more specimens. There you see the 'True Lover's Complaint', with the picture of an elephant above it; over the 'Fall of the Petticoat', a bitter satire on the ladies in the English quarter, sits an ape; while the 'Bonny Labouring Man' is honoured with a donkey.

I was most struck with the party ballads. It is notorious that the great mass of the Irish people know only two parties: one consists of Catholics, patriots, and the shamefully oppressed; the other of Protestants, Orangemen, unjust landowners, and oppressors generally. The ballad is naturally on the side of the former party, and it is the predominant mode in which its hatred and passion find a vent . . .

Hatred, fury, and revolt cannot be more clearly expressed; and it would be inexplicable that the English government allows the sale of such writings in the public market, if it were not perfectly well aware what value to place on the hatred, fury, and revolt of the Irish people. Its cry of pain is a cry of impotence, which dies out without producing any effect; its moan for help is of a traditional nature, and bears no consequences for the present. The English government has nothing more to fear from the abject, sunken Irish people; and the little outbreaks and night murders are things which belong to the assize court, and do not come before the political forum.

Thus I reached the Haymarket, which forms the frontier between the Irish and the old English town. The English settlers had a passion for adorning the mud cabins and impassable streets of Ireland with pleasant names of home. But where is the proud frontage of the London Haymarket? Where the stately doorways and arcades? Where the throng, so noble by day, so frivolous by night? There is nothing of all this; it is a large desolate court, covered by a wooden roof resting on wooden pillars. The glory of Ireland rests on wooden pillars, the end of which has already rotted away in the boggy soil. In the entire space, scarce anything was to be seen save old clothes, which, hung out for sale, fluttered in the breeze; the other principal article was buttermilk, which was brought in large tubs in donkey carts, and drunk by the thirsty souls out of large tin cups. In the old English town — for there is also a new one — Newtown Pery, in which the fashionable world of Limerick reside in a few neat houses . . . things do not look much better than in the Irish town. Here you find a whole street full of old clothes shops, and in the cellars the same stench, the same collection of dirty men and dirty goods. Even on the quays . . . the fresh breeze from the water and the neighbouring ocean cannot quite overcome the wretched smell of rags. In the main street there is an impenetrable medley of cobblers, donkey-carts, wretched men, herring-casks, low women, dirty children, and clothes shops. The side streets are gloomy and silent. I saw nothing of the venerable houses with gabled roofs which Macaulay describes in such elegant language; I did not find that 'the aspects of the streets is such, that the traveller who walks through them can imagine that he is in Normandy or Flanders'. On the contrary, with the sole exception of George-street, I did not see a house within the banlieue of Limerick in which the roof was not fallen in or the door broken, or at least a few panes of glass smashed. I remember walking through a large house in which only the walls were standing, the window holes could still be distinguished, and a few rags of paper still hung from the walls; and not only here, but also in Newtown Pery, the pride of Limerick, I saw entire rows of ruins; even in the centre of the broadest part of the Shannon, where there was no road or bridge, two large crumbling houses stood, without roof or window. Whence this frightful mass of old clothes shops in all the streets, these roofless ruins in the stream of busy life? I do not know . . .

An old corporal, in a red coat, and with a nose of the same hue, was sitting on a post in the doorway, and smoking his pipe. He must have been occupied with important thoughts, for he did not move till I stood close by his side.

'Eh, comrade!' I said, 'will you be my guide?' . . . 'Come,' he said, after noticing the interest I took in them, 'I will show you the towers.' . . .

We walked across Thomond Bridge. On the other side, not far from the last arch, on the right, is a large black stone deep sunk in the ground. Time has gnawed at its edges, and it has been rent by the rain of ages. But the upper surface can still be distinctly traced, which covers the whole like the top of a table.

'That is the treaty stone,' the corporal said.

I stopped to draw its outline in my notebook. A few steps further on is M'Donald's whisky store, a small thoroughly Irish house, in which there is usually a very decent row going on. M'Donald is a zealous patriot, and the patriots collect at his house and drink his whisky and curse the Englishmen within his four walls, where no one overhears them.

M'Donald was standing on the threshold while I stopped by the stone. The corporal went up to him, and I was invited to step in. The room was small, and many men with heated faces were seated on casks and benches, and the host's neat little wife stood behind the bar. She came forward to salute me.

'Take the strange gentleman up-stairs,' M'Donald said, as he gave the corporal a glass of strong whisky.

The woman went first and I followed her up a small narrow flight of stairs: then we walked into a lighter room, which looked like a palace compared with the lower one.

'Here, dear sir,' she said, 'you can read it;' and she pointed to a large glass frame on a table. It contained the articles of the treaty of Limerick. I was bending over it when M'Donald came in and said, 'We will go down and read it,' and he took the articles down stairs, where we followed him. His customers, the men with the heated faces, with the corporal at the head, who had already drunk more than one glass of whisky to my health, and at my expense, collected round the landlord and listened as he read the articles, one after the other, with considerable pathos. When I asked him presently what connexion there was between the articles and the stone, he replied: 'These articles were subscribed on that stone, and the Englishman broke this article, and this one,' and he pointed to the first, third, and seventh.

'He broke them all, he did not keep one!' a man with a large brown beard shouted, a perfect Hercules, rather decently dressed, and possessed of some slight degree of education. 'You want to know', he said, as he leaned against the wall, 'what that stone means. It is an eternal monument of English faithlessness and Irish bravery.'

An old man with grey hair, but cunning look, and who was held in great respect by his comrades, said that he hated the English and . . . 'O'Leary of Limerick bids you welcome, and hands you his glass to drink with him to the welfare of Ireland.'

I did not dare refuse, but I certainly felt uncomfortable, for the atmosphere was stiflingly oppressive, and the spirit-inflamed tempers of the whisky drinkers were beginning to grow dangerous . . .

'Bravo!' . . . shouted the little corporal in her Majesty's coat, with a sudden outburst. 'Hurrah! I am no worse Irishman than the rest of you, and I drink with you all to the health of our country and our people!'

'There will be bloody work yet in Ireland,' a very aged man said, who was cowering in a corner on a low stool. His eye had the cold lustre of age, and his voice, as he raised it, had something prophetically deep in it, which moved me. 'Bloody work,' he repeated, 'and battles upon battles . . . '

At this moment, when M'Donald, interrupting the deadly silence which followed these words, had walked to one of the casks to fill the corporal's glass again, the door opened and an old acquaintance walked in — the recruiting sergeant of the morning. His English face was red with cold, and the gay ribbons in his cap, damp with fog and rain, hung down in a bundle. But he was not alone; he was followed by four or five young fellows in torn coats, who had taken the Queen's shilling. Some coloured ribbons were fastened on their shoulders too. All was silent when the new party entered: the Herculean man, and the cunning-looking man, and the corporal, crept into the corner round the prophet, and looked as if they had not spoken for a week. But the recruiting officer was all the more loud: 'Hallo! Whisky here for my lads,' he shouted, almost before he entered; 'whisky here for her Majesty's light brigade! And he is a villain who doesn't join in when I say "God save the Queen!"'

The lads did not reflect long; they looked as if they had not eaten anything for some time or drunk for much longer. They swallowed the glass of whisky, and devoured the rolls handed them, and shouted, with their mouths full, between the bites, 'God save the Queen!' The others, however, were silent.

'Why do you sit there so mumchance?' the sergeant said, turning round impudently. 'And you, corporal there, why don't you shout when we drink the health of our most gracious Queen?'

'My good sir,' the corporal said, whose pipe had gone out in his fright, 'my glass is empty, and—'

'And you wish her Majesty's servant to fill it? Very well: in the Queen's name, fill his glass.'

M'Donald, whose face, during the whole scene, had been gloomy, walked to a cask and filled; but he did not say a word. The sergeant, with his fellows and the corporal, collected and hob-and-nobbed, till the cry of 'God save the Queen!' echoed through the same room which had a few moments before been the witness of the enthusiasm for Ireland's freedom and Ireland's faith. A new row, exactly opposite to that which had greeted me, commenced. The new guests sat down noisily in the seats of the former guests, who disappeared silently one after the other, and the Limerick articles were quietly carried up-stairs again. I went too, and the corporal with me. But he walked behind me silently and with drooping head; he evidently felt as he would after a defeat, and for a long time did not dare look at me or address me. And thus, undisturbed by this man, who walked after me like the pitiable destiny of Ireland herself, I proceeded along the banks of the rushing Shannon. I had taken another glance at the fermenting heart of the people, and it had not been satisfactory. English faithlessness and Irish 'bravery' had fought a new battle in my presence, and its result had not edified me.

From A *Pilgrimage through Ireland or the Island of the Saints*, Charles Griffin and Company, 1860

Majestic River
Mr & Mrs Hall

The great attraction of Limerick, although by no means the only one, is however its majestic and beautiful river, the Shannon . . .

It runs for a distance of upwards of 200 miles from its source to its mouth, which is between Loop Head and Kerry Head; it waters ten counties in its progress, and affords facilities for commerce and internal intercourse such as are unparalleled in any other portion of the United Kingdom. Yet, unhappily, up to the present time its natural advantages have been altogether neglected . . .

For a long space its course is so gentle that the ancient writers supposed its name to have derived from *Seen-awn*, the slow river, but for many miles, between O'Brien's Bridge and Limerick, it rolls so rapidly along as almost to be characterised as a series of cataracts. At the falls of Killaloe it descends twenty-one feet in a mile and above one hundred feet from Killaloe to Limerick — and yet there is scarcely a single mill at work all that way.

Nearly all along its course its banks are of surpassing beauty. As it nears Limerick, its adjacent hills are crowned with villas, and upon the sides are the ruins of many ancient castles. Castle Connell, a village about six miles from the city, is perhaps unrivalled in the kingdom for natural graces, and immediately below it are the Falls of Doonas where the river rushes over huge mountain rocks, affording a passage which only the more daring will make, for the current, narrowing to a boat's breadth, rushes along with such frightful rapidity that the deviation of a few inches would invariably result in destruction. This, although the most remarkable of the falls, is succeeded by several others between Castle Connell and Limerick . . .

The city lies in a spacious plain, the greater portion of which is scarcely above the level of the water. However, at a short distance there are some of the most interesting ruins in the kingdom which lie in the midst of scenery of surpassing beauty. Of these the tourist should first visit Carrig-o-gunnel, next Adare, and then Castle Connell, the most beautiful of the many beautiful places upon the banks of the noble Shannon . . .

The whole central district of Limerick is indeed studded with remains, both religious and castellated, which most emphatically speak of the former power of the Geraldines but they are mostly ruined and decayed now. A chain of towers may be traced in continuous succession from the Shannon to Kilmallock, indicating the territorial supremacy of the Fitzgeralds, whilst their numerous ecclesiastical structures tell of wealth, munificence and taste.

In the centre of an extensive valley stretching out from the eastern base of Knockfeerena, stand the remains of a small but very ancient church whose era belongs to the very earliest period of Christianity in Ireland. It is a plain oblong, about forty-six feet in length and eighteen broad. On one of the jamb stones of the door are a number of scores which is a circumstance worthy of remark, because a number of such scorings have been frequently found on or near other Romanesque remains, and are supposed to have some affinity with the Ogham character.

Ten feet north of the church stands one of those round towers so peculiar to Ireland, and so fruitful of controversy to antiquaries. It is fifty feet in height, and fifty feet in circumference at its base. The door, which has a semicircular head, is sixteen feet from the ground. Above this are three windows at different heights. One of them is round-headed, while the others are pointed. The upper portion of the tower, with its conical cap and upper windows, has been destroyed. The floors were placed on rests formed by diminishing the thickness of the walls. The peasantry call it *Clogawse-na-desart*. *Clogawse* signifies a growth of stones and bears reference to its supposed sudden growth in one night . . .

We may now quit the county of Limerick which is in many respects the most interesting and important county of Munster, not only in reference to the number and magnificence of its ancient remains, and its grand scenery, but also as regards those modern improvements in agriculture, manufacture and commerce, by which it is rendered honourably conspicuous among the counties of the south of Ireland.

From *Hall's Ireland: Mr & Mrs Hall's Tour of 1840*, Vol. 1, edited by Michael Scott, Sphere Books Limited, 1984/Hall, Virtue, and Co., 1841

Cigars and Apple-Women
William Makepeace Thackeray

The next morning a car carried us to Tarbert Point, where there is a pier not yet completed, and a Preventive-station, and where the Shannon steamers touch, that ply between Kilrush and Limerick. Here lay the famous river before us with low banks and rich pastures on either side.

A capital steamer, which on this day was thronged with people, carried us for about four hours down the noble stream and landed us at Limerick Quay. The character of the landscape on either side the stream is not particularly picturesque, but large, liberal, and prosperous. Gentle sweeps of rich meadows and corn-fields cover the banks, and some, though not too many gentlemen's parks and plantations rise here and there. But the landscape was somehow more pleasing than if it had been merely picturesque; and, especially after coming out of that desolate county of Kerry, it was pleasant for the eye to rest upon this peaceful, rich, and generous scene. The first aspect of Limerick is very smart and pleasing; fine neat quays with considerable liveliness and bustle, a very handsome bridge (the Wellesley bridge) before the spectator, who, after a walk through two long and flourishing streets, stops at length at one of the best inns in Ireland — the large, neat, and prosperous one kept by Mr Cruise. Except at Youghal, and the poor fellow whom the Englishman belaboured at Glengariff, Mr Cruise is the only landlord of an inn I have had the honour to see in Ireland . . .

Now, beyond this piece of information regarding the excellence of Mr Cruise's hotel, which every traveller knows, the writer of this doubts very much whether he has anything to say about Limerick that is worth the trouble of saying or reading. I can't attempt to describe the Shannon, only to say that on board the steam-boat there was a piper and a bugler, a hundred of genteel persons coming back from donkey-riding and bathing at Kilkee, a couple of heaps of raw hides that smelt very foully, a score of women nursing children, and a lobster-vendor, who vowed to me on his honour that he gave eightpence a-piece for his fish, and that he had boiled them only the day before; but when I produced the guide-book, and solemnly told him to swear upon that to the truth of his statement, the lobster-seller turned away, quite abashed, and would not be brought to support his previous assertion at all . . .

They say there are three towns to make one Limerick: there is the Irish town . . . the English town . . . and finally the district called New-town-Pery. In walking through this latter tract, you are, at first, half led to believe that you are arrived in a second Liverpool, so tall are the warehouses and broad the quays: so neat and trim a street of near a mile which stretches before you. But even this mile-long street does not, in a few minutes, appear to be so wealthy and prosperous as it shows at first glance: for of the population that throng the streets, two-fifths are bare-footed women, and two-fifths more ragged men: and the most part of the shops which have a grand show with them, appear, when looked into, to be no better than they should be, being empty make-shift looking places, with their best goods outside.

Here, in this handsome street too, is a handsome club-house, with plenty of idlers, you may be sure, lolling at the portico; likewise you see numerous young officers, with very tight waists and absurd brass shell-epaulettes to their little absurd frock-coats, walking the pavement — the dandies of the street. Then you behold whole troops of pear, apple, and plum-women, selling very raw, green-looking fruit, which, indeed, it is a wonder that anyone should eat and live: — the houses are bright red — the street is full and gay, carriages and cars in plenty go jingling by — dragoons in red are every now and then clattering up the street, and as upon every car which passes with ladies in it you are sure (I don't know how it is) to see a pretty one, the great street of Limerick is altogether a very brilliant and animated sight.

If the ladies of the place are pretty, indeed, the vulgar are scarcely less so. I never saw a greater number of kind, pleasing, clever looking faces among any set of people. There seem however, to be two sorts of physiognomies which are common; the pleasing and somewhat melancholy one before mentioned, and a square high-cheeked flat-nosed physiognomy, not uncommonly accompanied by a hideous staring head of dry, red hair. Except, however, in the latter case, the hair flowing loose and long is a pretty characteristic of the women of the country; many a fair one do you see at the door of the cabin, or the poor shop in the town, combing complacently that 'greatest ornament of female beauty', as Mr Rowland justly calls it.

The generality of the women here seem also much better clothed than in Kerry; and I saw many a one going barefoot, whose gown was nevertheless a good one, and whose cloak was of fine cloth. Likewise it must be remarked, that the beggars in Limerick were by no means so numerous as those in Cork, or in many small places through which I have passed. There were but five, strange to say, round the mail-coach as we went away; and, indeed, not a great number in the streets.

The belles lettres seem to be by no means so well cultivated here as in Cork. I looked in vain for a Limerick guide-book: I saw but one good shop of books, and a little, trumpery, circulating library, which seemed to be provided with those immortal works of a year old, which, having been sold for half-a-guinea the volume at first, are suddenly found to be worth only a shilling . . . Besides the book-shops, I observed in the long, best street of Limerick a half-dozen of what are called French shops, with knick-knacks, German silver chimney-ornaments, and paltry finery. In the windows of these you saw a card with 'Cigars'; in the book-shop, 'Cigars'; at the grocer's, the whiskey-shop, 'Cigars': everybody sells the noxious weed, or makes believe to sell it, and I know no surer indication of a struggling, uncertain trade, than that same placard of 'Cigars' . . . I asked one of the ten thousand fruit-women the price of her green pears. 'Twopence a-piece,' she said; and there were two little ragged beggars standing by, who were munching the fruit; a book shop-woman made me pay threepence for a bottle of ink which usually costs a penny; a potato-woman told me that her potatoes cost fourteen-pence a stone; and all these ladies treated the stranger with a leering, wheedling servility, which made me long to box their ears . . .

To return to the apple-women; — legions of ladies were employed through the town upon that traffic; there were really thousands of them, clustering upon the bridges, squatting down in doorways and vacant sheds for temporary markets, marching and crying their sour goods in all the crowded lanes of the city. After you get out of the main street, the handsome part of the town is at an end, and you suddenly find yourself in such a labyrinth of busy, swarming poverty and squalid commerce as never was seen — no, not in Saint Giles's, where Jew and Irishman side by side exhibit their genius for dirt. Here every house almost was a half ruin, and swarming with people; in the cellars you looked down and saw a barrel of herrings, which a merchant was dispensing; or a sack of meal, which a poor dirty woman sold to people poorer and dirtier than herself; above was a tinman, or a shoemaker, or other craftsman, his battered ensign at the door, and his small wares peering through the cracked panes of his shop. As for the ensign, as a matter of course, the name is never written in letters of the same size . . . High and low, in this country, they begin things on too large a scale. They begin churches too big and can't finish them; mills and houses too big, and are ruined before they are done; letters on sign-boards too big, and are up in a corner before the inscription is finished — there is something quite strange, really, in this general consistency.

Well, over James Hurley, or Pat Hanlahan, you will most likely see another board of another tradesman, with a window to the full as curious. Above Tim Carthy evidently lives another family; there are long-haired girls of fourteen at every one of the windows, and dirty children everywhere. In the cellars, look at them in dingy white night-caps over a bowl of stirabout; in the shop, paddling up and down the ruined steps, or issuing from beneath the black counter; up above, see the girl of fourteen is tossing and dandling one of them, and a pretty tender sight it is, in the midst of this filth and wretchedness, to see the women and children together. It makes a sunshine in the dark place, and somehow half reconciles one to it. Children are everywhere — look out of the nasty streets into the still more nasty back lanes; there they are, sprawling at every door and court, paddling in every puddle, and in about a fair proportion to every six children, an old woman; a very old, blear-eyed, ragged woman, who makes believe to sell something out of a basket, and is perpetually calling upon the name of the Lord. For every three ragged old women you will see two ragged old men, praying and moaning like the females; and there is no lack of young men, either, though I never could make out what they were about: they loll about the street, chiefly conversing in knots, and in every street you will be pretty sure to see a recruiting sergeant, with gay ribands in his cap, loitering about with an eye upon the other loiterers there. The buzz, and hum, and chattering of this crowd is quite inconceivable to us in England, where a crowd is generally silent: as a person with a decent coat passes, they stop in their talk, and say, 'God bless you for a fine gentleman!' In these crowded streets, where all are beggars, the beggary is but small: only the very old and hideous venture to ask for a penny, otherwise the competition would be too great.

As for the buildings that one lights upon every now and then in the midst of such scenes as this, they are scarce worth the trouble to examine; occasionally you come on a chapel with sham gothic windows and a little belfry, one of the Catholic places of worship; then, placed in some quiet street, a neat looking dissenting meeting-house. Across the river yonder, as you issue out from the street, where the preceding sketch was taken, is a handsome hospital; near it the old cathedral, a barbarous old turreted edifice, of the fourteenth century, it is said;

how different to the sumptuous elegance which characterises the English and Continental churches of the same period! Passing by it, and walking down other streets, — black, ruinous, swarming, dark, hideous, — you come upon the barracks and the walks of the old castle, and from it on to an old bridge, from which the view is a fine one. On one side are the gray bastions of the castle; beyond them, in the midst of the broad stream, stands a huge mill that looks like another castle; further yet is the handsome new Wellesley bridge, with some little craft upon the river, and the red warehouses of the new town looking prosperous enough. The Irish town stretches away to the right; there are pretty villas beyond it, and on the bridge are walking twenty-four young girls, in parties of four and five, with their arms round each other's waists, swaying to and fro, and singing or chattering, as happy as if they had shoes on their feet. Yonder you see a dozen pair of red legs glittering in the water, their owners being employed in washing their own or other people's rags.

From *The Irish Sketch Book, 1842–4*, Oxford University Press, 1863 edition

The Law of Landlordism
Alexander Somerville

Limerick, 22nd March 1847

Though a previous letter was dated here, I have not yet described Limerick city and county. Even now the city must be omitted, but the county has pressing claims to notice.

Its greatest length from east to west is fifty-four miles; its greatest breadth from north to south is thirty-five miles. It is chiefly a plain lying south-east of the Shannon, gently undulating. The soil is fertile beyond anything that can be expressed in common agricultural language. With good roads in some parts, and the best of hard stone to make good roads everywhere; with intersecting streams that drive mills and make meal and flour; with other rivers navigable from the Shannon inland, with the Shannon, broad and deep, all along the western boundary, rolling to the Atlantic, with water more than sufficient to float all the ships of the world at once; with the city of Limerick situated on that river, containing docks and harbourage, and affording a first-class market for agricultural produce; with all those advantages, Limerick county is still a poor one, if we may judge it by the employment it gives to the population and the wages paid by its agriculturists to their work people, ninepence and tenpence per day in ordinary years; one shilling per day in this extraordinary year of high prices received for their corn and cattle; still a poor county, if judged by the enormous proportion of its people unemployed by its own resources; still poor, if judged by the common evidences of poverty and disorder, an overwhelming military force in the principal town, barracks for soldiers in the smaller towns, stations, seventy in number, for the armed constabulary in the villages; still poor, if judged by the crimes committed in the struggle to sustain human life on the smallest amount of food now, and on the worst quality of food always before now, which human beings ever subsisted on; but a rich county if judged by the amount of rent paid to its landowners, and by their grandeur of castles, parks, mansions, equipages, ancient family lineage, and new dignities outshining family lineage.

There is Sir Lucius O'Brien, and William Smith O'Brien, MP for the county, and other O'Briens, all descendants of the kings of Munster. There are several O'Gradys; and there is 'the O'Grady' of Killyballyowen. There is John Fitzgerald Fitzgerald, 'the Knight of Glin' Castle, Glin on the banks of the Shannon, very ancient; and next door to him, at Mount Trenchard, there is Lord Monteagle, almost brand new. There is the Earl of Devon, owner, but I regret to say, only as yet nominal owner, of a large tract of the very richest land near Newcastle. There is William Monsell, Esq. of Tervoe, who writes so fervidly in favour of a poor-law which shall authorise rates to be levied on each estate separately, according to the pauperism on that estate. And there is the Earl of Dunraven, his father-in-law, whose great estates are, like his own, so well cleared of population and paupers. There is the Earl of Clare, Lord Guillamore, Lord Clarina, Lord Cloncurry, Earl of Kingston, Lord Muskerry, and about a hundred other proprietors, resident and non-resident, for whose names and titles space is not allowable in these columns. One of them, Squire Westropp, may be named, however, as it was from a part of his estate that the sub-sheriff, constabulary, 55th infantry, and 8th hussars were employed about a month ago in ejecting tenants for the non-payment of rent.

And this fact recalls to my mind that the English Earl of S__ owns an estate in this county from which some years ago, before English newspapers took much note of Irish affairs, and before Irish papers dared to publish and comment on the acts of landlordism, 1,500 persons were turned out homeless, landless, penniless, and potatoless, at the point of the bayonet, in one day. Mr Doolan of Fairy Hill, Portumna, county of Galway, formerly commandant of the police in Limerick county, told me a few days ago that he had the command on that occasion, and that he saw many of those people lingering on the roads and dying of want months after. Some of them are still paupers in the towns and villages.

Mr Doolan also stated, and authorised the use of his name in connection with it, that while in that command he was employed in obtaining evidence in cases of murder, and in paying the witnesses to go to America after they had given evidence. One case of murder was as follows:— A farmer was distrained upon for rent, and his potatoes, stored in a pit in the haggard, were under distraint watched by two keepers. The farmer's family had no other food but those potatoes. The keepers would not allow them to have any potatoes, the orders being against it. In desperation the family at last rose upon the two keepers and murdered them. They were tried and hanged, but not all at once. The father was hanged first; next two sons; next their mother was hanged; and at last one of the daughters. The whole expense of the trials and the rewards to witnesses was £10,000, for which Mr Doolan holds vouchers, and to the correctness of which he says he is ready to make oath. He says that his undoubting opinion is, that had the most ordinary feelings of humanity, simple fair play, been observed towards those people, no murder would have been committed. The two lives of the keepers would have been saved, and the five lives of father, mother, daughter and two sons, would not have been given to vengeance and the gallows. And there would have been saved £10,000, expended on a special commission, on different trials, on prosecuting, counsel, witnesses and hangmen; besides the saving to England in not being called upon to augment the garrisons of Limerick and the other towns with additional cavalry, infantry, and artillery.

But the most extraordinary part of this drama of cruelty, vengeance, and judicial butchery, is probably this, that the owner of the property on which the distraint for rent was made and the murder committed, lived at the time in Yorkshire, lives there still, draws, it is believed, about £60,000 per annum out of his Irish estates, chiefly in the county of Limerick; has not been in Ireland once during the present century, though an Irishman born; and averred to Mr Doolan, on the latter paying him a visit a few years ago, that he had never, before Mr Doolan told him, heard of the distraint, the murders, the trials, and the executions; that he left everything to his agents, and that it was their business, not his, to know those things.

Mr Doolan was concerned, as commandant of the police, in another murder prosecution, for which there was a special commission which cost, with the outfit of the witnesses to Canada, £30,000 — *Thirty thousand pounds* of national taxes, besides extra military expenses, for one murder; that murder occasioned by the inhuman conduct of an Irish landlord with the law of landlordism at his command.

From *Letters from Ireland during the Famine of 1847*, edited by K. D. M. Snell, Irish Academic Press, 1994

The Lady of the Restaurant
Seán O'Meara

Of all the womenfolk I knew
The lush, the gamey-eyed, the gaunt
Not one could hold a candle to
The Lady of the Restaurant

In Limerick City I sat down
A-weary of the stranger's face
For 'tis a pain to be alone
In such a populated place

I asked a man who chanced to pass
If he could recommend to me
A place where I could break my fast
And drink a mug or two of tea

He pointed and I wandered in
Where there were lights and people sat
By china-covered table cloths
Passing the hours in idle chat

There as I tilted up the cup
And gorged my belly out of want
Who should I see, then, looking up:
The Lady of the Restaurant!

I whispered low, now child of grace
What a predicament you're in
With muddy lanes writ on your face
And hairy acres on your chin

For could you but have seen her, boys,
With health or wealth you'd gladly part
Or with your wisdom if you're wise
To set her image on your heart

Within her love and beauty lurk
Her hair is pressed into a bun
No daubing brush's handiwork
Would dare to tarnish such a one

O boys my wonder was threefold
To see a mouth so ripe and sweet
A limb that had so fine a mould
The fluted leather on her feet

All things shall come to one who waits
By God I waited far too long
Around me were the nodding pates
But she had vanished in the throng

For me the Fates select such tricks
I drank no more when she was gone
She was a siren of twenty six
And I a year of twenty one.

From *Skinner's Fancy: Poems by Seán O'Meara*, Profile Poetry, 1979

A Dogfight
William Bulfin

I strolled along the southern fringe of the city farthest from the river, struck out from a remnant of the old wall in Clare Street, and headed westward through a labyrinthine jungle of back lanes, alleys, and roofless houses. It appeared to be rather an exclusive quarter in a certain sense, and I doubted, after I had enmeshed myself in its sinuosities, that the general public patronised it very extensively as a place of recreation, or exercised the right of way through it, if such a right existed. It was a bow-legged dog with a fighting face that fixed this latter conclusion upon me by coming forward with all his hair standing and fire in his eyes, barking furiously. He was quickly joined by other dogs of excessive lung power. They stripped their teeth at me and advanced inch by inch, whether on a bluff or on real business, I could not say. To retreat would have been madness. To advance unarmed would have been imprudent. To remain inactive would have been to invite disaster. I therefore, in all modesty, and on a very small scale, engaged in diplomacy. In other words, I instigated and fomented a dog fight. I said: 'Catch him, Spot;' 'Bite him, Terry;' 'Beat him, Lad;' 'Choke him, William the Third, or whatever your name is' (he was a hook-nosed, select-looking, taciturn kind of dog that did most of his vituperation inwardly, as it were). I addressed the meeting in this strain for a few seconds, after which the battle began with great pomp and circumstance. One after another the dogs went out of commission, howling with pain, until only two champions were left — Lad and William the Third. I left them, hoping that William would get the worse of it.

From *Rambles in Eirinn*, Roberts Wholesale Books Ltd; first published 1907

'A Shrine of Relics'
Geoffrey Grigson

1 February 1980

You ask how I came to write about Limerick. Looking for dolmens, caves, sheila-na-gigs and limestone flora, we had been staying in Co. Clare with friends of the Irish poet Geoffrey Taylor. My wife was agonised by getting something in her eye which felt large as the capstone of a dolmen. The something wouldn't be dislodged, and on our way home we stopped in Limerick and in a smart doctors' street, found a very handsome young Irishman, who whisked out a speck of dust and said to my wife as he did so that she couldn't be English, from her accent. She said, no, she came from Vienna. 'How much do I owe you?' asked my wife. 'Nothing,' said the eye-doctor, 'a present from one Viennese to another.' A good omen, so we stayed on for a while in Limerick.

Yours sincerely
Geoffrey Grigson

In Limerick, the intermixture of past and present slightly distresses an English nose and an English morality. Not far from the station, clean, trim, with blue-uniformed maids disappearing through well-painted, brass-plated doors under the fanlights, an Irish Harley Street runs towards the Shannon. In the consulting rooms of surgeons, physicians, eye specialists, gleamingly equipped, one may see from the framed diplomas on the wall, that a degree was taken, first at Trinity, then, not in London, but in the medical schools of Vienna. Not so far away, if one continues down hill to the Shannon, walks along its open waters by the wide quay, one's enjoyment of the windy air of an open-and-shut day is interrupted suddenly by a smell, the smell of decay and dirt and being poor. Dirty-legged children appear, dirty Rowlandson-like women slipper-slopper by under black shawls.

As one turns the corner of Honan's Quay, the smell, the whiff, becomes a stench, the dirty, indescribable, formless rubbish on the stone of the quay increases, the children and the women multiply; and with astonishment one sees the long tall cliff of eighteenth-century tenements, which deliciously — at least in the architect's intention — face the openness of the river. Broken, black windows. Broken, black fanlights, leading in, and in (the door having gone), into heaven knows what heart of blackness, what squalor, what indifference . . . The children weave in and out, the black shawls congregate by the doorless doorways. Through an open window, a woman between seventy and eighty, with the lower lids of her eyes sagging down and showing the watery red. And above all, around all, in all, the stench, the stench, a bit sweet with the near-bitter intensity and obscenity of saccharine. Mixed with the stench the high voices, shouts from one window to another, from window to quay, quay to window.

At one end the upper portion of the tenement cliff is blind. The wall has tumbled out, and in a great U, the brickwork has been replaced, but without windows. One house in the tenement empty, because dilapidation has gone too far. The windows without glass, and the wind off the Shannon blowing in and blowing out through the roof, yet powerless to cleanse, powerless to obliterate the stench. One remembered O'Casey — O'Casey's slum doors 'scarred with time's spit and anger's hasty knocking', the streets which were 'long haggard corridors of rottenness and ruin'. Only here, because the brick face stared with its corrupted eyes across the Shannon, towards trees and hills, because of all this, the effect was absolute, as if one looked at an aged, noseless syphilitic on a green lawn surrounded by flowers . . . Cromwell's Ireton died in this city, of the plague, and here were nose-plugged houses (in which fantastically life was possible) dying still of a plague.

Two turnings deliver one from the tenements into Patrick Street, and Patrick Street merges into the long run of George's Street, painted, and clean, alive with the great jars of coloured water in the 'Medical Halls', with fine gilt lettering, elaborate graining. Here are hotels, solicitor's offices, shops emitting the smell of newly roasted coffee; and a stream-lined motor-bus from the Atlantic air-port; and children still from the tenements who clutch one when asking 'Any gum, chum?' Half-way up a new church opens to the street, people of all sorts moving into it to pray and dip their fingers into holy water. A slick interior of marble and white, blue and pink statues, and black tubby priests. Then, two bookshops in George's Street, with that strange blend — strange at least to an Englishman — of theology, pietism, and the secular. One could buy in them the new number of *The Bell*, Evelyn Waugh, St Thomas Aquinas, Webb's *Irish Flora*, a fascicle on early Celtic art, and almost enough pietistic pamphlets to drive out the smell of Limerick's poverty, and replace it with the smell, and emptiness, of whiteness and water. Bookshops and the slick church, the cheaply printed piety and the smooth marbles, were portions of the new Ireland, not superimposed but growing nastily out of time's spirit.

In between them and the tenement Ireland, in a side street leading back to the

Shannon, one came into a crowded cave where Ireland of the town, of the tenement, and of the country all crowded and mixed into a painting of Ostade's: prams, parcels, saddles, saucepans, sacks, young girls and children, long farmers, round nuns, hags under shawls, a hairy hunchback, filling the dark cave around a stove, from which a pipe straddled along to a soot-rimmed hole in the wall. In the centre of the gloom, to which one struggled through bodies and parcels, a wooden box from which a clerk — since this was the bus station — sold tickets and gave, endlessly, information and times. Full buses endlessly moved up and emptied their cargoes into the deep etching of the cave and moved off: long-distance buses which tied together all of the south of Ireland. The cave once more, in its darkness, shabbiness, elderly improvisation, its bare wood, its hot human steam and crowdedness, was an Ireland without date, the fecund, active Ireland, so unself-consciously alive, so bewildering to notions of betterment, and tidiness and social services . . .

One may think, between the bus station cave and the tenements of Limerick, that a visitation of plague is not the prerequisite required for the squalor of Irish towns; and one realises how foreign the whole concept either of town or village must be to the Irish, how the towns have been imported by the English and foisted upon a tribal, rural Irish . . .

In Limerick, still one other Ireland was visible, as the dust flew up in stinging curves against the dirty and the clean. Patrick Street has a large curiosity and junk shop. Books, bed-pans, gilt mirrors, gilt wall brackets held up by cherubs, bamboo tea-tables — the expected jumble of the newer meretricious and the older solid. The delicate gilt furniture told of auction sales within the walls of a demesne, of the decay and the death of the Anglo-Irish. And here were their books — Thomson's *Seasons*, the poems of Aubrey de Vere, the *Spectator* in calf, Hervey's *Meditations*, *The Rambler*, the annuals and the Books of Beauty, John Locke, Paley, an early edition of *Modern Painters*, armorial bookplated inside, with Latin crests of a moral bravado; and with them the last layer, Farrer's *English Rock Garden*, E. A. Bowles's *My Garden in Summer*, books by 'Elizabeth', even a few volumes of Turgenev, alongside a history of the Boer War. In England the Farrer and the Bowles would be expensive, in Limerick, they cost a shilling or two the volume.

Beside the junk shop, one should see, last of all, Limerick's museum, which is less a museum, despite torques and blunderbusses and sherds and corporation maces and insignia, than a shrine of relics of 1916 and the rebellion. IRA proclamations, letters of Irish political martyrs and fighters — all are mucked up with the Bronze Age and with the eighteenth century and (again) with Aubrey de Vere in book and manuscript, in a medley of untidiness indifferent to the stratifications of time. But it is the IRA proclamations which have pushed the gilt cherubs into the junk shops.

From *The Mint*, edited by Geoffrey Grigson, Routledge & Kegan Paul, 1946, reprinted in *The Old Limerick Journal*, No. 3, 1980

Drumcollogher
Percy French

I've been to a great many places,
And wonderful sights I've seen
From Aghernavoe to Ballinasloe
And back to Ballyporeen.
But when they talk of the towns that
Over the ocean lie —
When they say to me, 'Pat, what do you think of that?'
I ups and I says, says I —

Chorus
I suppose you've not been to Drumcollogher?
Ye haven't? Well now I declare,
You must wait till you've been to Drumcollogher,
And seen the fine place we have there.
There's only one street in Drumcollogher,
But then, 'tis a glory to see;
Ye may talk till you're dumb, but give me ould Drum,
For Drum is the place for me.

They tell me there's Isles of the Ocean
By India's golden shore,
Where life all day long is a beautiful song,
With flowers and fruits galore;
They tell me the sun does be shining,
With never a cloud in the sky —
But when they have done with their clouds and their sun,
I ups and I says, says I —

Chorus
I suppose you've not been to Drumcollogher?
Ye haven't? Well now I declare,
You must wait till you've been to Drumcollogher,
And seen the fine sun we have there.
There's only one sun in Drumcollogher,
But then, 'tis a glory to see;
Ye may talk till you're dumb, but give me ould Drum,
For Drum is the place for me.

I was over in London quite lately,
I gave King Edward a call;
Says the butler, 'He's out, he isn't about,
An' I don't see his hat in the hall;
But if you like to look round, sir,
I think you will have to say,
Apartments like these are not what one sees
In your country every day.'

Chorus
Says I, 'Have you been to Drumcollogher?
Ye haven't? Well now I declare,
You must wait till you've been to Drumcollogher,
And seen the fine house we have there.
There's only one house in Drumcollogher,
For hardware, bacon and tea;
If your master would come we would treat him in Drum,
Oh! Drum is the place for me.'

From *The Second Book of Irish Ballads*, edited by James N. Healy, The Mercier Press, 1962

Portrait of an Irish Town
Heinrich Böll

Who, thinking of Limericks, could approach Limerick without picturing a cheerful town? Where the roads had been dominated by cheerful schoolchildren, complacent cows, pensive donkeys, now suddenly they were empty. The children seemed to have reached school, the cows their pasture, and the donkeys seemed to have been called to order. Dark clouds came up from the Atlantic — and the streets of Limerick were dark and empty. Only the milk bottles in the doorways were white, almost too white, and the seagulls splintering the grey of the sky, clouds of white plump gulls, splinters of white that for a second or two joined to form a great patch of white. Moss shimmered green on ancient walls from the eighth, ninth and all subsequent centuries, and the walls of the twentieth century were hardly distinguishable from those of the eighth — they too were moss-covered, they too were ruined. In butcher shops gleamed whitish-red sides of beef, and the pre-school children of Limerick showed their originality here: hanging on to pigs' trotters, to oxtails, they swung to and fro between the hunks of meat: grinning pale faces. Irish children are very inventive; but are these the only inhabitants of this town?

We parked the car near the cathedral and strolled slowly through the dismal street. The grey Shannon rushed along under old bridges: this river was too big, too wide, too wild for this gloomy little town. Loneliness seized us, we felt sad, deserted between moss, old walls, and the many painfully white milk bottles that seemed destined for people long dead; even the children swinging from the sides of beef in the unlit butcher shops seemed like ghosts. There is a way of fighting the loneliness that can seize one suddenly in a strange town: buy something; a picture postcard, or some chewing gum, a pencil or cigarettes: hold something in your hand, participate in the life of this town by buying something — but would there be anything to buy here in Limerick, on a Thursday at half-past ten in the morning? Would we not wake up all of a sudden to find ourselves standing in the rain beside the car somewhere on the highway, and Limerick would have disappeared like a mirage, a mirage of the rain? So painfully white were the milk bottles — not quite so white the screaming gulls . . .

In Dublin we had been told: 'Limerick is the most devout city in the world.' So we would only have had to look at the calendar to know why the streets were so deserted, the milk bottles unopened, the shops empty: Limerick was at church, at eleven o'clock on a Thursday morning. Suddenly, before we had reached the centre of modern Limerick, the church doors opened, the streets filled up, the milk bottles were removed from the doorways. It was like an invasion: the inhabitants of Limerick were occupying their town. Even the post office was opened, and the bank opened its wickets. Everything looked disconcertingly normal, close, and human, where five minutes ago we seemed to be walking through an abandoned medieval town.

We bought a number of things to reassure ourselves of the existence of this town: cigarettes, soap, picture postcards, and a jigsaw puzzle. We smoked the cigarettes, sniffed the soap, wrote on the postcards, packed up the jigsaw puzzle, and went cheerfully off to the post office. Here there was a slight hitch — the postmistress had not yet returned from church, and her subordinate was unable to clarify what had to be clarified: how much did it cost to send printed matter (the jigsaw puzzle) weighing eight ounces to Germany? The young lady looked imploringly at the picture of the Madonna, with the candle flickering in front of it; but Mary was silent, she only smiled, as she has been smiling for four hundred years, and the smile said: patience. Strange weights were brought out, a strange scale, bright green Customs forms were spread out in front of us, tariff books open and closed, but there remained only one solution: patience. We practised it. After all, who would want to send a jigsaw puzzle as printed matter from Limerick to Germany in October? Who does not know that the Feast of the Rosary, although not a whole holiday, is more than a half-holiday?

Later on, though, long after the jigsaw puzzle lay in the letter box, we saw the scepticism flowering in hard, sad eyes: melancholy shining in blue eyes, in the eyes of the gypsy selling pictures of saints on the street, and in the eyes of the hotel manageress, in the eyes of the taxi driver — thorns around the rose, arrows in the heart of the most devout city in the world.

Evening

Ravished, robbed of their seals, the milk bottles stood grey, empty, and dirty in doorways and on window sills, waiting sadly for the morning when they would be replaced by their fresh, radiant sisters, and the gulls were not white enough to replace the angelic radiance of the innocent milk bottles; the gulls bobbed along on the Shannon, which, pressed between walls, increases its speed for two hundred yards. Sour, grey-green seaweed covered the walls; it was low tide, and it almost looked as if Old Limerick were exposing itself indecently, lifting its dress, showing parts that are otherwise covered by water; rubbish was waiting to be washed away by the tide; dim lights burned in the bookies' offices, drunks staggered through the gutters, and the children who that morning had swung from the sides of beef in butcher shops now showed that there is a level of poverty for which even the safety pin is too expensive: string is cheaper, and it works just as well. What eight years ago had been a cheap jacket, but new, now served as jacket, overcoat, trousers, and shirt in one; the grown-up sleeves rolled up, string around the middle; and held in the hand — innocently shining like milk, that manna that is to be found, always fresh and cheap, in the last hamlet in Ireland — ice cream. Marbles roll across the sidewalk; now and again a glance at the bookies' office where Father is just putting part of his unemployment pay on Crimson Cloud. Deeper and deeper sinks the comforting darkness, while the marbles click against the worn steps leading up to the bookie's office. Is Father going on to the next bookie, to put something on Grey Moth, to the third, to put something on Innisfree? There is no dearth of bookies here in Old Limerick. The marbles roll against the step, snow-white drops of ice cream fall into the gutter where they remain for a second like stars on the mud, only a second, before their innocence melts away into the mud . . .

The sea had not yet allowed the kindly water to rise, the walls were still naked and dirty, and the gulls not white enough. King John's Castle reared grimly out of the darkness, a tourist attraction hemmed in by tenements from the twenties, and the tenements of the twentieth century looked more dilapidated than King John's Castle of the thirteenth; the dim light from weak bulbs could not compete with the massive shadow of the castle, everything was submerged in sour darkness . . .

Where was he, the dark, blood-stained drunk, who had had enough string for his jacket but not for his shoes? Had he plunged into the Shannon, into the gurgling grey narrows between the two bridges which the gulls used as a free toboggan? They were still circling in the darkness, they alighted on the grey waters, between one bridge and the other, flew up to repeat the game; endless; insatiable.

Singing came flooding out of churches, voices of chanting priests, taxis brought travellers from Shannon airport, green buses swayed through the grey darkness, black, bitter beer flowed behind curtained pub windows. Crimson Cloud *has* to win.

The great Sacred Heart shone crimson in the church where the evening service was already over; candles were burning, stragglers were praying, incense and candle warmth, silence, in which only the shuffling footsteps of the sacristan were to be heard as he straightened the curtains of the confessionals, emptied the offering boxes. The Sacred Heart shone crimson.

How much is the fare for these fifty, sixty, seventy years from the dock that is called birth to the spot in the ocean where the shipwreck occurs?

Clean parks, clean monuments, black, severe, well-behaved streets: somewhere near here Lola Montez was born. Ruins from the time of the Rebellion, boarded-up houses that are not yet ruins, the sound of rats moving around behind the black boards, warehouses cracked open and left to the disintegration of time, green-grey slime on exposed walls, and the black beer flows to the health of Crimson Cloud, who is not going to win. Streets, streets, flooded for a few moments by those coming from evening service, streets in which the houses seem to get smaller and smaller; prison walls, convent walls, church walls, barrack walls; a lieutenant coming off duty props his bicycle by the door of his tiny house and tumbles over his children in the threshold.

Incense again, candle warmth, silence, people at prayer who cannot bear to part from the crimson Sacred Heart being gently reminded by the sacristan please to go home. Head-shaking. 'But—,' whispered arguments on the part of the sacristan. Head-shaking. Firmly glued to the kneeling bench. Who is going to count the prayers, the curses, and who has the Geiger counter that could register the hopes concentrated this evening on Crimson Cloud? Four slim fetlocks, there is a mortgage on these that nobody is going to be able to redeem. And when Crimson Cloud does not win, the grief must be quenched with as much dark beer as was needed to nourish the hope. Marbles are still clicking against the worn steps of the pub, against the worn steps of churches and bookies' offices.

It was much later that I discovered the last innocent milk bottle, as virginal as it had been in the morning; it was standing in the doorway of a tiny house whose shutters were closed . . .

Limerick slept, under a thousand rosaries, under curses, floated on dark beer; watched over by a single snow-white milk bottle, it was dreaming of Crimson Cloud and the crimson Sacred Heart.

From *Irish Journal*, Secker & Warburg, 1967

Pound Devalued in White House
John Liddy

It was suggested to the
Proprietor that he remove a
Photograph of Ezra Pound
Before Robert Graves and his
Entourage of chosen literati
Entered Gleeson's old world
White house in the thrice
Sieged City of Limerick.

The erudite barman,
Understanding the critical
Implications of such a request,
Promptly placed
The out-of-favour Pound
Behind a snap-shot of local
Poet Gerard Ryan.

And there he remained while
The eminent Don
Sat recalling the times
When his father drank whiskey
From the same barrel
And heated his rump
By the same fireside.

When the hour came round to
Leave
Mr Graves autographed a
Photograph of himself
For Mr Gleeson.

Today it hangs beside Mr Pound
And still not a word between
Them.

From *Castle Poets* (III), George McKern, 1977

Cow Country
Peter Somerville-Large

Ardpatrick is locally regarded as the highest green hill in Ireland, and the fields lap its base all round. The Limerick plain to the west and north is the richest pastureland in Ireland, the centre of the dairy industry. The landscape is dominated by Queen Cow; where the fields are not brilliant green with lush grass, there is scarcely a clod of earth that isn't dented with a cloven foot or enriched with manure. From the summit of the hill the view is of a country drawn with a Dutch perspective, full of rolling shadows, patterns of fields with distant towers and church spires shining in the sun — and dotted all around, the browsing flicktailed herds of cows that Cuyp would have posed and painted . . .

In winter very often there were days when the whole plain was covered with mist. I remembered a remark of a friend who lived near Kilmallock. 'All Limerick villages are ghastly. It's something to do with the dairy industry.' . . .

At the turn-off for Elton I passed a small river which rejoiced in the name of the Morning Star. Near here I joined forces with the local postman wheeling his bike, dressed in yellow cape and gaiters with a sort of bonnet over his cap. We trudged on together past a fortified house of the O'Hurleys full of rooks complaining about the weather. Suddenly the Scarteens burst towards us, a torrent of steaming horses and hounds filling up the road. Behind the famous black-and-tan hounds, panting and flecked with mud, came the riders, their elegance just beginning to be crushed by the rain. We thought we saw one or two drenched Americans. Behind them the followers were all dry in their cars, and behind them again a few laggards trotted briskly in an effort to keep up.

'All done for pleasure,' said the postman.

From *From Bantry Bay to Leitrim: A Journey in Search of O'Sullivan Beare*, Victor Gollancz Ltd, London, 1980

Publishers' Acknowledgments

The Editor and Publishers thank the following for the use of prose and poetry extracts which are in copyright:

Mr Peter Carr for *The Big Wind*.
Fr Gaughan for *Thomas Johnson, 1872–1963* by J. Anthony Gaughan.
Mr Eugene McCabe for 'Limerick Pageant'.
Mr Michael O'Riordan for *Connolly Column*.
Mr Jeremy Sandford for *The Farm by Lough Gur* by Mary Carbery.
Mr George T. Sassoon for *Sherston's Progress* by Siegfried Sassoon.
Mr Kieran Sheedy for *The Clare Drama Festival at Scariff*.
Mr Mainchín Seoighe for *Dromin Athlacca*.

Anvil Books for *Limerick's Fighting Story* by J. M. MacCarthy.
Blackwater Press for *The Good, the Bad and the Rugby: The Official Biography of Tony Ward* by John Scally.
Brandon Book Publishers for *Fall from Grace* by Joe Broderick.
Cambridge University Press and Professor J. I. Cronin for *Gerald Griffin 1803–1840: A Critical Biography*.
Curtis Brown for *From Bantry Bay to Leitrim* by Peter Somerville-Large.
Four Courts Press for *The War in Clare 1911–1921* by Michael Brennan.
David Higham Associates for *Presentation Parlour* by Kate O'Brien.
The Irish Times for 'The First Radio Pirate'.
The Lilliput Press for *The Franciscans in Ennis* by Patrick Conlan OFM.
The Limerick Leader for 'The Cranberries' by Frank Corr, and for 'Séamus Ó Cinnéide' by Desmond O'Grady.
Macmillan for *Richard Harris: A Sporting Life* by Michael Feeney Callan published by Sidgwick & Jackson.
The O'Brien Press for *Voices of Ireland* by Donncha Ó Dúlaing.
The Observer Press, Newcastle West, and Mr Michael Hartnett for 'Maiden Street Ballad'.
Peters Fraser & Dunlop for *The Midnight Court* translated by Frank O'Connor and published by Maurice Fridberg; for *Irish Miles* by Frank O'Connor published by Macmillan & Co.; and for *Leinster, Munster and Connaught* by Frank O'Connor published by Robert Hale Limited.

Poolbeg Press for *More Kicks than Pence: A Life in Irish Journalism* by Michael O'Toole, and for *The People who Drank Water from the River* by James Kennedy.
Reed Books for *Irish Journal* by Heinrich Böll.
Routledge for *Stone Mad* by Seamus Murphy published by Routledge & Kegan Paul.
Sporting Books Publishers for *The High Rollers of The Turf* by Raymond Smith.
The Sunday Tribune for 'The Most Maligned Place' and 'Those Old Sweet Songs' by David Hanly.

The Publishers have used their best efforts to trace all copyright holders. They will, however, make the usual and appropriate arrangements with any who may have inadvertently been overlooked and who contact them.